ISBN 978-1-333-28860-0
PIBN 10484072

This book is a reproduction of an important historical work. Forgotten Books uses
state-of-the-art technology to digitally reconstruct the work, preserving the original format
whilst repairing imperfections present in the aged copy. In rare cases, an imperfection in
the original, such as a blemish or missing page, may be replicated in our edition. We do,
however, repair the vast majority of imperfections successfully; any imperfections that
remain are intentionally left to preserve the state of such historical works.

1 MONTH OF
FREE
READING

at

www.ForgottenBooks.com

By purchasing this book you are eligible for one month membership to ForgottenBooks.com, giving you unlimited access to our entire collection of over 1,000,000 titles via our web site and mobile apps.

To claim your free month visit:

www.forgottenbooks.com/free484072

English
Français
Deutsche
Italiano
Español
Português

www.forgottenbooks.com

Mythology Photography **Fiction**
Fishing Christianity **Art** Cooking
Essays Buddhism Freemasonry
Medicine **Biology** Music **Ancient**
Egypt Evolution Carpentry Physics
Dance Geology **Mathematics** Fitness
Shakespeare **Folklore** Yoga Marketing
Confidence Immortality Biographies
Poetry **Psychology** Witchcraft
Electronics Chemistry History **Law**
Accounting **Philosophy** Anthropology
Alchemy Drama Quantum Mechanics
Atheism Sexual Health **Ancient History**
Entrepreneurship Languages Sport
Paleontology Needlework Islam
Metaphysics Investment Archaeology
Parenting Statistics Criminology
Motivational

NEW-YORK HISTORICAL SOCIETY.

PUBLICATION FUND.

———

II.

COLLECTIONS

OF THE

NEW-YORK HISTORICAL SOCIETY

FOR THE YEAR

1869.

PUBLICATION FUND SERIES.

NEW YORK:
PRINTED FOR THE SOCIETY.
MDCCCLXX.

F
116
N63
1260

Officers of the Society, 1870.

EXECUTIVE COMMITTEE.

FIRST CLASS—FOR ONE YEAR.
AUGUSTUS SCHELL,   ERASTUS C. BENEDICT,
ROBERT LENOX KENNEDY.

SECOND CLASS—FOR TWO YEARS.
JOHN ROMEYN BRODHEAD,   EVERT A. DUYCKINCK,
JAMES WILLIAM BEEKMAN.

THIRD CLASS—FOR THREE YEARS.
SAMUEL OSGOOD,   WILLIAM CHAUNCEY,
CHARLES P. KIRKLAND.

FOURTH CLASS—FOR FOUR YEARS.
EDWARD F. DE LANCEY,   WILLIAM T. BLODGETT,
JOHN ADRIANCE.

ERASTUS C. BENEDICT, *Chairman.*
GEORGE H. MOORE, *Secretary.*

[The President, Recording Secretary, Treasurer, and Librarian, are members, *ex officio*, of the Executive Committee.]

COMMITTEE ON THE FINE ARTS.

JONATHAN STURGES,   THOMAS T. BRYAN,
ANDREW WARNER,   EDWARD SATTERLEE,
WILLIAM J. HOPPIN,   HENRY T. TUCKERMAN.

JONATHAN STURGES, *Chairman.*
ANDREW WARNER, *Secretary.*

[The President, Librarian, and Chairman of the Executive Committee, are members, *ex officio*, of the Committee on the Fine Arts.]

INTRODUCTION.

THE undersigned, a committee charged with the preparation and publication of the Collections for the Year 1869, respectfully submit this volume to the Society and the public. Unwilling to forestall the labors of writers of history, by anticipating the use of the new materials presented in the following pages, they have not encumbered the text with notes or comments of their own; nor deemed it expedient to vary from the general principles laid down in the introduction to the preceding volume, the first of the series.

The Clarendon Papers, which occupy the first place in this volume, are copies from the original manuscripts preserved in the Bodleian Library at Oxford, England. They were procured by Mr. GEORGE H. MOORE, in the course of researches for his collection of the Statutes at Large of New York from 1664 to 1691. In placing them at the disposal of the committee for publication, Mr. MOORE desired that due acknowledgment should be made to the Librarian, Rev. H. O. COXE, M. A., Corp. Christ., for his courtesy in promoting the objects of the inquiry which led to this valuable result. These documents cannot fail to be regarded with peculiar interest, for the light which they throw on the origin, progress, and results of the Royal Commission of 1664 and the American Colonial policy of Clarendon's administration. Nor is their value diminished by the fact that they have so long remained untouched in the repositories of the University, and are now for the first time made available with us for the history of the important transactions in America to which they relate.

The first of the Tracts relating to New York which are here reproduced, is printed from the original in the collection of the late Reverend Dr. HAWKS, for which the Society is under lasting obligations to the judicious liberality of WILLIAM NIBLO, Esq. It contains some interesting particulars of the French expedition into New York in 1689–90, as well as the massacre at Schenectady, which are not to be found in the current history of those events.

The second is a reprint of one of the early New York tracts, printed by Bradford, which illustrates the course of legislation in the colony during the administration of the Earl of Bellomont. No portion of our history is more important than that which relates to this period, when the parties formed during the Leisler troubles were organized and consolidated. Their influence continued to be felt to the end of the colonial government.

INTRODUCTION.

Of the Miscellaneous Documents—the additional letter by Lieutenant-Governor Colden on Smith's History is printed from the original, recently presented to the Society by SAMUEL W. FRANCIS, *M. D. Dr.* FRANCIS *found among the papers of his honored father, the late* JOHN W. FRANCIS, *M. D., the entire series, more complete than the drafts among the Colden Papers, from which the other letters were printed in the volume of Collections for the year* 1868. *With characteristic liberality he has added the whole to the Society's collection. The papers relating to New Albion furnish an interesting and important addition to the materials for the history of that unfortunate attempt at colonization in America. Taken in connection with the Documents printed by* Hazard, *in his* State Papers: *vol. i.* 160–174, *they may help to correct serious errors of historical writers on that subject.*

The Notes, etc., on East Hampton and Gardiner's Island, are printed from the author's original manuscript. Prepared at the request of the late Rev. Dr. SAMUEL MILLER, *in* 1798, *they form a part of the collections which he made with a view to writing a history of New York and gave to the Society when he abandoned that design. In Dr. Lyman Beecher's historical sermon at East Hampton in* 1806, *he acknowledged the great assistance he received from these notes, and they have been freely and copiously extracted by various writers since that time ; but they are now for the first time printed entire.*

The Documents concerning New York and the New Hampshire Grants conclude the volume. By an Act of the Legislature of New York, 21st October, 1779, " *the Honorable* James Duane *and* John Morin Scott, *Esquires, and* Egbert Benson, *Esquire," were nominated and appointed Commissioners, to collect and procure Evidence, Vouchers, and Materials, for manifesting and maintaining the Boundaries and Jurisdiction of the State, and the Rights of the Grantees under the same, which were drawn into question in the disputes respecting a certain district of country on both sides of Connecticut River, then commonly called the New Hampshire Grants. The result of their labors is to be found in this collection. Should it be deemed proper hereafter to print the formal statement of the evidence and argument founded upon these documents by* James Duane, *from the original manuscript in the possession of the Society, it is believed that the vindication of New York may be rendered complete. Apart from this consideration, these papers will be found to have an interest independent of their connection with a controversy long since determined, and to embrace historical materials of much value to illustrate other topics.*

ERASTUS C. BENEDICT,
EVERT A. DUYCKINCK,
GEORGE H. MOORE.

NEW-YORK: *January,* 1870.

CONTENTS.

I. THE CLARENDON PAPERS.

II. TRACTS RELATING TO NEW YORK.

III. MISCELLANEOUS DOCUMENTS.

THE CLARENDON PAPERS.

THE CLARENDON PAPERS

I.

CONCERNING NEW NETHERLAND, OR MANHATTAN.

THAT pte of America (by the Dutch) called the New Netherlands lieth in 40 deg^{rs} od minutes of northerlie lat^d the place of the residence of the Dutch Gouer^r (who stiles himselfe Director Generall of New Netherlands, & Admirall of the northerne ptes of America) is vppon an Isl^d by the Indians called Manahataus which lieth in the mid-waye betwixt Boston in New Engl^d and Virginia vppon the sowthwest point of the s^d Isl^d they haue a considerable ffort of some 30 peeces of ordinance brasse, Canon, demi Culuerin, & others, since the yeare 1647 they haue much emproued their buildings aboute it, that it is now Called the ffort & Cittie of New Amsterdam, allthough in the yeares 1641, & 1642 there was not six howses of free Burgers in it, but now there is many, so that they make vpp two Companies vnder the Comand of their seuerall Captaines besides the maine garrison which is Constantlie kepte there which att most neuer exceedes 70 besides officers.

They haue had two seuerall warres with the Indians, the first in the yeare 1641 : the Indians first killed two Dutchmen att seuerall times in seuerall places vppon pretence of their vsurping & taking away their land without giueing them satisfaction, att the which the then Gouern Will Kieft was faine to conniue at for

the present, and the sᵈ Indians being forced to retire
more towards the sea side for feare of the Highland
Indˢ. putting themselues vnder the protection of the
Dutch ffort. seating themselues within Canon shott
thereof: neuerthelesse the sᵈ Dutch Gouernʳ Kieft
made oute a ptic against them and killed some 60 men,
women, & children, in the night time, when they little
expected any such matter from the Dutch, but in requitall the Indians presentlie betooke themselues to
their Armes & killed more of the Dutch, burning their
farmes destroying their Cattle; But the Dutch Gouernʳ
(findeing himselfe to weake for the Indians & planting
time Comeing on) pswaded them to accept of a peace
and that all differences on either side might be forgotten
which the Indians as seeminglie for their owne ends
embraced, and held verie faire Correspondencie vntill
such time as they had got in their Crop of Corne

    In the interim the sᵈ Dutch Gouernʳ as aforewritten
findeing his forces to weake for the Indians inuited
seuerall of the English in New Englᵈ to come & liue
vnder his gouermᵗ promising them many & large priuilidges vppon which many that were tyranised ouer by
the partialitie & rigidnes of that gouermᵗ both in the
ecclesiasticall & Ciuill pollicie thereof, & for the better-
ment of their accomodation in lands betooke themselues
vnder the protection of the Dutch, and the Indians the
yeare followeing (not forgetting the former iniurie of
the Dutch & their daily vsurping vppon their rights)
renued the warre with more violencie then euer, and
had then vtterlie rooted oute the sᵈ Dutch, had it not
bynne for a small ptic of the sᵈ English that were entertained in pay which gaue a Checke to their pceed-
ings; neuerthelesse yᵉ Burgers and ffarmers were so
affrighted that by comon Counsell of them all they
were resolued to haue put themselues & lands vnder the
absolute Comand, & ptectiō of the English in New
Englᵈ had not the Gouernʳ himselfe & the English
that Came from thence mainlie opposed it, & enter-
taining more of them in pay, whom the Indians did

more feare then all the Dutch saying oftentimes to the
s^d English what wrong haue we done to yow? that
yee should fight for the Dutch against vs telling them
that if they would leaue the Dutch to themselues, they
would kill them all & give them the land. so that for
the reasons affores^d I may trulie say that those of New
Engl^d were and are the cheif Cause that the Dutch are
growne to that height, and their encroachments vppon
his Maties rights in those ptes. So that now They make
Claime to a large Tract of land, & that to begin att the
Westermost point of land leading into Deleware riuer
by them called Cape Hinlopen, & from thence Eastward to Cape Cod by them renamed Cape Mallebar,
in the which is included all Prouidence pte of New
Plimouth, & all Connoticot and Newhauen Collonies
with all the Isl^d adiacentent (sic) to the eastward, and
all that portion of land to the Westward granted by
pattent to Sr Edmund Plowden, & in pursuance thereof
have attempted seuerall wayes either by force or pollicie for the displanting his Maiesties subiects in those
partes, vnlesse they would submit to their gouerment
and acknowledge them as Lords paramount of the said
lands as shall be made to appeare by seuerall perticulars
in the ensuing relation

The s^d Cittie New Ansterodam is very delightsome
& conuenient for scituation especiallie for trade haueing
two maine streames or riuers running by, with an excellent harbour; the end of the s^d Riuers or Streames is
ye ordinary passage from & to New Engl^d and Virginia,
the other up a riuer most comonlie called Hudsons
riuer, as being first discouered by one Hudson, an Englishman. Many ancient Indians report that it was an
English fflag they first saw in the s^d riuer & that an
Englishman was the first that traded with them & that
for certaine Kettles, Hatchets, Kniues & other trading
ware they gaue the s^d Englishman that land, where
the Dutch Fort & Cittie now standeth. some 40: or
50 leagues vp the s^d Hudsons riuer they haue a small
plantacion or Collonie called Renchliew's Wicke, with a

small fort Called Ourania belonging to the West Indie Chamber of Ansterdā in Holland, where they haue a very greate and rich trade with a nation of Indians Called the Mohocks, & that for most sort of furres especiallie Beeuer Skinns, principallie in exchange for powder, gunnes and lead, by meanes whereof as they haue generallie learnt the vse of those sort of Armes & to keepe them very well fixt, so they are become very expert marksmen, and being plentifullie supplied by the Dutch. haue many times inuaded the French themselues, & French Indians vppon Canada, & being sensible of their owne strength the Dutches Covetousnes & timerousnes keepe the s^d Dutch themselues there in a very slauish Condition & is feared may proue very preiudiciall if not distructiue to his M$_a$^{ties} Westerne Collonies of New Engl^d

In the yeare 1641 : Captaine Daniell How & other Englishmen purchased a considerable tract of land, of the Indian proprietours on the westerne pte of Long Isl^d beginning to settle themselues there, the affores^d Gouern^r Kieft sent a Company of souldiers & seised the psons of the s^d English putting them in Irons threatning them to send them prisoners for Holland, vnlesse they would promise him to desert the s^d place thereby forcing them to quit their right & interest they had thereunto

In the same yeare certaine psons of qualitie of the English nation inhabitants of Newhauen in New Engl^d disbursing Considerable summes of money & to emproue ye English rights in those ptes purchased seuerall tracts of land of the Indian natiues in Deleware riuer, & setled certaine families there, the affores^d Gouern^r Kieft Combining with the Swedish Gouern^r then there disposessed the s^d English of their rights, ceising vppon their Armes & goods, to the losse of the aduenturers in the generall of aboue 1000^l sterling besides what the pticular plantors suffered therein, & were not wanting of an Amboina plott in imprisoning one Mr Geo : Lamberton the principall pson then there of the English nation, threatning to take away his life vppon pretence of his Complotting with the Indians against him.

In the yeare 1647 : the present Dutch Gouern[r] Peter Styvesant succeeding Kieft in the gouernem[t] so for their further prosecution of their designe in vsurping vppon the rights of the English. some two moneths after his settlem[t] in his said gouernm[t] (in an hostile way) surprised a ship in Newhauen harbour, of very good value belonging to a Dutch merchant who had put himselfe vnder the protection of the English & was admitted as a plantor amongst them the then Gouern[r] of Newhauen, M[r] Theophilus Eaton by his letters directed to the s[d] Styvesant protested against the s[d] Violence & breach of peace, but the said Styvesant (insted of giueing satisfaction) added a further iniurie in Claiming by his letters responsitorie the s[d] Newhauen as a member belonging to his gouerm[t] & vppon that pretence made prize of the s[d] ship & goods.

The same yeare M[r] Thomas Pell of Newhauen affores[d] furnisht & rigd oute a Vessell to trade with the Swedes and Natiues in Deleware riuer, and the vessell only retourning by the Manahatans the Comon & vsuall passage, the affores[d] Dutch Gouern[r] Compeld them to pay (as they call it) recognition what he pleased to demand, for whatsoever they had traded for in the riuer, allthough the Dutch had not then any Considerable interest in the s[d] riuer, not by the hundred pte att least to what the English had bought and paid for to the Indians the right owners, haueing likewise a better right to it then any other nation in Europe, neuerthelesse hee would not pmit any English vessell to passe by the said Isl: of Manahatans vnlesse they would first put him in securitie for the payment of the said recognition, & acknowledge him as proprietour of the s[d] riuer by accepting Comissions from him, which all refusing they lost the opportunitie of their intended voyages to theire very great damage

The Comissioners for the vnited Collonies of New Engl[d] taking into theire considerations these and many other wrongs done to the English by their letters of seuerall dates directed to the s.^d Dutch Gouern^r Styvesant protested against his s^d violences & required satisfaction, to the which he would neuer answere in the generall, but by seuerall letters to the Massachusets & Plimouth Collonies in pticular, hopeing in regarde of some interest hee had in certaine merchants of either place that traded to the Manahatans hee might by their meanes gaine a ptie amongst themselues there to ballance (if not ouer) whatsoeuer Complaint the wronged Collonies should bring in against him, so that very confidentlie

In the yeare 1650 : hee gaue a meeting to the said Com͞issioners att Hartford vppon Conneticot where after some debate aboute former passages, for the Composing whereof & setling prouisionall limits it was thought meete to referre it to a Com͞ittee of fowre psons vizt one of the Massachusets another of Plimouth Collonies with two such as hee himselfe should make choice of, satisfaction by the wronged Collonies being required and the iniuries made to appeare those things for the time present were put of, the Massachusets & Plimouth Collonies not much vrging it, howeuer prouisionall limits with some other matters being agreed vppon, and some questions arising aboute the right of lands in Deleware riuer, the English of Newhauen produced seuerall euidences for seuerall Tracts of land purchased by them of the Indian natiues in the said riuer, but the Dutch Could not make oute any right hee had there by any one euidence hee could produce but that of his owne words, howeuer by the Delegates it was agreed vppon and desired that either ptie might improue their iust right and Interest they had in the s^d riuer, in peace & loue without disturbing the one the other.

The yeare followeing many of the inhabitants of Newhauen in expectation of the pformance of the s^d agreement disposing of their estates there, shipped them selues and goods with an intention to settle themselues in Deleware, & the vessell passing by the Manahatans, one of the principall of then (sic) went on shoare to deliuer a letter to the s^d Dutch Gouern^r from the Gouern^r of Newhauen, wherein mention was made of their intentions and desires of a neighbourlie compliance with him, the s^d Dutch Gouernour desired of the s^d ptie a sight of his Comission which (vppon his faithfull promise of a present redeliuerie) was graunted neuerthelesse the s^d Styvesant deteined the Comission & Comitted the pties entrusted vnder a guarde vntill such time as they promised & engaged to proceede no further, & so enforced them to retourne backe againe to the exceeding great losse and discouragem^t of the s^d men for euer attempting the setling themselues in the s^d riuer.

The affores^d yeare 1651 ⠂ the s^d Styvesant with what force hee Could possiblie raise marched ouer land to Deleware, & all the Interest the Dutch had then in the riuer was a small trading howse Called Fort Nassaw with 4 : or 5 : smaller bowses adiacent, and a small peece of barren land aboute 40 : leagues vp the riuer, two dayes before his arriuall there, his agent by order from him seised vppon an English barque belonging to a merchant of Virginia, allthough his s^d Agent had giuen a full discharge the very day before to the merchant for whatsoeuer the Dutch West Indie Company could or might pretend against him, neuerthelesse the s^d Styvesant deteined the merchant as a prisoner with the vessell & goods vntill such time as he enforced him to pay him 100^l sterl : for the which the Honorable 'Sr William Berckley then Gouern^r of Virginia wrott to the s^d Styvesant aboute it requiring satisfaction to be giuen for such an apparent and manifest wrong.

Att the same time hee sent for seuerall Indian Sachemacks or Lords and desired to buye of them a certaine Tract of land on the West side of the riuer some 14 leagues lower, & within 4 or 5 mile of the principall fort of the Swedes called Christina, but the Indians vtterlie refused to sell it him, yet through his much importunitie they tould him they would giue it him, the whole quantitie of the s^d land not conteining much aboue 12 : acres

it being in the nature of a peninsula, so quitting ffort
Nassaw and sailing to the place vppon a point thereof
very convenient to comand the riuer. hee erected a prettie
considerable peece nameing it ffort Cassimere haueing
12 peeces of ordinance mounted in it ; the then Swedish
Gouern^r Collonell John Prince protested against his
vsurpation of the s^d lands, allthough not purchased by
either, The s^d place being very conuenient for trade
with a nation of Indians in Virginia Called the Sus-
quahanouhs, & by the Dutch the Mincques, it being
formerlie the vsuall Custome of the Dutch to Carrie
their trading wares vpp into the s^d Indians Countrie
some ten or twelue dayes iourney there being then some
30 trading barques then in the Riuer belonging to the
Dutch ; the s^d Gouern^r Styvesant Caused a platt of a
towne to be laide oute neere the ffort, & the Dutch that
were then there began to build howses aboute it, so that
it is now become a pretty small towne.

In the yeare 1654 or thereaboutes a Swedish gent :
being emploied and empowred with Comission from the
late King of Sweden for the regulating and setling the
gouerm^t of the Swedes in the riuer & to bring them a
supplie the Dutch Comander of the said Fort Cassimere
went aborde the Swedish vessell, & was so Ciuillie entertained by the s^d gent : that in requitall hee pmitted
him to Come in and view his s^d ffort with 12 : firelocks
for his guarde, the gent : tooke his present aduantage
& Comanded those Dutch souldiers that were then
there to submit themselues & ffort to the Crowne of
Sweden, which was very peaceablie obeyd by them all.

The then Dutch Gouern^r Styvesant not haueing sufficient forces to resubdue the s^d place acquainted his
masters the Dutch West Indie Company therewith who
vppon reasons best knowne to themselues & likewise
apprehending it might be of greate charges to them to
attempt the regaining of it, and keeping of it against
such as haue a better right to it then themselues, surrendred vp their right (which in realitie is none att all)
to the Cittie of Ansterdam in Holland, and that vppon

the specious pretence for the sending thether many pore decayed families.

Vppon which the s^d Cittie in the yeare 1655 sent ouer a ffrigat of 36 gunnes called the ffrigat Ansterodam with all sorts of amunition, & instruments of warre & an order to the s^d Styvesant to endeauour the subduing of the s^d place by force of armes. vppon which the s^d Styvesant made what preparation hee could for the accomplishing of it, and for that end raised what forces hee could, which of souldiers and seamen in paye and voluntiers plantors & others might amount to the number of 400 : or 500: men with fowre ships and the affores^d ffrigat for the transport of his forces to Deleware, but the Swedes haueing sould most of their amunition to the Indians for beeuer skins & other ffurs had not wherewithall to maintaine their Strengths and thereby after a small seige were necessitated to surrender vppon articles all their Forts & submit themselues to the gouerm^t of the Dutch, so that the Dutch are nowe become absolute masters of that famous riuer, that was discouered & posessed by the English long before the Dutch had any Footehoulds in any of those ptes. But in that interim of tyme the Indians aboute the Manahatans fell vppon the the (sic) Dutch & in their first furie killed all they could light vppon, burning their howses destroying their Cattle, but vppon better considerations spared the liues of such as they tooke & put them to ransome especiallie for powder & lead, & in one place att one time tooke 70 : of them prisoners, & would not ransome them without a good quantitie of powder & lead, by report 24 small barrells with lead proportionable, besides other Comodeties And that to such an ashtonishment & terrour of the Dutch that the bowers or ffarmers generallie left their habitations, & betooke themselues to their Cittie New Amsterdam, where the affrighted burgers or Cittizens themselues were as readie to gett aborde such ships as were then in the harbour, with what goods they coulde and to bid an vltimum vale to their New Netherlands : the said ash-

tonishment or terrour did not only continue vppon them
as men strucken with a suddaine pannicke feare but
with a Certaine deliberate expectation of haueing a
greater blowe to fall vppon them from the incensed natiues for their intrusion into and vsurpation of their
lands, and all the time of their s^d furie they were very
peaceable to the English that liued vnder the Dutch
very ciuillie sending to the English of the seuerall
townes vnder y^t gouerm^t desiring them not to be troubled att any thing betwixt the Dutch & them, for as
they had nothing against the English for any iniurie or
wrong they had euer done them so they would not in
the least measure harme them either in their persons
goods & Cattle, & were as good as their words, only
burning downe the ffarme howse of an English gent:
that was Capt of the Dutch ffort saing in excuse hee
was an English-Dutchman.

That the s^d Dutch Gouern^r Styvesant att his retourne from Deleware by all the arte and industrie hee
had first Courted them to a Cessation and for the gain-
ing thereof pmitted them to come in theire Cittie New
Amsterdam and to passe and repasse freelie without
any molestation or disturbance to sell and dispose to
other of the Dutch nation what the Indians had plun-
derd from others of their Countriemen, and did seeme
to take noe notice of what the Indians had formerlie
done in killing his Countriemen, so that for the present
the buisnes was smothered vp on both sides allthough
the Indians I am Confident waite only an opportunitie
of doeing them a greater mischief.

The warre betwixt the two nations arising the s^d
Dutch Gouern^r Styvesant by himselfe, and Agents
(by the Confession of many Indians) hired the Mohocks
with the other High land Indians to Cut of and Massacre all the English that that (sic) were in those ptes,
whereby as New Engl^d was put into a ve[r]y sad Al-
larme & to a very greate Charge, so the English that
were vppon that pte of Long Isl: which hee claimed
to be vnder his gouerm^t were necessitated all of them

to leaue their labours & to stand vppon their guardes
day & night for feare of being exposed to barbarous
Crueltie or Dutch treacherie, & the s^d English sending
to him for a supplie of am̄u[ni]tion it was denied them,
allthough the Indians were then very plentifullie sup-
plied by the Dutch : The affores^d Comission^{rs} for the
vnited Collonies being then att Boston, the Comis-
sion^{rs} for the two Westerne Collonies vizt Conneticot
and Newhauen being nighest the danger much pressed
the Comissioners for the Massachusets & Plimouth
Collonies that some speedie Course might be taken for
the preuention of it, which they of Boston & Plimouth
seeminglie embraced by making a greate noise of greater
preparations of raising forces to subdue the Dutch,
which all turnde to nothing, but made the Dutch Gouernour more stronglie fortifie, both ffort & Cittie farre
stronger then they were euer before.

Maior Robert Sedegwicke being emploied with Co-
m̄ission & power for the subduing the s^d place, many
of the English next adiacent to the Dutch vppon Long
Isl : being well affected to the right of their nation to
those ptes, many of the Dutch bowers themselues being
very willing to submit to an English gouerment being
wearied with the oppressions & exactions of the Dutch
Gouern^r Corresponding with them togeather with a
greate ptie of the low land Indians who were readie to
engage against the Dutch in the behalfe of the English,
& daily waited for the word or order from the English.
who sent for a Comission by an expresse to Boston
for that purpose, which as they were enformed was denied by Captaine Leuerets meanes, and allthough the
two Westerne Collonies were in a readie posture to
aduance, & in all probabilitie the designe might haue
bynne very easilie accomplished without the shedding
of one drop of bloude ; yet the execution of the said
Comission was so long retarded (as supposed) by his
former Compliants of the Massachusets & Plimouth
Collonies y^t the generall peace betwixt the two nations
interuened before the accomplishment of it, and that to

the greate preiudice of his M^{a}^{tie} and subiects in loosing such an opportunitie of firmelie establishing his Maiesties rights to those ptes & the greate profit that might haue redounted to his Maties subiects not only of their settlem^{ts} in the best pte of all that Northerne Empire, but likewise the greate profit of the trade with the natiues, so that I may trulie say that as New Engl^{d} in the generall (for the reasons affores^{d}) were the first Cause of their populating it: so Boston & Plimouth in pticular of their fortefieing and keeping of it euer since.

Mr Thomas Pell affores^{d} in Consideration of a valuable summe of money purchased a considerable Tract of lands (of the Indian natiues the right & true owners thereof nere adiacent to the s^{d} Isl: of Manahatans) in the time of the late warre & was seised & posesst thereof & kept posession thereof in the time of the late warre, setling certaine families there, & erected the small beginning of a towne called Westminster, neuerthelesse the s^{d} Dutch Gouern^{r} Styvesant after the conclusion of the generall peace betwixt the late Vsurper Oliuer & their States, & Six moneths after his owne publique proclaiming of it in those ptes, in a hostile way and by force of Armes inuaded the lands of the s^{d} English, surprised their psons Carrieing them prisoners to their Cittie New Amsterdam, & kept them there in prison so long vntill such time as he enforced them to subscribe to an instrum^{t} in writing to acknowledge the Hollands West Indie Company as Cheif Lords & patrons of the said lands & to submit to his gouerment vnder them & to accept & obey such Magistrates which he should from time to time Constitute ouer them, the said lands were formerlie in the yeare 1642 setled by certaine English families that were banished oute of the Massachusets the cheif whereof were Mrs Anne Hutchinson and others & that vnder the gouerm^{t} & protectiō of the Dutch, the Dutch Gouern^{r} pretending a right thereunto, but the Indians disowned that euer they had giuen or sould the Dutch Gouern^{r} any pte or pcell of the s^{d} lands & therefore forewarned the s^{d}

Mrs Hutchinson to departe or else to buye & giue them
satisfaction for the same, the which they delaying vppon
the promise of the s^d Dutch Gouern^r fullie to satisfie
the Indians himselfe, which hee not doeing the s^d Indians killed the s^d Mrs Hutchinson with many more
English that were there, burning their howses and killing their Cattle, so that allthough the s^d place was first
setled by the blood of the English, & since lawfullie
purchased as abouesaid by the Consent and willing
desire of the s^d Indian owners for the English to settle
there, yet the place is still deteined from the s^d Mr Tho :
Pell. whom I haue often heard say that he could make
it appeare by his accompts the purchase of the s^d lands
& what he had disbursed aboute the settlement of it,
stood him in very neere 500^l sterl :

By what hath bynne formerlie written it may eui-
dentlie appeare that the Dutch haue entruded into his
Mat^{ies} rights in the very best pte of all that large
northerne Empire & haue from time to time encroached
more & more thereuppon by their force & pollicie
& seuerall wayes abused and wronged his Maties subiects, of those ptes after their first settlem^{ts} there fined-
ing (sic) so gainfull & beneficiall trade with the Indian
natiues allthough Contrarie to the wills & desires of the
s^d natiues, who euer since most comonlie once in two
yeares killed some of the Dutch in destation & dislike
of them for taking their lands away, so that after the
great massacre of the Dutch when their Gouern^r was
at Deleware, and his base submission by begging a
stilstand or Cessation of Armes from the s^d Indians, an
intelligent Indian discoursing with some English aboute
the opportunitie they then had lost by their asistance to
haue rooted oute the Dutch & to be reuenged for wrongs
done them and setling the gouerm^t and lands vppon
themselues, asked this question ; I wonder what for
men you englishmen are, the ptie desired to knowe a
reason of his question, to whom hee very readilie re-
plied ; Wee of the Indian nation loue and feare your
nation ; your nation feare the Dutch, and the Dutch

are affraid of vs, vpbraiding our nation with Cowardice vntill such time hee was satisfied by telling him our hands were tied vpp by the peace that was made in Europe; so that to myne owne knowledge as the Indians haue oftentimes denied to sell their lands to the Dutch so they are desirous of the English to settle amongst them, & for that end I am very Confident would be very ready to asist the English against the Dutch with a Considerable ptie of them, if euer occasion should require.

In septemb. 1659. a fort belonging to the Dutch, lyinge about 80 : miles aboue Manhatas beinge some weekes belegured by some thousands of Indians, their Corne burnt, and many slayne, and they not able to relieue it, They requested Sr Henery Mody to raise a foote Company for theire assistance, wch he did, and wth the Countenance of them, they entered the fort and sett vp the English Coulors, wch the Dutch keepe to this day, to be supposed to make vse of on the like occasion. One Mr Abraham Sheares who caryed the Colou^{rs} is now heare and can giue a fuller relation.

And now by letters from New England we are informed, the Indians, are on the same termes as formerly.

Endorsed in Lord Clarendon's hand-writing—" *Concerninge the New Nether-landes, or Manahatan*," and in another hand, " *During Ld Clarendon's Ministry.*"

II.

THE CASE STATED, AS IT RELATES TO Y^E DESIRE OF HAVING ONE GENERALL COLLECTION TOWARDS CARRYING ON Y^E WORCKE OF PROPAGACŌN OF Y^E GOSPELL AMONGST Y^E INDIANS.

Some English being formerly planted amongst ye Barbarous Indians in America, apprehended it a duty incumbent on them, not only to endeavour ye Civilizing of those Natives, but as much as in them lay after some

Comerce wth them, ye pswading of them to forsake their accustomed paganish Charmes & sorceries, & other their Satanicall Delutions, and instead thereof to acquaint y^{em} wth ye knowledge of ye only true God in Christ, and wth his everlasting Gospell. By the blessing of almighty God vpon wch indeavours, & smale beginnings, many remarkeable instances & testimonyes were had & given of the Gospell made knowne amongst them, by enlightning their mindes & turning them from ye miserable darknes, by wch they were kept in Captivity, to serve ye living God in ye Gospell of his sonne.

The Knowledg of soe glorious a worke soe hopefully begun comeing into England, stirred vp divers about ye yeare 1648. to move ye Lords & Comons y^t then were, not only to Constitute a Corporacōn for ye managem^t of y^t service, but to grant Liberty for one generall Contribucōn throughout England & Wales, for incouragem^t of fitt instrum^{ts}, and pvisions requisite, for civilizing & employcing of ye Natives, and for what might bee necessary for carrying on soe good a worke, the desires & motives of wch persons being granted, divers sumes were raised, & by meanes thereof ye worke hath had a verie considerable pgresse, in having ye Gospell preached to ye Indians in their owne Language, the new Testam^t a few chapters whereof were only done at first, being now throughout printed in their owne Language, and many Natives brought over to imbrace ye true Christian Religion.

His Ma^{ty} considering ye Consequence of soe glorious a worke, hath lately erected a Corporacōn to carry on and pfect this worke, who at y^{er} first entrance cheifely by meanes of Collonel Bedingfeild, for ye space of neare two yeares past, interrupting their possession, and receiving ye pfitts of Lands purchased of him wth ye greatest parte of ye Moneyes received by the former Collections doe finde their charges have of late much exceeded their incumbs, and their Revenue much to smale at present, to enable them to carry on soe chargeable, as well as charitable a worke. And therefore doe humbly desire ye grant of a free Collection, wch they hope wilbee lesse scrupled at, because ye benefit intended by ye first Collections was not received there being divers Countyes in the Kingdome, and severall parishes in ye Citie, in wch noe collections for this worke have yet bene made.   •

Endorsed—"*The Case of the Corporation for New England.   C: (61.)*"

III.

CAPTAIN THOMAS BREEDON TO THE COUNCIL FOR FOREIGN PLANTATIONS.

MY LORDS AND GENTLEMEN

Having received a Sumons to appeare before yor Hono^{rs} of his Ma^{ts} Counsell for forraine plantacōns this day being the xj^{th} of March 1660 to give informacōn of the present State Condicōn & Governm^t of the severall Collonies of New England. I doe here in the first place present you wth the booke of Lawes for Massachusetts Colonie Whereby your Hono^{rs} may vnderstand the Governm^t thereof better then myself, wch governm^t they assert to be, by Patent from ye King: wch patent, I never saw therefore cannot tell how agreable to their Patent they act. What Lawes are not mencōned in this booke are in the Magistrates breasts to be vnderstood. The distinction of Freemen and Non-Freemen Members & Non Members is as famous as Cavalleeres and Roundheads was in England and will shortly become as odious, and (I hope) abandon'd. The grievances of the Non Members who are really for the King and also of some of the Members are very many wch I referre yee to others more able then my selfe to relate them. And since his M^{a}^{tie} hath graunted a Generall pardon it will not become mee to say they had somuch as a stinking breath, although they apprehended a Gentleman not many yeares agoe supposing him to be the

King) Resolving to send him for England, had not Sr Henry Moody and others better knowne his Matie. It is not vnknowne to you that they looke on themselves as a Free State, and how they sate in Counsell in December last a weeke before they could agree of writeing to his Matie there being too many against owning the King or their haveing any dependance on England. Their Peticōn I have not seene but by informacōn vnderstand they acknowledge their Allegiance to his Matie vpon wch I Quere. First: Why doe they not proclaime his Matie. Secondly why doe they not act in his Ma^{ts} name Thirdly why doe they not give the oath of Allegiance to his Matie but in stead thereof force an oath of fidelitie to themselves and their governm^t as in booke of lawes page: 62: 63: & 84: As the arrivall of Whalley and Goffe who came to New England vnder the names of Richardson and Stephenson I knowing them comānded them before the Governo^r and acquainted him they were two of the Kinges Judges declared Traito^{rs} and Murderers and therefore advised him to secure them who answered without a Com̄ission from England none should meddle wth them. For my service herein I was abused by many by Calling mee Malignant. And the Marshall generall of the Country before severall in Court time, vsed these expressions grining in my face Speake against Whalley and Goffe if you dare if you dare, if you dare. Afterwards came to my hands the Act of Parliam^t and Kin'gs Proclamacōn wch some vilified and said they were malignant Pamphletts I had pickt vp. Hereupon I wrote a letter to the Deputie Governo^r (a copie whereof I humbly present yor Honours) sent it by my man who is able to testifie it and to that purpose brought him over wth mee) the Deputie asked him whether it was my writing he answered it was, & that I ordered him to bring his answere, who bad him be gone told him he had nothing further to say to him, By the booke of Lawes yee may vnderstand that none but Freemen who will take the oath of fidelitie are capable of bearing Office in Military

2

or Civile affaires. And though the Officers are Free-men, yet 2 thirds of the soldiers are Non-Freemen who (though at present) obey the comand of their Officers would (I am confident be glad to have Officers by the Kinges Comission and doe desire and expect a Governo͏ʳ to be sent from the King, others feare it and say they will dye before they will loose their liberties, and privi-leges, by wh^ch it may appeare how difficult it is to recon-cile Monarchie & Independency   There are many also desire his Matie may be proclaimed there, and to be governed by the Lawes of England: but in the booke of Lawes, page the 9th it is enacted That whosoever shall treacherously or pfidiously endeavo͏ʳ the alteracōn and subversion of their frame of politie or governm͏ᵗ fundamentally shalbe put to death: And if any speake for the Kinges interest they are esteemed as against their frame of politie or government and as Mutiners vnder wch pressure many groaned at my comeing away being (as I may say) debarred of their Allegiance by a law.   Wherein their Lawes are contrary to the Lawes of England.I leave to yo͏ʳ Hono͏ʳ to judge: of how great concernem͏ᵗ it is that there should be a speedy course taken for settling and establishing this Country in due obedience and subjection to his Ma^ty may appeare by the two Hectors Whalley & Goffe dayly buzzing in their eares a change of Governm͏ᵗ in England & also by multitudes of discontented persons of their Gang goeing and sending their estates thither what the effects will be is to be feared: Vnles a speedy course be taken they being the Key of the Indies, without wch Jamaica, Barbados & the Carybee Islands are not able to subsist there being many thousands Tonnes of provisions as Beefe, Porke, Peas, Bisquett Butter, Fish, &c. carryed to Spaine, Portugall, and the Indies every yeare besides sufficient for the Countryes vse.   I doe further assert That the French and Dutch tradeing into the English plantacōns in America is verie much to the preiudice of England and to the losse of his Matie in respect of Cus-toms many thousand poundes, yearely   Now whereas

there are many shipps and persons bound for New-
England sodainly, vpon accompt of libertie and to secure estates, I leave it to yor Hono^{rs} wisedome whether
it may not be requisite That the Merchants of England
that trade thither and those of New England should
not give securitie for their friends allegiaunces in New
England or else Whether it may not be expedient to
lay any Imbargo on all shipping bound thither vntill
his M^{atie} shall conclude of sending over for establishing
and settling that Country in firme peace and due obedience.

What I haye here declared I have done out of my
duetie to his M^{atie} and my love and respects I beare ; to
them of New England in generall haveing received
many comon favours from them as to my personall
affaires and as few in respect of his Ma^{ts} interest.

New Englande 11th Mar. 1661.

IV.

SAMUEL MAVERICK TO THE EARL OF CLARENDON

RIGH^T HONORA^{BLE} AND MY VERY GOOD LORD

Hauing formerly p^{r}sented to p^{r}sent to you^r Hon^r my
generall obseruations of the nature of the places, and
Constitutions of ye seuerall Gouerm^{ts} in the northern
pts of America, So shall I now in all humilitie lay open
my pticular thoughtes, what in my weake Judgm^t
may most Conduce, to ye regaininge of his M^{aties} rights
in those pts from Intruders, And reducinge the English
to dew obedience. The concernem^{ts} of it. And the
easiest way as I conceiue to effect it.

And shall therefore first humbly assert, that as his
Matie hath a genera^{ll} right to those pts, by vertue, of the
first discoueries, So likewise a pticular legall right, aboue,
aboue and before all other Princes o^r states in Europe.
First by antient possesion freely giuen by the Natiues, to

the subiects of his M^{ties} p^rdecessors, and by them taken, to theire vse and theire suckcesses. Secondly by keepinge the said possesion euer since by the English in seuerall pts thereof. Thirdly by ye purchasinge of seuerall tracts of land both on the Continent and adiacent llands by his M^{ties} subiects, and all hath beene donne by ye desire & volentary consent of ye natiues in generall. Queene Elizabeth of famous memory granted Pattents to diuerse of her subiects fo^r Virginia and places more southerly towards Florida. King James of like famous memory also granted letters Pattentes, to some noblemen, gen^t, and marchants, for all the lands lyinge betweene the degrees of thirtie fiue and fortie of north latitude, about the yeare 1609. And afterward also granted to some gen^t, and marchants, intituled the Plymouth Company, all the lands and Ilands betweene fortie and fortie-eight degrees, naminge it New England. So that I humblie conceiue, there can be no Intervale betweene either, for any prince or state to settell any of theire subiects there, nor can it be donne wthout Intrenchinge on his Maies^{ties} Rights And yett the Dutch, haue since these Patents were granted, And many English settled on both sides, intruded into the most considerable pt of both, for trade and Comerce wth ye natiues gettinge yearely from them aboue one hundered Thousand Beauar skines, besides much other good Pelterey. The land also is exceedinge good, There are also two gallant riuers runninge farr vp into the land And it lyeth most Commodious for comerce from and wth all pts of the West Indies, and may in tyme on that Account, proue very aduantagious to ye Crowne of England if Regained, and as p^riudiciall if not.

As for those English in New-England wch haue gotten the power in theire hands, you^r Lord^{sh}i^p hath beene informed how they stand affected to his Maies^{ties} Gouerm^t, they are a greate and Considerable people, and ye sooner reduced the better, They p^rtend seuerall Pattents to beare them out in what they doe, as Plymouth a grant from his M^{ties} royal grandfather, Mes-

sachusetts and seuerall others from his M^{aties} royall
Father, who also since granted a large tract of land
to S Ferdinando Gorges intituled ye Prouince of
Mayne, wh^{ch} included seauen or Eight of ye lesser Pattents, granted to seuerall others before, And since in
Oliuer Cromwells tyme another was granted for a
large tract of land, to Collonell Alexander Rigby
vnder the title of ye Prouince of Ligonia, And he by
his agen^{ts} contended fo^r Jurisdiction, ouer pte of the
Prouince of Maine and some other Pattents, But
while they were contendinge Messachusetts swallowed
vp all, The two sowtheren Collonyes Conecticott and
Newhauen haue no Pattents that I know but gouern
by Combination amongst them selues, but in a strange
confused way, and in this Confusion and ye gouer-
m^{ts} in New England at p^rsent, and I conceiue will be
no otherwise vntill his Maies^{tie} be pleased to call all
againe in to his owne hands, and disposall, wch I
supose may be donne wth out Iniury to any, there
beinge, none but haue some way or other forfaited
theire priuiledges And now my Lord in all humilitie I
craue pardon, for what I may haue erred in, in the
p^rmises, And humbly begg you^r fauou^r to giue me leaue,
to shew wth what facilitie, I conceiue the Dutch Plantations may be regained & ye English reduced. For the
Dutch I know by credible information they haue not of
theire owne Nation, forteene hundred wch can beare
armes, and there are neare fower hundred able English
men wch liue amongst them, These all both Dutch and
English, are extreamely burdned wth heauie taxations
as the tenth pte of all the land produceth, And vnheard
of Excise, not only on all goods, brought to them or
caryed from thence, but also on what they eate and
drinke. S^r I am very Confident, if his Matie doe but
send and demaund a surrender lettinge them enioy theire
lands and goods, and mittigatinge the burdens they now
lie vnder, there will be littell or no dispute about it.
Yet for the more honora^{ble} caryage on of the worke and
the more surely to effect it, It will be Convenient if his

Maies^{tie} please, to haue one good frigott and two smaler ones, a hundered or two of well experienced soldiers, one thousand spare armes wth some powder shot &c. And for what men else may be needfull in case they should at first refuse surrender, the English Plantations wthin twentie or thirtie leagues can suddenly furnish.

As for reducem^t of the English, the diuisions amongst themselues, the members and freemen, against the non members and non freemen, is such, as that if the former of these should refuse to submitt, the latter I am very confident, (are wch farr the greater number) will wth much Joy, receiue and obay his Maies^{ties} Commands, and then there can be no dispute. And howeuer debarringe them from trade a few monethes, will force them to it But care must be had, that they may enioy libertie of Concience in some reasonable large measure, And be as littell burdned by taxes or otherwise as may be,

As for the diuidinge of this large and greate tract of land in to seuerall gouerm^{ts}. The nominatinge, of some fitt and able Comisioners there. And the raisinge some reuenew to the Crowne, when regained and reduced, my selfe and one or two more well experienced there shall att all tymes waite on you^r Lord^{ship}, to shew ou^r weake apprehensions, if desired. And I shall now humbly craue leaue to subscribe my selfe.

Sr You^r Lordshipes most humble servant,

SAMUELL MAVERICKE.

V.

LETTER TO LORD CHANCELLOR CLARENDON.

RIGHT HONO^{BLE}

May it please yo^u, as to ye question once propounded to me, whether those in New England owned his Ma^{ts} Soverainty ouer them, to ye best of my observation I take 3 quarter parts of the inhabitants in the whole Country are loyall subiects to his Ma^{te} in theire harts, But as for those of ye Massachusets which made there adress to his Ma^{te} I shall humbly crave leaue to acquainte your Lord^{hp} with a few of theire actings by which it may be iudged how they stand affected.

1. Fyrst, as for the oath of Allegiance it was never administered to any although some haue desired to take it) but insted there of, they force all aboue 16 yeares old to take an oath of fidelitye wch is to be subiect to the Govern^t of that Comon wealth and to be faithfull to ye same and to yeeld assistance wth person and Estate to mainetayne ye libertyes and priviledges there of, and to submitt to ye Laws made by the same as in theire booke of Lawes.

2. Aboue 20 yeeres since they made a Capitall law, that whoeuer should atempt, any invasion Insurrection or rebellion against that theire State or Comonwealth or should indeavor the suppressing of any towne or townes fortes &c. or should goe about to alter the frame and politye of Goverm^t of that theire Comonwealth should be put to death, upon wch 7 persons for petitioning to haue a body of Lawes establisht and published as neare as might be agreeing with the same of England, for freholders to haue votes in Elections or to be exempted from publicque Charges, And that persons of knowledge and inoffensive in theire lives and Conversation might be admitted to ye Sacram^t of the Lords supper and there Children to Bapptissme for this, besides with hazard of ther lives they weare fined aboue 1000 pound, And notwithstanding there appeales, forced to pay it and there Court records about that business almoste totally falcifyed.

3. Thirdly they contemptiouslye defaced all the English Collours brought out of England; about the same time they drew vp all theire Companies in armes declareing it was to Resist there landing of a Generall Gove^r which they heard was Sent by ye King, when theire vnhappye breach began here in England (to in-

cite men to come over) Sermons were preached fre-
quentlye. on that text Curse ye Merosh. and many
came came (sic) ouer that tyme. Some to serve in y^e
Armie against his Ma^{te} others to Sowe the seede of Rebellion and Sedition amonge the rest. Peters and Weld
were sent over and for some yeeres mainetayned on y^e
Countryes cost here,

4. At the Arrivall of the said Newes of his Ma^{ts}
death most of them seemed to reioyce and Some of y^m
expressed soe much in words being then at Supper together,

5. He was not thought to haue taken a pertinent
text, if not Such as these He pulls downe ye Mightye
from there Seate and Exalts the humble and mecke.
And I will overturne overturne.

6. In all those times of Division here they forced all
Commanders of Vessells to giue great bond with Secu-
retye not to trade with any which held out for his Ma^{te}
they also permitted ships belonging to places in obedience to his Ma^{te} to be taken vnder theire forts wch they
might haue rescued and none of the other partye were
molested.

7. Theire mainetaineing and (sic) Agent here all
Olivers tyme shewed there goodwill towards him, Theire
last Agent sayd not long sence that rather then New
England should admitt of appeales to England, or be
subiect to it, they would deliver it vp to the Spaniard,
proved by Substantiall oath to his face in Drs Com-
mons. this person slipt a board the night after we were
before the Right Ho^{ble} Councell, and is gon for New
England, he was Generally Suspected to haue a great
hand in Conveyance away of Goff and Whalye, whose
Courtious intertainement by those in power theire shewes
also how Loyall they are.

8. In Ollivers tyme one Mr. Cason a gentleman of
Some qualitye, for Speaking words against the then
Vsurper Oliver was Committed to ye Goale and a great
waite of Irons layed on him for many weekes. thus
brefly to that question, by which I humbly conseave it

evidently appeares. that they haue hetherto gon on in a Constant course of Disloyaltie. I meane those which made the late adress * to his Ma^te. And truely S^r as I haue beene informed the Sending of it was carryed but by one or two voates, where as there would haue come a petition vnder thousands of hands desireing a Generall Governor to be Sent had they durst to haue don it for feare of the Capitall Law aforenamed.

But here another question maybe made, how a Gove^r can iustlye be imposed on those which haue had Pattents formerly granted for tracts of lands and Gover^t. Truely S^r I am confident all but the Massachusets and those three Sothern Colloneys in Combynation with them) of which two of them haue noe patent at all that I know of, will freely and ioyefully surrender and submitt to such Gover^t as his Ma^te shall appoynt over them. And for the Massachusets. I am fully assured that if all the Legall free-holders with in y^t Jurisdiction might freely voate for it, It would be caryed by three parts of foure at least, And I humbly Conseave his Ma^tes Royall Father in his grant to them, Intended although some few persons were named and theire Successors that all freholders should haue voats in election of officers Civill and Militarye, and be Capiable of chuseing and being chosen according to their Seaverall qualityes, But the Messachusets haveing gotten the Militia into their owne hands, debarr thre parts of foure this privilidge, dew to them and intended for them, and all vpon this Ground because they cannot ioyne with them, in theire Church Covenant, for noe Church member noe freeman, Noe freeman no voate, And by this meanes the Countrye looseth the Improvement of the abilityes of many hundred persons, and where as they should by patent haue Eighteene assistants at least, as I remember they haue not now, nor a long time haue had aboue 12. And the Gove^r that now is hath held

[* The Petition and Address of the General Court of the Colony of Massachusetts in New England, December 19, 1660. See *Massachusetts Records:* Vol. IV., Part I., page 450.]

the place 8 or 9 yeeres, I conseaue for want of fitting
choyse, this defect in Number of Maiestrates I humbly.
Conseaue is a breach of theire Charter, and wheras
the end of the grant for Euery privilidge, they are
limited not to doe or inact any thinge, Contrary or repugnant to y° law of England, Notwithstanding they
haue made, that Capitall law before mentioned, which
if any vpon the account of Loyalty to his Ma^{ts} breake he
may die for it, as some of those formerly mentioned or
one of them at least now like to doe, y° Maiestrates
being publiquely exhorted and pressed Soe to doe, by
one Mr. Rogers a minister in his Sermon before the
Court, they haue likewise lately taken away the life of
three quakers by some law or other they haue lately
made, two also were exsicuted for adultery by a law
theire made (in other perticulers I beleiue they haue
broken theire patent, but suppose it be not broken and
they will not Surrender it, They may procead as a Corporation with in theire owne iust bounds, if they can
find men willing to elect officers or be elected, And yet
I humbly conseaue it is Convenient and very necessary
that a Generall Gove^r be sent with all convenient Speed,
whoe may Setle the bounds of euery patent, Now all in
confusion as I sayd before, and in case of appeales to See
iustice don Impartially and without delay for want of
which benefitt of appeales many haue suffered deeply
there.   If resolved on, then whether one Single person
or Some Commissioners may I be soe bold with you^r
Lord^{shp} as to shew my weake apprehentions either may
doe well, but a Single person is more honorable And
truly my Lord the place is not despicable, it is the greatest Scoape of land, most improved and populated of all
his Ma^{ts} Collonies in America, and indeed without it,
most of the others could not haue gon on, nor will not
well Subsist for the future.
     If there be any doubt of their receaveing A Governor
or Commiss^{rs} my Lord pardon my bouldness.   I am
confident theire wilbe little or noe opposition.   I am
very well assured thre quarters parts of the Inhabitants

will ioyefully and thankfully receive them, as the restorers of them to libertye from long bondage, both in Civill and in eclesiasticall respects. howeuer for the more hon^{ble} carying on of the business, two or three Ships not great ones wilbe convenient some armes, these will awe them if they refuse, and keepeing of them from trade a few moneths or weekes doe the worke, And also regaine the Dutch plantation if soe ordred, And truely my Lord. that is a business of great consernement to his M^{tes}_a interest in America. Now some propositions must be layd downe, I beseach you^r Lord^{shp} once more to pardon me if I shew yo^u my poore and weake apprehentions.

Fyrst the act of indemnitie to be extended to them as conserning life and although they never allowed any libertye of Conscience to those diffring never soe little in iudgm^t from them haveing debard soe many thousands the Sacrament of the Lords Supper, though of Competent knowlidge and in offensive in theire lives and Conversations, and many thovsands of the Children of those parents are vnbaptised. Some aboue 30 yeeres old, neither would they Ever permitt any minister that would to doe it. And also haue Compelled although of another iudgment to come euery Sabboth day to theire meeteing, or for default to pay 5/s euery time and haue also made them to Contribute largely to those ministers which would not officiate as aforesayd, Yet my Lord if it may stand with the good likeing of his Ma^te and H_o^{ble} Counsell, I could wish, that contributeing according to theire estates towards and (sic) orthodox allowed minister his competent mainetaynance in Euery parish, all which is noe more then they haue made others to doe for many yeeres past. I say I wish they might haue libertye to hear whear they please, this libertye to be inioyed tell abused.

As to Civill libertye if they freely submitt to his Ma^te. I wish they may inioy all libertyes belonging to subiects. although they haue debard many thousands for many yeeres of theirs, Certainely these things offred to them

cannot but ingage them to a free and willing returne
to obedience, haveing with all the protection of theire
owne Gratious King and his confermation of the Lands
they now posses or shall heare after take vp.

Now my Lord how a revenew shalbe raysed, truely
in this I am to seeke what to say, onely this I apprehend there is noe one but will willingly pay Some Small
annuall rent to his Ma^te for the lands he shall conferme
to them as one halfe penny p Acre, which in tyme will
amount to reasonable Somes, the Customes also in time
will pve considerable, As towards the mainetenance of
a Gove^r or Comm^rs, I could wish there might not be
Soe much imposed on the people as formerlye, Some
reasonable Some reasonable Some (sic) I am sure they
will willinglye give, the rest for present must necessari-
lye be made vp some other way, the Customes of march-
andise imported from forraine parts and Some exported
to forraine parts will helpe.

And now my Lord haveing given yo^u Some perticulers of theire actings and transactings in New England, and wherein I conseave they haue forfited there
Charter, also how necessary I conseave it is that a
Gove^r or Com^rs be speedily sent over, the probabilitye
of there free reception there And to Seaverall other
perticulers, I haue presumed to show my poore and
weake apprehentions, leaveing all to you^r Lordships
Serious consideration.

VI.

SAMUEL MAVERICK TO THE EARL OF CLARENDON.

RIGHT HONO\i A^BLE AND MY GOOD LORD.

When I appeared before you^r Lordship, and the rest
of the righ^t honorab^le Councell, expectinge other inter[ro]-
gatories, I declared not so fully as I should, as to the
question, whither they euer ownd his Maties souerainty

ouer them, I declared some actions wh^ch I humbly conceiue rendered them of another Judgment as defacing
the English Coulors. Bringinge theire forces in armes
and declaringe it was to resist ye landinge of a generall
Gouerno^r sent by the Kinge. The rage betweene
Brookes and Ewers. Theire pmittinge shippes belonginge to places in obedience to the Kinge to be taken
vnder theire forts wh^ch they might haue prevented.
Byndinge all bound from thence in those tymes, not to
commerce or trade wth any people that held out for his
Maies^tie A Cappitall law in the 12th page of theire law
booke is, That who euer shall Indeauou^r the alteringe of
the frame and politie of Gouern^t of that theire Comonwealth shall be put to death. Many other thinges I
omitted. As in the begininge of the late troubles to incite men to come ouer sermons were frequently preached
on that text Curse yee Merosh &c. At the first newes
of his M^a^ties death the gouerno^r and magestrates sittinge
att supper, one asked if it were good newes, another
answered the best that euer came and no contradition.
And p^rsently after, he was not thought to haue taken a
ptinent text, yf not such as these. He pulleth down
the mightie from theire seates and exalteth ye humble
and meeke. And I will ouerturne &c. for the Oath of
Allegance it was neuer administred to any although
some haue desired it, but insteed there of the oath of
fidelitie hath beene forced on all aboue 16 yeares of
age. Wherein euery one must acknowledge himselfe to
be subiect to the gouerm^t of that Commonwealth, and
to be faithfull to the same, and yeeld assistance wth pson
and estate, to maintayne, the Liberties and privilidges
thereof. And to submitt to Lawes established by the
same.

Many acts of high Iniustice haue beene donne, but
more remarkable that ag^t Docto^r Child and six others,
who for desiringe to haue a body of lawes established, and
as neare as might be agreeinge wth the lawes of England.
Liberty as freeholders to haue votes in election of publique officers, or to be freed from publique charges. And

psons of competent knowledge and inoffenciue in theire liues and conversations to be admitted to the Sacram^t of the L. Supper, and theire childeren to baptisme for this wth hazard of theire lyues, they were besides fined about one thousand pound, And appealinge for England it was peremptoryly refused. And the recorde of that buisiness, almost totally falsified, as was there in Court since Justified.

As for liberty of Conscience the p^rtence of theire going ouer, they neuer yett allowed any to those neuer so littell differinge in Judgment from them, There are many thousands haue not received the sacram^t since they went ouer, and many thousands more borne there in the like Condition, although they are of Competent knowledge, and ready to giue account of it in publique, and liue not scandalously, And many thousands are vnbaptised of whome some are aboue thirtie yeares old.

My Lord, yf on what Complaynts haue come again^st these psons, a small pte in Comparison of the rest of the Considerable freeholders, The Kings Maiestie, re-solue not on sendinge ouer a generall Gouerno^r wth ex-pedition, his Maties loyall subiects there wch are three pts of fower, will be frustrated of theire expectations, remayne disconsolate, and still sufferers, on both ac-counts civill and Eclesiasticall.

I assure yo^u my Lord the worke will proue more dificult, if not speedily p^ruented, when we appeared be-fore your hono^rs, that Impudent and inconsiderable pson Scott thrust in after vs, And we have iust cause to sus-pect as a spie. for that night one Capt Leuerett a proud spirited pson slipt privatly abord one of the shippes bound for N. England ridinge in the downes, It is that pson who in Oliuers tyme and since, was the N. Eng-land agent, And did not long since say, that before New England should admitt of appeales to England, they would deliuer it vp to the Spaniard, proued by a sub-stantiall psons oath before a Comitee in Doctors Com-mons. And in these shippes are gonn also aboue one hundered other psons wch are gon hence in discontent, and are not like to further the reducem^t but may doe much to hinder it if not speedily p^ruented. I leaue this to you^r Lordships wise Consideration, And to pardon the bouldness of

Sr You^r Lord^{ships} most humble servant

SAMUELL MAVERICKE.

To the righ^t Honorab^{le} Edward
   Earle of Clarendon Lord Chan-
   cellor of England
        these humbly p^rsent.

VII.

SAMUEL MAVERICK TO THE EARL OF CLARENDON.

RIGHT HONORA^{BLE}

I was yesterday wth the Lord Privie Seale, who intended this day to wayte on you^r Lord^p. I make bould heare inclosed to send yo^u a breefe acc^o of what hath past betwene his Lord^p and my selfe, in refference to N. England. he put me to a taske yesterday, wch accordinge to what he propounded, and as the tyme would afford I haue ready to p^rsent to him, before he come to you^r Lord^p, And probably may shew it to yo^u. In what I may be short therein of what is expected I shall God willinge make vp wth expedition My Lord I pceiue some haue no desire that those psons in New England should be reduced: And shall make bould to put you^r Lord^p in minde, that if any thinge be resolued on that way the tyme of the yeare calls for expedition, and surely my Lord the longer it is defferred the more difficult it will be to effect it Truly my Lord what euer I haue declared is truth, I haue no selfe end in what I haue donn, only a desire (yf it may be) that as I saw the first settellmen^t of those p^{ts} so that I may see the reducement of them of them vnder his M^a^ties obedience. wch is the earnest desire of

You^r Lord^ps most humble seruant,

SAMUELL MAVERICKE

To the right Honora^ble Edward
Earle of Clarendon Lord Chan-
cello^r of England these humbly
p^rsented.

VIII.

SAMUEL MAVERICK TO THE EARL OF CLARENDON.

RIGH^T HONORA^BLE,

May it please you^r Lord^p? The tyme seemes long since I had the happines to be admitted to you^r p^rsence, I am in duty bound to acquaint you^r Lord^p, that we haue certaine intelligence from Holland that the Dutch haue latly sent one shipp and are p^rparinge three more, for the strengthninge the New Netherlands. My Lord I am affrayed Whaley and Goffe, haue a hand in the buisines, and I wish some in New England be not also involued. There are many discontented psons heare also wch are p^rparinge to goe ouer speedily, 4 or 5 shipes are already designed, what the issew may be I know not. I haue had thoughts of late to propound to you^r Lord^p a p[s]on I aprehend fitt for a Commando^r ther. It is Collonell Francis Louelace, a pson euery way accomplished for such an Imploy and very well beloued in all those pts. I leaue it to your Lord^ps consideration, being alwayes ready to wayte on you, I am S^r

You^r Lord^ps most humble seruan^t

SAMUELL MAVERICKE.

To the right honora^ble Edward
Earle of Clarendon Lord high
Chancello^r of England these be
humbly p^rsented.

IX.

SAMUEL MAVERICK TO THE EARL OF CLARENDON

RIGH^t HONORA^{BLE}.

May it please you^r Lord^p I am a daily obseruer of the many great and waightie affaires of the nation passinge thorough you^r Lord^p hands. Yett in the middest of the Croud I most humbly craue leaue, to acquaint your Lordsh^p that wth in a moneth past or there about there haue gonn of from hence for New England many seditious factious psons, Convayinge ouer considerable estates, Three shippes more are preparinge for the same designe, and for ought we know to transport the like Cargo, for what else we cannot imagine. These added to those of the same humo^r alr[e]dy there, may make y^t worke proue difficult and chargable, wch if sett on wth expedition would be easily effected, Good my Lord pardon me, I can truly, and wth confidence affirme, that neither avarice, ambition, or desire of reuenge, hath put me on what I haue donn in this buisines from first to last, It is zeale to his M^{aties} seruice, and affection to the many thousands of his M^{aties} loyall subiects and my sufferinge freinds, wch hath made me so bould att this tyme as formerly to be troublesome to you^r Lordship. The summer passeth away, and winter is not for any designe in those pts. My Lord the Earle of Marlebourgh is ready at any tyme yo^u shall appoynt to wayte on you^r Lordsh^p So is also

You^r Lordships most humble servant

SAMUELL MAVERICKE.

To the righ^t honora^{ble} Edward
 Lord Hide Earle of Clarendon
 Lord Chancello^r of England.
 these be humbly p^{r}sented.

3

X.

SAMUEL MAVERICK TO THE EARL OF CLARENDON.

RIGH^T HONORA^{BLE} S^R

May it please yor Lord^p since I had the happines to kisse your hand I haue had seuerall discourses wth the Earle of Marlebourgh, and the Lord Winsor about theire seuerall designes, I haue propounded to theire Lord^{ps} Considerable psons for Commanders such as (by discourse wth and full information from others) theire Lord^{ps} rest fully satisfied wth, as to theire abilities, for carying on the seuerall designes, but thus I finde and they vnders[t]and, that vnfitt psons striue hard for, and hope to, carry the cheife Commands, vnlesse yor Lord^p interpose as for the East Indies, one Capt Minus, and Capt Jerimiah Blackman, in whose roome some of the East India Company indeauou^r to bringe in two others who were neuer there. And for the west Indis Capt Minges, well knowne by all and approued of by my Lord Winsor, is like to be outed, and in his roome put one Capt Ffearnes, inconsiderable in respect of the other, as may easily be made appeare. Thus much I make bould to acquainte y^r Lord^p wth desiring his Maties designes may prosper. Capt Mings desires to kisse yor Lord^{ps} hand when yo^u please to afford him that hono^r, so also doth

You^r Lord^{ps} most humble seruan^t,

SAMUELL MAVERICKE.

I haue beene often wth Collonell Venables, about the New England buisines and cannot vndersta[n]d w^{tt} is doun about it, I humb[l]y desire to haue the happines to speake wth you^r Lord^p wher yo^u please to appoynt, &c.

To the righ^t Honora^{ble} Edward
    Earle of Clarendon, L: Chan-
    cellor of England these be hum-
    bly p^rsented.

XI.

SAMUEL MAVERICK TO THE EARL OF CLARENDON.

Righ^t Honora^{ble}:

May it please you^r Lord^p I haue lately spoken wth Collonell Venables, and finde him not altogether of from the New-Eng^d designe, but backward because there haue beene no propositions made to him. I haue seene some wch he hath drawne vp, to haue p^{r}sented to you^r Lord^p but fearing it might be ouermuch p^{r}sumtion hath hitherto forborne. They are many and how you^r Lord^p will ap-p[r]oue of them all I know not, yf euer they come to your view, I leave that to you^r wise Consideration. And shall now humbly craue leaue breefely to repeate the heads of what I haue formerly spoken as to the well settellm^t of New England.

Good my Lord it is the considerablest of all his M$_a$^{ties} Collonyes in America what if it were by Act of Parlam^t annexed to the Crowne of England, I meane N. Eng^d from 40 degrees to 48. that bounde beinge al-loted and that name giuen to it by Kinge James his M$_a$^{ties} royall Progenito^r.

How euer it will require a diuision into three Pro-uinces, and Commissioners appointed by his M$_a$^{tie}, in either of them.

The oath of Allegance to be taken by all, as a toutch stone to try theire loyalty to his Matie.

The Militia to be in the hands of such as his M$_a$^{tie} may confide in, wch will enable him the better to Pro-tect them.

The act of Indempnitie to be extended to all these as to life.

Pattents not apparently forfaited to continew Cor-porations according to the teno^r of theire Gran^{ts} all free holders wth in their seuerall bounds having voats in Election of officers.

The iust bounds of euery Pattent fourthwth to be laid out.

Appeales on Just grounds to be admitted of, to his Maties Comissioners.

The lawes to be reformed. And reduced as neare as may be to ye lawes of Eng^d.

Liberty of Consience in a large measure allowed, prouided they rase not fundamentalls, And to be enioyed till abused, the want of this hath much hindered the increase of that Plan^t for neare twenty yeares past, and the affordinge it, will speedily much increase it.

Taxes to be abated as much as conveniently may be.

I hope my Lord I haue at tymes made euidently appeare his Maies^tie^s titell to that great, and most considerable tract of land vsurped by the Dutch yf intended to regaine it, three shippes will be necessary, and some armes and ammunition. yf not one or two, will serue, and may in the way (if spedily dispatched) helpe to carry people wth my Lord Winsor, from the windward Iland to Jamaica. Or else as a Convoy to seuerall Considerable shippes bound for New-England; and may there take in Provision for Jamica, and in the way take in Passengers, if any p^rsent in New England or else from Barmodaes, Barbadoes and other Carieba Ilands.

My Lord I humbly conceiue, there must be from heare, a pson fitt for Conduct, and an able lawier, for there is not one in New Eng^d that p^rtends any thinge as to the knowledg of the Lawes of England, and whom else his Matie shall please to send from hence. some there will be found there, to doe him seruice on seuerall imployes, and the impowring of such, will much please the maio^r pte of the people there.

As to the raisinge a revenew to his Matie I am still to seeke, the Customs will in tyme be Considerable, and yearly one halfpenny on euery acker taken vp will amount to much. My Lord I beseech yo^u consider, how the Inhabitants hauc brought it to what it is, at theire owne cost & charges, wth out any help of the state heare,

And the charge now for resetelmᵗ and keeping it in order for the future is not greate, and will alwayes grow lesse. as the place doth grow more populous. And truly my Lord, there are some hundereds intend ⁎ ⁎ for that place wᵗʰ theire families this yeare, and will proceed if they can but vnderstand what liberty they shall there enioye. five shippes are already designed for that place, and I beleiue more will speedily. .

My good Lord I beseech yoᵘ pardon my pᵣsumption, Mʳ Winthrop Capᵗ Breedon and my selfe, and another or two, are ready all wayes to wait on youʳ Lordᵖ and I alwayes am,

Sʳ youʳ Lordᵖˢ most humble seruanᵗ

SAMUELL MAVERICKE.

To the righᵗ Honoraᵇˡᵉ Edward
  Earle of Clarendon Lord high
  Chancelloʳ of England. be these
  most humbly pᵣsented.

XII.

SAMUEL MAVERICK TO THE EARL OF CLARENDON.

RIGHᵗ HONORAᴮᴸᴱ

May it please youʳ Lordᵖ since Thursday last I heare Mʳ Norton and Bradstreete boast much that by the assistance of some great psons they haue obtayned what they came for. I besech yoᵘ good my Lord Consider from whome they were sent, euen from those wᶜʰ for so many years stiled themselues a state and Comonwealth & neuer owned his Maᵗⁱᵉˢ Soueraignitie ouer them vntill they saw there was no avoydinge of it. Yea they frequently bragged they were the elder Commonwealth. Consider also I humbly beseech yoᵘ who they are wᶜʰ are sent, euen such as for many yeares in theire seuerall wayes spoake & acted vyolently agaᵗ his Maᵗⁱᵉˢ Interest. I wish my L. yf yoᵘ shall think it fitt, that the oath of

Allegance may be tendered them, and see also how they
like the act of Vniformitie, although it may not be convenient at p^{r}sent to Impose it there.   Truly my Lord if
what they desire be granted wthout limitation New E.
will soone be in a shattered Condition.

And now once more good my Lord I most humbly
beseech yo^u to take into you^r serious Consideration the
bad neighborhoode New E. will haue of the Dutch if
they grow more potent, sad experience hath shewed it
in seuerall places, and the sooner the p^{r}uention of this is
sett about, wth more ease and lesse charge, it will be
effected, and also New England settled.

I humbly begg the favo^r, at some tyme yo^u shall
thinke fitt, to admitt me to you^r p^{r}sence, wth out these
psons.   Accordinge to you^r Comand I shall attend this
afternoone, and at any tyme else.   And euer remayne.

You^r Lord^{ps} most humble seruant

SAMUELL MAVERICKE.

To the righ^t Honorable Edward
  Earle of Clarendon Lord Chan-
  cello^r of England. be these most
  humbly p^{r}sented.

XIII.

SAMUEL MAVERICK TO THE EARL OF CLARENDON.

RIGH^T HONORA^{BLE}

I most humbly beseech you^r Lord^p that I may haue
another hearinge before the New-England affaire be
fully concluded on, where I shall affirme, (and no man
shall be able iustly to contradict it) that those wch haue
had the Comande in the Mesachusets Gouerm^t, and by
vsurpation ouer many other gouermen^{ts} haue shewed
them selues disloyall (as I conceiue) in many pticulars,
wth yor Lord^p fauou^r I shall mention some.

Disloyaltie. 1. The first wch I obserued was defacing the

English coulors terminge it a badge of the whore of Babell.

2. On a rumo^r of the arivall of a Gouerno^r sent by the Kinge they were all in armes to resist.

3. They made a Capitall Law that who euer should atempt any Invasion, Insurection, o^r Rebellion, against that their Comonwealth, or Indeauou^r the surprisall, of any towne or fort, or the alteration, of theire frame and politie of Gouermen^t, should be put to death, wch hath kept all in awe, in so much as at this tyme, the Considerablest pte of the Inhabitants dare not make an Adresse to his Matie.

4. The Oath of Allegance was neuer administered to any, but an oath of fidelitie to them selues forced on all aboue 16 yeares.

5. When the vnhappie breach began heare in England, to incite men to come ouer, sermons were frequently made on that text Curse yee Meroch, and many came ouer and serued against the King, and were heare highly p^rferred, others were sent to sow sedition, as Peeters and Weld, and were for some yeares maintayned by the Cunterey.

6. After the sad newes of the Kinges death he was not thought to haue taken a ptinent text if not such as these. He putteth downe the mightie from theire scates, and exalteth the humble and meeke. And I will ouerturne ouerturne.

7. They pmitted shippes belonginge to places in obedience to the Kinge to be taken by Parlament Comission vnder Command of theire forts. And forced all Commanders bound fourth, to enter into greate bonds, not to Comerce or trade wth any place wch held out fo^r the King.

8. They maintayned an Agent heare in Cromwells tyme wch shewed theire affection to him.

9. Theire Courteous Intertaynem^t of Goffe and Whaley, many monethes, after they knew they were proclaymed traytors and transportation offered for them, shewes also how loyall they weare.

10. In Cromwells tyme a Gen^t one Cason, for sayinge he was a Rebell and a Trayto^r was Committed to prison and heauie Irons laid on him, for many weekes, and had once a resolution to put him to death.

Iniustice.
As for their acts of Iniustice they haue beene many.

1. I shall name a few.

They gaue a Comission to one Capt Cooke to march wth a foote Company aboue fivetie miles beyond theire boundes, and there by force of armes to sease on one Mr Gorton and seuerall of his neighbours, and aliue or dead to bring them to Boston wth all theire Cattell to a great number, wch was accordingly pformed, And they in tryumph brought in to Boston, theire Cattell sould, and they comitted to prison fo^r a long tyme wth heauie Irons on, And at last dispersed in to seuerall townes, out of the bounds of wch they were not stepp vpon payne of death. theire heauie Irons still on.

2. One Mr Morton a gen^t of good qualitie, vpon p^rtence that he had shott an Indian, wittingly, wch was indeede but accidentally, and no hurt donn, they sentenced him to be sent fo^r England prisoner, as one who had a designe to sett the Indians at varience wth vs, they further ordered as he was to saile in sight of his howse that it should be fired he refusinge to goe in to the shipp, as hauinge no buisines there, was hoisted by a tackle, and neare starued in the passage. No thinge was said to him heare, in the tyme of his abode heare, he wrote a booke entitled New Canan, a good description of the Cuntery as then it was, only in the end of it he pinched to closely on some in authoritie there, for wch some yeares after cominge ouer to looke after his land for wch he had a patent many yeares before, he found his land disposed of and made a towneship and himselfe shortly after apprehended, put in to the goale wth out fire or beddinge, no bayle to be taken, where he remained a very cold winter, nothing laid to his charge but the writinge of this booke, wch he confessed not, nor could they proue, he died shortly after, and as he said

and may well be supposed on his hard vsage in prison.

3. The case of one Ratclife whome they handled cruelly, as most seuerely whiped his eares Cutt and banished on payn of death, no c[r]ime legally proued against him.

4. The sufferinges of Docto^r Childe and Company were very remarkeable, no crime proued against them, only accused for petitioning, and appealinge from theire sentence. besides the hasard of theire liues Imprisonmen_t^s monethes and some for yeare (sic), they were fined aboue one thousand pounds, Six of the scaven paid the fines, the other was three yeare or thereabout prisoner, wth Irons on, because he could not pay it.

5. Theire forcinge so many Gouerm^{ts} vnder theire Command wch had as ample and more antient Patents then theires.

6. Their banishinge so many Considerable psons, who were forced to shelter them selues vnder the dut[c]h, wher some whole familyes of them, were shortly after, all murdered by the Indians or Captiued, theire Crime was only difference in Judgement.

7. Theire forcinge men and weomen, who are of Contrary Judgm^t, to come to theire church meetinges, or to pay 5/s for euery default.

8. The puttinge to death so many quakers, strict Imprisonment, Cruell scurginges, heauie and insuportable fines laid on others, and strictly exacted to the vallew of a thousand pound and more.

9. Neither is there to be left out, that hard measure wch the owners of the Iron workes mett wth all, the workes wch cost them forteene thousand pound, beinge taken from them, wth a full stocke of mine and Coale, vpon p^rtence of a debt of three thousand three hundred pound.

My Lord I know no man can disproue what I haue said, much more I could say on either accoun^t,

As to theire petitioning for a Continuance of theire priviledges, Good my Lord I humbly conceive, if they could wthout scrupell, take away by force the priviledges, and dispose of the land of more then a dozen Paten^{ts} many granted and po[sse]ssed before theires, his $M_a{}^{tie}$ doth them no Iniurie if he take away theires, beinge wth all many other wayes forfaited, All others I am sure will freely submitt to what his $M_a{}^{tie}$ shall order.   I beseech Your Lord^p pardon me for givinge yo^u this trouble,

You^r Lord^{ps} most humble seruan^t

SAMUELL MAVERICKE.

To the righ^t Honorable Edward
    Earle of Clarendon Lord High
    Chancellor of England.
        be these humbly presented.

XIV.

SAMUEL MAVERICK TO THE EARL OF CLARENDON.

RIGH^T HONORABLE.

May it please y^r Lord^p yf I misvnderstood yo^u not, yo^u ordered me to draw vp the heads of what might be thought requisit for those of the Messachusetts to Condescend vnto, vpon the Continewation of the Charter. I most humb[l]y conceiue they may be such as these followinge.

That all freeholders may have voats in Election of officers civill and Military.

That all psons inoffenciue in life and conversation may be admitted to the sacrament of the Lords supper, and theire childeren to Baptisme.

That such lawes as are now in force there, derrogatinge from the lawes of England, may be repealed.

That the oath of Allegance may be administered in steade of that wch they tearme the oath of fidelitie.

That they goe not beyond theire iust bounds, euen those wch fo^r neare twentie yeares they were content wthall.

That they admitt of Appeales on iust & reasonable grounds.

That they pmitt such as desire it, to vse ye Common prayer.

That all writts &c. may be issewed out in his Maties name.

My Lord I hope you are pswaded of the greate necessitie there is of sendinge ouer some Commissioners for the further and better setlinge of those Collonyes, now out of order. I most humbly beseech yo^u that all convenient expedition may be made, the summer passinge fast away.

As for the Dutch I haue p^rsumed to giue yor Lord^p notice, how they incroach and increase and what course they haue taken to invite people to them, and how seuerall of o^r English familyes are lately gonn to them. I leaue all to you^r Lor^{ps} most wise Consideration, and shall alwayes attend you^r Commands. Remay[n]inge

You^r Lord^p most humble seruant

SAMUELL MAVERICKE.

To the righ^t Honora^{ble} Edward
  Earle of Clarendon L. high
  Chancelo^r of England be these
  Most humbly p^rsented.

XV.

JOHN SHAW TO THE EARL OF CLARENDON.

MY LORD

His M^{atie} was Gratiously Pleased to make Mr John Mann Surveyor Generall of Jamaica, where arriuing he found some opposition by the then Governor in pursuance of his office, vpon which he preferred a Petition vnto his Ma^{ty} that he would be pleased to giue order vnto the Lord Windsor present Gouernor now going to the Iland that he might be Incouraged in execution of his office to measure and sett out land to the Planters according vnto his Pattentt And further he humbly desirs that his M^a^tie wold be Gratiously Pleased to grant him the keeping Records of the sayd Lands being Duely Capable of the same by vertue of his surveyors Place wch Petition is by his M^a^tie Referrd vnto my Lord Windsor to be grattified in his Requestt or otherwise to Certify what his Ma^ty conceiue fit to be done theirin.

My humble request vnto y^ur Lord^pp is before my Lord off Windsor Leaue England to Recomend the sayd John Mann vnto his Lord^pps fauour he being & will approue him selfe a most vsefull Person hauing at his one Charge made a survey off the Iland whereof he hath made a Draughtt & sentt itt vnto his Matie.

Yo^ur Lord^pps most humble servant
JOHN SHAW.

23th Aprill 1662.

Endorsed—" *A Memoriall towching Mr John Mann Svrueyor off Jamaica April 23th 1662,*" and " *A Lre from Jo. Shaw for Ld Clar^d to recommend Mr J. Mann surveyor of Jamaica to Ld Windsor ye Governor.*"

XVI.

JOHN CLARKE TO KING CHARLES II.

MY LORD O KING

I humbly and earnestly craue yor Majesties favour according to y^or Royall word, for a speedy dispatch of a good & ample Charter for ye Colonie of Rhode Island & Providence Plantations, and that ye Charter lately granted unto my neighbo^r Mr. Wintrup may againe be reveiwed by yor Majesty, for as much as therby he hath iniuriously swallowed up the one half of o^r Colonie: And y^t now by yor wisdome, through a cleer information of ye state of those Parts, such certaine & equall bounds & limitts may be set between us both, as may

best stand with ye growth & flourishing of those Planta-
tions & with ye Permanent hono^r of yor Majesty & yor
Petitioners shall take themselues greatly obliged

JOHN CLARKE.

May 14. 62.

XVII.

SAMUEL MAVERICK TO THE EARL OF CLARENDON.

RIGH^T HONORA^{BLE}

May it please you^r Lord^P (if I know my selfe) I have
beene for some tyme, becne a faithfull Intelligencer, as
to the New-England affaires in psuance of wch I heare
wth humbly p^rsume to p^rsent to you^r Lord^P a trew representation of the affaires as now they stand there,
colected out of seuerall letters lately come from thence
and also by report of many psons lately arived euery
pticular, and more, will be playnely made out if re-
quired. I leave all to you^r Lord^{P[s]} wise Consideration,
and am att all tymes ready to attend you^r Comandes.
And shall euer remayne

You^r Lord^{ps} most humble seruant
SAMUELL MAVERICKE

My Lord I haue much more to say, so hath Capt
Breeden and others, yf yo^u please to Command vs att
any time to wayte on yo^u.

To the righ^t honora^{ble} Edward
    Earle of Clarendon Lord high
    Chancellor of England these be
    must humbly presented

Endorsed—" New Englande. B: No. (12.)"

A Representation of the state of affaires in New England as Collected out of Seuerall Letters & by reporte of Seuerall persons wch Lately came from thence as followeth.

One Mr Kellon Who formerly had the Kings Warrant fo^r aprehending Whaly & Goffe. Whome he followed making dilligent inquiry after them as farr as Newhauen, where being Credibly informed they were in two houses, ye s^d Kellon went to ye Gouern^r Mr Leete for his asistance and Liberty to search, wh^ch the said Gouern^r refused should be don vntill such tyme as their did a Court sitt about it, wh^ch delay the s^d Mr Kellon Credibly beleues was an opertunitie giuen to Escape away wch he suposes they did from the s^d two howses, & that wth the consent of Some of the Chieff Magistrates, ye said two Coll. being reported to bee at the said place two dayes after Mr Kellons going away and yett no Care taken to aprehend them.

The said Mr Kellon informing of a french Vessell that Came to Boston to trade Contrary to the Act of Nauigation, and prosecuting according to ye s^d act in his Maties behalfe was condemned to pay ye Charge of the Court, though he fully proued the Information.

One Mr Lositer a fusition taking notice of ye delay of Newhauen Gouern^rs & their Neglect to Yeild Obedience to ye Kings Warrant for Whaly & Goffe, in the name of him Selfe & diuers of his Neighbours to quitt themselues from ye Guilt of that neglect, drew vp a protest in Writting against itt, w^t their reasons for so protesting, wch they gaue in to the Governo^rs, & for ye protest the said Mr Rossiter was a forthnight Imprisoned.

Its frequently taught & preached as a duty to hide ye fugitiues of Moab, the Kings M^atie is spoken slitely of, & prognostick of a Sudden Change in one yeare more & Such Like things are blowne about in New England to keepe vp a party in a hopefull Expectation of an alteration here.

Diuers Youths lately p^{r}secuted att Boston for making bonefires on Gunpowder treason day at night, it being kept as a thankesgiuing for ye returne of New England Agents, Y^e Youths being Willing to Conforme to ye practise that Such a tyme affords in old England, for this the parents of the Youths were fined, but ye Children of ye Church Members Who Were guilty as much as Others. Scapt all Scott free.

One Capt Scott is reported to haue had ample power from ye King & Councell, W^{ch} in a little tyme in Long Island he putt forth to ye Imprisoning diuers, Others he threatned much, Especially ye Gouern^r of Rods Island, butt hauing strick Comand from the Kinge to returne Wth all speede, hee Could not stay to Effect his intended designes, this Cap^{tt} Scott by his Confident boasting of his fauor at Court is Entertayned of their Cabinett Councell at Boston, & now reported to bee in some imployment for them to England, One Thomas Joy but for asking him Whether he did not once keepe Cows, was asaulted w^t two or three boxes on the Eare & vpon Complaint of the s^d Scott to ye Comission^{rs} the s^d Joye was fined 200lb bound to his good behauior, and Since his Estate all Seized on.

Cap^{tt} Scott confidently affirmes that my Lord Chancello^r in his heering & in publick audience asked Mr Clarke iff hee where not ashamed so Impudently to Vilify and acuse Mr Winthrop (and Mr Winthrop being present) my Lord Chancello^r should say he wondered how Mr Winthrop Could have the patience to bare itt.

Cap^{tt} Scott is much made of att Boston and reputed as their Sauiour, pretends to bee a greate fauorite att Court Weares about his Neck the Kings picture in gold, Wth a gold chayne, wch hee affirmes heere ye King gaue him and before his going over to New England he afirmed the Duke of Yorke gave it him.

Diuers inhabitants of Roade Island Colony have been imprisoned att Boston aboue 12 moneths for keeping possession of Lands bought of the Indians wch is not wth in the bounds of their pattent, and notwthstanding their Apeales to his M^a^tie when the Agents of the respectiue Collonyes where p^r^sent in England, are not yett releast butt more strictly Confined vpon the returne of ye s^d Agents.

The Libertyes of New England are nothing att all inlarged, notwithstanding his M^a^ties orders in his Letter, the Gene^tt^ Court spent about 3 Weekes tyme in descanting vpon itt what his Maties meanes and disputing whether the King w^th^out the Parliment Cann Impose such things on them, and many doe Openly Expresse they neuer intend to Obserue his Maties Comands and Will dye before they Will Yeald to him, and are more seuere against the Kings friends than Euer they were.

Strange Reports are Raysed and blowne about concerning the diuisions of England the the (sic) King is gonn to Windsor Castle and dares nott Come to London. Thereby to discorage all the Kings freinds here, and to keepe vp the Sperits of others in Expectation of Sudden Changes and alterations. Which are frequently pronosticated here.

Endorsed—"*Extracts of* 5 *Seuerall letters from New England. Feb.* 1662. *B:* N^o (13)."

XVIII.

SAMUEL MAVERICK TO THE EARL OF CLARENDON.

RIGH^T HONORA^BLE

May it please you^r Lord? As I haue ptly vnderstoode w^tt Indeauours there haue beene to obstruct the settelm^te of the Gouerm^t of New England, so I also vnderstand that some (vnder the name of Inhabitan^te of, and adventurers to New England,) haue indeavored to render me vncapable, of bearing any share (as a seruant) in that worke, this hath not beene vnknowne to many who haue beene, and are much concerned there on wch some for p^rvention of secret scandalls wch might hinder me of being the meanest seruan^t in this worke haue drawne vp, and subscribed, this inclosed testimony and presse me humbly to p^rsent it to you^r Lord.^p they are not many yett enough, And truly my Lord these are the men wch long haue, and still doe driue on the trade in that place, and it will euedently be made appeare, that those, who haue indeauored to obstruct, are no way Considerable, nor cannot stand in competition wth these. I humbly leaue it wth you^r Lord^p, and am ready at all tymes to attend your Commande humbly cravinge the fauou^r from you^r Lord.^p that at some convenient tyme I may haue the happines to speake wth yo^u : And I shall euer Remayne

You^r Lord^{ps} Most humble seru^t

SAMUELL MAVERICKE.

To the righ^t Honora^{ble} Edward
    Earle of Clarendon Lord high
    Chancello^r of England. These
    be most humbly p^rsented.

Endorsed—" 8. *Mr. Mavericke* 28. *March.* 1662. *testimoniall frō the Merchants.*'

[DOCUMENT REFERRED TO IN THE PRECEDING LETTER.]

These are to certify all whome itt may concerne that the bearer heereof Mr Samuell Mauerick, hath a long tyme dwelt in New England (allmost since the first plantation thereof by ye English) inioying the loue & friendly respects of ye Generallitye of the inhabitants their, amongst whome hee hath had his coñuersation inoffensiuely, & not iustly liable to any obiection so farr as wee can heere or vnderstand saue that (for conscience sake) hee could not subiect to bee a Church memb^r, Butt otherwise in greate esteeme as a person whose desiers & endeauours haue allwayes bin for ye generall good of ye Cuntry, & for the inlargement of those iust Libertyes & priuilidges (wch through the corruption of the tymes) the inhabitants their hauе bin depriued of, & haue greate hopes of beeinge restored vnto, by the endeauors of the sayd Mr Mauerick, Whose retorne to New England in the effectuall accomplishment thereof would bee

4

exceedinge ioyfull to farr the Maior part of the people
their,   To the truth whereof wee who haue liued in
those parts, and others of us who haue long tyme held
correspondence, & bin frequent traders wth ye inhabitants thereof (for preuention of secrett scandalls obstructing his endeauours) haue thought fitt to giue him this
testimoney to wth wee haue subscribed our names this
20th of Ma^{rch} 1662.

John Beix	Robert Lord
J Davy	Dauid Ashley
Will. Beeke	Edward Godfrey
Will. Hiecoke	of Yorke in New Eng- lan^ some times an Inhabitant 27 yeres.
J, Pococke.	T. Breedon
Tho. Goodlake	John Winder
Wee whose names are aboue menconed sie the Com^any of Ad- venturers for the Iron Works in ye Masse- chosetts in New Eng- lan^.	Tho : Kellond
[Name illegible.]	John Breedon
John Dand	Tho : Bell
	David Yale
	Sam : Hutchison.

XIX.

Col. Thomas Temple to the Earl of Clarendon.

My most Honored Lord.

I thought it my duty to giue your Lo^{sp} this short
accoumpt of Noua Scotia and our affayres therein.   At
my Ariuall into these parts, it was the begining of
winter, which broake not vp heer vntill May.   The latter end of which month the Generall Court sate heer in
Boston ; to whome I addressed my selfe for thier freind-
ly assistance against the French or any other persons, in
order to ye preseruing his Ma^{tis} right in this Country.
which I obtayned ; haueing found the Country inuaded
by the french on that part borders on Canada ; vnder
the Comand of two brothers Called by the Tytles fo
Monsieur de Cowdray. and Monsieur Bell Iles. sonnes of

one Monsieur le Borgne. a Rochell marchant; they pretending the King of France his Comission; which I neuer saw; for though I have Monsieur Belle-Ile. one of the brothers heer prisoner he shews noe Comission, but says his brother hath one. at my first Comeing all though it were winter I sent out a little frygatt & a Catch of my owne. & surprised both hime and a vessell. he had taken from me; that lay before his fort; within Pistoll shott; & hearing that there was some french men of war vpon our Coast; which gaue forth great braggs what they would doe this summer I procured two very fine frygatts. built heer one of 28 gunns. the other of 18. both well mand. to scoure along our owne Coast. & mett with none but one man of war, whoe was sent me in hether. & finding he had a Portugall Comission. He was freed; I haue in this few months prouided all necessary furniture; for to build a fort at La Heaue the nearest place In my iurisdiction. to the french and have mounted. twenty good gunns. the fort will be vp. & fitted by october. & then I feare noe power eyther of Pyratts or interlopers. a fort I have alsoe fitted to place vp in the Indians country our enemys. which will be built and mannd in the Spring. Soe that I hope to giue his M^{tie}a a good accoumpt of this Country; being now in Treaty. With the chiefe persons of Dartmouth & Plimouth, to begin a fishing desygne in these parts. & bring all the fishermen at New found Land hether, if that fayles—this being the fruit fullest place of fishing knowne in the World; which if god gives a blessing to my endeauors will proue of great aduantage to his Matie poeple & subiects, and his owne reuenues. for the fish, will be brought into London from hence. & other parts of the Kings Dominions which now is suplyd by hollanders; whoe takes nothing but mony for it, and that in vast summes whereas his M^{tis}a subiects will make their returns in the manifactures of his owne Kingdomes. Nauigation & shipping mightily encreased and in short My lord in a few yeares, when his Matie is master of all the fishing trade in the North

of America he will be master of the King of Spaynes, may without fyghting or makeing war for it. but whether doe I ramble ; I beseech y^{re} Lo^{sp} pardon my boldnes. For the Copper I told his M^{atie} off to speake the Naked truth. I have not mony to open the mine which at first will aske a good summe to entertayne miners & thier prouisions. but this I will performe. if his M^{atie} please to send any or imploy any knowing person hither I will shew hime the place and truly, (as I beleeve) the richest mine of that sort was euer knowne. Mr Chyuins can shew y^{re} lor^{sp} a farther patterne both of the Copper & the Mountayne ; some of the stone. the Marchants y^r Lo^{sp} writ about haue obstructed me both in this & the fishing all in their power Good my lord forgiue this boldnes and pardon this Romantick paper. tyme may posibly persuade your Lo^{sp} there is more reason & truth in it ; then I confess there there is (perchance) manners or wisdome. good my lord pardon for this once the want of both. if you shall iudge it such. in
My most honored lord Your humblest seruant
T. TEMPLE.
Boston. August the 21th 1663.

MY NOBLE LORD.

I humbly wish this letter may fall into your lo^{sps} hands as you ride in your Coach. to Hampton Court or Twitnam. that your Leasure alone may beg pardon for my presumption.

XX.

COL. THOMAS TEMPLE TO THE EARL OF CLARENDON.

MOST HONORED, AND MY SINGULAR GOOD LORD.

I receaued yours of the 25 of Aprill (63) wherein to my noe small Comfort, I found the Continuance of your Lor^{sps} great goodnes, iustice, and noblenes shewd to me in my poore affayrs, (howeuer vndeseruing) in giueing me leaue, and tyme, to answer for my selfe, which fauor in all due humility I must euer thankfully acknowledge My lord it hath bin an extreame affliction to me, (vnder which I still languish,) to be noe otherwise knowne to your Lo.ᴾ then by the clamarous complaints haue bin presented to you ; though altogether vniust ; neyther was anything wanting in me to haue freed your loˢ·ᴾ from farther trouble in this kinde, a thing I infinitely desyred & noe less indeauored ; haueing made at my ariuall into these parts ; as I thought & belieued ; a friendly and finall agreement betwixt Cap. Breedon & my selfe, Concerning all differences, debts, & matters of accoumpts, or security what soeuer betwixt vs which I did chiefly in respect & obedience to your Loˢ·ᴾˢ Coāands though to my loss and in my owne wrong some thousands of pounds. he haueing receaud as apears by accoumpt 5000ᵉ yᵗ yeare of my absence in Peltry and gaue me noe other accoumpt, but that it was all spent in charges. his owne amounted to 500ᵉ more, all which I allowd off besides the 1000ᵉ I allowd time by his freinds articles in London. and Truly my lord I was very much surprized at the receipt of your loˢ·ᴾˢ, and the more when at the same tyme Cap. Breedon had desyred me to vse my interest at the Generall Court to take of the Fine they had imposed vppon hime which contrary to all mens expectations and beliefe I obtayned, though it was Carryed but by two or three voices. and giuen vnto me. which I gaue to his Atturnys heer. neyther doe I insert this heer out of vanity but to shew your loˢ·ᴾ plainly vpon what tearms Cap. Breedon & I parted. the true state whereoff, and of yᵉ Country as I found it, I made. bold to informe your Lo.ᴾ off in a letter sent by a Gentleman. one *Mʳ John Richards* at the same tyme, but your Loˢ·ᴾ being ill. & not to be spoaken with he gaue it into yᵉ gentlemans hand that wayted whoe gaue hime this accoumpt that he had presented it into your Loˢ·ᴾˢ own hands.

My lord to answer in Particular to what I am charged withall by Cap. Breedon although I could easily make it; yett to enter into particulars, (or re-crimininations a thing I naturally hate.) I feare it would be both vnseasonable and tedious to your lo:ᵖ whose minitts are pretious, especially in a letter. Therfore I shall humbly beg leaue to make motion to your Loᵖ That you would please to impower some one person or persons heer, eyther by way of Comission or otherwise whoe may iudge and determine all matters betwixt vs eyther in matter of security, or accoumpts; I shall waue all aduantages I might pretend by any articles made with his brother, or others or himselfe. Nay my lord I shall with pardon offer yett more. Cap. Breedon hath left heer two very honest, able and sufficient men his atturnys to looke after his estate; one of them a marchant partner with hime in the Company: furnisht me with goods. The other, a Merchant that kept all our accoumpts betwixt both the Company & my selfe. the fittest men to settle busines betwixt vs. I will be Content if it may stand with your loᵖˢ pleasure; & ease your farther trouble, to stand to their finall iudgment & determination.

My lord you were gratiously pleased to intimate in yours that you would not Countenance any vnreasonable demands. and since honest and generous mindes haue euer giuen place to reason; to that, and your loᵖˢ Comands I shall euer equally and cheerfully render all humble & readdy obedience. Indeed fortunes liberality haueing denyed me any better way at present; to express my humble accknowledgment, and due thankfullnes; for all those many vndeserved fauors and reall benefitts, you haue Confered vpon me vnless it be in my feruent prayers to allmighty god, to Continue & encrease your prosperity heer; vntill he shall change it into eternall happines. Soe prays my euer honored good lord.

Your most humble most obedient & most faythfull deuoted Seruant

T. TEMPLE

Boston, August the 21ᵗʰ 1663.

Endorsed—" *Coll. Temple from New Englande. Aug. 21ᵗʰ 1663.*"

XXI.

COL. THOMAS TEMPLE TO THE EARL OF CLARENDON.

MY LORD,

After I had writt my letters to your Lo⁸ᴾ vpon perv-sall of yours to my selfe and Cap. Breedons petition, I thought my selfe obliged to giue your Lo⁸ᴾ this short accompt more, which is.

That I am content to giue any farther security, vpon the land or otherways, as Concerning the Peltry trade which shall be produced. there wauing all former articles.

And for the rest I am charged withall. to haue stopt thier Peltry. at once. 800 £ an other tyme 1400 £ the first I did when there was a report heer that Mʳ Newgat & Mʳ Harison were Comeing to seize vpon the forts. Soe soone as it Came & we had news that Cap. Breedon was Governor. I gaue it euery skin into his Corespondents hands. Mʳ Vsher his partner.

for the 1400 £ I stopt which he says they payd for extrauagant expences of mine; first it was not any such summe, but being forced to take vp goods of other men, & they backward to pay them. I writ them once word from the fort that if they did not pay them as they ought I would, & see they payd them off. this is the whole truth.

for his first article, of 2500 £ that I ow them on the old Companys accoumpt. it is vtterly false. in euery word & sillable. they indeed sent ouer a partner of thiers in that ship brought me yʳᵉ Loᴾ letters. whoe sued me heer in Court, in two actions about it, in both which I cast them. and proued them fully payd.

for the forfiture of the morgage or the land. I haue Cap. Breedons bond of 8000 £ for performance of his Old Articles. which I will make proofe he hath often and sundry ways broaken to my damage aboue the sayd summe. My lord, in short, I shall refer my selfe, ey-ther to any arbitration, or your loᴾ owne iudgment.

& waue any aduantage by my new Articles made in
London.

Since I was vnhapily engaged wth these men, or
knew the stratagems of merchants ; which is about
seauen years. I have payd them. betwixt 30. or forty
thousand pounds reserving to my selfe but 200 £ a yeare,
and I believe I can make it a peare that for most of their
goods I have payd a hundred in the hundred aduance.
Besydes. the Comodity I payd them in was in furrs.
which as I am informed they haue many tymes doubled.
by which y^{re} Lo^p may iudge they may well render any
one insolvent as they terme it.

I and my friends are really out vpon this Country.
5000 £ & they never a penny. except ye goods they receaue aduantage by. good my Lord : pardon this trouble
I am forced to giue you and if I doe not proue every
word I have writ to be true & all thiers falce, be pleasd
my Lord not only to take away my Comission but punish me wth death.

> I am My ever honored Lord Your most humble &
> most obedient seruant

> T. TEMPLE.

Boston. August the 22th 1663.

XXII.

SAMUEL MAVERICK TO THE EARL OF CLARENDON.

RIGH^T HONORA^{BLE}

May it please yo^u since I spoke with you^r Lordship,
we haue received Intelligence from New England, of
what daylie and ernest expectation there is (by the
loyall ptie there) for the arrivall of his Maties Comissioners, who may free them, from the bondage, they
haue so long lyen vnder, they also informe, that very
littell or nothinge is pformed, of what was promised
before you^r Lord^p by the Mesachusets agents last yeare,

they also lett vs know that there are many hundreds this
yeare arrived there from hence generally disaffected to
his Maties Gouerm^t both civill and ecclesiasticall, And
from the Manhatas we heare the dutch Gouerno^r hath
sent for a supply of men and ammunition, and that they
intend wth all expedition to build a fort on Niott poynt,
wch who euer hath, will inioy, that braue riuer, and the
rich trade there in : I therefore must humbly beseech
your Lord^p to be pleased wth all conuenient speede to
dispatch away the Comissioners. Collonell Griffith is
goinge downe to Cornebury to kisse yor hand, and to
p^rsent to yo^u seuerall proposalls many of wch we humbly
conceive will (being granted) proue vsefull, fo^r the better settlemen^t of those Collonyes, And to wayte on him
there goes to psons wch I am well assured may (wth yor
Lord^ps approbation) be very vsefull. the one Capt Jno.
Manninge who hath for many yeares beene a Commander
vnder Maio^r generall Morgan, who hath given him a large
and ample Certificate, wch he will shew you, many more
he might have had if desired, he is well knowne and beloued in New England, and will be fitt for any imploy-
m^t in the Militia. he is very desirous to goe, and hath
wayted for this imployment aboue 18 monethes, The
other pson is Mr Mathias Nicholes who hath beene
bred a scholar, and a studient in Lincolnes Inne, and a
good proficient as by many I haue beene informed, and
had he had now tyme, he could haue brought Certificates from some sariants at law and other eminent
psons) by what I haue heard and seene, I (most humbly Conceive he may be fitt for a secretary to the Comissioners, and I hope after your Lord^p hath had some
discourse wth him, approue of him so to be.   My Lord
I leaue all to your Lord^ps Consideration, Craving pardon for my bouldnes, I shall euer Remayne
          S^r you^r Lordp^s most humble seruant
                              SAMUELL MAVERICKE.
    Septemb^r 1th 1663.
To the righ^t honora^ble Edward Earle of Clarendon Lord
    high Chancello^r of England these most humbly be
    p^rsented.

XXIII.

John Winthrop to the Earl of Clarendon.

Right Honorable

Vpon the happy arrivall of his Maiesties Com̄missioners I had the high favour of your Lordships letter: Duty and affection inforceth me humbly to acknowledge your lordships accumulate goodnesse to your servant, & this Colony of Coñecticut and all New-England: Your Lordships Comañds, for reception of the Honorable Com̄issioners, shalbe attended wth all imaginable indeavours, according to the capacity of this our wildernesse condition, and wth all dutifull observance. I have been to waite vpon their hon^{rs} at their first com̄ing to the West End of Long Iland, and continued that service, till, vpon the 28th of August last, I saw ye towne vpon the Manatos Iland reduced to the obedience of our Soveraigne Lord the Kinge, Wherby there is way made for the inlargment of his Maties Dominions, by filling y^{t} vacant wildernesse, in tyme, wth plantatiōs of his Maties subiects, and we hope also it wilbe a meanes of ye future peace, & good of these his Maties adioyning Colonies.

I humbly beseech Your Lordship; be pleased still to favour these plantations, wth the continued extention of y^{r} goodnesse, wch hath appeared thus farre over this vast Ocean: And y^{t} the Lord of Heaven would multiply your Lordships yeares, wth all abounding fœlicities, wilbe their continuall supplications, together wth his, who is ever devoted to be,

My Lord your Lordships most dutifull Humble
        Servant
                                JOHN. WINTHROP.

Hartford in New-England
        Sept. 25, 1664.
For the Right Honorable Edward Earle of Clarendon
Lord High Chancellor of England.

XXIV.

THE COURT OF NEW PLYMOUTH TO H. M. COMMISSIONERS.

The Courts answear to the propositions made by his Majes-
ties commissioners.

1. To the first we consent; it having been the practice of this Court in the first place to insert in the oath of
fidelity required of every housholder, To be truly loyall to our Souveraigne Lord the King, his heires and
successors. As also to administer all acts of justice in
his M^{a}J^{tie} name.

2. To the second we also consent, it having been our
constant practice to admit men of competent estates, &
civil conversations, though of different judgements. yet
being otherwise orthodox, to be freemen, and to haue
liberty to chose, & be chosen officers both civil & military.

3. To the 3.^{d} We cannot but acknowledge it to be a
high favour from God, & from our Souveraign, y^{t} we
may enjoy our consciences, in point of Gods worship,
the mayn end of transplanting our selues into these remote corners of the earth; & should most heartily rejoyce, y^{t} all our neighbours so qualifyed as in that proposition would adjoyn them selues to our societies,
according to the order of the gospell for enjoyment of
the sacraments to themselues & theirs. But if ,through
different perswasions respecting church government, it
cannot be obtained, we would not deny a liberty to any
according to the proposition that are truly consciencious
although differing from us, especially where his Majesty
commands it, they maintaining an able preaching minister for the carrying on of publick Sabboth worship,
w^{c}h we doubt not is his Majesties intent, & withdraw
not from paying their due proportions of maintenance
to such ministers as are orderly setled in the places
where they liue, untill they have one of their own; &
y^{t} in such places as are capable of mayntaining the
worship of God in 2 distinct congregations. Wee being

greatly encouraged by his M_a^{ties} gracious expressions in his letter to us, & your honors further assurance of his Royall purpose to continue our liberties, that where places, by reason of our paucity, & poverty are uncapable of two, it is not entended that such congregations as are already in being should be rooted out, but their liberties preserved, there being other places to accomodate men of different perswasions, in societies by themselues wch by our known experience tends most to the preservation of peace & charity

4. To the 4th we consent, y^t all lawes & expressions in lawes derogatory to his Majesty, if any such be found amongst us, wch at present we are not conscious of, shalbe repealed, altered, & taken of the file.

The league between the 4 colonies was not (with any intent y^t ever we heard of) to cast of our dependance upon England; A thing wch we utterly abhor intreating your honors to belieue us, for we speak as in the presence of God.

The Court doth order Mr Constant Southworth Treasurer to present these to his Maj. commissioners at Boston withall convenient speed.

By order of the Gen^{ll} court for the jurisdiction of New plimouth.

NATHA. MORTON secret.

New plymouth, May 4, 1665.

Endorsed—"*The Court of New Plymouths answear to 4 propositions &c.* 4 *May*, 1665."

XXV.

GOVERNOR BELLINGHAM TO THE EARL OF CLARENDON.

RIGHT HONO^RABLE

May it please yor Lordship this Court having had ye hono^r of perusing yor Lordships letter * of March 15. 64. directed to the Governour & Councill of this his

* [Printed in Hutchinson's Mass. Vol. I. Appx. XVII.]

Majesties Colonie upon seriouse consideration thereof returne your Hono^r our humble thanks for your favourable respect & freindship therein exprest Assuring you that it cannot but very deeply affect us that our application to ye Kings most Excellent Majestie should carrie ye least appearance of any shortnes of Expression of that due submission & acknowledgement which might answer his Matie Royall favour in so bounding the hono^{r}able Commissioners by Instructions wherewith being at that time wholly unacquainted, though since they have ben made known unto us, we were left under the sence of such extent of the Commission as was represented by its Expressions to us & indeed since y^t we have found them so to insist on ye Exercise thereof as to render those our fears not altogether groundlesse The account whereof being rendred will manifest that there hath not been so clear a convey of his Matie Grace as (we dare not but believe) is lodged in his Matie royall breast towards us. The consideration whereof doth the more depresse us that we should by any shortness of expressing argument for our request occasion his Matie to have such a sence of our humble Application & supplication to him as is manifested in the Hono^{ble} Secretary Moris his l^{e}re of 25 Feb 64 Being truely sensible how much it is incumbent on us to act in all things according to our duety whereby his Gracious Matie may find in himself why he may be pleased to continue that Grace to us of which we haue so high a value & so great need in this our exile capacity though we cannot deserve it. It is most true that ye Complaints exhibited against us by persons not so studious to serve his Matie as themselves by his Matie authority with their suing for iustice at his royall hands could not giue us cause to expect other than his Matie pleasure hath put forth. But of those complaints we haue not received any notice from y^e hon^{ble} Commissioners save one relating to Mr Thomas Dean & of that in a way whereby they would haue subjected to themselves the authority which hath ben derived to this Court & so long enjoyed by us from

y^e Favour & Grace of his M$_a$^{tie} & his royall predecessors. viz by summoning this Court to appear as Delinquents at the barre which we could not submit unto
without forfeiting our Allegeance to his M$_a$^{tie} in betray-
ing the trust comitted to us for y^e carrying on that
work which is the great good & maine end of y^e Pattent
& our transportation into this wildernesse. For rend-
ring account of any thing alledged against any proceedings of Court or Person in Authority we haue tendred
unto them that whereby we might giue his Majesty
satisfaction, which hath been refused by them. & therefore we haue sent the Narrative of our proceedings with
them that they may be presented & submitted to his
Majestie. By which we hope that we shall clear it that
this Court hath not any such præsumption that his
M$_a$^{ties} subjects in this Colonie are without hope of redresse appeales being ordered from inferio^r Judicatures
of his M$_a$^{tie} to them that are superio^r & ourselues being
ready at all times to render a faithfull & humble account
unto his Majesty. & we assure your Lordship we præ-
sume not to expect a continuance of happines in our
enjoyments But in the way of duetifull obedience to
God & the King Of which we shall indeavo^r that there
may be no ground of doubt from the whole of this his
M$_a$^{ties} Colonie. In the Assurance whereof we Crave
the Continuance of your Lordships favour & end with
humble & earnest prayers unto God to præserve his
M$_a$^{tie} & your Lordship

    remaining Right Hono^{r}able Your Lordships most
humble servants

RI. BELLINGHAM, GOV^R

In the name & by the order of the generall
Court of the Masachusets.

Boston. In New England 30th of May 1665.

These ffor the right Hono^{rble} Edward Earle of Clarendon
    Lord High Chancellor of England & of his Majestjes
    most Hono^{rble} Privy Council be humbly presented

XXVI.

Governor Bellingham to Robert Boyle.*

HONOURABLE S.

Itt is a great favor in your hon', had it beene no more then the taking notice of this smale colony of the Massachusets, circumstanced wth both meaness & remotenes, but to shew this respect, at such a tjme when loaded wth many calumnies & reproaches from evill minded persons, is as well a great addition to this favour on your part, as of obligation to the reall acknowledgment of the same on ou^{r}s;

Although we hope the righteous God will in his due time make it manifest to his Majesty & to our Deare Nation & people from whom we are this day voluntary exiles, that ou^{r} accusers are such who designe not the honor of his Majesty, but through the glosse of spetious pretences doe ajme only the advancement of their particular ends, & contriuements yet tending to the great obstruction of his Majestjes reall interest & the jnevitable ruine of his good subjects heere. That any clause in our last addresses should carry any appearance of reflection vpon his Majestjes wisdome, & Iustice or be wanting in that due respect which we owe to his Majesty as it ministers vnto us matter of much' exercise, so we can truely say, it was far from our jntencōn, who doe acknouledge ourselues so abundantly obliged in the chearefull discharge of our duty to his Majesty, for the reitterated assurances given us of the full & peaceable enjoyment of all the libertjes granted vnto us, by his royall charter, & particularly & in speciall wise expressing the same in his jnstructions given to his honou^{rble} Comissioners for the regulating of them in the excerting the power & authority to them given by their comīssion, so far as the same relateth to this colony.

[* Compare Endicott to Boyle: Oct. 19, 1664, in Birch's Boyle; Appx. 450, and Boyle to Endicott: March 17, 1665 in 2 M. H. S. Coll. VIII. 49.]

S^r

Your expressions of tender respect for our good coming wth so much reallity christianly counselling & cautioning of us in the way of duty the only & sure way for the obteyning of our just desires, doeth embolden us with the greater freedome to give you^r honou^r this further trouble, humbly crauing this favor from you^r hon^r, that so far as you^r wisedom shall find any just plea in what we present, you will please to improve the same, according to the oppertunity the lord hath given you for our just vindication & in anything you find lesse pertinent, or jnconvenient to be insisted on, that the same may be burjed in your oune breast The result of the late negotiation betweene his Majesty^s Comissioners & this his Majesty^s colony, we know not how better to comunicate to your hono^r, then by the transmitting true Copies of all that haue passed in conference betweene us, the which we haue caused to be done vnder the hand of the Secretary of our Generall Court herewith inclosing the same.

Vpon pervsall whereof your honour will easily perceiue where they & we haue disagreed, as also the reasons why we could not submitt to their proposalls & Comands to ou^r generall Court & all our officers both military & ciuil in such wise as appeares by the warrant vnder their hands.

The ample assurance given us by his Majestje that he hath not the least intencōn nor thought of violating or in the least degree Infringing his Royall charter heretofore granted by his royall father as more particularly is fully exprest in his Majesty^s letter. to this colony of Aprill 23^d 1664 doth encourage us to hope & expect that we shall yet haue the continuance of his royall favour towards us, & that he will not charge us wth the denyall of his Soueraignty for our non obseruance of those Comands of his Comisioners as were expressly derogatory to his Majestjes honōr & authority heere as contrary to his Instructions given them to obserue in the exercise of their Comission in this Colony; as by

comparing his Majestjes letter of Aprill 23ᵈ 1664 sect.
2ᵈ his Instructions to his Comissioneʳs sect 2ᵈ? 3ᵈ? & 8ᵈ
with their warrant for protection of John Porter Junʳ,
their third reply to our returnes made to their proposall,
on the eighth Instruction; the peticōn of the President
of the Colledge & sundry other gentlemen the same will
fully appeare.

And whereas It is a grand priuiledge of his Majestjes subjects in this colony as is conteyned in his Majestjes royall charter that wee & our children after us shall
haue & enjoy all libertjes & jmunitjes of free & naturall
subjects wᵗʰin any of his Majestys Dominions to all intents constructions & purposes whatsoeuer: Giving &
Granting vnto the Gouernoʳ & Company liberty from
tjme to tjme to make lawes &c for the well gouerning
of the people of this Colony not contrary to the lawes
of England, & appointing the said Charter or the duplicate or exempliffication there of for the putting the sajd
lawes in execution to be a sufficjent warrant to discharge
&c: all this being pleaded by us in conference that we
had with them, together with our rejtterated tender by
both word and writing, to give them an account of the
grounds of our proceedings in any matter or case that
his Majestje had comāanded them, or themselues sawe
meete to make inquiry into; and we willingly grattified
their desire wᵗʰ giving them a Copy of a letter wee received in the time of our Conference from Sʳ Willjam
Morrice, wherein his Maᵗʲᵉ although manifesting himself
not well pleased with our last addresse; is graciously
pleased to declare that his intent in sending them in such
a capacity to this place is out of his speciall favour to
us; & that he might be truely informed of those many
complaints against us, as well by neighbour colonjes,
particular persons, & the natiues, & in case they could
not compose matters themselues, then to give an account
of the true state of any such case to his Majesty; all
which we willingly submitted vnto, as may appeare in
our returnes to them before recited, yet neuerthelesse they
still jnsisted vpon our Submission to them as a Court of

5

Appeales & proceeded to sumon the Gouerno^r & Company being Assembled in generall Court with some others in such wise as their writting expresseth to appeare before them that they might heare & determine such complaints as should be exhibbited against us,

1. And vpon the Question put to them by a Comittee (at their request) appointed by the Court to conferr wth them about these matters, first by what lawes they would proceed in Judgment they answered by the lawes of England

2ly. Secondly whither they would haue a Jury to passe on such cases as they tooke cognizance of, they answered no

Now hoño'd S^r the premises considered be pleased to give us leaue to propose first whither our Submission to such their Comands would haue rendered us to his Maj^{ty} fitt persons to be betrusted with the administration of Justice here for the punishment of Malefacto^{rs}, & maintenance of ciuil right, wherein the honour of God & his Majesty is so much concerned.

And whither such a submission be consisting with the priuiledges of Englishmen especially for a whole Colony of his Majestjes subjects, that haue purchased their libertjes, by planting his Majesty a Colony at so great a distance from all civil Nations, & at so deare a rate as wee haue done: As also the necessity we were put vpon (after their refusall of so many tenders as is aboue-recited, together with their manifest Interposing with the authority here in such wise as we haue done) to declare our non compljance wth them in their proceedings, for the timely preventing of great danger that might haue acrewed therevpon & the mantenance of his Majestjes peace here, according to the constitution of our charter to all which we stand obliedged by ou^r oathes to God to his Maj^{ty} & to his good Subjects of this colony.

Wee doubt not but his Maj^{ty} will receaue full information by his aboue said commision^{rs} of the falsnes of many of the complaints & misreports made concerning vs as to the great diuicōns of the people here & their disaffectednes to the Gouernmen^t according to our present constitution, that it is not groune to so great a heigth as represented to his Maj^tje by the petition* of Mr Samuell Mauericke, (& by his Majesty referred to the Hono^ble Comissioners of forreigne plantations the 5th of August 1663) boldly therein affirming that our diuissions were groune to such a heigth that we were ready to rise in Armes one against another, or remooue to the dutch or other places, and wee hope in the Issue our Innocency will further appeare touching those cases where of ou^r enemjes haue so greatly aspersed us to ou^r Lord the King

S^r if to all your favo^rs yor hono^r will be pleased to Add this to pardon our boldnes in giving you^r hono^r so great a trouble you will thereby the more obliege vs dayly to pray to God to fill you^r hon^r wth such guifts & graces of his holy spirit as may fitt & enable you to discharge the duty^s of so great a place & trust to wch he hath called you whilst you are here, that when you are to be no more he may take you to himself in Glory wch is the praje^rs of S^r.

You^r Hono^rs most Humble Servants

RI BELLINGHAM GOV^R

In the name & by order of the generall Court of ye Massachusets.

Boston in New England, 31th of May 1665. ·

These For the Hono^rble Robert Boyle Esqr Gouerno^r of the Corporation for the proppogation of the Gospell amongst the Indians In New England present

Endorsed—" *Colony of the Massachusetts to Mr Boyle, May* 31. 1665."

[* The original petition was stolen out of the Secretary's Office in Whitehall by one Capt. John Scott and delivered to the magistrates at Boston. Letter of Colonel Nicolls in *N. Y. Col. MSS:* III. 136.]

XXVII.

THOMAS DEANE TO THE EARL OF CLARENDON.

Boston the 22th June 1665.

My Lord

I was honoured with yours of the 16th March for which I most humbly returne your Lordsp my most hearty thankes, the enclosed I deliuered accordinge to directions.

Yo^r Lord^{sps} Comaunds vppon me to giue a free relation of all that passes, putt me on a great Streight, beinge fearfull to incurr your Lordships displeasure either by silence, or writeinge what I vnderstand not, the truth is my Lord the transactions of his Majestys Comissio^{rs} and the Genera^{all} Court of this Collony, were all priuate and wee Catch Nothing but by the Ecco, Exceptinge thus, The Comissio^{rs} were pleased to Lay the Stresse of what followed on my case, which if it might haue been without disseruice to his Majesty I could haue wished had been otherwise and not the first Case as I acquainted them, but their Wisdome saw other caus and I submitted thereto, His Majestys Comissi^{rs} went into the Gen^{all} Court and Summoned the Gouern^r and Comp^{ie} to appeare before them next morninge at the hous of Capt^e Breedons which Sumons insteed of beinge obayed occationed the publishinge of a Declaration by order of the Gen^{all} Court next morninge by sound of Trumpett in seuerall places of the towne, the Last whereof was vnder the window of Capt^e Breedons hous where the Comiss^{rs} were then mett, vppon which the Comiss^{rs} gaue vp, I doubt not but yor Lordship hath seene the Courts Declaration, and there by will sufficiently see their Speritts. The next day after this Coll: Nicholls repaired to his Comaund at New Yorke the others since gone Eastward, vppon this after two days the Gen^{all} Court Comaunded me and Thomes Kellond (a merchant concerned with my selfe in the Seizure) to appeare and offerred a tryall before them to which my Answere was, that in regard we appealed to the Kings Comiss.^{rs} wee could not thinke it be came our Duty so well (since they pmitted not the Tryall to be before so equall Judges) to haue it tryed there. Therefore with seuerall other psons (who seeme to haue iust caus of Complaint) and were thus hindred from the iustice they expected to be done them) wee must wait with patience vntill his Majestys further pleasure be Knowne. It cannot but be troublesome to yor Lords^p for me to giue my sence of thes people's disposition, you will better pceiue it in the Papers they Answere the Comiss.^{rs} with, and the requitall they haue made for his Majestys Royall grace and fauour towards them.   Butt my Lord you may be assured and wilbe informed, his Majesty hath many Loyall Subjects here which I hope wilbe so considered, as not concerned in this Courts proceedings

My Lord

I'me here for some yeares setled, and am obliged for my owne security as well as I can to temporize.   If heareafter I may be made happy with your Comaunds you will conferr the greatest honour Imaginable vppon

My Lord yor hono^{rs} most humble Seruant

THO. DEANE.

To the Right hono^{able} Edward Earle of Clarendon Lord high Chanceller of England & one of his Majstys most honou^{able} priuie Councle humbly present

Endorsed—" *Tho' Deane from Boston (in America) to the Ld Chan June 22* 1665. *R.*"

XXVIII.

SAMUEL MAVERICK TO THE EARL OF CLARENDON.

RIGHT HONO^{BLE},

May it please your Lord^{pp} by Capt Harrison I hope you have received two letters from me, one by the Capt

owne hands, the other from the hands of Mr John Breedon brother to Capt Brcedon.

In one of which I gave your Lord^p a breife accoumpt
of what passed at the court of Election: what kinde of
persons were chosen into office; who amongst the whole
Court of Magistrates, & Deputies I conceive to be loyall,
& honest: who otherwise: How that the Major part,
not the wisest disowned his Majesties authority over
them, & in effect proclaimed it by sound of trumpet, for-
bidding us to act any more (within their jurisdiction)
on his Majesties Commission, to us granted.

In the other, I presumed to declare to your Lord^p
my opinion, how these people may most speedily, &
with more safety to the innocent be reduced, As by
seizing on some of their estates in England, I named a
ship now in the King's service, belonging most part of
her (if no fraudelent coveighances have been lately
made) unto persons of this place, & none of his Majesties best subjects, her name the Society Christopher
Clark Comander, untill shee was pressed into his Majesties service. An other way I propounded was the prohibiting of all trading with any of his ^{M}a^{Jties} Colonys in
America or into any part of Ewrope, without Certificat
first had, & obteined from such as his Maj^{tie} shall here
authorize to give such Certificates, that they belong to
such or such a Colony who are in obedience to his
^{M}a^{Jtie} or to such or such a person in any other Colony
who are knowne to be loyall Subjects to his Majestie.
A third way which I presumed to propound was, the
keeping of two small vessells, on this coast, who may
probably hinder all commerce with the Massachusets.

Since which time I have met with some able, &
honest men, who are of opinion, that, the ordering of
two, or three (of the most refractory persons) to be sent
for England, will soone do the work. but there must
be force to backe it, The fittest psons for p^{r}sent to be
sent for are Richard Bellingham Gou^r Daniell Gookin,
Will: Hathorne Rich: Waldron or Walden James
Oliuer.

Colonel Cartwright becomīng fit for travell, on the 8th of June we began our journey to the Eastward parts: At Salem, Ipswich, Newberry, & Hampton we found kind entertainment: ffrom Hampton we went (accompanied by severall persons) to see the place where the bound howse once stood, a person living close by, shewed us the very place where it stood, & when the howse fell, he placed a barrell of a gun in the place where it stood, which hee shewed us standing, as the bounds of Massachusets eastwards: Between this place & the Province of Mayn are the townes of Hampton, Exeter, Dover, & Portsmouth, the three last lye in Pascaraquay river: In all those places we acted nothing; but passed over the river into the Province of Mayn, & first summoned the inhabitants of Kittery to appeare at Major Shapleys howse, to heare his Ma^{jties} Commission read: They generally all peticōned, that they might be taken under his Ma^{jties} immediat go^rvm^t not being willing any longer to remaine under the Massachusets, and as unwilling to be subject to Mr Gorges: with what expedicōn we could we went unto all the townes within the Province of Mayne & found the Inhabitants generally desiring, & peticōning for the same favour, as will appeare by a generall peticōn now sent to his Ma^{jtie} by Colonel Cartwright: To satisfie them for the present, till the Kings pleasure were further knowne, we freed them from being under either of the aforesaid Governments & appointed certaine Justices of the peace to order the affaires of that Province.

Yesterday in the towne of Wells they kept the first Court, to the great joy of the people, who had been long in a confusion; Sr Robert Carr & myself were present. Not withstanding those of Massachusets knew what we had don, yet on the 4th of July they sent two of magistrats, & other officers, to keepe Court at York: but finding the people would not submit to them & unexpectedly finding Sr Robert Carr, and myself there, & the foot company in armes, they forthwith returned.

When we were at Casco in this Province, the Sagamore of Wesapaguaqueg* & of severall other places, came & surrendered his Country (under the hand & seale of himselfe, & other great men) to his Maj^{tie} humbly craveing his protection of them; It is a far better country then Narraganset, Colonel Cartwright hath the deede in his keeping.

The whole province of Mayn is claimed by severall persons who had distinct Patents from the Councell of Plymouth for it, all subscribed by S^r. fferdinando Gorges, as he was one of that Councell, & done long before he got the Patent for the Province: And as I have said before the Inhabitants, humbly desire they may be free from that government, and truly My Lord, neither that, nor the Massachusets will ever flourish, nor will the major part of the people be satisfied, untill they be fixed under his Maj^{ties} immediat government. If all the ffreeholders may have liberty to assemble they will vote that the patents may be delivered up to his Maj^{tie} & it will be carryed by ten to one.

On the 9th of Julie, we received his Maj^{ties} letter of the 28th of January, & forth with in prosecuçon of what was commanded, we sent warrants to the foure townes on Pascaraquay river, ordering the inhabitants to meet us on severall dayes at their usuall places of meeting to heare his Maj^{ties} letter read, & to consult with them about fortifying that river. On the 13th of Julie being the day of meeting at Portsmouth, the Governor & Councell of the Massachusets, by two of their Marshalls sent a prohibition to the people, & a letter to us, which put a stop to our indeavours, for the present.

Indeed, if it may please your Lords^p it is very necessary that, that river should be secured: the harber is very good, & spacious, there is usually loaden thence above twenty ships yearly: at this time there are 7, or 8 ships lading, one of which is laden for the most with

[* " In this province also an Indian Sachem, who lives neare to the great " lake, from whence flows Merimack River, petitioned his Ma^ty to take him " under his protection, which is also lost." *Commissioners' Account of the Province of Maine*, in Folsom's *Catalogue, &c.* p. 67.]

masts, & the best that ever went hence. It is very great pitty to see how naked, & open they lye, even a booty, to any small Pickaroone. Colonel Cartwright can give you an exact accoumpt of this, as of any other things you shall desire informacōn in, especially what gunnes, ammunition &c. may be needfull, & are not here to be had, not only for securing this river, but Road Island, & other places also, who haue yet no kind of defence.

My Lord, if it had not been for the stubborness (if not rebelliousness) of the Massachusets, his ^{Ma}j^{tie} might by this time have had a better accoumpt of affaires here, then now he can. The far greater part of the people feare they shall still remain in bondage to their old masters the governour and Councell of the Massachusetts; Those in Hampshire are not yet freed from them, although much desired by them. Those in the Province of Mayn (although freed for the present) yet fear they may be returned again under either the Massachusets or Mr Gorges government, & then look on themselves & posteritys as miserable.

Good my Lord, I beseech you hasten what you may the setlement of these poore people, I am much affraid, there may be, else, bloudshed. I assure your Lords^p we have used our indeavours according to our skill & have not forborn to travell in extreamities of cold, & heat any where, where we might have hopes to do his Maj^{tie} service your Lords^p hath formerly been pleased to intimat that their was a suply for us, either sent, or to be sent, of which we yet heare nothing, I beseech you to consider, that our expence is great, far more, when we are travelling, then when we are in Boston in our quarters, & it can not be avoided with honour. And I hope your Lordship will not forget to procure something from his Maj^{tie} towards the expence, & trouble I was at in England in following this New England business, I shall desire Mr Breedon to waite on your Lords^p about it.

Your Lordship knows I informed nothing but what was true, and as I said there, all things have come to pass hitherto here, I did prognostik the rebellion of the

Massachusets governour, & councell; & now they have made good what I said. I am the man they looke on to be their cheife enemy, & on that accoumpt make no conscience of abusing me: yet I praise God for it, they have nothing justly to say against me. and may I but retein your Lordships favour, I care not for what they can say or doe, which favour I humbly beg, & shall endeavo^r in any thing I may in some measure to deserve. And shall much rejoyce, if while I live, I be any wayes serviceable to his M^a^{jtie} his Highness or your Lordship, & shall ever remaine

your Lord^{pps} Most humble Servant
SAMUELL MAVERICKE.

July 24th 1665.

Endorsed—"*Mauericke* 24 *July* 1665 *R*"

XXIX.

RICHARD NICOLLS TO THE EARL OF CLARENDON.

July ye 30°. New-Yorke 1665

MY LORD,

Capt. Carterett, who ariued in May at Virginia, sent mee yor Lord^{pps} of the 11th of Feb with the inclosed Duplicate of a former which never came to my hands, these arived heere the 22th of June, and this is the first opportunity which presented to returne answer from hence to virginia, and soe into England, My Lord those high expressions of yor Lord^{pps} care for a supply to bee sent to the releife of our necessities keepes up the spiritts, both of Planters and soldiers, who will be contented to goe naked in his M^a^{ties} service, wee haue rather hopes then feares of De Ruyters arivall, being allready better fitted then any other Plantacōn in America, insoemuch that the Dutch heere who have Long hoped for and expected De Ruyter, begin to pray that hee may never attempt a peece of service to their soe certaine ruine I

must not flatter yor L^{dp} with the Imaginary strength of
the ffort which is truly inconsiderable against Land
forces, but all his ffleet shall doe vs noe preiudice, I haue
sett double stockadoes round, and mounted 40 pcice of
Cannon vpon the Walls & Batteryes I haue 200 men
heere for the defence, besides the other Garrisons which
may not bee Left naked. I haue furnisht all the English about mee with Armes & amunicōn, and disarmed
only ye Burgers of this place in this posture our affaires
stand, Tis his Maties and his Royall Highnesses their infinite goodnesse to countenance my poore endeavours in
these parts with their Royall approbacōn, I shall dayly
endeavour to become worthy of soe high an honno^r My
Lord I was soe much sollicited to bee present at Boston
in hopes of a fayre Issue of his Maties Comīssion, that
after haueing settled every thing in good order heere I
made a journey through the Woods to Boston, and returne back in a moneths tyme, Of those transactions
Coll Cartwright will giue yor L^{dpp} a full account, who
hath taken great paynes in the Employment, and is now
vpon his returne into England. from him yor L^{dpp} will
allsoe be more fully informed that the late Indenture
made to my Ld Berkley and Sr George Carterett is to
the manifest destruction of the Dukes Collony, for my
lord, the very name of the Dukes power heere, hath
bine one great motive for weell affected men to Remove
hither out of other Collonies, men well affected to Monarchy, and haue found that our new Lawes are not con-
triued soe Democratically as the Rest, and when I was
last at Boston, I did engage a hundred famillyes to re-
moove, and dispersed printed papers for their Encorag-
ment, but good land is none of the least Arguments to
a Planter which was then to bee found in the Dukes
Pattent, but now is wholly giuen away, In discharge of
my duty to his Royall Highnesse, and the trust reposed
in mee I begg pardon for being very plaine in the matter,
My Lord, all that part of the Duke's Pattent ioyneing
to Nova Scotia is not worth a farthing, when it comes
to Long Island which is a place of common fame, I as-

sure yo[r] L[dpp] it is as barren a soyle as any part of New
England, meanly inhabited by a poore sort of people
who are forct to labour hard for bread and cloathing,
the whole revenue which can bee drawne from their
Labours is but 200[£] of this country pay, which is litle
aboue a hundred pound sterling, with which sume all the
courts of Justice and other Publique charges are to bee
maintained, I durst not endeauo[r] to stretch their purses
farther in the infancy of this change least their affections
should bee perverted, and wee doe not want ill neighbours to doe us ill offices in such occasions But by this
meanes all their mouthes are stopt, and the first 3 sessions haue bine held with good satisfaccōn to all the
Collony, in 7[ber] is held a generall Assizes the Governour,
Councell, and Justices upon the Bench, where the lawes
are againe to bee reviewed and amended, in case any
reasonable obiections bee made, otherwise to bee confirmed heere, and remitted over to his Royall Highnesse
for his Royall hand, to make them authentick, and then
if they were printed and imediately sent over they would
bee fully satisfactory to these parts, and of some consequence to his Ma[ties] Interest, in relation to the other
Collonies, Your L[dpp] will allsoe perceiue by this inclosed
determinacōn, betweene the Comission[rs] with the Gov-
crno[r] and councell of Conecticutt that those Townes
upon the maine to the Eastward of N. Yorke did properly belong to their precedent pattent, soe that there
remaynes only, One small Towne to his Royall highnesse, of all that tract of land from Conecticut Riuer to
Hudsons Riuer, soe that up Hudsons River which is
all the North part, and soe cold that few or none will
bestow their Labours, Only one Towne is seated w[th]
Planters to which or very neare the Indenture reacheth.
aboue that 70 myles is Albany seated, who are noe
planters but only a towne of Trade, with the Indians,
Thus the extent of the Dukes Pattent is described to
yo[r] L[dpp] and I humbly begg your L[dpp] to take the whole
matter into serious consideracōn, for if the Duke will
improove this place to the vtmost, Neither the trade, the

Riuer, nor the Adjacent lands must bee devided from this Collony, but remayne Entire, But if his Royall Highnesse bee weary of the hopes of his new Acquisition It were much better for the publique good to devest himselfe of the whole and then I might haue hopes to bee recalled to the hono^r of a domestick . . . . .
In which, or any other Employment I shall most cheerfully pay my duty as long as I liue,

I most humbly recomend my selfe and the necessityes of this place to your L^{dpps} protection, not doubting but with an vnwearied dilligence and constancy both officers and soldiers, and every man heere in his capacity, will in some measure deserve yor L^{dpps} fauo^r, of which though I am the most vnworthy yet noe man is more ambitious than I am to bee knowne.

My lord Your L^{dpps} most obedient & most faithfull
    Servant

RICHARD NICOLLS

To the Right Honble the Earle of
  Clarendon Lord High Chancel-
  lour of England

XXX.

SAMUEL MAVERICK TO THE EARL OF CLARENDON.

RIG^T HONOR^{BLE}

May yor good Lord^p please once more to giue me leaue to begg in behalfe of those who haue so long beene sufferers vnder the Mesachusetts Gouer^t and yett finde no releife. On ou^r arivall they had great hopes of it, but seeing nothing donn, they feare they shall be in a worse condition then formerly, And if his Matie doe not take some spedey course, those who haue declared them selues against them will be vndon, the case of the loyall ptie heare, being all one as it was not long since in England, although they are two for one at least, yett they are so ouer awed that they cannot helpe them selues, And if his Matie should yet longer suffer these people to goe on in theire way, hauing so much declared them selues, against his authoritie ouer them, those wch are well affected will neuer dare heareafter to declare them selues. besides all those ill consequences wch must necessarily follow the loyall pte being daylie threatned, and this day the extraordinary generall Court setting it is rumored abroade, that we shall be commited and that they will send fourth forces in to the Prouince of Mayne to subdue those who latly renownced them, and so freely submitted to his Matie Good my Lord pardon my bouldnes the groanes, and continewall complainte of these poore people constraine me to it. I shall endeauou to keepe vp theire spirite what I may, in hope of a speedy releife.

We supposed the supply we haue heard of had come by one Capt Carteret, but he hath beene long in Virginia and many haue come thence / and we hear nothing of any such thinge / ou^{r} expences must necessarily be great / and w^{t} we haue receiued heare hath beene to a full quarter pte losse, And for credit we must expect none heare, vpon the acc° we are on Coll Cartwright and my selfe haue not had one farthing worth of all the plunder taken at Delawar it was worth they say about Ten thousan^{d} pound, but how squandred away or to whome giuen we know not, a runagat seruant of his confessed he had 400^{ll} I mean Sr Robt Carr, he heares he is not to haue the gouerm^{t} of Delawarr and therefore now moues the Inhabitants of the prouince of Mayne to petition that he may be Gouerno^{r} ouer them / he indeauours to be very popular / and accepts of Courtesies fron such as are not of the roghtest. I shall trouble you^{r} Lord^{p} no more at p^{r}sent but subscrib my selfe

You^{r} Lord^{ps} most humble seruant,

SAMUELL MAVERICKE.

Boston, Augt 11th 65.

Endorsed—" *Mr. Mavericke of Boston to the Ld. Chan: Aug. 11th 1665.* R."

XXXI.

Samuel Maverick to the Earl of Clarendon.

Right Hono^{ble}:

May it please your Lord^p. By Capt. Hide an account was given by us of our proceedings to that day, which was Novembr: 24th last, which came safe to hand, as your Lord^p. was pleased to writ to me. By Capt. Harrison May 30th: we gave a full relation of what had past to that day; but not hearing whether that ship ever arrived, I herewith send you a copy of that letter, which I sent by him: but the particulars of the transactions wth the Gen^{all} Court of the Massachusets, was sent to New-York: one copy also was sent by Colonel Cartwright, besides that formerly by Harrison. The Court promissed to print it but since refused to do it.

What business was done in the Eastern parts, from the 8th of June, to the last of July Your Lord^p. may be pleased to see in the copy of the letter sent to M^r. Secretary Bennett, the originall of which was sent by Colonel Cartwright.

On the third of August a gen^{all} Court extraordinary, began at Boston to consider (as many supposed) how to mannage theire opposition: And being informed, that they had commissionated Maj^r. Gen^{all} Leverat, Maj^r. Lushar; & Damforth, three of their Champions, to go into Hampshire, & the Province of Mayne to call the inhabitants to an account, for their submitting to his Matie and peticoñing to him, that they might be freed from them Sr Robert Carr went shortly after thither, expecting their coming. I remained here, to watch their motions; at last about the 4th of October, they set forth, & coming to the hither side of Pascataquay river, it was expected they would have gone over the river into the Province of Mayn; but receiving a letter from Sr Robert Carr (then being on the other side) they forbore, onely went to Dover, where they had ordered a

Court to be kept that day ; & demanding a reason from the inhabitants, why they had peticoñed to be freed from under their governm^t, and receiving an answer (to be supposed) not according to expectation ; within two howers came away for Boston.

On the news of Colonel Cartwright's being taken (as 'tis by most imagined he is) the Gen^{all} then sitting, ordered a gen^{all} day of Thanksgiving, to be kept, in all their Jurisdiction ; some frivioulous reasons they give for it ; but the main is, that God hath yet been pleased to lengthen out the injoym^t of their liberties.

Last night Mr Delavall came from New York hither, haveing been, but 50 howers coming. all are well there : There wants nothing but a supply of money, or goods ; which Colonel Nicolls & we all desire, may be sent, if not allready done ; for without it the Garrisons cannot be maintained, nor we live, as (for his Maties hono^r) we ought to doe.   We carry it on as well as we can, desiring, not to let the people know that we are any way straightned ; which to know, would cause some to rejoyce, & insult.

I shall trouble your Lord^p no further at present humbly desiring your Lord^p to be pleased to be referred to Mr Secretary Bennet for further information, of what iherea is wanting ; for to him by this conveighance we send   copy of a Letter sent him by Colonel Cartwright. A copy of the Massachusets declaration ; A Copy of J. Porters peticōn, & the protection we gave him, which they so much are troubled at ; A copy also of the prohibition they sent to the Constable of Portsmouth, & of theire letter to us, & our answer to them.

These we send fearing the former may be lost.   By all oppertunities I shall acquaint your Lord^p with all materiall passages here ; Humbly craveing the continution of your Lord^{ps} wonted favours towards me ; and I shall ever remaine

Your Lord^{ps} most humble serv:

SAMUELL MAVERICKE.

Boston Novembr: 7. 1665.

XXXII.

Sir Robert Carr to the Earl of Clarendon.

My Lord

May it please your Lord.ᵖ When Colonel Cartwright returned for England I made bold to trouble you by him with a lᵉre, which if he be taken by a Dutch Privateer, as we have it reported with us in Boston, that hee is : I feare, that that with others miscarried. But the result of what I then sent, was to let Your Lord.ᵖ understand, that, That prejudice which is throwne upon me by some malicious persons, I do not yet understand what it is ; though assured by yoᵣ Lord.ᵖˢ letter to Mᵣ Maverick, that there is some against me. It was so long before I saw your Lord.ᵖˢ letter, that I had not time to write more.

I had received a fall, by which I had hurt my leg, at Delaware, and that kept me so long, before I could attend the Commission : but before I could well weare a Boot, I went to New-York, & so to Boston : and ever since we begun, which was the 20ᵗʰ of ffebruary, I referr myself to Colonel Cartwrights relation : I hope I shall not loose your Lord.ᵖˢ good opinion (which I most highly esteeme) by a single, & a mistaken report.

That little which I had gotten, by the hazarding of my life, at Delaware, I heare is given away and one come over to take possession of it : Wherefore I beseech your Lord.ᵖ if any thing of my concernes comes before your Lord.ᵖ that you would give a dispatch unto it.

I have some suspicion of the persons who have prejudiced me, & misrepresented me unto your Lord.ᵖ I doubt not to make it appeare to be too rashly, if not maliciously done of them : & shall referr myself to Col: Nicolls, & Col. Cartwrights relation for my vindication : I shall speak evell of no man, but I wish that Those persons had demeaned themselves in these parts

6

so acceptibly as I have done, and things might have beene otherwise then they are.

I beleive, ere long, you may receive an account of our deportments, if you have not already, and shall submitt to your censure, & his M^{aties} sentence thereupon, as to my particular concerns: This aspertion occasioned my boldness to send a letter to be presented to his Matie. The copy whereof is inclosed.

I hope you will not too hastily conclude me guilty (my Lord) of any thing may render me disloyall; and shall desire your pardon for troubling you with this relation, desiring you to give his Matie an account thereof, at yor best oppertunity, and I shall ever acknowledge my self

Your Lord^{ps} most obliged, faithfull, & humble Servant,

ROBERT C . . . .*

Boston Decembr. 5. 1665.

To the Right Hono^{ble} Edward Earle
of Clarendon Lord High Chancellor of England

———

XXXIII.

ACCOUNT OF MASSACHUSETTS, BY COLONEL CARTWRIGHT, 1665.

The Colony of the Massachusetts was the last, & hardlyest perswaded to use his Majesties name in their forms of justice.

In this colony at the first going over of the Commissioners were many untruths raysed, & sent into the other colonies, as that the King had sent the commissioners thither to rayse 5000^{£} yearly for his Majesties use &c. where upon Major Hawthorn at Salem made a seditious speech at the head of his company; and their

[* The name is torn off in the MS.]

late Governor made another in their meeting hous, at Boston, but neither of them were so much as questioned for it by any of their magistrates.

The Commissioners visited all the colonies before this, hoping both that the submission, & condescension of the other colonies to his Majesties desires would haue abated the refractorinesse. wch they much feared in this colony; and that the assistance of Colonell Nicolls, whom they expected, would haue prevaled much. But nether examples, nor reasons could prevayl with them to let the Commissioners hear & determine so much as those particular causes (Mr Deans, & the Indian Sachims) wch the King had commanded them to take care of, & to doe justice in; And though the Commissioners (who never desired y^t they should appear as delinquents, but as defendants, either by themselues, or by their atturnies) assured them, y^t if they had been unjustly complayned of to his Majesty, their false accusers should be severely punnished, & their just dealing made known to his Majesty, & to all the world, yet they proclaymed by sound of trumpet, That the generall court was the Supremest judicatory in that province; That the Commissioners pretending to hear appeales was a breach of their priviledges, granted them by the Kings royall father, and confirmd to them by his Majesties own gratious letters, and that they could not permitt itt. By wch means they haue for the present silenced about 30 petitions, wch desired justice against them.

To elude his Majesties desire of their admitting men civile, & of competent estates to be freemen, they haue made an act, whereby he who is four & twenty years old, a hous-keeper, & brings one certificate of his civile life, another of his being orthodox in matters of fayth, & a third of his paying 10^s, besides head-mony, at a single rate, may then haue liberty to make his desire known to the court, and it shall be put to the vote. The Commissioners examined many townships, & found y^t scarce 3 men in 100 payd 10^s at a single rate; yet if this rule was generall, it would be just. But he, who is a church member, though he be a servant, & pay not 2^d may be made a freeman.

They will not admitt any who is not a church member to the communion, nor their children to baptisme, yet they will marry their children to those whom they will not admit to baptisme, if they be rich. They did imprison & barbarously use Mr Jurdain, for baptizing children, as himselfe complaynd in his petition to the Commissioners. Those whom they will not admitt to the communion they compell to come to their sermons, by forcing 5^s from them for every neglect; yet these men thought their own paying of 12^d for not comming to prayers in England was an insupportable tyranny, and they yet constantly pray for their persecuted bretheren in England.

. They haue put many quakers of other provinces to death, (for wch also they are petitioned against) first they bannisht them as Quakers upon payn of death; & then executed them for returning. They haue beaten some to Jelly, & been otherwayes exceeding cruell to others, & they say, That the king allowes it in his letter to them. Indeed they haue misconstrued all the kings letters to their own sence.

They haue many things derogatory to his Majesties honor in their lawes of wch the Commissioners made a breviat, & desired y^t they might be altered; But they haue yet donne nothing in it. Amongst others, who ever keeps Christmas day, is to pay $5^£$.

They caused at last a mappe of their terratories to be made; but it was made in a chamber, by direction, & guesse. In it they claym Fort Albany, & beyond it, all the lands to the South Sea. By their south line they entrench upon the colonies of New plymouth, Rode island, & Conecticot, & on the East they haue usurped wholly the pattents of Mr Mason, & Mr Gorges; & say, y^t the Commissioners had nothing to doe betwixt them & Mr Gorges, becaus his Majesty commanded them ether to deliver possession to Mr Gorges, or to giue his Majesty reasons why they did not.

The Commissioners being at Piscatoquay, when they received his Majesties command to see the harbours fortifyed, sent their warrants to 4 towns upon that river requiring them to meet at a certain time & place to hear his Majesties letter read &c. one of these warrants was sent post to Boston, from whence 2 marshalls were sent the next day post by the Governor & councell with another warrant to forbid those towns either to meet, or to doe any thing commanded them by the commissioners, at their utmost perills; and withall sent an unbecoming letter to the Commissioners.

Colonel Whaley, & Goffe were entertayned by the magistrates w^{t}h great solemnity, & feasted in every place, after they had been told that they were traytors, & ought to be apprehended. They made their abode at Cambridge untill they were furnished with horses, & a guide, & sent away to Newhaven, for their greater security. Captain Daniell Gookin is reported to haue brought over, & to manage their estates, & the Commissioners being enformed y^t he had many cattle at his farm in the kings province, w^{c}h were suspected to be Whaleyes. or Goffs, caused them to be seized for his Majesties use, till further order, But Captain Gookin standing upon the priviledge of their charter & refusing to answear before the Commissioners as so, there was no more donne in it. Captain Pierce, who transported Whaley & Goffe into New England may probably say something to their estates.

They of this Colony say, y^t King Charles the first gaue them power to make lawes, & to execute them, & granted them a charter as a warrant against himselfe & his successors, & y^t so long as they pay the fift part of all gold & sylver oar w^{c}h they shall gett, they are free to use their priviledges granted them, & that they are not obliged to the King, but by civilitie, & y^t they hope to tyre the king, the lord chancelor, & the Secretary too with writing, They can easily spinne 7 yeares out with writing at that distance and before that be ended a change may come. Nay, some haue dared to say, who knowes what the event of this dutch warre may be.

This colony furnished Cromwell with many instruments, & those who haue retraited thither since his Majesties happy return are much respected & advanced to be Magistrates. They did sollicit Cromwell by one Mr. Wensloe to be declared a free state, & in making their lawes did many times style themselves, this State, this Commonwealth; and now beleeues themselues to be so They demand what taxes they pleas, but their accounts could never yet be seen, some few soldiers & a Captain they keep their at Castle, the Governor hath 100£ yearly, every magistrate 30£ about 80£ they giue yearly to the Colledge. about 1500£, or 2000£ yearly they rayse

If the Commissioners had stood in need of their assistance to reduce the Dutch, they did intend to haue made them pay eleven shillings a week for euery foot soldier.

They convert indians by hyring them to hear sermons, by teaching them not to obey their heathen princes, & by appoynting rulers amongst them over tenns, fifties &c. Those whom they say are converted cannot be distinguished by their lives, manners, or habitts from those who are not.

This colony wᶜh hath engrossed the whole trade of New England hath many towns within its just limitts, wᶜh the commissioners suppose to be Seconet brook on the South West, Merimuck river on the north east, & 2 right lines drawn from each of those 2 places till they come to Coneticot river; (wᶜh will make it a very large province) or at the furthest till they come within 20 miles of Hudsons river (wᶜh is supposed to be at the least 250 miles, from Boston) that river is already planted there abouts, & granted to his royall highnesse. Boston is the cheife town, seated upon a peninsula, in the bottom of a bay, wᶜh is a good harbour, & full of fish, it was fortifyed this year 1665 with 2 blockhouses; they had before a small castle upon an isle in the rode where ships must passe about 5, or 6 miles from the town. Their houses are generally wooden, their streets crooked, & unpaved, with little decency, & no uniformity. There nether dayes, months, seasons of the year, inns, nor churches are known by their English names.

At Cambridge they haue a small colledge, (made of wood) for the English; and a small brick pile for the indians, where there was but one; one was lately dead, & 3, or 4 more they had at schole, as they sayd. It may be feared that this colledge may furnish as many scismaticks to the church, and the Corporation as many rebelles to the King, as formerly they haue donne, if not timely prevented.

In this colony too the King hath many very loyall subjects, who petitioned their generall court at his Majesties first comming in, for the owning of his Majesty, & now lately for complying with his Majesties commissioners, but haue had neither answear, nor good look since. They are sorry y^t so few should carry on so strong a faction, for there are scarce aboue 8 of the most factious; yet they are so overawd, y^t they canne doe nothing to remedy it. They say, it is now with them, as it was with the Kings party in Cromwells time. One of these was derided for being so civile as to accompany one of the Commissioners from the town he dwelt in to Boston. And others of Boston derided some of Rodeisland for having yeilded so much to his Majesties desires.

In Boston lyes ten iron gunns taken in the French fort in Cromwell's time, wch would help well to defend the harbour of Piscatoquay where the masts are laden, if they be the Kings.

Endorsed—" *Massachusets* 1665 *B. No.* (28) *N. B. This paper is writ by Col. Cartwright, one of the King's Commissioners on his Return from America.*"

XXXIV.

CARTWRIGHT'S ANSWER TO THE MASSACHUSETTS NARRATIVE OF TRANSACTIONS WITH THE ROYAL COMMISSIONERS.*

The relation of the Commissioners first comming to Boston, and the coppies of the Kings letters, & of the Commission are most probably tru.

p. 9. [Mass. Rec. IV. ii. 164.] That those 2 commissioners were not satisfyed with the Courts answear to their proposall is also tru; & the reason was, becaus it was so delatory.

p. 12. [Mass. Rec. IV. ii. 166.] This resolution of the court put in generall terms needs expounding, The duties expressed in their patent, as they say, is onely paying the 5^t part of all gold & sylver oar; & then they are obliged to no more.

p. 13. [Mass. Rec. IV. ii. 167.] The Com: desired what forces they could spare; and the Court orders y^t the volunteirs should not exceed 200

As to the charges. The Captains of the frigots took for each frigot a pilot from Boston to the Manhatoes; one of wch complayned to Col: Cartwright in Nov: 1664 as he was going to Virginia, y^t he was unpayd; his name was Throgmorton. And another of them (namd Cole) was payd, that winter, in Boston by Col: Cartwright, after he had been refused by Maj: g^{ll} Leveret: As to the soldiers, the Com: never heard that there were above 12 raysed. Their present charges were to haue been defrayed by the country, But the Court expected y^t the Com: should haue repayed them; and they allowed eleven shillings a week to each soldiers. In w^{ch}, their courtisie to the King had not been much.

The Courts order for admission of freemen is a mere

[* The document to which this is a reply—"A breife narrative of the late negotiation betweene his majestjes colony of the Massachusets & the hono'ble Colonell Richard Nicolls, Sr Robert Carr, Kn^t, George Cartwright, & Samuell Mauericke, Esqr, his majestjes comissioners"—is printed in the *Massachusetts Records;* Vol. IV. Part ii. pp. 157-265.]

juggle to deceive his Majesty. The Com. have examined the lists or rowles of many towns and find, y^t
scarce 3 men in 100 pay 10^s at single rate, besides head
mony. But the order will speak for it selfe.

p 14 [Mass. Rec. IV. What was donne, or sayd by Mr Maverick
ii. 168.] at Piscatoway was not known to Col:
Cartw: till now; nor does he now see what caus they
had, from w^t, (they say) he did, to write such a letter
p. 15. [Mass. Rec. IV. to his Majesty. That letter sayes so much,
ii. 168.] y^t no more need be sayd to prove, y^t y^y
look upon themselues as a common wealth, & not obliged
to the King further then paying the 5^t part of all gold
& sylver oar. Or if they had cause to suspect Mr Maverick, who had (as many other relate) received great
affronts, & high jnjustice from them, they had no caus
to suspect the other 3 at that time, or to accuse them
for expecting great matters there.

p. 22. [Mass. Rec. IV. The Com: being told by severall men of
ii. 173.] quality, y^t the non-freemen were not acquainted with any of the kings letters, nor with any
thing donne by the Commissioners, sent such letters to
5, or 6 gentlemen, as is set down.

The motion of having the Country come in was
made by Mr Maverick, & when it was violently spoken
against by some of the magistrates; Col: Cartw: replyed
y^t it was not desired, y^t all the country should so come
in as to leaue the towns empty; but y^t such as might
with their own conveniency, & were willing to come,
might not be hindered. for many had complayned y^t y^y
had never seen nor heard the kings gratious letters; &
that the kings favours might be known to all, was the
onely caus of this motion. Whereupon S^r Ro: Carr
saying something to the same purpose, Col. Cartw: reply'd, it was so reasonable a motion, for a thing so just
& necessary, y^t none could refuse it, but would giue
caus to be suspected a traytor; or to y^t effect. Never
the lesse they appoynted traynings on the day of Election, or near it, purposely to hinder all they could. They
here wholly forget (as y^y did page 9th when mention was

made of his Maj: letter of June 28. 1662) y^t the Com: desired them to prepare a mappe or draught of their country.

P. 23. [Mass Rec. IV. ii. 174.] The Com: being to compose the differences in the province of Rode-island & there being to be a tryall between Joseph Torrey & the persons mentioned, thought it necessary they should be summoned, & therefore sent that Warrant. The Com. were enformed y^t Roger Plaisted had a hous in that province, both he & the rest had 14 dayes time; he who carryed the warrants made oath of serving them. But at a private consultation it was agreed y^t he should not appear; it being against their charter to appear before any, but their own magistrates: as, afterwards it was [Mass. Rec. IV. ii. 175] told to the Com: The 2 first clauses of the declaration concerning the Nanhiganset country were in direct obedience to his Majesties commands. As to the 3^d, it is first observed, y^t there may be a mistake in coppying; For it was ordered y^t when ever (not whatever) ether of the Sachims &c. And they thought, y^t y^y had good reason to doe so. For the Indians never knew what selling of land, or mortgaging meant, till the English taught them, yet it was proved before the Com: that the Indians sent to know where y^y would haue the mony payd, before the time in the mortgage was expired; and answear was returnd, they could not receive it now, becaus Mr Winthrop was in England, yet after that seized upon the country as forfeited.

24. [Mass. Rec. IV. ii. 175.] To the 4th claus, it was proved before the Com: y^t Cachanaquand (of whom they pretended to haue bought land) was younger brother to Pessicas, & by custome of those Indians had not power to sell land. For there the cheife Sachim onely sold land, and disposed of the under sachims; as Miantonimo had sold Rode-island, Cononicut, & prudence isles, the township of Warwick, and Providence, & had disposed of those under-sachims. But besides it was proued, y^t Cachanaquand is simple, and y^t he was se-

duced, being máde drunk, & kept so for some dayes, & carryed to Boston, where this 'sale was made, about 6000 acres of the best in that province for about 25£ (300 fathom of peag). In this purchase, & in another pretended to by Mr Brown, as also in the Mortgage, Mr. Winthrop governor of Conecticot, Major Wenslo of New Plymoth colony were joyned together with these of the Massachusets; Mr. Winthrop being by, at the hearing of the cause, did openly declare, that he knew nothing of it; & y^t his name was made use of w^thout his consent, & w^thout his knowledge; wch made it look like a combination (as it was afterwards confesst to be) that the Commissioners of the Vnited colonies, being alwayes the cheife men of those 3 colonies, & New-haven, (for Rode island was excluded) might alwayes make orders in favour of the purchasers against Rode-island, and so they did. But besides all this, there was an order made by the G^ll Court of Rode-island, That none should buy land in that province of the Indians w^thout consent of the court upon penalty of forfeiting what they bought; it was openly proved, y^t this order was made, before these purchases. Such an order had been long before made in all the other colonies, & exe-cuted against Mr Brenton eleven years after possession, & 7 years after having built an hous upon some pur-chased land in the Massachusets colony. as he com-playnd in a petition. The Com: did not think them-selves bound to expresse all these particulars in their declaration. That all these things, & more had been proved might haue appeared, if the papers had not been lost at sea.

p. 24. &. 25. [Mass. Rec. IV. ii. 175-6.]. That declaration there mentioned was also made by the Com: The Case this. The Massachusets give away a tract of land, on the Eastern side of Pawcatuck river, within the Colony of Rode-island, pretending, they had conquered it from the Pequit indians. Betwixt their conquest & their dona-tion of land, by their own relation, there are aboue 20 yeares. The Com: could not perceiue where in their charter theire own militia was so much put into their owne hands as to make an invasive. To defend themselves is permitted them; but to make an offensive warre, & so farre out of their own bounds, to conquer nations, & to dispose of the conquered lands is not to be found there. And as this prerogatiue was not granted to any one colony; so neither was it granted to them all joyntly. For they never had any such charter.

They had made a combination amongst themselves (but left out Rode-island) in immitation of the States of the united provinces, & styld y^m selves, the Vnited Colonies, by this y^y took more power then was ever given, or entended them, as by the copy, if not lost, might haue been seen. That there should be an agreement amongst all the severall colonies, for assisting of each other, & for keeping a good correspondence betwixt each other, as y^t servants, debtor, & murtherers, or theeves might not be defended against their just prosecutors, is absolutely necessary. But then it ought to be under a head, so long as there is a king, nether then are they to exercise the Kings prerogative without his leaue & consent.

But it was proved before the Com: That Myantonimo the Nanhiganset Sachim had conquered that very tract of land On the east side of Pawcatack from the Pequits some yeares before that the English warre begunne, & had given it Soso, & that Myantonimo with 500 indians did assist in that warre against the Pequitts, & so did Unkas another Sachim, yet these had no share of the conquest. Pessicus & Ninicroft the present Nantiganset Sachim acknowledged this to be true also. Of this Soso the Rode-islanders bought it. Notw^t standing divers protected by the Massachusets, build there; and authorised thereto by violence seized on, & carry'd away the persons of the rode-islanders prisoners to Boston, keept y^m them there severall months; they beat the constable & took away his staffe, and committed many other outrages, whereby the purchasers were very much damnefyed; all this was proved. & to haue been donne

since his Majesties happy return into England. Vnlesse violence, & expression be a good tytle, the Massachusets had no reason to complayn of that order.

The Pequits country lay cheifely betwixt the rivers
of Pawcatuck & monhegon. that country is now given
by his Majesty to the Colony of Conecticot as conquered
by them (& so indeed it seemd to be by a relation of
that war made to the Commissioners) Some of these
Pequits were ordered ether by the Vnited Colonies, or
the Massachusets to plant on the East side of that
river. Those of the Massachusets party would them
plant on y^t land the Rode islanders held, the Rode
islanders, on that land w^{c}h the Massachusets held, so y^t
betwixt both the indians were denyed, or hindered to
plant at all. Now the Commissioners had prevayled
with Mr Winthorp the Go^r of Conecticot, to provide a
place for those indians in y^t wh^{ch} had been their own
country against the next planting season, & he promised to see it donne. upon this reason the Com: made
that part of the order not to hinder the indians from
planting there this sommer.

p. 25. [Mass. Rec.
IV. ii. 177]
PORTER^{rs} C.^{a}SE. That w^{c}h y^y call Porters protection the
Com: wrote under his petition, in answear
to it. But, he never appearing, how the
originall was produced in open court may be questioned.
But if they had sent a coppy of the petition (w^{c}h most
probably was produced when the answear was, being
both on one peece of paper) the reason of that answear
would appear. John Porter, at Warwick in the province
of Rode-island, complaind in a petition to the Com: y^t
he had been unjustly imprisoned at Boston, by the Massachusets, for being undutifull to his parents, as was
onely pretended, & was sentenced to be banisht or to
pay 200$^£$, w^{c}h he refusing to submit to, was threatend
to be sent to some forrain plantation; and that he had
often petitioned the G^{ll} Court, but could not be heard;
Becaus Major Hawthorn hindred it, who was his onely
accuser, witnesse, & judge; & had marryed his daughter
to the petitioners younger brother, & now endeavoured

to disinherit, or banish the petitioner. And desired the Com. to doe him justice.—And he sayd by word of mouth y^t Mr Endicot the then Governor who had stayed the sentence from being wholly executed upon him, whilst he lay very weak, charged him y^t he should be sure to escape to the Com: as soon as he was dead. The Com. being assured, y^t the aboue named Ma: Hawthorn was the same man against whom y^y had had so many informations for making a seditious speech at the head of his company, & y^t the late governor had really befriended Porter, and considering the reasonablenesse of the petition; and their duty to relieve the oppressed, & considering the necessity of securing his person from being sent away, if they entended to doe justice, and knowing y^t there were some in that Colony, who to gratifie the Massachusets would be ready to betray the petitioner to them, underwrote that order; and with all told him, y^t they feared the Massachusets would not consent y^t the Com: should hear any complaints against them, & therefore advised him, to keep himselfe out of their reach, untill they saw w^t the Massachusets would doe, w^{c}h w^{t}hin 5 dayes, y^y thought, they might know, (for the court was to begin on the 3^d) & if he could get any friend to attend for that time, he should haue word, when to come, For if y^y would not obey the kings commission, that order would doe him no good in their province. Upon some intelligence they serched the outskirts of the province for him, and sayd, he should fare the worse for having appealed to the Commissioners.

p. 26. [Mass. Rec. IV. ii. 177] When the Com: had donne all y^y had to doe in Rode-island colony, the Governor & gentlemen were ernest to haue them goe & stay at Rode-island 8, or 10 dayes, having time enough after to goe to the Court at Boston. Sr Rob: Carre consented. Mr Maverick having several friend[s] to visit would make use of that time. Col: Cartw: was sent to prepare the instructions & other papers to be given in to the court; & being resolved to see both the head & stream of

Charles river, & the converted indians by the way, he would not break the appointment he had made. upon this occasion y^y came severally into Boston. To haue sent them word, y^t y^y were comming was to haue begd a reception; & would haue been too great a peece of vaynglory for a sober man to be guilty of.

And all this respect & honorable reception wch they so often mention was the having of some few soldiers in arms; for wch the Com: stayd 2 howers when y^y went out in February, before y^y could be gotten ready; and with the charge of wch they might haue apbrayded the Com: & exasperated the country, as they had donne before for the charges of the soldiers, & the reception of the Com: in July 1664. That, & the many false reports wch they had raysed, & severall disrespects made the Com: wisely sleight what they saw, they could not haue there. Col: Cartw was a whole month lame of the gout, & in all y^t time Mr Bellingham whilst dep: gov: & governor did not so much as send to see him, nor in 2 months before.

[Mass. Rec. IV. ii. 178-195] The relations (from p. 27 to p. 44) of the THE CONFERENCE. severall papers wch passed betwixt the Com: & the court are tru, & need no coment. The last wch was the occasion of a conference sayes playnly, y^t the Kings instructions were an infringement of their charter; for wch the Com: had reason to be dissatisfyed; & endeavoured to proue by severall clauses in their charter, y^t appeals did belong to the King. And sayd they are tyed by their charter not to make lawes contrary to the lawes of England, now to hinder any caus from comming to the King's bench, or the Chancery is certainly contrary to the lawes of England, The King is judge of those 2 courts; but instead of causing y^m to come thither to answear, his Maj: had sent Com: hither, for their greater ease &c. Moreover the Com: sayd the King was to expound any passage in their charter; for he who granted knew best what he had granted, and if they would beleeue his Majesty, he had told them, y^t he desired nothing but w^t y^y were obliged to by their Charter, (in the 9th instruction) & what was necessary for the support of his Majesties government there, (in his Ma: letter of Ap. 23. 1664.). and in the beginning of that letter, his Majesty sayes, y^t to see good government established, and justice duly administred in the Massachusets colony, is as much his duty as to see them in his nearer dominions; and how can his Maj: discharge this duty, if appeales be not made unto him? They say dalso, y^y by their charter, y^y were obliged to make wholesome, & reasonable lawes; who should be the judge, whether those lawes be reasonable & wholesome but the King? Or who will not judge them to be nether wholesome but the King? Or who will not judge them to be nether wholesome, nor reasonable when they deny the king that great prerogatiue of hearing appeales? They sayd also that it was most plain by their charter, y^t y^y were to be impleaded by the name of the Corporation &c. & y^t by their charter y^y were made but a corporation, & had no more granted to y^m in gencrall terms then the priviledges of a Corporation, & y^t no corporation in England could refuse an appeal to the King, & all these particulars, & more were shown, & read to them.

The Com: were not so sencelesse (as they report) to plead y^t John Porter had sustayned great wrong by the court, when y^y had not heard the cause, & had onely seen the petition wch he gaue them. They took y^t petition to be no more gospell then what the court sayd. But if the Com: did say, y^t John Porter pretended y^t he had sustained great wrong &c (as it is most probable they did not) yet it was no presumption, as they term it. This phrase ought to haue come from a Commonwealth at least.

The Com: having sayd w^t is before written concerning John Porter, & a great deal more added, y^t if he appear to be w^t y^y say he is, They shall be so farre from protecting him, y^t having first punnisht him for slaundering of the Colony, they will deliver him to be proceeded against, as the Court shall think good. But it

was in vayn to say any thing to them, who from the
first were resolved never to grant appeales.

At this conference there was nothing written, yet
the very occasion of it showes, y^t it must be the businesse of the Com: to prove, that the kings instructions,
& the protection of Porter (as y^r call it) were no in-
fringings of their charter. The coppies of the Kings
letters, & their charter were produced & very many arguments were used, but all these are waved; and it is
well they are; for the answearing of them might haue
spent 100 pages more. if their replyes (as they set them
down) will satisfy his Majesty, the Com: cannot be
further concernd.

To the question, whether the Com: would use a
jury or no, it was answeared If they were to hear a cause,
where matter of fact was to be proved, they would use
a jury. But in this case of Mr Deans; where the fact
was already proved, & confessed, they would use none;
And w^{t}ever determination they should make there;
they would make a just report of it to his Majesty.

p. 46. [Mass. Rec. IV. The answear to the question, by w^t law y^y
ii. 197.] would proceed, y^y report rightly, by the
law of England. But leaue out the reason. The Com:
were commanded by the King, in the 11th instruction
to giue such reparations to Tho: Dean as upon the mer-
ritts of the cause, & by vertue of the sayd act of parliment he ought to receiue. But if y^y had been to haue
heard John Porters caus y^y would haue considered the
lawes of that colony.

The Com: also pleaded the submission of the 3 other
colonies, who had suffered appeales to be made to, & determined by the Com: & yet had nether lost their charter, nor any of their priveledges granted them, nor were
forced to quit their habitations, nor had yet any cause
to complayn. But all of them returnd thanks to his
Majesty for sending commissioners to them. But from
the first time these saw the Commission, they resolved
w^t to doe, & ever since mayntaynd y^t resolution.

The Com: did entend to haue been as good as their

word, & to haue presented the Courts jugglings, equivo-
cations, & denying his Majesties authority in their own
words, & therefore sent Coll: Cartwright over wth those
very papers & about 30 petitions against tyranny, & op-
pression.   But all those being taken by the Dutch, they
humbly referre the Courts own coppies to consideration,
& can say no more then' what they haue there written.

p. 63. [Mass. Rec. IV.
ii. 211.]
The Com: exceptions to their lawes would
haue been much plainer, if the book had
not been lost, by wch y^y might haue been compared.   But
the Com: never understood, y^t y^y had donne any more
to those exceptions, then coppyed them out.   Themselues say no more.

p. 64. [Mass. Rec. IV.
ii. 214.]
Their Southern bounds are not controverted.   Becaus new plymouth hath made
an agreement with them; & are contented to stand to
it, though it be to their losse, yet are sensible of the injury.   Both Rode-island, & Conecticot complaynd y^t
the Massachusets had strecht their southern line too
Southerly.   The Com: seeing y^t y^y would not submit to
any judgement but their own, & y^t y^y had denyed the
Commissioners authority, resolved to leaue their bounds
to be determined by his Majesty.

P 65 [Mass. Rec. IV.
ii. 214.]
This order was made in their hott bloud.
For, y^y entended y^t the Com: should sitt
by, & hear y^m examine the businesse, & affirm in it, y^t
this was the entent of his Majesties Commission, & instructions to y^m.   This order had some had some (*sic*)

[Mass. Rec. IV. ii.
199.]
relation to their answear to the 7 & 8th instruction (p. 48) where y^y say, They are to
govern all the people of this place, whether inhabitants
or strangers, by wch word they meant the Com: as in
discourse one of themselues expounded it.   And y^y did
beleeve, for they sayd it, y^t the Com: were obliged to

p. 66. [Mass. Rec. IV.
ii. 215.]
obserue their order.   But upon the Com:
reply The zelots were contented in that
point to be perswaded by the more moderate, after consideration to doe nothing in the businesse.

   The narratiue of John Porters case may be tru.

P. 67. [Mass. Rec. IV. ii. 216.] The Com: did not know it when he gaue them a petition. There was enough sayd of this before. It is not possible in nature, y^t the court could think, y^t the Com: when y^y had heard the case as judges would ether haue acquitted John Porter, or haue blamed y^m for their sentence against him, if this case was tru. Their shoe wrung not here, But as y^y had resolved (Aug. 3. 1664. page 12^t) to adhear to their patent, the duties & priviledges thereof, & to be their own expossitors. (for y^t also is granted them in their charter) they were resolute not to forgoe that priviledge, of being their own judge. And here it is to be remembred, y^t y^y forgot to sett down an order made by the Court Sep. 10th 1664. to deterre all people from complayning against them.

p. 69 [Mass. Rec. IV. ii. 218.] The Courts narratiue of Mr Thomas Deans case may be tru. And if it giue his Majesty satisfaction, the Com: will not complayn for having been sent so farre to no purpose. For their own relations might haue served in all cases, as well as that.

p. 71. [Mass. Rec. IV. ii. 255.] The long Apologeticall reply &c will be best answeared by Mr Gorton, whom 3 of the Com: heard preach twice: They could not perceiue any sparks of that spirit of malignity in his sermons, nor no sparks of revenge in his discource. But a great deal of learning in his sermons, of zeal in his prayers, & of loyalty in his actions they did perceive; he preserved the deed of surrender made by the Nanhyganset Sachims to K: Charles the first for 20 yeares.

p. 87. [Mass. Rec. IV. ii. 219.] It is most tru y^t y^y doe improue the narratiue very well to the end they designed it, y^t is to tyre his Majesty, the Councell, the Lord Chancellor, & the Secretaries too. The narratiue set down in 84 pages in folio, they say is breifly given; the improuement truly makes up 111 pages.

But (letting passe their divisions, & subdivisions) by comparing w^t y^y say here, They took the oath of Allegiance, wth w^t y^y sayd p: 50 (considering how I stand

[Mass. Rec. IV. ii. obliged to the Kings Majesty, his heires,
201.]   & successors, by our charter, & the government established thereby, doe swear accordingly &c) it
will easily appear how farr y^t oath binds them.   By
their charter, y^y say, they are onely obliged to pay to
the King the 5^t part of all gold & sylver oar for all
duties &c.   And so, they swear accordingly

P. 88. [Mass. Rec. The liberty there mentioned will be best
IV. ii. 220.]   expounded by their own words, p. 50 ;
concerning the use of the common prayer book—And

[Mass. Rec. IV. ii. to haue the same set up here, we conceiue
200.]   it is apparent, y^t it will disturb our peace
in our present enjoyments.   And if all their lawes concerning their churches be read, it will easily appear the
common prayer book was never entended.   And the
banishing of Mr Williams, Mr Wheelwright, Mr Gorton, Mr. John Clark &c. and indeed all who differed so
farr from them, as would not come to their meeting
houses, or quietly pay 5^s aday for missing showes y^t
they never entended any other worship should be set up,
but their own.

p. 88. [Mass. Rec. Touching those priviledges &c   There
IV. ii. 221.]   is scarce one non-member y^t hath had land
given him, & scarce a member that hath not had. Divers
haue complayned to the Com: of this very thing : as
would haue appeared by the papers lost, if here.

P. 89. [Mass. Rec. The repealing of that law wch appointed
IV. ii. 221].   officers of trust to be church-members onely
signifies nothing, whilst those officers are chosen by the major part of members, but onely to elude his Majesties desires.

And is no other than what is required of his Majesties subjects in England   here they speak plain. They
haue as much power to set up what church discipline
they pleas, & to oblige all people to obserue it within
their jurisdiction as the King hath in England.   And
when y^y say, it is no barre, &c. they forget, or dissemble
their own Act; he y^t is not a church member, must pay
10^s at a single rate (wch is a great deal there) or he cannot be a freeman.

[Mass. Rec. IV. ii. 222.] They say, the reassuming of the former practice was readily submitted to they mean, using the King's name in their forms of justice. But it cannot be denyed, they were the last & longest before they did reassume it. And it may easily be proved, y^t when they were both petitioned, & sollicited to make an address to, & to own the king (about the year 1660) they answeared, Let us first see whether the king will own us, before we own him.

p. 100. [Mass. Rec. IV. ii. 222.] In repeating the Kings grace to them in his letter of June 28 (62) they will not obserue Provided alwayes, & it being our declared expectation, &c. about the middle; nor presuming y^t they still merrit the same, by their duty & obedience, in the end of that letter. Nor in his Majesties letter of Ap. 23 (64) will they take notice of what the King sayes is their duty, & that he expects a full complyance to all those his desires. with out w^{c}h complyance it is a reall presumption to expect the continuance of his Majesties favours.

p. 104. [Mass. Rec. IV. ii. 227-8.] But these gentlemen say, They shall not proceed to execute the sentence of justice legally passed against a notorious offendor, but they will protect him, untill they haue again heard & determined the case. One might think these gentlemen had a priviledge by their charter too of saying what they pleas, be it never so false, or so sencelesse for their own caus. There hath been a great deal more then enough sayd to haue satisfyed any reasonable man, that the Com: in honor, prudence, & conscience could not undoe what they had donne for Porter, before they had heard him speak for him selfe.

P. 105. [Mass. Rec. IV. ii. 228.] it is very probable, y^t these Commissioners were the first that ever were faulted for saying, they would proceed according to discretion. if they, who complaynd, had well vnderstood what discretion had been, they would not haue thought that proceeding according to discretion had been a crime.

By their letter to the Com: they used an artifice to

p. 107. [Mass. Rec.
IV. ii. 230.]
try if they could make the Com. giue them an account of their proceedings, y‘ they might the better haue shown themselues to be the Supreme judicatory of y‘ province. But fayling of that, they will not misse to slaunder the proceedings of the Com: though donne with great care, consideration, conscience, & equity. as the severall cases will testifye.

If cheating of the indians by a mortgage, & a fraudulent purchase; if pretending a conquest where they made none, & selling the lands pretended to be conquered without their own limitts; if oppressing of their neighbours be to be justifyed by magna charta, then their title to those lands claymed are good; and their combination to destroy Rode-island is effectuall. For all those lands they speak of are the onely lands wch the Nanhyganset Sachims submitted to his Majesty in 1664, and the onely lands now granted to Rode-island by his Majesties charter, & before by the Lords & commons.

MR BROWNS CASE. The Com: are also blamed by some for doeing another peece of injustice; w^ch, these gentlemen having overslipt, shall be here set down.

Tocomano (a petty Sachim) giues to Mr Brown a tract of land about 1652, whether Mr Brown did accept of it then, or no is uncertain. but it is certain, Mr Brown did not draw any writing for it then, as afterwards he did; but goes that year to old England, & was Sr Henry Vanes steward at Raby. In 1660, when he saw y‘ the King was to return into old England, he returned into new England. But before he came thither, though in the same year, Tocomano sells that tract of land to trustees for Rode-island, and they, before they bought it, sent to Newplymouth, in whose jurisdiction Mr Browns family was, to know if they had any obligation upon that land. They returnd answear, Tocomano might sell it to whom he pleased. Thereupon writings are made, and sealed by Tocomano, & his sonne, & his grandsonne and 40^£ payd the same day, and 20^£ more the next day, both to Tocomano himselfe.

Then in the yeare 1661 Mr Brown makes a writing, & getts the same 3 men to seal it, wch sayes thus, Where·as I Tocomano about 9 yeares since gaue such a tract of land to Mr Brown to make an English town on, but then he could not becaus he was to goe to old England. But now being returnd, and having a mind to make an English town, and having taken for his associates Mr Winthorp of Conecticot, Major Atherton of Boston, Major Wensloe & Mr Willet of Newplymouth &c all whom I approue well of, I doe confirm unto the sayd Mr Brown the sayd tract of land &c. presently after this Mr. Brown dyes, & Mr Willet (his sonne in law) sayes, y^t Tocomano came to him, and askt, if his grandchild could sell to Rode-island men y^t land wch he had given Mr Brown. Mr Willet answeared, No. Tocomano replyes, but he hath sold it, & gotten a great deal of peag, what must be donne? Mr Willet answeared, take the peag from him, least he spend it. Upon this Toco-mano goes away, & within a short time returns wth a bag of peag, wch Mr Willet kept ever since, & w^n this caus was heard at Warwick in Rode-island province, where the land lyes, he delivered the peag to the Comis-sioners. Since then Tocomano is dead. But his sonne appeared before the Com: and when he saw both the writings, he sayd, he had sealed them, and showed wch was his fathers, and wch was his sonns seal, at each deed; and y^t his father had received 60£ of Rode-island men; but y^t nether he, nor his sonne had received any of it.

The deeds, both were seen and so dated. The an-sweare returnd from Plymouth was proved on oath, the sealing of the deed, and the paying of the mony then to Tocomano himselfe was proved by 3 oaths. The Com: judged the purchase of Rode island good, if Mr Browns deed had been before the other; yet buying it without the consent of the Court would haue barrd him by the practice of all the other Colonies.

My Lord.

In that thing, cald the improvement of the narrative,

there are so many falsities, and repetitions, y^t they are not worth the answearing in particular.

The judgements wch the Commissioners gaue concerning those lands in the Nanhiganset country were grounded upon those evidences wch were produced before them, and are set down in each particular case, (marked p. 23. p. 24)

[Mass. Rec. iv. ii, 175-6.] That there was a designe to ruine the Colony of Rode-island may appear by the Massachusets refusing them ammunition, in a time of very great danger; and by the inserting of the names of some of the principall men of Conecticot, & New-plymouth into all their pretended purchases, and mortgage of the Nanhyganset lands; as will appear by their deeds,

That the United colonies did usurp authority is certainly plain in that, y^t the authority of disposing of lands, without the limitts of their respectiue limitts, wch they exercised, was not given them by the king; if that act be justifyed, they may dispose of all new England both when, and as they pleas.

What was donne to John Porter is truly set down [Mass. Rec. iv. ii. 177.] here (marked p. 25) and what they report was as well to maligne the Commissioners, as to improve their narratiue. And peradventure we speed here, as in another place, where I was complemented by a magistrate with this speech, y^t if we found not that respect wch was due to us, as the Kings Commissioners, we might lay the fault on Mr Mavericke. For we found lesse, becaus he was with us.

The summoning of the whole Corporation to appear before us, is another great crime layd to our charge with much rethorick, & some little abusing of Gods name. In this we required no more, then what was their duty; wch we showed them in their charter, That they are to be impleaded, & to answer by the name of the Corporation &c. and this too at the conference, but not one word of that in their relation, nor in their long imprisonment, nor of that unhansome letter they sent us to Piscatoway, nor of their warrant to forbid all people to obay us, sent by 2 marshalls, when by his Majesties espetiall command we were taking order to haue that harbour. fortifyed. But they haue reserved liberty to enlarge themselves upon occasion.

If all causes heard in the King's court of Chancery require not a jury, these gentlemen needed not to haue troubled themselues, if any of the Commissioners had sayd, they would not use a jury. But that was a mistake, and had been easily pardonable, if they had asked their question for speeding of the businesse, & not for quarrelling. It did not concern them how we would proceed in a tryall, when they were resolved before hand, that they would not be tryed by us.

That his Majesty should send us with a commission, and instruction so contradictory in them selues, & so contrary to his Majesties charter, and letters to them, & so distructiue to his Majesties authority amongst them is strange, if true. To affirm it, sure cannot be lesse then Scandalum magnatum. For it concerns more than his Majesty.

The papers, wch are sayd to haue passed betwixt us, are, to the best of my remembrance, true. For the matter in them, & the manner of delivering y^m we humbly submitt to your Lordships censure; & humbly begge your Lordships favour, and pardon, if we haue not manifested as much discretion in, as affection to his Majesties service.

If this folio of 111 pages was answeared by one that delighted to put words in rank & file, 7 years would scarce serue for 2 or 3 replyes. But it being apparent that they never entend y^t his Majesty shall haue the hearing of appeales : and it being as certain y^t they haue forfeted (their great idol) their charter by exercising authority beyond their bounds, at Pawcatuck, at Warwick, at Block-island, by imprisoning Mr Gorton, & by putting the Quakers to death for religion : and it being as plain that his Majesties promises were made with a proviso, wch they neither haue, nor ever will perform; The shortest way to reduce them to obedience, is to take the forfeiture of their charter; and then his Majesty may extend what grace & favour he pleaseth, to them afterwards. And also provide for his loyall subjects there, who otherwise (it wilbe feared) shall never haue baptisme administred to their children, nor the Eucharist to them selues; And also prevent all disputes with the Massachusetts for the future, by giving them such a charter as they cannot misconstrue. For the misconstruing of their charter makes them misreport what the Commissioners haue donne, & misenterpret all the king's letters, nether beleeving what he sayes, nor doing what he desires. That, & a little propensity in some of them to a temporall independency, as well as a spirituall, are the onely grounds of denying his Majesty that, wch all his other colonies most readily yeilded him.

I humbly hegge your Honors pardon for having set down myn' own opinion, when the other 3 commissioners, having declared what was donne, humbly referred to your Lordships great wisdome what was to be donne: and for not giving your Lordship more measure in, when I could not adde more weight to, the answear of this false, impertinent & very tedious improvement. Beseeching your Lordship to take notice of that relation wh^{ch} I presented to your Lordship of the Massachusets, before I saw their narratiue I humbly subscribe my selfe

Your Honors most humble servant
GEORGE CARTWRIGHT.

Jan. 5. 1665.

Endorsed—" *Jan: 5th 1665–6   Geo: Cartwright one of ye kings Commissioners to N England A. No* (46).''

XXXV.

MEMORANDA BY COLONEL CARTWRIGHT.

A MEMORIALL CONCERNING THE MASSACHUSETS.

1. That Mr Richard Bellingham the governor of the corporation of the Massachusets, and Major Haw-thorn, & 2 others be sent with the return of these ships hither to answear such things as are layd to their charge, by his Maj. commissioners.

2. That the sayd colony of the Massachusets meddle not with the government of the province of Mayn, but let it continue, as the Commissioners haue left it, untill his Majesty shall otherwise determine.

3. That Mr Corbet of Portsmouth in Newhampshire, and all others imprisoned for petitioning the Commissioners be set at libertie, & their bayles discharged forthwith, without paying fees. And that none hereafter be anywayes molested for making applycation, or showing respect to the Commissioners.

CONCERNING RODE-ISLAND, &c.

4. His Maj: commanded the Commissioners, y^t, if y^y found, his Maj. had a just right to the Nanhyganset country, they should enter on it in his Majesties name, & call it the Kings province, & promise those princes his Royall protection; All wch the commissioners did doe. For some of those Indian princes were aliue, & did own their former deeds, & did actually surrender themselues & ther country into·his Majesties protection & ernestly desired so to continue. But this Nanhyganset country being almost all the land wch is granted to the colony of Rode-island &c. if it be continued severall will make that patent of little, or no valew; it is humbly desired that his Majesty would ether appoint a governor over that province, wch was, by his Royall command, calld the King's province; or giue it again to the Colony of Rode-island & providence plantations.

5. That Doctor Alcock an honest & ingenious phy-sitian, who first planted Block-island, may not be dis-possest of his purchase of it; though he bought it of the Massachusets, who had no right to sell it.

6. That the temporary bounds set by the Commis-sioners betwixt the colonyes of New-Plymouth & Rode·island may still continue to be the bounds betwixt those 2 colonies untill his Majesty shall see just reason to alter them. And that Mr Brenton continue his pur-chase from Sachim Phillip within those controverted bounds, untill he hath the wholle price thereof repayd unto him. And y^t this 6^t memoriall be also made known to the Governor of New plymouth.

7. That all the English colonies, by their deputies meet, & agree together, assoon as is possible, to assist each other, against the Dutch, or any other of his Ma-jesties enemies, who shall attempt any of his Majesties terratories in those parts.

8. That there might be a supply sent to the Commis-sioners for the discharging of their quarters, & bringing them back to England. But if any of the commission-ers think it more convenient for them to stay in those parts, that they may haue leaue to doe so. For Mr Maverick hath his mother, wife, children, & brothers living there, and nether estate, nor employment here.

Endorsed—" *Coll. Carterett concerninge New Englande. After the Restora-tion.*"

XXXVI.

Francis Moryson to the Earl of Clarendon.

To the Right Honble Edward Earle of Clarenden Lord high Chanceller of England.

An Humble Addresse in the behalfe of Virginia.

May it Please yor Lo^rp

The only Shipp that is likely to goe this yeare being

wth in few days ready to Sayle occasions this Speedy and most humble Addresse to yor Lo^{pp}

The narrative delivered to yor Lo^{pp} att Salisbury sett forth the Two maine parts of my instrucc̄ons from Virginia To represent Marylands dissent from them in the Stint for planting, To gett Bristoll Patent for Rapahanock revoakd, I shall not trouble yor Lo^{pp} wth perticulars in either.

ffor the first, The com̄on calamitie hath a little raysed the price of our comoditie wch perhapps will supply his Lo^{pp} wth better Arguments then formerly to oppose vs, Soe that I shall lett that rest as it doth, wholy to decline it, I dare not vntill further Order from the Countrie.

ffor the Bristoll Patent Since I vnderstood that it was yor Lo^{pps} oppinion, That it would appeare hard to oppose a new Graunt to those hono^{ble} Persons concernd in the Old, therefore I shall only p^{r}sent the same necessary restrictions of my former Narrative, and most humbly leave it to yor Lo^{pps} determination.

ffirst That there might bee noe alteration in point of Governm^t, altogether inconsistant wth the peace of the rest of the Countrie. Secondly. That the Rights of the p^{r}sent Possesso^{rs} may bee p^{r}served, Their Rents not raysed nor new ffines imposed or their Tenures altered. Thirdly That there may bee time perfixed for peopling of the Places soe granted or in case of ffaylure, Liberty to others to take vpp the Lands. My Lord this is a Law as old as the first planting the Countrie, and a most wholsome one, for otherwise perticuler men would keepe great Tracts of Land in their hands, in hope of getting a great Rate for it, and neither people the Places themselves nor lett others that would doe it, If the time seemes to short that the Law injoynes, I shall most humbly leave it to yor Lo^{pp} to inlarge it. only desiring y^t his M^a treasure may be consulted wth before the grant passes.

But my Lord the maine busienes of this Paper is to p^{r}sent some generall Propositions to make the neighbourhood of Maryland lesse p^rjudiciall to vs. If they shall appeare (vpon yor Lo^{pps} view) Reasonable, Then most humbly to desire y^r Lo^{pp} to Signifie soe much by yor Letter to the Countrie wch will both infinitely satisfie them, and cleere yor Represento^r from neglect in their Service.

ffirst I most humbly Propose That his Lo^{pps} Countrie may bee concluded in all orders wth Ours from King and Councell, where either Trade is concern'd, the Comoditie the Same, and mannaged wthout any inconsiderable inequallitie, or of State ; Civill or Ecclesiasticall, especially where there is any necessitie of laying a Tax vpon the People for the executing of those Comands.

My Lord this will appeare att first Sight a Proposition rather of envy ag^t Maryland then of Advantage to Virginia, But if yor Lo^{pp} pleases to looke into the Reasons you will finde yor Represento^r in this, Labours to p^rserve, from a necessary Ruine the Poore Countrie that hath intrusted him.

All taxes (my Lord) wth vs are by Pole not Acre, the losse of the poorest man as great to Virginia as the richest, all paying equall, Soe that if any comand comes from hence, that requires men or money to effect it, his Lo^{pps} Countrie lyes ready att the Doore, to invite them wth as good Land as they leave and free of all Incombrances. By this meanes wee yearely Loose considerable numbers of People, and by it have fewer hands to Act any thing for our Advantage, or for the Advance of his M^a^{ties} Service and fewer Purses to pay for it.

My Lord this is no Ayrie notion of mine, wch I should not have p^rsumed to offer to soe great a Minister of State as yor Lo^{pp} Vnlesse I could demonstrate the truth, by the Sadd effects of it.

His Maties instructions by Sr William Berkley, though they did not positively enjoyne the building of a Towne, yet they soe recommended it to vs, that wee must have Showne a supine negligence if wee had not att least indeavord it, Our poore Assay of building ffower or ffive houses lost vs hundreds of people wch I hope will wipe of that odium that is throwne vpon the Governm^t, That wee vse our people worse then Maryland, and therefore they Leave vs, and flye to them, But the true reason (my Lord) is, That wee are ready vpon all comāands to expresse our zeale to his Maties Service to the vttermost of our abilitie.

I shall trowble yor Lo^{pp} wth an other Demonstration of the reasonableness of this Proposition, This Parliam^t. made a Law, That noe Sectary or Quaker shall bee transported to Virginia or New England, Wee were extreamely ioyfull of it, hopeing wee should have beene securd from those disturbances, That those people make where they come, But my Lord it was Soe farr from workeing the good effect wee hoped for, and I am confident the Parliament intended, that it hath proved most infinitely ruinous to vs, ffor his Lo^{pp} takeing his Maryland for part of neither, and soe not concernd in the Law, grants a Tolleration to all Sorts of Sects, wch by their neighbourhood (a River only severing of vs,) Infect our People and by that drawes them from vs, or spreads their Venome amongst vs, Thus (my Lord) by not bringing both Countries vnder One Standard, wee cannot have benefitt of any Act of Grace, though made never soe much to our Advantage.

My Lord, I aime not by this, to bring Maryland Subordinate to Virginia, But I desire they may bee both Soe, to King and Councell, nor doe I att all intend any thing in this a Complaint ag^t soe hono^{ble} a Person as his Lo^{pp} but rather Admire his prudent management, That never Omitts to improve the least occasion to his Advantage, I know (my Lord) it is his Lo^{pps} interest to gett People to him, as it is ours, to fix them wth vs, for it is an vndoubted truth That the Riches of all Plantations cheifely consists in the well Peopling of them, ffor had wee Mexico and Perue vnder ground, and wanted People to bring it above Ground wee should for all that, remaine as poore and indigent, as though Planted on Bagshott Heath, the barrenest Peece I know.

Peace and Warr is vndoubtedly (my Lord) his

Maties Prerogative, in all his Dominions, If Virginia and Maryland · have not the Same ffreinds and Enemies, wch allwayes they have not, it must of necessitie bee a Consequence, That att one time or other wee shall fight English and Indians, ag^t Indians and English, Soe that the reasonableness of this Proposition appeares in every pticular can bee imagined.

But (my Lord) after all I shall humbly follow that part of my Instructions to Acquiesse in yor Lo^{pps} decision (for there the Countrie hath laid it) I would I has as well pformed the other part of soe fully Stateing their miserable Condition, That they might receave redresse for it;

Haveing expressed this zeale to his Maties Servis, and the Countries Good, I should bee loth to bee soe partiall to myselfe as not to remove the least Obstruction that any Interest of mine can bee to either, I therefore (my Lord) most humbly p^{r}sent you wth my Comission, desireing of yor Lo^{pp} That when there is a ffort built, for it hath beene a Castle only in the Ayre this 30 yeares) yor Lo^{pp} will bee pleased that my nephew Charles Morisson may have the comand, a Youth every way (if my neerenes to him doth not make mee misstake) capeable of the Place, my Lord of ffawkland gott it for his ffather, the only compensation any of vs had, for the Lievtenantshipp of the Ordnance purchased by my ffather, and settled vpon my elder Brother, by the Composition wth Sr Edward Villers for Munster, and disposed of by his Matie to Sr William Heydon wth a promise to conferre vpon my Brother a place of equall Vallew, But (my Lord) I intend not to Capitulate but most freely render it vpp, leaving both my Selfe and nephew to yor Lo^{pps} Goodnes and ever remaineing

    yor Lo^{pps} most humble and Dutyfull Servant
      and Creature

                      FRANCIS MORYSON.

If yor Lo^{pp} pleases to pervse this it will lessen yor Lo^{pps} trowble in my dispatch.

Endorsed—"*An Address to his Lo^{pp} vpon the goeing a way of the last Shipp this Yeare for Virginia.* 1665."

XXXVII.

RICHARD NICOLLS TO THE EARL OF CLARENDON.

MY LORD

Being uncertaine whether any vessell hath arrived in safety with Letters from mee in twelue moneths past, & hearing that Colonell Cartwright was taken at Sea & carryed into Spaine, I haue long resolved to send this expresse in relation to the whole Affayres wherein I am so deepely concern'd, but from the beginning of November till now wee haue beene frozen up, which hath not happed formerly in mans Memory, The upper parts of Hudsons Riuer are not yet open, from whence I expect very considerable newes every houre, which will deserue a perticular relation. My Lord I haue herewith sent the Copies of all the Transactions at Boston & according to Instructions remitted them to the Secretary of State wherein will appeare the obstinacy of their few Rulers to comply with his Maties just demands for Justice between Man & Man, & a shuffling sort of discowrse to evade the discovery of their hearts So that wee were necessitated to bring their Allegiance to the Touchstone in Mr Deanes Case, finding that in other matters of Lesse Consequence they did onely contriue Delayes with faire words to put the Countrey to great Charge & make the people weary of hearing from his Ma^{ty}, & in briefe to represent to his Ma^{ty,es} best subjects in America for no small burden that their Courts should bee held so long together; By this meanes they do hope to render any Message from his Ma^{ty} dis-agreeable to the humo^{rs} of the People, The papers will shew how farre & in what Method wee proceeded in Treaty with them, but wee ceas't after they had by sound of Trumpett publish't their Manifesto, because they disown'd us for a Co^{rt} & would bee their owne Interpret^{rs} & Judges in all Cases. This Manifesto of theirs might haue drawne ill Consequences upon vs for t'was ordered to bee read at ye doore

8

of the house where wee were mett together, & so it was accordingly performed, with a great Rabble of people attending, but the people were more civill then their great men imagined they would haue proov'd after such a publicke Invectiue against us, howeuer wee were sufficiently exposed to danger. Thus ended our affaires at Boston so that as Comission.^{rs} wee haue setled onely the bounds of the three Colonyes of Conecticutt Plymouth & Rhode Island & yett haue not fully visited Conecticutt where indeed at our coming there will not bee two dayes worke for us, & not the least appearance of a refractory disposition in them, nor any considerable Complaints made against their Policy.

My Lord I haue according to yor Lordshipps Comands of the of ffebruary used all my Endeavo.^{rs} to keepe up the spiritts both of the Merchants Planters & Souldy.^{rs} in dayly hopes of the supplyes mentioned, I. haue run my selfe into debt both here & at Boston, I haue consum'd a considerable sume which I brought of my owne, I haue charged my small Estate & friends in England with neare two thousand pounds sterling by bills of Exchange, wherein I have manifested my utmost power to discharge the trust reposed in mee by his Royall Highnesse with faithfullnesse & Reputation knowing that his Royall Highnesse will not suffer mee to perish under the burden, for had I not thus engaged my selfe & friends, The souldy.^{rs} must haue either perisht and with them his Ma.^{tyes} Interest, or by them the Planters must haue beene eaten out, who haue enough worke to support their owne meane Conditions & ffamilyes; Our neighbours of Boston haue made good use of our Necessityes in raysing the price of their Goods, but this poore Colony hold downe their heads & see their feet & Leggs without shoes & stockings, or shirts to their backs, & all meane Necessaryes at an Invincible Rate ;. I cannot with modesty expresse all perticulars least I should seeme to doubt of that Consideration which is due to this place, & may probably haue miscarryed in the voyage hither the last Yeare.

My Lord I haue severall wayes wrote to yor Lordship the true state of this place & Delaware, but now
the bearer hereof Ensigne Stocke who hath served at
Delaware as Comissary ever since the Reduction of the
ffort, will (viva voce) informe yor Lordship most perticularly in the affayres & Interests of that place. My Lord
some few yeares past the West Indya Company tooke
Delaware from the Sweedes & annext it to this Government, but finding the charge thereof to exceed the Revenew, they made sale thereof to the Burgemasters of
Amsterdam. upon certaine Conditions, One whereof is
very necessary to bee preseru'd, which was that the
Burgemasters should not challenge any propriety or
priviledge of Trade or planting further then ten miles
from the East or North East side of Delaware Riuer,
& the west Indya Company also obliged themselues not
to clayme any Propriety or priviledge within that Pre-
cinct, but to content themselues with the trade & Emoluments which should arise neare or from Hudsons Riuer
& the adjacent parts; To the End that diversity of Interests & Constitutions, might not interrupt both their
well lay^d foundations.

Now so it is that his Royall Highnes by misin-
formations and such specious pretences (wherewith My
Lord Berkely & Sr George Carteret haue beene themselues misled) hath giuen by Indenture the whole &
onely Tract of Land which in progresse of time would
haue ennobled his Territoryes & enricht this place, but
that is not all, for the west side of Delaware Riuer
where the ffort stands, & all the Plantations are seated,
is by this Late Graunt so straitly pent up with the Lord
Baltimores Patent to the westward, that whereas they
haue formerly cutt their Hay upon the East side of the
Riuer which is now denyed them, of Necessity they
must remoue their stations. Thus at once hath his
Royall Highnesse undone two fayre Colonyes, & twill
bee soone found that the new Colony of New Jersey
will fall of it selfe, for in grasping at too much in y^e
first setling, the whole will bee lost. I begg pardon for

intruding this as my certaine knowledge, yet I cannot but discharge both my duty & my Conscience wherein I am trusted.

My Lord I could urge the protection given to crim- inall persons already, but there are so many other con- tingencies of greater moment that I shall onely mention two which wee cannot but expect hereafter; The one is that his Royall Highnesse by Patent hath all Hudsons Riuer with all the Customes proffitts &c graunted by his Ma.^{ty} The Duke hath giuen away all the tract of land to the West of Hudsons Riuer with all his Rights thereunto, Now whether the Duke meant to giue away the Customes & proffitts which cannot but swime vpon Hudsons Riuer, is not exprest, or cleare to mee, How- euer I did not exact any from Capt Carterett; Neither are Islands mentioned in the Graunt, yet hee has putt in his Clayme to Staten Island, whereby wee must see o.^r selues absolutely besieged on all sides, The Riuer will remaine but the Customes are lost.

The other Point is that since New Jersey (to make it selfe a Colony) must advance farre into the woods, amongst divers Nations of Indyans, who seeing them few in Number, will haue Encouragem.^t suitable to the promptnesse of their Natures to doe mischeife to Chris- tians, whereupon a Warre may ensue, & I should bee very much griev'd to heare that o.^r English Neighbo.^{rs} are murder'd by the Natiues & not concerne my selfe therein; but when I shall concerne my selfe in another Colonyes defence (who may probably giue occasion suf- ficient to the Indyans) from whence shall I defray the Charge of such assistances; Nay this Colony will say, shall wee expose o.^r selves, estates & familyes to justify the actions of another Governo.^r & Councell; Some de- bates haue of late passed amongst the Indyans, how farre it was probable I would take part or revenge any mischeife done in New Jersey, T'was concluded they would not doe any violence without my leave, because I haue w.th Guifts and a good Garrison, gain'd some In- terest & power amongst them. Yet they are of late highly sensible of o^r wants, whereas the Dutch alwayes supplyed them with Plenty & upon easy Termes so that both Christians & Pagans generally suffer by the dearth of the Trade. My Lord after yor great Patience to read our just Grievances & sad Complaints, bee pleas'd to take into yor Lordshipps care and countenance the advancing of this place & Delaware, both which had no other Staple Comodity or fix't Trade but Tobacco, brought for the most part by English small Vessells from Virginia & Mary Land, Long Island never afforded aboue one thousand Hogsheads yearely, by this meanes all the Neighbo^r English were in a cheap and plentifull manner supplyed with all sort of Necessaryes from ye Dutch, receiving sometimes three styvers, never under two & one halfe, or the like value in Goods for each pound of Tobacco. The trade of Beauer is an uncertaine Comodity, yeilding Communibus annis the Customes of twenty or twenty five thousand Beauers, all these Customes were taken at tenn per Cent here, by the officers of the West Indya Company, The goods which came from Holland payd there the Dutyes to the Company & none here. All shipps from other parts were either prohibited, or wth leave first obtained paid tenn per Cent for all sort of Goods, So that in breife by a Graunt from the States Generall, the Customes both outwards & homewards bound were giuen to the Company alone, by which meanes this place did not onely subsist but encrease, but now the whole property is alter'd, Tobacco cannot bee a Comodity of that value to English, & the Dutch cannot hope for it, Beaver is an uncertaine trade at all times, & this onely can remain to us hereafter, The whole Dutch factory must fall & consequently the People must quitt the Countrey, because all their hopes of proffitt is destroyed, & their correspondencies broken :

My Lord I am so sensible in this point that without speciall order from his Royall Highnesse I shall not put in practise that Rigour of Seizing some few small Estates of Hollanders now lyeing darkely in the hands of their Agents here, Notwithstanding that I know the law of Nations would beare mee out, but my Master would doubtlesse blame mee for being Rigourous or Scrutinous in small Trifles to the discouragement & detriment of the future hopes of Trade or of Strangers to continue or come to liue amongst us, which hopes haue hitherto kept up the hearts of many, and yet they are no better then Ayery fancies, Vnlesse his Royall Highnesse can obtaine either a Generall Liberty for some Terme of yeares to the better Encouragement of this Place, that shipps of any Nation may Import or Export into or from hence all sorts of Merchandize whither they please, onely paying to his Royall Highnesse his vse such Customes & Dutyes as his Royall Highnesse shall Establish; which point would more readily passe the House of Lords & Comõns then the Comĩssion^rs of the Customes; But Tangier is one Example & all New Colonyes haue very great Priviledges graunted them; Otherwise my Lord in regard this whole Colony is peopled with three parts Dutch, why may not (the warrs ended) a permission bee given onely to foure or six Holland Shipps to trade yearely hither with Comõdityes of their owne Growth & Manifacture, & from hence to returne directly home, payinge onely dutyes to his Royall Highnesse.

My Lord some such like Overture for Trade must bee accepted or this Colony is ruin'd, Surely his Royall Highnesse will concerne himselfe for them, & the rather because the Strength & flourishing Condition of this place will bridle the ambitious Saints of Boston, & is at present a key to the whole Countrey, Wee want onely materialls to make a Locke to the Doore. My Lord at this present during the Warres with Holland wee cannot expect the good affections of the Dutch here to the English, but this I presume to affirme, that in all other occasions they would manifest their good Obedience to his Matie in better Termes than some of the Vnited Colonyes.

My Lord I haue remitted for confirmation to his

Royall Highnesse the present Lawes of this Colony collected out of the Lawes of the other Colonyes, onely
with such Alterations as may reviue the Memory of old
England amongst us, ffor Democracy hath taken so
deepe a Roote in these parts, that y° very name of a
Justice of the Peace is an Abomination, wherefore I
haue upon due Consideration of his M^{ties}a Interest layd
the foundations of Kingly Government in these parts so
farre as is possible, which truely is grievous to some
Republicans, but they cannot say that I haue made any
alteration amongst the English for they had no setled
Lawes, or Government before.

Tis not easily to be imagin'd what paines I haue
taken how much patience I haue exercised towards a
sort of People of such refractory & peevish dispositions
as are not knowne in old England, yet for my Masters
service I can suffer much more, and to shew the Planters that his Royall Highnesse intended rather the settlement of his M^{ties}a Authority in true English words
& formes, then his proffitt, I thought it a part of sound
discretion to lay little or no burden upon their meane
Estates;

These Lawes haue beene put in practise the space of
one yeare with some Amendments upon Reviewe, &
such is the unfortunate Condition of these parts, that
some Points of the Lawes must of Necessity admitt of
Alterations or Abolitions yearely, & yet by the Dukes
Instructions I am narrowly bound up to the space of a
yeare for his Highnesse Confirmation, otherwise the Law
is voyd, By which Instruction fully executed, wee
should at this present haue no Law in force; I hope his
Royall Highnesse will giue a larger Latitude to the
next Governo^r in that point, & dispatch this New body
of Lawes in print without Alterations.

Possibly yor Lords^{pp} hath mett with some bold vn-
dertakers & vaunters of themselues for Trade into this
Place, especially one Mr Winder, yet I doubt not yor
Lord^{pp} will sooner giue Creditt to these Motions &
Informations, then to any Man besides, all which I

haue fully comunicated to M.ʳ Coventry. I haue presumed to giue yo.ʳ Lordsᴾᴾ this tedious Account wherein
I haue at once discharg'd my duty & manifested my
owne weaknesse, out of both which (in you.ʳ great wisedome) I shall hope some good Resolutions may bee
drawne, & possibly where my Expressions are not full
enough, or that good forme or Method is wanting, I
beseech yo.ʳ Lordsᴾᴾ to excuse my Incapacity, & yet to
take a further view of my letters to his Royall Highnesse, to M.ʳ Secretary Bennet & M.ʳ Coventry.

Lastly I beseech yo.ʳ Lordsᴾᴾ to take my owne hard
Condition into yo.ʳ kind thoughts, that I may not see
my owne Ruine both at home & abroad, So long as I
demeane my selfe a Loyall Subject, a dutifull Servant,
& in all things an honest Man, vnder which three Characters I may confidently assume the hono.ʳ of being

My Lord yo.ʳ Lordsᴾᴾˢ most humble and most
obliged Servant

RICHARD NICOLLS

April the 7ᵗʰ [1666]
ffort James in N: Yorke

XXXVIII.

THOS. LUDWELL TO THE EARL OF CLARENDON.

Virginia July 18ᵗʰ 1666

RIGHᵀ HONORAᴮᴸᴱ:

Did not yᵉ performance of my duty to your Lordship far out waigh all other Considerations with mee, I
should not now haue bin soe impertinently presumptious
(as to trouble your Honor with any of the Concernes
of this Country well Knowing how greate a parte your
Lordship must necessarily beare in yᵉ Conduct &
p.ʳservacōn of three Kingdomes at once threatned with
yᵉ Combined force of almost all their neighbours, the
Success of which greate action I hartely pray may bee

for y° Glory, and Safty of y° King & his Kingdomes, & y° honor, reputacōn, and prosperity of you^r Lordship, but my Lord that I may avoid that tediousness I my Selfe condemne, I shall humbly take leaue to informe your hono^r that vpon the arrivall of his Maties Genn^ll Commands for y° building one, or more forts for y° securitie of y° ships trading hither the Assembly after a serious Consultacōn had vpon y° most effectuall Way of obeying y° said Commands, concluded, that since some Riu^s were to wide to bee secured, and that many forts would bee a Charge insupportable to the Country, it would bee best to build one at James Citty, and mount all the ordinance Wee had upon it which are foureteen, a place in y° hart and Strength of y° Country and sufficiently capeable of all the ships that trade hither besides it being y° place where y° Assembly and all y° greate Courts are held, It would bee an Ornament, Security, and advantage to it to haue ye forte there where y° Inhabitants of the place would bee a strength sufficient (but in y° times of Danger) to keep it without Charge to y° Country in order where vnto y° Assembly voted Eighty Thousand Pounds of Tobacco to bee leavied vpon the Country for y° building y° same, and at one hundred pounds Charge weighed and brought y° Guns in place, but after all this Trouble and expence y° Bristoll men (whose trade lyes aboute y° mouth of y° Riu^r) brought in a particular Command from his Ma^ty to build it at poynt Comfort on y° Mouth of y° Riuer, a place where Ships cannot securely hall on shore, and consequently any man of Warr who hath but y° boldness to run by a ffort (a matter of noe greate danger) may be master of y° whole Riu^r, and all y° Ships in it, besides it is a place soe nere y° Sea that wee can haue no Intelligence of y° arrivall of y° enimy till hee is vpon vs, whereas at James Towne being fifty miles within the Riuer they must haue severall winds and tides to come to it, and consequently wee should haue notice time enough by Land to provide against them furthermore wee must bee necessitated to keep a Continuall force in pay att Poynt Comfort which would amo^{u}nt to much more then ye p^{r}sent revenue of ye fort would discharge wch as I have already said would bee avoided at James Towne yett y^{e} Gou and Councell fearing that their deviations from his Maties Commands (though more for his service) might bee adjudged contumacy haue ordered y^{e} fort to bee built at y^{e} Riuers mouth and doe Carry on y${}_{x}^{e}$ Worke with all possible expedic$\bar{o}$n. But the reversing our first Councells & rendering our preparations & first Charges for a ffort at James Towne vselesse by his Maties second Commands doth very much trouble y^{e} mides of y^{e} people because they find their hopes of a ffort at James Towne frustrated and much of their money paid in vaine a thing they seldom parte with willingly how just or necessary soever ye occasion bee, or in what parte of ye world soe euer it bee demanded Besides my Lord it gaue vs all most insuperable feares by casting vs soe far back in our fortifications, that vpon ye arrivall of a dutch Caper who aboute ye 7th Instant tooke a ship of ffoy within our Capes Wee knew not what Course to take for ye securitie of those Ships then in harbour haueing noe fort ready to protect them, But it pleased God that all ye men escaped in their Boates to the Shore who forthwith gaue notice to ye Gouerno^{r} and hee in his owne person with infinite Labour and trouble to ye ships who rode soe securely careless haueing most of their Men aboard fetching in Tobacco that had ye Enimy pursued his advantage hee might haue made himselfe Master of most parte of the Ships in the Country which makes vs sadly reflect vpon our Condition here who haue noe Latitude Left vs of putting our owne Councells in Execution for owr better protection, and yett must justly feare a severe censure vpon euery Misfortune, for prevention of which, I shall humbly offer this expedient that since wee are here vpon ye place, and thought fitt by his Ma^{ty} to bee entrusted with ye Governm^{t} of it, & consequently must bee better informed of ye Dangers to bee avoided, and ye meanes of avoiding them that his Ma^{ty} and the Lords of his most Hono^{ble} privy Councell will bee pleased in all their Comands relating to this place to refer something to the opinions of the Gou and Councell here, where experience as well as parts is necessary to act by, of wch first ye King, and those Honored Lords can haue noe more then what is p^rsented vnto them by psons to often byassed by their owne Intrest; This my Honored Lord would secure us all from those terrible fears wee are in for ye Country in gennerall, for our owne Reputations, and this would take from vs of the Councell our greife to see ye Gou^r soe violently agitated by ye sharpe since hee hath of ye hazard his Hono^r is exposed vnto whilst hee hath not Lyberty to act according to ye Dictates of his Zeale and Judgm^t for his ^Ma^{ties} and ye Countryes service, a Condition that would bee insupportable to him were hee not soe Confident of his Owne integrety & ye Affections of ye whole Country as to relye vpon their ready assistance vpon any Invasion, haueing noe other meanes left him to serue himselfe with all, for ye protection of ye same, I shall now humbly offer one thing more to your Hono^{rs} Consideracōn that is wether it bee an vnfitt thing for vs to begg of his Ma^{ty} that (in regard wee are a flat open Country full of Riu^{rs}, and consequently ships of Warr may ride out of any danger & supprise m^{ch}t men comeing in from Sea who can haue noe notice of any Such from vs, and are from this Capers experience aboue mencōned Likely to attempt ye same) hee will bee gratiously pleased to send vs one, or two ffrigatts to ride here for ye prevencōn of ye abouesaid inconveniences, I think it is noe more then what hee hath gratiously granted ye Careebees, and our Customes are worth more then all theirs I haue many more perticulars to informe you^r Hono^r of but shall refer them to ye next fleet, & shall now add only this one very greate One wch is that, bee our danger what it will without, Wee shall be necessitated to haue a Warr with most if not all our Indians who haue at severall places and at severall times within these last two Months killed eight, or nine of our people, and dayly shew themselues vpon our fronters in

greate Bodies but wee shall soon lett them feele ye Efects of their vnjust molestacōns, & and although ye remoteness of their aboad and their sculking way of Invasion may draw our Revenge into some Length yett wee shall secure our selves from any greate Mischeife, & had ere this begun our just Revenge had wee not vpon ye arrivall of this Caper suspended a while ye execucōn of what wee had before resolved on, that wee might see wether he had any more Company, & Consequently more to bee provided against   I press this Indian Warr soe much ye more to your hono^r from ye hopes I haue that your Lordship will bee pleased soe to represent it to ye King that his Ma^{ty} vpon a just Consideracōn of our p^{r}sent necessities will bee ye more inclined to grant vs his assistance of ye navall force I mentioned before, My Most Hono^d Lord my thoughts are soe filled with ye p^{r}sent subject of my discourse that I had almost forgotten to acquaint your Lordship that wee haue at Length in Virg^a, Maryland, & Carolina granted to y^e Genn^{ll} Wishes & desires of y^e people a Law for a totall Cessation from planting Tobacco in y^e year 1667 but doe humbly submitt y^e same withall others to his M$_a$^{ties} & y^e Lords approbacōn, and Confirmacōn, if it shall appeare prejudiciall to his M$_a$^{ties} Intrests in poynt of Custome, or any way elce, his Maties dissent signified to vs is sufficient to make that Law void, and wee doe humbly pray that wee receiue either his Confirmacōn of it, or y^e Contrary soe soon as may convenietly bee that the people here may know how to imploy themselves   I will now trouble your Lordship noe farther but shall for Euer pray that God will bless my good Lord with ye Choycest of his Blessings, and mee With ye Continuation of your Lordships fauours vpon
My most Honored Lord You^r Lordships

MY MOST HONORD LORD
haueing been vexed wth a feauo^r these ten dayes last past I am forced to begg your Honnors pardon for sending only a duplicate of my former and that in my clerks

hand not being able to wright soe much my selfe ; may God for euer blesse yor Lors^p wth health and happiness I am

    Right Hono^{ble} yor Honnors most humble & obedient serut

                      THO: LUDWELL.

17th Sept. 1666 Virginia

XXXIX.

RICHARD NICOLLS TO THE EARL OF CLARENDON.

MY LORD

    I must ingeniously confesse and humbly acknowledge yor transcendent care of mee and of all that are concern'd with mee in these remote parts, and it is to admiration that your Lo^{pp} should not forgett such small concernments amidst a Million of those great affayres wch daily passe yor Lo^{pps} hands, Truly my Lord I may say (yet with due Respect) no Correspondent is so punctuall as yor Lo^{pp} is pleas'd to bee, and I can as truly answer for my selfe, that I have not once fail'd to trouble yor Lo^{pp} with an unpolish't Narratiue of these affaires, when euer I could heare of an oppertunity, though I find severall have miscarried. My Lord I shall not tire out your patience with many Lines at present for I am certainly informed that my Letters of the 7th of Aprill last by Mr Arthur Stocke are safely arriu'd in London, therfore I send no duplicates; By them y.^r Lo^{pp} will haue understood my present condition, for though the Ammunition and Cloathes for the souldyers is well arriu'd by Bendall & Groome, yet my Condition is very sadd without yor Lo^{pp} pleaseth to continue your Care that shipping may come hither early in the spring.

    If y.^r Lo^{pp} pleaseth to peruse my Letters to his Royall Highnesse, to Secretary Morrice and to Sr William Coventry, the summe of all our affaires are more at Large:

Mr Maverick will bring the Duplicate of this and all the rest along with him into England. Sr Robert Carr has layne sicke ten weekes in this Towne. T'is a vast charge and no proffit to his Royall Highnesse to keepe Delaware in his hands: I wish my Lord Berkley and Sr George Carteret had it in Exchange of their Patent, for then they might reape benefitt, and the Duke bee no looser. The Massachusett Colony will not understand his Maties last signification to them, I haue humbly propos'd to Mr Secretary and Sr William Coventry my conceptions thereupon, I hope yor Lo.^{pp} will prevayle with his Royall Highnesse that I may bee recall'd, and some other fitt person sent in my place, vnlesse his Royall pleaseth to giue mee a Latitude to establish a Temporary settlement of Government in my absence, which indeed will bee a very hard taske for mee to contrive. It remaines that I should thankfully acknowledge the Honour of yor Lo.^{pps} letter bearing date the 13th of Aprill & a duplicate of the same Tenour & date with a Postscript bearing date the third of June full of highly obliging Expressions of your Lordshipps goodnesse to mee, which I shall endeavour to meritt with all that Respect & service which is Most due to yor Lo.^{pp} from

My Lord y.^r Lo.^{pps} Most humble devoted servant,

R NICOLLS

ffort James in America
   octob. ye 24th. 1666.

XL.

SAMUEL MAVERICK TO GEORGE CARTWRIGHT.

EVER HONO.RD S.^R

Captain Peirse ariveing Augt. 7th I rec^d from him a packet, wherein was enclosed his Maties significacōn of his pleasure concerning the Massachusets, & his confirmacōn of what we had done as to the Province of

Main, his order for ye release of some prisoners if any such were on account of petitioning to his Matie or us his Coṁissioners; and also a confirmacōn of the temporary bounds, set betweene Plymouth, & Rhode Island till his Maties pleasure was further knowne. In it the King commands the Councell to send four or five persons forthwith into England, ordering Mr Bellingham, & Major Hawthorn to be two of them. I gave the Governor notice that I had such a significacōn, to deliver when his Councell was assembled, & notice given of it. It was nere five weekes after (notwithstanding all I could speake, or write to presse it) ere I could have opportunitie to deliver it, according to Sr William Morrice his order, which was to the Governor, & Councell assembled. On Sept. 5th both the Generall court, & court of Assistants sitting I deliverd it, and had it read, with much adoe. The Generall court after six dayes spent about Anabaptists, Quakers, & I know not what, tooke the significacōn into consideracōn; and it was voted that noe person should be sent, notwithstanding his Maties expresse command; on which or a little before the considerablest in Boston, & other townes peticōned, that complyance with, & humble submission might be made to his Matie by them who were the representative of the Country; if not, they let them know they would peticōn his Matie to distinguish between the innocent, and the nocent, as by the peticōn a copy of which Capt Breedon will send you with this, yo^u will see. There was an order presently made to summon into the next court eight of the peticōners, most of them you know. Mr Dean, Capt Savage, Mr Bratle, Mr Glover of Boston. Mr Batter of Salem. Capt Apleton of Ispwich. Capt Gearish of Newbury. & Capt Pike of Salisbury. What they will say to them I know not, & I am sure they care not. Capt Hubbard of Hingham should have bin amongst them, having with nere all the inhabitants of that towne, subscribed the peticōn; but their unworthy deputy delivered it not. Many were very hot for degradeing these Cap^{ts} presently: Major Dennison, & Mr Broadstreet, and Cap.ᵗ Pincheon, as I heare, entred their dissent, amongst the Magistrates. Mʳ Browne, & Curwin, Cap.ᵗ Davis, with severall others of the deputies, likewise dissented; and had their dissent entred. They now begin to thinke & feare that, the major part of the people will not stand by them. And (as I have ever thought, & said) not ten will stand by them: Yet some of them seeme to be resolved to beare it out to the last. One sayes, If they must be ruined, it were better to be torne in pieces by a Lyon, than gnaw'd in peeces by ratts. An other says they are resolved, not to be trampled on by any. Cap.ᵗ Breedon (I suppose) will informe of this more at Large.

Sʳ The 600ˡ worth of goods sent by Mʳ Bendall, I rec.ᵈ at Boston, and about ten dayes since, they were divided. Colonell Nicolls his part is, by his order, put on board the sloape I lookd for here for my transportation to York, if shee come not in, I will away by land within two dayes, although (you know) it is a long journey. Wee humbly thank my Lord Chancellor for his ordering the aforesaid summe for us: and you for your care, & paines about it. The goods are not yet disposed off, only divided. Cap.ᵗ Breedon, Mʳ Deane, and Mʳ Lynde are desired to see how the Draper dealt as to the goodnesse, & price; (having looked superficially over them) they suppose there is 25: per Cenᵗ charged above what they had them charged for ready money, As to the goodness it is not yet seene. I mean when I came from Boston.

Sʳ Robert Carr gott in his travills to Delaware, & Maryland a Feavoʳ, & Ague, & I do not heare that he is yet recovered.

I only write these lines to you, fearing the fleet may be gone before my returne. And with this Cap.ᵗ Breedon will send you as many copies of papers, as can be procured, Within a few days I have bin at Yorke you shall have a better account, if this come to you before. I am now at Mʳ Brentons who thanks you for your letter, & will write to you in answer. All your friends here, &

elce where are well, & remember themselves to you, & desire the injoyment of your company. I do not meane as those of the Massachusets; With my best respects presentèd to you, & thankes for all favours remaine

Your very affectionat friend

SAMUELL MAVERICKE.

Major Phillips of Saco being here present desired me to present his service to you.

To the Hono^ble Colonell George
Cartwright Esqr at Mr Lavand-
ars a Cook at the Talbot in the
Strand these present.

XLI.

THO: BREEDON TO THE EARL OF CLARENDON.

Boston octob^r 22th 1666

MAY IT PLEASE YOUR LORDSHIP

Being Com̄anded by m^r Mauerick to giue your honour as good an accounte as I could in reference to seuerall transactions here; I have in ord^r thereunto demanded of ye Secretary m^r Edward Rawson, copyes of seuerall as p the note, and he answered he was prohibbited by the courte to giue some, whence may be gathered, they are ashamed of theire actions, yet persist in their way, and if obedience be better then sacrifize (as I am informed) haue sente two masts which Cap^tt Peirce cales the one Gouorno^r Bellingham, the other majo^r Hawthorne; some more Loyall then others petitioned the Generall Courte a Copy whereof goes herewith, some were selected to answer for it but the charge being refused to be sighned by the drawers vp thereof, the petition^rs were dismist wth a kinde of reproofe which the Secretary refused to giue me a Coppy of: if fame be not a Lyer I must say that Cap^tt Peirc and m^r Samuell

9

Wilson are two that do more mischeife by theire reports
they bringe from England (what Euer Elce they may
on the Exchange) then any men I know, By their re-
reports here his Maj^{tys} comands from Secretary Morrice
with his maj^{tjs} signe is (besids what could I say more)
slited & the Comission's sent by his majesty looked on
as an ould almanack out of Date ; not that I can or doe
excuse any persons that are of themselfs disloyall or in-
clyned to disloyall principls, that haue with Oliuer
joyned & would if it were possible rake up his ashes,
had he been here buryed they would if possible by them
haue raised him from the dead but to speake for the
major parte of this jurisdiction (that are ouer awed by
some that haue the sword in their handes) I must say
that his maj^{ty} need not doubt of theire Loyalty, Some
experience haueing been made by some of ye memb^{r}s of
the generall courte which I forbeare to name: Yo^r
Hono^r will here of them by the title of dissenters from
the rest: being also required by Coll Nicholls to giue
into the courte a coppy of his Comission from the Lds
Comission's of the prize office and to know theire sence
there of, the Secretary gaue me this answer, that the
Courte would not concerne themselfs in any thinge was
giuen in by worde of mouth: 2^{ly} : that the courte Questioned the Coppy as not witnessed, to which m^r mauerick
& my selfe tendring to witnes the major Generall m^r
John Leueret tould me he would Satisfy Gouornour
Nichols that the Kings Comission's had not to act any
thinge here, by which may be gathered, that his maj^{iy}
hath giuen away all power from himselfe by his Charter
saue the 5th parte of mynes royall as they say: but to
implead their charter deny to send any acording to his
maj^{tys} comands, I hope his maj^{tys} loyall subj^{ts} may not
sufer wth the rest: the fleete is hasting away & I begg
your pardon for this trouble & shall for Euer remaine,
my Lord

Yo^r hon^{r}s most oblidged Seruante
THO: BREEDON.

I forgot to acquainte your honour that m^r Deane and m^r Gibbs sett out one priuate man of warr wch tooke two prizes, and my self & friends another that took two more, und^r comission of this Collony, which its possible they apply to the Collony: But indeed my Lord it was but four or fiue of us, and we are in much trouble by reason here is not the Comission^{r}s deputys allowed of by the Courte: I haue not farther to add, but that I am as before:

Yo^{r}s to serue

THO: BREEDON.

To the Right Honnorab Edward Earle
  of Clarendon Ld High Chancellor
  of England this psent

p Hope Bendall Commander of ye Ship: Trijall

[DOCUMENTS REFERRED TO IN THE PRECEDING LETTER.]

I pray call for these Coppies from Mr Rawson.

The declaracōn of the Gen^{ll} Court with sound of trumpett and the Commissioners reply therevnto.

John Porters petition and the Commissioners order there vpon.

The Messachusetts Commission to Mr Symonds and m^r Danfort June 2^d 1665.

The Messachusetts warrant to the Constable of Portsmouth and their letter to the Kings Commissioners and their reply.

A warrant for summoning a speciall Gennerall Court to be held Augt 1st and the order of that Court.

The summons for Mr Corbett to appeare at the gennerall Court at Boston October 11th 1666.

his sentence at that Court with the Mittymus to ye Jaylor, and the warrant from the gennerall Court to the Marshalls of Dover and Portsmouth for aprehending of Mr Corbett.

To the Honoured Generall Courte now assembled In Boston.

MAY IT PLEASE THIS HON^RED COURTE

Yo^r humble pettition^rs being informed that lett^rs are lately sente from his majesty to ye Gouourn^r & Councell, Expressiue of his ill resentment of ye proceedings of this collony wth his Comission^rs, lately sente hyther & requiring also some principle persons therein, wth comande vpon theire allegiance to attend his maj^tys pleasure in order to a finall determination of such differences & debats as haue hapned between his maj^tys said Comission^rs and ye Gouernm^t here, and wth declaration of his maj^tys your pettition^rs looking at as a matter of the greatest importance justly calling for most serious consideration, that they might neither be wanting to your selfs in wth houlding any incoragem^t that theire concurance might aforde in so arduous a matt^r, nor to themselfes and to ye Country in being inuolued by their silence in ye dangerous mistake of (otherwise well minded persons) inclining to disloyall principalls they desire they may haue liberty without ofence to propose some of theire thoughts & feares aboute this matt^r unto yor more serious deliberation your petition^rs humbly conceiue that those who liue in this age of ye world are no less than oth^rs concerned in that aduise of ye wise man; to keep ye Kings commandm^t because of ye oath of god, and not to be hasty to goe out of his sight that doth whatsoeu^r pleaseth him, wherefore they desire that seeing his maj^ty hath already taken no littell displeasure against us, as if we disowned his maj^tys jurisdiction ouer us; efectuall care may be taken least by refuseing to attend his maj^tys ord^r for ye clearing of our pretences unto right and fauor in that particuler, we should plunge our selfs into greater disfauour: And danger; our receiuing a Charter from his maj^tys Royall predecesso^rs for ye planting this Collony, with a confirmation of ye same from his royall person by ye late addres sufficiently declares this place to be parte of his dominions and our selfs his subjects in testimony of wch also ye first Gouorn^r m^r mathew Craddock

stands recorded Juratus de fide et obedientia, before one
of ye mast^rs of Chauncery, whence it is Euident y^t if any
proceedings of this Collony haue giuen any occasion to
his maj^ty to say that we beleiue he hath noe Jurisdiction
ouer us, what efectuall course had need be taken to free
our selfs from ye incuring his maj^tys further displeasure
by Continuance in so dangerous an offence, and to giue
his maj^ty all due sattisfaction in that pointe, such an as-
sertion would be no less distractiue to our welfaire then
derogating to his maj^tys honour, the doubtfull interpretation of ye words of a pattent, wch there can be no reason
to hope they should euer be Construed ye diuesting a
Souoraigne prince of his Regall power ouer his naturall
subj^ts & Leige people is to fraile a foundation to build
such a transendent Imunity & preuiledge vpon: Yo^r
pettion^rs shall Euer be willing to acknowledge to y^e
Vtmost how much they are bounde to your selfs &
others in ye like Capasity for your aboundant care &
paines in Carrying on ye gouernment of ye Collony & in-
deauoring to vphould ye libertys thereof & should not be
unwilling to ruñ any hazard wth yow for ye regular defence
& ye security of ye same & would be most unwilling to
reflect upon ye persons of them they so much honour &
resp^t by an unnessisary disenting from them in some
things wherein they could not approoue ye reason of y^e
proceedings, but in matter of so greate concernm^t as is
ye matter now in agietation wherein ye honour of god &
ye credit of religion as well as ye interest of their owne
persons & estates are all concerned they earnestly desire that no party will so irresistably carry on any designe of so dangerous a consequence as to nessessitate
theire brethren equally engaged wth them in ye same un-
dertakeing, to make theire perticuler addres to his maj^ty
and declaration to ye world to cleare themselues from the
least imputation of so scandelous an Euell as ye apear-
ance of disafection or disloyalty to ye person and Gou-
ernm^t of theire lawfull prince & Souoraine, would be;
Wherefore your petitioners do here humbly entreate
that if any occasion hath been giuen to his maj^ty, so to

resente any of our former actions as is in his last letters
held forth that nothing of that nature be farther proceeded in, but contrarywise that aplycation be made to
his maj^{ty} by meete persons imediately to be sente for that
end to cleare the transactions of them that gouerne this
Collony from any such construction, Least otherwise
that wch duely improoued might haue been as a cloude
of ye latter raine be turned into that wch in conclusion
may be founde more terrible then ye roaring of a Lyon:
thus craueing your fauorable interpretation of what is
here humbly presented : Your Petitioners shall euer be
oblidged to thankfulnes

THOMAS BREEDON	SAMUELL BROADSTREET
JOHN FFREAKE	THOMAS SAVAGE SENI^R
THOMAS KELLOND	RICHARD WHARTON
THOMAS DEANE	HENRY TAYLOR
HABAKKUK GLOUER	JAMES WHETCOMB
JOHN JOLLIFFE	W^M TAYLOR
ROBERT GIBBS	JOHN CONEY
BERNARD TROTT	EPHRAIM TURNER
ANTIPAS BOYSE	THOMAS BRATTLE
RICHARD PRICE	SYMON LIND
SAMUELL SCARLET	JOHN BUSHNELL
NICHOLAS PAGE	JOHN WOODMANSEY
	RICHARD PATTESHALL

ffrom Ipswith subscribed this pettition . . 73 :
ffrom Salem 36
ffrom Hingham most parte of ye towne, but their
    deputy did not deliuer it : hundreds more might
    haue been had

XLII.

H. M. COMMIS^{RS} FOR N. ENGLAND TO THE GOV^R & COUNCIL
OF THE MASSACHUSETTS.

GENTLEMEN
    Although we were credibly informed before your

Generall Court sate in September last, and by divers circumstances were alarmn'd that the Significacōn of his ma^{ties} pleasure to your selves, under his Maties Signe manuall, & subscribed by Sr William Morice principall Secretary of State, would not meet with a full complyance in your Generall Court: Yet wee gave very litle credit to reports so derogatory to your dutifull Submission to his Maties commands: and haveing seene the copy of an humble addresse to your Generall Court, under the hands of many considerable persons, eminent for loyalty, and estates within your Jurisdiction, wherein the Peticōners did with a modest importunity, offer to their Representatives, their deep sense of the calamities, which may ensue, if his Maties just displeasure should be kindled against the disobedient. Wee were full of hopes that the Generall Court would have given his Matie due satisfaction to his commandes, & particular thankes to those Gentlemen the petitioners; But being fully informed, that yor resolucōns are neither to send Mr Richard Bellingham your present Governo^r, with Major Hawthorne, who are expresly required upon their allegiance to attend his Matie nor to make your choice of two, or three other persons, as his Matie is pleased to direct you: and further that you have not only discountenanced, but laid heavie charges against those loyall, & dutyfull petitioners, We conceive ourselves, at last, highly obliged (as Commissioners from his Matie) solemnly to manifest, declare, and protest, in the name, & behalf of his Matie

1. ffirst, That his Maties significacōn of his pleasure to his Colony of the Massachusets, is an originall signed by his Matie Subsigned by Sr Wm Morice Principall Secretary of State, which ought to be received for authentick in all his Maties dominions; & is so entertained in all the other his Maties Colonies in New-England, to their joy, & satisfaction, though with some blot upon record in your Scutcheon.

2. Secondly, That, his Matie will be justly displeased with your resolution against sending the persons nominated in the Signification, with such others as you are

positively commanded to make your owne choice of to attend his Matie whoe expects from all his Subjects, obedience, as much more acceptable than Sacrifice.

3. Thirdly, That his Matie cannot but approve that humble petition presented to your Generall Court; and by the Lawes of England (which must be the touch stone) those Gentlemen, ought not to be molested, fined, or imprisoned for any matter contained in the said petition, so full of duty to his Matie of respect to your Generall Court, and tending to the peace, and welfare of the whole Colony.

4. Lastly. Wee ourselves fully concurring with the substance, and to those good ends manifested in the petition, do earnestly sollicit you to resume the whole matter into your most serious consideracõns, that his Matie may be honoured with the reall obedience of his Subjects, and thereby encouraged plentifully to power forth the riches of his goodnesse upon his Colony of the Massachusets, To which we are hearty wellwishers, & will contribute our best endeavours, at all times, & in all places, when by your submission to his Matie we shall be encouraged to remain.

Your very affectionat friends, & Servants his Maties Commissioners for New England

R. N.   R. C.   S. M.

Fort James at New York
November 3^d 1666.

Mr RAWSON

This inclosed letter (directed to the Governor, & assistants of his Maties Colony of the Massachusets) we have particularly remitted to your hands, in respect to the office you beare as Secretary to the Colony, that so it may have a more easy addresse, & access to them: as also that we may have a full, & speedy answer thereunto, To which end we desire you to deliver the same as a paper important to his Maties Service, from

Yo^r affectionat friends his Maties Commission^{rs} for New England

R. N.   R. C.   S. M.

Be pleased to deliver the answer & resolution of the Court to Mr Samuel Maverick, or whom he shall appoint.

Fort James at New York
Novembr 3^d 1666.

Endorsed—"*A Copy of a letter sent from his Maties Commissioners for N. England to the Governor and Councell of the Massachusets &c*"

XLIII.

EDWARD RAWSON TO COL. RICHARD NICOLLS.

RIGHT HONO^{BLE}

These few lines are to give your hono^r an account of the reception of you^{rs} by the hands of Mr Mavericke bearing date the 3^d instant, on the tenth of the same, with such answer thereto, as our honord Governor with such of the assistants as were with him on the thirteenth were pleased to signifie to me, that so Mr Mavericke might be acquainted therewith, and haveing waited on him for that end, understanding of an opportunity willingly lay'd hold thereof to give the same unto your self and Sr Robert Carr & is That they finding the contents of yo^{rs} doe referr to the actings of our Generall Court which was dissolved Sundry dayes since, that their re-returne to the Hono^{ble} Sr Wm Morice was dispatched & gone for England in the last month, yet at the first opportunity for the assistants meeting your letter shall be communicated according to the direction thereof. Presenting my humble service to yor Hono^r & to Sr Robert Carr not haveing wherewith to give yor Hono^r further trouble take leave to subscribe my self S^r

Yo^r Hono^{rs} most humble Servt

EDWARD RAWSON.

Boston the 14th November 1666.

These for the Right Honour^{ble} Colonel Richard Nicolls Governor of New York be presented.

Endorsed—"*A Copy of an answer to the Letter sent from his ma^{ties} Comissioncrs for N. England to the Govern^r & Councell of the Massachusets. 14 Novr. 1666*"

XLIV.

PAPERS IN THE CASE OF CORBETT.

To THE MARSHALL OF DOVER & PORTSMOUTH.

Yo^w are hereby required in his Majestyes name &
by virtue of an order of the Generall Court sitting in
Boston the 11th Instant to App^rehend & seaze on the
person of Abraham Corbett & that forthwith. & him
safely to Convey to Boston & to bring him before the
Governo^r or Magistrates at Boston to answer for his tumultuous & seditious practises against this Government
to be proceeded with as in their wisdomes they shall
finde cause hereof yo^u are not to faile at your perrill.

Dated at Boston 26 october 1665.

By order of the Generall Court

EDWARD RAWSON *Secrety.*

That this is A true Copie Compared with the originall warrant on file

Attest. EDW. RAWSON *Secret^y.*

Vnde^rwritt.

Jno Robe^rts marshall of Dover came before the
Governo^r & majo^r Generall Jno Leuerett & brought wth
him m^r Abraham Corbett whom he had seazed on the
13th Instant & acording to this warrant brought him &
p^rsented him to the Governo^r & majo^r Generall to be
proceeded with accordingly this 15th of November. 1665.

as *Attest.* EDWARD RAWSON *Secrety*

To THE KEEPER OF THE PRISON IN BOSTON.

Yo^w are hereby required in his Majestyes name to
take into you^r Custody the person of Abraham Corbett & him safely keepe till the next Generall Court of
Election that he may there appeare & answer for his
tumultuous seditious & disorderly carriages ; which hath

been to the disturbance of his Majestjes peace. Vnlesse he give bond with two able suertjes for his appearance before the sajd Generall Court & in the meane time that he be of Good behauiour for your so doing this shall be your warrant   Dated in Boston this 15th of November 1665.

RI. BELLINGHAM *Gove^rn^r*
J^{N°} LEUERET *Asistant*

That this is A true Copie Compared wth the originall left on file Attest.

EDWARD RAWSON *Secrety*

Mr Corbetts Crime was for getting hands to a petition to his Maiesty wch petition I suppose Coll Cartwright hath a Coppy of or at least can attest the same as I doe   Witnesse my hand

THO: BREEDON

XLV.

PETITION FROM RHODE ISLAND AND PROVIDENCE PLANTATIONS.

To the Kings Most Excellent Ma^{tte},

The humble Peticōn and Address of the Gouern^r and Companie off His Maties Colonie of Rhode Island and Prouidence Plantations in New England.

MOST HUMBLIE SHEWETH

That whereas yor Maties most humble Subjects and Supplicants, as soone as wee heard ye joyfull tidings off yor Maties happy restoracōn to the Possession of yor Royall Crowne and dignitie, makeing our humble addresses by Peticōn vnto yor Royall Matie in wch wee imployed that faithfull & trustie Agent Mr John Clarke, did thervpon by yor Maties Royall bountie obtaine a

most Free & Ample Charter of incorporacōn, for our
possessing Emproueing and Gouerning the Lands and
Islands in and off the Narragansitt Bay and Countrie
in New England, wch grante Yo^r Matie was gratiouslie
pleased to make firme and good to vs and o^r Successors for euer vnder the Greate Seale, and that
alsoe done after yor Matie had taken cognizance of
the Indian Sachems submission of the said Countrie vnto yor Matie in the yeare 1662 in wch they
remembred an address of the same nature made
some 18 yeers before to Y^r Royall Father of Blessed
memorie, which their address was neuer, nor could bee
taken notice off vntill their late adress aforementioned
in 1662, In meane time, wee liuinge and gouerning
here by virtue of a Charter granted in his late Royall
Maties Name by the Lords and Comons in 1643. The
said Indians sold seuerall considerable tracts of the Narragansitt Countrie vnto people of this Colonie, and receiued therfore full satisfacōn, as in their said late address they doe acknowledge: And indeed some Thousands of pownds it hath cost the people of this Colonie
in those Purchases: Euen more than the other Colonies
hath expended for ten times as much which they possess, who yett could not content themselues, but in-
croached on this small corner, not onely dispossessing,
molesting, captiuing and finening your Majesties Leige
people here liueing; butt also claimeing all the Countrie by strang pretences of free purchases & gift's by
forced mortgages from the Indians, therein including
the Indians rights vnsould; with those aforesaid sould
to some of this Colonie: whervpon itt pleased yor Majestie in your Royall wisedome to send yor Honble Com-
mission^{r}s to enquire into those matters, who haue with
exceeding Trauell and care, paines and patience, judgment and discretion, accordinglie most Hoñ^{bly} discharged the trust in them reposed: And vpon findeing
the Indians to owne their subjection former and latter,
and seeing the hard dealings by the other Colonies vsed
to them and vs; did for a present expedient distinguish

those Lands from the rest of this yor Majesties Colonie by the name of The Kings Prouince and prohibited all Colonies from exercise of Jurisdiction therin, And after by a spetiall comission vnder their Hon^rs hands & seales did comitt the gouernm^t to the Gouerno^r & Councill off this Colonie, till yor Majesties pleasure bee further knowne, All which being the effect of yor Majesties gratious and fatherlie care of vs yor poore vnworthie subjects : Therby wee feele much ease at present from great oppressors : And for itt wee returne all humble thanks as in dutie bownd : And howeuer by this late result, our Charter seemeth to be very much impaired, and as it were in parte suspended for the present, Yett wee in all humilitie doe confess & owne yor Majesties royall wisedome, and the justice of those Honble Persons yor Maiesties Commission^rs : Beleeiuing ther is not any the least intent to make voide our Charter in any parte, butt rather to reconfirme or enlarge itt, Wherfore wee haue made bold in some other papers humbly presented to the Right Honble the Earle of Clarindon, Lord High Chancelor of England to declare some reasons why of right and necessitie the whole Countrie of Narragansitt as in the very letter of the Charter shuld beelong to his yor Maties Colonie As also why the Line between Y^r Maties colonie of New Plimouth & vs, shuld bee settled accordinglie, though at p^rsent somewhat shortened : And for the more cleere demonstracon of the same matters, Wee haue caused a draught to bee made of Plimouth & Connecticott & more perticularlie of this yor Majesties Colonie lying between them and herewith humblie presented itt

Therfore in the great experience of Yo^r Maties most wonderfull grace and Fauour shewed vnto vs, Wee prostrate ourselues in all Loyaltie and Humilitie at Yo^r Majesties feete Most humblie imploring Yo^r Royall Grace & Fauour to restore yor Majesties Royall Grant to its former state and extent, by readjoyning the Kings Prouince to the rest and soe reconfirme vnto vs, that yor Majesties said late

Royall grant as it is vnder the Great Seale: And to sett and settle our Eastern bounds alsoe accordinglie, Soe shall wee bee encouraged to goe on in propagating plantacōns of that which lyeth wast, and by Gods help and Yo^r M$_a$^{ties} gratious Fauour shall bee enabled to serve yor Majestie in Protecting and directing the Indians here liueing, instructing their Children in learning and Ciuill educacōn ; as alsoe in putting this Colonie in a Posture of defence, promoteing off Trade, Husbandrie, and Fishing, And gouerning ourselues in peace & justice vnder Yo^r Majestie, and for euer deuoted to pray for Yo^r Maties Long life and greatness here & Eternall Glorie hereafter

WILLIAM BRENTON
WILLIAM BAULSTON
JOHN CLARKE

This is a true Copie of what was sent by the Hon^{bl} Collon^{ll} Cartwright one of his M$_a$^{ties} Hon^{bl} Comission^{rs} for New England ordered by the Genl Asembly to be signed by the Govr and part of the Consell

---

XLVI.

WILLIAM BRENTON, WILLIAM BAULSTON AND JOHN CLARKE
TO THE EARL OF CLARENDON.

RIGHT HON^{BLE}

Howeuer ther are vpon vs soe very many and great obligacōns to yor Lordshipp for those vnmeritted Fauours hithervnto Extended vnto this his M$_a$^{ties} Colonie; which here to recount, would butt add to Yo^r Lordship trouble to read, and to our selues greater measure of shame in that Wee haue nott, nor as yett cañott saue in emptie words any way returne Yo^r Lordship any the smallest token of our acknowledgm^{ts} Butt are Euen in a wanting & consequently in a crauinge condition for yor Lordships Fauour to bee still o^r defendo^r and releife:

May itt please Yo^r Hon^r this Poore suppressed & allmost Extinguished Colonie next vnder God and his M_a^{tie} owe euen their All vnto yor Lordshipp: And howeuer haue nott wherein else to shew their gratefull acknowledgm^{ts}: did designe to choose & sett apart out of this small Tract, a competent, and convenient quantitie of Land for a Farme of a thowsand acres or therabouts, and to haue begged yor Lordships acceptance of the same, soe as to owne and dispose of itt att yor Hono^{rs} Pleasure: And shuld take itt as the greatest Fauour possible, yor Lordshipps acceptacōn therof: Now itt soe falls, that a present seeming cloude passing ouer o^r Colonie hath Ecclipsed the splendor of our Charter, and rendered vs in a sort vncapable of disposing ought in the farr greater Parte of his Royall M_a^{ties} Grant, and of our absolute cleere Purchasees from y^e Indians Butt beleeuing ther is no intent, butt that all will bee restored to its cleere and full extent vnto vs, in which, wee humblie Emplore Yo^r Lordships fauour to bee o^r helper & Protector: some reasons Wee·haue made bold to present to yor Lordshipp in two Papers shewing why of right and necessitie, that now called the Kings Prouince, bee still continewed and adjoyned to the rest of this Colonie, and why the line betweene Plimoth Colony and vs bee established as in the Mapp described, itt being according to the very letter of the Charter to vs Granted: And haue yett a further humble Peticōn to yor Lordshipp Concerning some help's or incouragment towards Fortification of this Bay: which in very deed is the most Excellent in New England considering the climate, most healthfull Scite most commodious in the midle of the Colonies; Harbors, most safe for the biggest ship's that euer sayld the sea, and of all sorts whateuer, and for outlett & inlett soe good, as none can equall itt, that in hardest winters, when the Masachusetts & others, to the

East and west are fast-locked vp with strong doores of
Ice, this is alwayes open : besides the conueniencie of
the Maine land and Islands at the very entrance soe near
each other easie to bee secured by Forts on eyther
Chanell, One meanes, may it Please yor Lordshipp to
Encourage the growth of & giue strength to this his
M_a^{ties} Colony would beè by some act off Grace extending some Peculiar Priuiledge in Point of freeness of
commerce hence to other his M_a^{ties} Dominions, with
some ease in some measure as to Taxes vpon that is Imported or Exported, though butt for some Yeares : Butt
Wee dare not direct yor Lordships wisedome but only
implore yor Honble countenance in what shall seeme best,
Onlie, one thing shall bee bold to Propose, Concerning
an Estate that is bequeathed in England for the Pious
end of Propagating the Gospell in Conuerting, or att
least instructing the Indians in the Knowledg of mor-
rall Virtues & by degrees to know God : Heere are the
greatest number of Indians, liveing in the Confines of
this little spott that are in any Parte of new England
besides : And howeuer those which are growne up to
ripe Yeares in their wilde and vnciuill manners, will
hardlie leaue their owne sensuall customes ; Yet were
ther a Schoole erected with meanes to mainteyne it for
the Bringing their children some to learning & some to
handy crafts, for the increase of manufacture, ther would
in a few yeares by the blessing of the Lord appeare a
very hopefull change, and in one Generation they would
in a great measure bee made happie, and also bee a
mean off good aduance vnto his M_a^{ties} interest in these
Parts vnder the Gouernm^t by his M_a^{tie} already heer
established vnto vs vnder the Great Seale, And ther-
fore Wee humbly Implore yor Lordship's fauour in
furthering this good worke if soe it shall in Yo^r Hon^{rs}
Wisedome appeare to bee.

And thus crauing yor Lordship's Pardon for our
extreame boldness & tedious Importunitie, Wee shall
humbly recommend to Yo^r Honble consideracōn the
Pervsall of our humble Peticōn to his Royall M_a^{tie}

herewith presented to yor Lordshipp's view, humbly craueing your Lordship's Fauour to couer or excuse our boldness, or any other Errors therin (to vs vnawares) committed, And soe farr to extend yor Hono^{rs} Fauour to vs as wee may therby bee restored to that happiness of injoying that most Ample Grante in itts full extent, the which wee owne our selues yor Lordship's very greatly obleidged for Procureing the same att first Butt most Exceedinglie bound to yor Lordshipp For those high fauours mentioned in Yo^r Honble Letter to Vs therin declaring such vnexpected regard to vs as was and is wonderfull, and hath imboldened vs thus to presume to glue Yo^r Lordshipp this further trouble by the hands, of this Noble & Honble Gentleman Colonell Cartwright, to whom and the other Honble Comission^{rs} Wee are most deeplie Engaged for that Exceeding Care Paines and Trauell taken in our behalues & the most vnbyassed resolutions by their Hon^{rs} Proceeds declared vpon the hearing of all differences, Soe as wee haue cause, & hope shall haue to bless the Lord and the King's Majestic, and returne all Humble thanks to yor Lordshipp for this happie visitation by those Honble Persons, wherby those vncredible oppressions wee endured, of Scorne & Contempt, Sclander & reproch, threatning & molestations, Captiuing and imprisoñing Fining and Plundering the People of this Colonie is now made cleer before their Hon^{rs} and therin cleerlie discouered a Combination of all the Colonies to roote vs vp and Expose vs to ruine, in seeking out new Places of the Willderness ther to strugle with all sorte of diffi culties, as in the beginning of this Plantacōn, they forced vs to: and denyed vs releife in greatest danger Which our sufferings could not be knowne to any butt God and ourselues vntill this time of hearing was come: Butt not to giue Yo^r Lordshipp more troble at this time Wee humbly cast ourselues and Cause at yor Lordshipp's Feet, And with all cheerfullness Subscribe our selues in behalf of this his Majesties Colonie of Rhod Iland and Prouidence Plantations

10

Yo.ʳ Lordshipps most humbly & faithfully deuoted
Servants

WILLIAM BRENTON
WILLIAM BAULSTON
JOHN CLARKE

Dated Nuport June 16.ᵗʰ 1665.

This is a true Copie of what was sent by the Hon.ᵇˡᵉ
Collon.ˡˡ Cartwright one of his Ma.ᵗⁱᵉˢ Hono.ᵇˡᵉ Comissioners for New England.   Ordered by the Gen.ˡˡ Assembly
to be Signed by the Go.ʳ and parte of the Counsell.

Thess To the Right Hon.ᵇˡᵉ Edward
   Earle off Clarindon Lord High
   Chancelor off England Most hum-
   blie Presented.

XLVII.

REASONS WHY THE " KING'S PROVINCE " SHOULD REMAIN TO
RHODE ISLAND.

Some Reasons humbly p.ʳesented vnto the Right Honor-
able Edward Earle off Clarindon Lord High Chan-
celor of England By the Gouern.ʳ and Companie of
his Majesties Colonie of Rhode Iland & Prouidence
Plantacōns: Shewing why itt is both right and off
necessitie that the parte of the said Colonie now dis-
tinguished by the name of the Kings Prouince shuld
remaine to y.ᵉ said Colonie.

1. For as much as wee haue had possession by Free
Purchase in some parte of the midle of the Narragansitt Country, by the Indians sale about seauen or eight
& twentie Yeares besides what was before or since
granted to the fowre Townes of Prouidence, Portsmouth
Nuport and Warrwick.
2. For that the s.ᵈ Country is wholie & clearlie Con-

teyned in the Grant made in his late M_a^{ties} name by the Lords & Comons in the yeare 1643 before the Indians surrendering themselues and Lands vnto his late M_a^{ties} gouernment and Protection, w^{c}h grant was since Confirmed, and that w^{c}h Mr Weld vnderhand gott of the same Country was prohibited being neuer past at Councill Table nor Registered.

3. For that the Indians since the s^d Grant haue sould seuerall pts of the s^d Country and taken full satisfacõn for itt off People of this Colonie, who bought & possessed itt quietlie vntill in these 4 or 5 yeares the other Colonies by Clandestine purchases & forced mortgages haue incroched both vpon that those people had purchased, as afores^d, and the rest as yett vnsould and this is fully cleered to bee true by the Indian Sachems owne acknowledgm^t in their Address to his Royall M_a^{tie} in Aprill 1662. w^{c}h address was by the Honble Commission^{r}s S^{ir} Robt Carr K^t George Cartwright & Samuell Mauerick Esq^{r}s here produced, and to y^e said Sachems read, and by them Cleerly vnderstood and owned.

4. Forasmuch as the whole is conteined in his M_a^{ties} late Royall Grante to this Colonie in 1663 and to deuide the same in two seuerall parts, will render both soe inconsiderable as that neyther will in any measure bee sufficient for any competent number of people to liue vpon besides the inconueniencies that will arise by the mixture of one with the other, w^{c}h would render both in a state of much trouble, and discouragem^t to people for building or settling vpon itt except conteyned in one entire Tenure as granted to the Colonie afors^d and vnder that one gouernment.

5. For that the whole as considered to bee fully granted in o^r patent vnder the great Seale conteyning all that is called The Kings Prouince, and the rest is no way answerable vnto the least of the other Colonies in quantitie as by a mapp calculated in that respect according to true informacõn & knowledg And herewith presented, it doth appeare. Soe that on eyther pt (if parted)

ther can bee no competencie to raise any considerable supplie of prouisions for trade to his M^aties other Plantacōns, nor can this Colonie grow to any maturitie, of strength to serue his Matie, but groan vnder the weight off Pouertie, & bee subjected still to the wills of the other Colonies to giue what they please for the little wee raise, wee being not able to transport itt, as being not worth while farr abroad, to make the best off itt because of the little quantitie theroff.

6. For that by experience wee haue found that by reason of the interruption this Colonie hath had in the possessing of the Narragansitt now called The Kings Prouince, wch interruption was by force from the other Colonies, as it is cleered to ye Honble Commission^rs aforementioned many of the people of this Colonie haue been forced to expose themselues to seek out other places to their vtter ruine & vndoing, And some into Plimouth claimes: 12 or 16: miles from Rhod Iland, wch had wee had the vse of that s^d Narragansitt Country would haue in a good measure sufficed & incouraged o^r owne People and haue giuen strength & growth to the Colonie to haue sett vpon trading Fishing &c.

7. And Lastly that Countrie of the Narragansitt of Right belongs to this Colonie not for the fors^d reasons onlie butt also for that, although the Sachems did about 20 yeares since submitt itt & themselues to his Majesties late Royall Father of glorious memorie, yett no cognizance could bee, or was then or euer after by his s^d M^atie taken of the same, nor vntill the Sachems made their last address vnto his Royall Matie in the yeare 1662 wch their address being taken notice of, And it mentioning ye said country & owning it to be conteyned in our former grant &c. his Most Royall Matie was thervpon & therafter howeuer, gratiouslie pleased to giue and grant the s^d Narragansitt Country expressly vnto this Corporacōn, All, itt & the rest vnder the name of the English Colonie of Rhod Island &c as in the s^d Charter vnder the great scale is more perticularly mentioned, wch s^d Grant wee humbly & Cheerfully expect

to bee firme & good, and will soe bee accounted & con-firmed by his M^{aties} Royall grace to vs and ours for euer, And the rather because his M^{atie} granted y^t wch the Indian Sachems had soe freely & fully surrendred to his Royall will & pleasure to order and dispose

WILLIAM BRENTON
WILLIAM BAULSTON
JOHN CLARKE

This is a true Copie of what was sent by the Honble Colln^{ll} Cartwright one of his Maties Honble Commission^{rs} for New-England: Ordered by the Gen^{rl} Assembly to be Signed by the Govo^r and parte of the Counsell.

XLVIII.

REASONS FOR SETTLING THE EASTERN LINE ACCORDING TO THE CHARTER.

Some Reasons Humblie p^rsented to the Right Honble Edward Earle of Clarindon Lord High Chancelor of England By the Gouerno^r and Companie off his Majesties Colonie of Rhode Iland and Prouidence Plantations, for settleing the Easterne Line according to the meaning and Letter of the Charter.

1. Because that Line intrencheth not on Plimouth Pattent (such as it is) for that it is not bounded by the Sea on the South in that Grant, butt by a riuer called Narragansitt Riuer, no such riuer being knowne.

2. Because Rhode Island, lyeth as inclosed, and in a manner imbayed within the Land which Plimouth would haue to bee, in their jurisdiction. And yett it is the Narragansett Bay and therfore good reason that thes maine Land inclosing and soe neare adjoyning to the Island shuld pertaine to itt, espetiallie being expresslie granted to his Royall M^{atie} in our late Charter

in express words; three miles to the East of the most
easterly and north easterlie parte of the said Bay.

3. Because this Island being small, scarcelie holding
three miles broad any great parte of itt or Fifteen
Long, The inhabitants espetially on that side the Island,
lying veric neare the Maine, are forced ther to winter
their Cattle, and otherwise also to keepe them ther, w^ch
Land hath otherwise neuer beene improued by Plimouth, but itt hath layne wast neare Forty Yeares,
since they first began that Plantacōn, besides manie of
ours for meer necessitie haue bought Lands neare the
water on that side, of the Indian owners and possessed
itt many Yeares peaceablie: it being soe very Remote
from Plimouth Towne and from any Towne of that
Colonie, as, that itt would bee of little vse to them if
they had itt.

4. Because the nearness of that Land on the east
side, is by experience an annoyance to this Gouernm^t,
by being onlie att present out of the jurisdiction of this
Colonie there being Farmes made by some of this Island
people, just ouer the Riuer within call of the Island;
wher any that are Culpable, or Conuicted by ye Law
here, make their escape ouer, and ther are out of reach,
Euen at this time: And Plimouth Towne soe very remote that vnder three or foure dayes time, we cannot
attaine their warrant to apprehend such whateuer the
occasion bee; in wch time the offendo^r is inabled to
make a finall escape nor can wee make the Cheife port
of this Colonie, butt on this Island hauing none elce
fitt, As this, which is indeed hard to bee equalized in
New England for reception & safe riding off vessells of
all sortes, and in all Seasons, and hardest Frostie Winters, wch is not soe in any other parts off this Countrie.

5. Because the Maine Land on the Eastside as
afores^d is soe near the Island & the Riuer beetween soe
Convenient, that a Towne on that side would answeere
to them on this side very comodiouslie on all occasions
of releife or defence, And indeed this Colonic cann neuer
bee secured from invasion if that side (for such a quan-

titie as is mentioned in our Charter) bee not in this Jurisdicōn and at its deuotion, itt lying soe remote from Plimouth as afore is said, that it cannott answere them to fortifie itt, itt being neare :50: miles from them by Land, butt aboue a hundred by watter.

6. Because the people of this Island ther settled & settleing themselues haueing beene vsed too, & liued in this gouernm⸤ doe earnestlie Long still to bee vnder the Protection & direction therof, as also they being so nearc vs, and soe very remote from Plymouth, by wᶜh meanes itt is very difficult for them to attend their Courts for justice.

7. Because the Natiue Indians both Sachems and others not onely and often in former times haue motioned and desired to bee in, or vnder this gouernment, but euen alsoe of late, since we receiued the Late Royall grante vnder the Greate Seale, haue by word and writting desired they might bee esteemed, deemed & owned within this Jurisdicōn hauing allwayes for neare :30: yeares had very neare, frequent and freindlie Com̄erce and entercourse with vs:

WILLIAM BRENTON.
WILLIAM BAULSTON.
JOHN CLARKE.

This is a true Copie of what was sent by the Honᵇˡᵉ Collonell Cartwright one of his Maᵗⁱᵉˢ Honᵇˡ Comissionʳˢ for New England Ordered by the Genʳˡ Asembly to be Signed by the Goʳ and parte of the Counsell.

XLIX.

WILLIAM BRENTON AND WILLIAM BAULSTON TO THE EARL
OF CLARENDON.

RIGHT HONᴮᴸᴱ
Wee being in some measure sensible how much yoʳ

Lordship is prest with the waighty affairs of the King-dome y^t dayly pursue you, And Conscious to o^r selves y^t wee haue heretofore By o^r Agent made no small Ad-dition to yor Lordships trouble and being also greatly ashamed at o^{r}selves y^t as yet wee have not found out a way in any measure to shew o^{r}selves gratefull shall not dare to presume at this p^{r}sent to give yor hon^r any fur-ther trouble then to signifie y^t this inclosed being super-scribed to yor Lordship is an exact Coppie of w^{tt} was sent ye last year by ye hand of y^t hon^{rble} trusty & pru-dent Commission^r Collonell Cartwright which also mis-carried in y^t unhappie disaster y^t befell himselfe, & Con-tains in it o^r humble addresse to his Matie, o^r thankfull returne to yor hono^r, & severall grounds & reasons why ye land on ye East and West of ye Island although otherwise stated Pro/tempore by ye hon^{rble} Commission^{rs} ought of right & good reason remain as is determined in expresse termes in his Maties late Royall grant bestow-ed upon us, Wee humbly crave the Continuation of yor Lordships unmerited favour towards us as to ye perusall thereof, & as to ye improving of yor Lordships interest on o^r Behalfe. The whole before express'd being as is deemed two parts of three of ye land express'd in o^r Charter a very necessary appendix to this Colloney with respect to ye good both of plantacōn jurisdiction & fortificacōn. That on ye West being ye land about which the Contest held so long & so strong between o^r Agent & Mr. Winthrop before his Matie & yor hon^r. That on ye East being Claimed by those who have no Charter from his Matie that Canne bee found upon Record, who have made no application unto his Matie to receive one who formerly in Combination with ye Massachusets & toge-ther with them stil'd ye English and Indians within their pretended precincts to bee their subjects, o^r honrd friend Collonell Cartwright can further informe. We also Crave yor Lordships favour in handing ye inclosed thankfull representation and humble Petition unto his Matie Wee shall not adventure to give yor hon^r any fur-ther trouble for p^{r}sent but to hegge yor pardon for this boldnesse, & so Committing yor Lordship in these troublesome & hazardous times, to the Councill, guidance, protection, & Blessing of ye Almighty, shall humbly tak leave to subscribe o^r selves

Right Hon^{rble} yor Lordships greatly obliged Servants

WILLIAM BRENTON
WILLIAM BAULSTON

These to the Right Hon^{rble} Edward
    Earle of Clarindon Lord high
    Chācellor of England most hum-
    bly presented.

Endorsed—" *Gouernors of Rhode Islande to me rec. January.* "

L.

PETITION FROM RHODE ISLAND AND PROVIDENCE PLANTATIONS.

To His most Excellent Majestie Charles the Second King of Greate Brittaine and of the rest of the Kingdomes Dominions and Territories to Him belonging

1he thankfull representation and Humble Petition of the Governo^r and Companie of your Majesties Colonie of Rhode Island and Providence Plantations in New England.

MOST HUMBLY SHEWETH
    That forasmuch as it pleased your M_a^{tie} vpon o^r first humble addresses by o^r Agent out of your Princely bounty without any the least desert of ours to signifie your Royall pleasure and good will towards vs in such memorable and greatly obligeing expressions as these, That your Matie had a speciall favour for vs, and would

take speciall care of vs, and countenance vs &c. And having given vs (your vnworthy yet Loyall Subjects) soe good a word, of soe greate a King, to trust vnto, have (as one resolved to rule by his word) ever since for o^r more cheerfull dependance thereon, vpon all occasions soe Graciously vouchsafed, to give forth such and soe many most signall proofs, that it was, and yett is on your Royall heart, to performe the same, (which as wee humbly conceive is the Glory of Princes, and the most facile, and forceable way and meanes they can vse to rule and sway even in the hearts of their Subjects) Wee cannot most Gracious Soveraigne without incurring the most Just censure of vnheard of ingratitude, but once againe renew, o^r most humble and hearty thankfull acknowledgements vnto your M$_a$^{tie} being thereto greatly obliged and also Provoked, As by the frequent and vnvaluable expressions of your Royall bounty towards vs and tender Paternall care over vs heeretofore Shewen; In taking such cognisance from the first of the true state of our case, with respect to the many streights and perplexities into which wee were plunged, by the envious and subtle contrivances of our neighbour Colonies round about vs, who were in a combination vnited together, to swallow vs vp that they might as is thought the more securely stand of themselves; In stretching forth your Princely and Potent hand, for o^r speedy releife, and to pluck vs as a spoil out of their teeth; In setting such boundaries between them and vs, as in your Maties late Royall grant to vs it doth appeare, beyond which without too apparent a casting of the yoke of Allegiance they cannot passe; In sending your M$_a$^{ties} Hono^{rble} Comissioners with speciall care to see that the boundaries soe sett be duely observed (for all which as in duty bound wee humbly return'd o^r hearty thanks vnto your M$_a$^{tie} as by an Exact coppie heerwith sent vpon the failer thereof will alsoe appeare) Soe by the late vnparraleld expressions of your royall M$_a$^{ties} singular favo^r in those Gracious Letters last sent, vnto vs, which being so fild with the Gracious acknowledgements of the good sattisfaction received in your Royall breast vpon the account returned by yor M$_a$^{ties} Hono^{rble} Comissioners as to the fidelity, Love, and Loyalty of yor Poore Subjects in this Colony both English and Indians, together with the ample and Princely assurances therevpon of being ever mindfull of vs, Soe as vpon all occasions to afford vs yor M$_a$^{ties} Constant Protection and Royall favour in all things which may concerne o^r safety, peace, and welfare, is soe rich and soe transcendent a favo^r of soe high and Potent a Prince, to such poore despised Pesants that Live soe remote in the woods, That wee want fitt and suitable words to give vent to those large conceptions of thanks that are formed in our hearts, and therfore must humbly crave your M$_a$^{ties} pardon therein, being minded with your M$_a$^{ties} Leave to place those Letters, and the former as precious Jewells in o^r choicest cabinett with your Maties Gracious Letters Pattents lately granted vs, as considerable seconds, if not a good confirmation of the said Grant; And while wee must needes take shame to ourselves, for o^r soe emprudent manageing of yor affaires in these hazardous times, that two soe rich and royall boones should come to our hands one after another from o^r Soveraigne Lord the King, before hee could receive soe much as one small mite of the tribute of thanks, from vs, Soe Wee cannot but heerby bee incouraged hopefully to expect, That although it pleased yor M$_a$^{ties} Hono^{rble} Comissioners in a prudent management of soe greàte a trust reposed in them (observing the temper or rather distemper of the Collonies about vs for a temporary settlement and vntill your Majesties pleasure bee further knowne) to state the boundary on the East for a greate part thereof three miles short of that Line exprest in o^r Charter; And on the west to state the whole Narragansett Countrey (being the Land in contest with all o^r neighbors) as more immediately shadowed over with yor M$_a$^{ties} wing, yet when the matter shall come before your M$_a$^{tie} and Demonstrations bee made by the Mapps wee have sent, That the tract and tracts aforesaid are clearly included already and that in expresse termes in yor M$_a$^{ties} late

Royall Grant, and confirmed vnto vs, vnder the Greate Seale of England, it will bee otherwise determined by yor M$_a$^{tie} and soe as to restore the same as is expressly determined in the said Grant, especially if your Royall M$_a$^{ties} more weighty occasions will permitt but a briefe pervsall of those grounds, and reasons sent by o^r much Hono^{red} Friend, and your Maties trusty and Prudent Comissioner Collonell Cartwright, and now againe transcribed and sent vnto the Right Hono^{rble} Edward Earle of Clarenden Lord High Chancello^r of England, wherein is showen, together with the equity the vtility, and vrgent necessity, with respect to the good both of Plantation, Jurisdiction, and fortification, and as it relates to the best emproveing and secureing of yor M$_a$^{ties} interest in these parts as well as our owne that soe it should passe.

Yo^r Petitioners therfore humbly pray yor Royall M$_a$^{ties} speciall favo^r, as to a speedy restoring of your late Gracious Grant bestowed vpon vs, to its full force, and extent, which for the present seemes to be vnder suspence, with respect to the one halfe, if not two parts of three of the Land, contained therein, And as to such other encouragements with respect to ammunition, fortification, and advance of trade as may make most for the Honor of yor Matie and for the peace, safety, and welfare of yor Colonie of Rhode Island and Providence Plantations   And now that the Majestie on high who is infinitely higher then the highest of men, being King of Kings and Lord of Hosts would Graciously vouchsafe to condescend soe as to afford yor M$_a$^{tie} his constant, sweet, influencing Prescence, Guidance, Protection, and blessing, and goe forth with your armies to make their way Prosperous, against all yor M$_a$^{ties} envious opposers. is and shall be the earnest, and constant Prayer, supplication, and Intercession of

Yo^r Majesties much Obliged Subjects
WILLIAM BRENTON.

LI.

WILLIAM DYRE TO THE EARL OF CLARENDON.*

RIGHT HON^{BLE}

The originalls of thess two papers, together with the Copies of the originalls sent by the Honble Coll Cartwright cosisting of a peticōn to his M^{atie} a Letter to yor Hon^r and two papers contayning certaine Reasons &c were all sent by the last fleet that went for England, about octob^r Last past

Yo^r Hon^{rs} humble Servt

DYRE

Nuport in Rhod Iland Dec 14th 1666.

Thess To the Right Honble Edward
Earle of Clarindon Lord High
Chancelor off England Most humbly Presented

———

LII.

ROBERT CARR AND SAMUEL MAVERICK TO THE EARL OF CLARENDON.

RIGHT HONOR^{ABLE}

May it please you^r Lord^p. In octob^r last were two letters writen to yo^u, and in my absence att New Yorke, were by Captaine Breedon committed to the care and trust of Mr Bendall and Capt Clarke, In this fleete are sent two pacquetts, the outward Couert is directed to Sr Will: Couentry, in those are letters to his royall highnes, you^r Lord^p and Sr Will: Morice, In all wch an account is giuen, how al thinges stand heare att this tyme. One Samuell Wheate will repaire to yor Lord^p. and

---

* Accompanying copies of the two preceding documents.]

present to yo[u], the coppie of a letter we wrote to the
Gouer[r] and counsell of the Messachusette, exhorting
them to obedience and theire answer to it. by w[ch] it is
euident, they intend to stand out as long as they can.
In the letters before mentioned were sent Copies of Petitions deliuered to the last Court subscribed by many
considerable p[s]ons of 'seuerall townes desiring they
would obay his M[aties] Commaunde.   And how the petitioners were delt w[th.] by that Court for theire p[r]sumption.

Good my Lord we most humb[l]y desire yo[u] would
be pleased to procure some speedy order may be taken
for the quelling of the rebellious, and incouragm[t] of the
loyall and well affected partie, for if they be suffered to
goe on in rebellion it will be an ill and daungerous
p[r]sident to the other Collonyes, Two yeares since we
p[r]sumed to shew o[r] opinion, how this might be donn
w[th] the least charge and trouble, and w[th] most securitie
to the Innocent.

At first by sendinge for some of the most eminent
offenders was this yeare doune but takes no effect.

next seisinge on their estate where euer found, and
prohibitinge them all trade w[th] any of his M[aties] Collonyes or in any other ptes, w[th] the subiecte of any prince
in league w[th] his Ma[tie], vnlesse they can p[r]duce a certificate vnder the hand and seale of such as his Maies[tie]
shall appoynt for that purpose, that they belong to such
or such a Collony w[ch] are in obedience to his Ma[tie], or
to such or such a pson in the Messachusets, who haue
declared them selues, and are certainely knowne to be
loyall subiecte. seuer[a]ll shipes w[ch] went in the last
fleete & now in this also, belong in whole or pte to disaffected psons, and goods to a great vallew.

another way may be the keeping of a small frigott
or two who may intercept all trade & comerce w[th] Boston
or any other port belonging to the Messachusette. w[ch]
will soone bring them downe. We humbly leave it to
consideration. My Lord if some speedy course be not
taken, those w[ch] haue submitted, or declared for his
M[atie] by petitioninge or otherwise will be in a miserable

condition. Yf we may be any wayes seruisable, we are at his Maties Comaund. So craving you^r Lord^{ps} pardon for giuinge yo^u this trouble we remayne.

Your^r Lordship^s Most humble seruants
Robert Carr
Samuell Mavericke.

Boston Janu: 10. 166⁶⁄₇.

My Lord I intended to haue come in this fleete and had all thinges ready abord. but the shippes being 20 dayes since driven ashore and and (sic) not able in 15 dayes to gett of, / in the meane tyme I was seased on by a fitt of sicknes wch hath so weakned me, as that by aduise of P[h]isitian and freinds, I am aduised not to aduenture. Pardon I beseech you these scribled lyenes in haste. I Remayne

You^r Lords^{ps} most humb^l servant
Samuell Mavericke

To the righ^t honora^{ble} Edward Earle
  of Clarendon Lord high Chan-
  cello^r of England these humbly
  p^rsent.

LIII.

Thomas Ludwell to the Earl of Clarendon.

Virg^a ffeb. 12. 166⁶⁄₇.

Right Hono^{ble}:

Wee being here in Generall and my selfe in perticular soe astonished and afflicted for the miserable deuastation of London by fire and beleeuing your Lord^p as much more conserned, soe very much more sensible of that most afflictiue misfortune I should not now haue troubled your honnor wth this addresse, did not my duty enforce me to take all oppertunities from hence to

giue your loid.^p as perfect an acco^t as I can of the condicōn of this collony wch is hitherto in peace and vndis-
turbed by any forraigne enimy, (that excepted who
tooke the Joy ship last spring) and this Gouernm^t will
take all possible care to preserue it soe in the maine,
though it wilbee impossible to p^ruent little damages w^{ch}
perticular howses may receaue by a skulking enimy who
(if he attempts it) may land and doe some mischeife,
and begon of to sea again before wee can come to theire
rescue whome he may attaque because we are in an open
flat country full of great riuers not to be wholy defended but by nauall force but to p^ruent such misfortunes
soe farr as wee can, wee haue ordred a fleet of boates and
shallops mannd and armed to be reddy in euery riuer of
this collony to oppose such attempts when they shalbee
made ; but for the fort att the mouth of James Riuer,
wee haueing struggled wth many difficulties, looseing
seuerall men & much of the materialls by stormes w^{ch}
broke our rafts in floting the timber to the place w^{ch}
admitts of noe other way of fortifycation being a loose
sandy foundation, wee are allmost in despaire of per-
fecting it in that place which would haue been donn wth
more ease att James towne and more effectuall, wee
haue been allreddy att seauenty thowsand pounds of
tob^o charge to effect it att poynt comfort and much of
it yett vndonn, but I shall trouble your lord^p noe further in this perticular till I heare more out of Engl^d,
but shall proceed to informe your honnor that haueing
had but fiue shipps here this winter and fearing from
this misfortune att London that there will come but few
from thence this yeare and consequently that those
great quantities of tob^o now vpon our hands will remaine soe, wee haue (wth the consent of Maryland and
Carolana) confirmed a cessation from planting tob^o in
the yeare 67, of which I informed your honnor in my
last and doe now send the transactions to coll moryson
to be p^rsented to your lord^p, I formerly prayd your honnor that if it were ill timed or contrary to his ma^{ties} intrest, that wee might receaue his ma^{ties} comands to the

contrary which only could haue diuerted the people here
from desireing it, but haueing receaued none such and
beleeuing that if the warr continues wee shall haue soe
few shipps here as that the tob? allreddy made will keep
them imployd vntill more be reddy, I hope w:th all hu-
millity that what hath been consented to for satisfacōn
of the people will not be p:riudiciall to his Ma:tie and may
put the inhabitants here vpon makeing more staple com-
odityes as silke flax &c w:ch for the future may diuert
soe much of theire labours from tob? as to keep that a
good comodity by w:ch now they could not liue did not
theire stocks find them victualls, I haue one thing more
to trouble your Lord? w:th all, w:ch is that when the
Gouer: came last out of Engl:d he brought w:th him a
Comission of oyer & terminer directed to himselfe and
many other iustices therein named but I obserue that
he is only of the quorum in it and consequently if he
should dye or depart this country, that comission is
voyd and wee left w:thout that most necessary defence
against those crimes tryable and punishable by it, which
(though I thanke god wee haue very rarely occasion for
it) would be a very great inconvenience, I shall humbly
propose a remedy and begging your Lord:ns pardon for
my p:rsumption) shall leaue it to your honnors approbation, which is, that that restriction to S: W:m Berkeley
may be enlarged by adding —— or our Gouer: for the
time being—though this be not vsuall in England yett
my lord our case is different for there any defect may
presently be supplyed, but here it cannot by reason of
our great distance, I should not haue p:rsented this to
your lord? but that I iudge it may be very dangerous att any time for the people to know that this gou-
ernm:t is not sufficiently armed w:th power to punishe
them if they offend and doe humbly hope your lord?
will pardon me for that consideracōn; and now my
most honnord lord I cannot forbeare amiddest our great
afflictions to expresse the consolation wee haue here for
his Ma:ties glorious successes ag:t his ingratefull enimies,
which euidently declares that your Lord? and all other

11

his ministers of state measured all your councells by the best rules of prudence, as his comanders haue theire conduct and actions by that of courage, and may god for euer sanctifie all his afflictions and prosperities soe as to make him glorious here and happy hereafter, and continually blesse your lord? in all your publique and priuate consernes./ I am

Right Hono^{ble} yor Honnors most humble obedient seruant

Tho: Ludwell

These to the Right Hono^{ble} Edward
    Earle of Clarendon Lord high
Chancellor of England &c.

II.

TRACTS RELATING TO NEW YORK.

PROPOSITIONS

Made by the Sachems *of the three* Maquas *Castles, to the* Mayor, Aldermen, *and* Commanalt *of the City of* Albany, *and Military Officers of the said City, and County in the City-Hall,* February 25th, 16$\frac{8}{9}\frac{9}{0}$

Peiter Schuyler Mayor, *with ten more Gentlemen, then present.* Interpreted by *Arnout* & *Hille.*

The Names of the Sachims, *Sinnonguiness* Speaker, *Rode, Sagoddiockquisax, Oguedagoa, Tosoquatho, Odagurasse, Anharenda, Jagogthera.*

𝔅𝔯𝔢𝔱𝔥𝔯𝔢𝔫,

WEE are Sorry and extreamly Griev'd for the Murther lately committed by the *French* upon our Brethren of *Shennechtady,* we esteem 'this Evil, as if done to our selves, being all in one *Covenant-Chain;* But what they have done is by way of stealth, by way of Robbery unawares; our Brethren of *New-England* will be sorry to hear of this sad Disaster, but we must not be discouraged. [They give a Belt of *Wampom,* according to their custome, to wipe off the Tears.

2. 𝔅𝔯𝔢𝔱𝔥𝔯𝔢𝔫, We lament and condole the Death of so many of our *Brethren* so basely Murther'd at *Shennechtady;* we cannot account it a great *Victory,* for it is done by way of *Deceit.* He (meaning the Governour of *Canada*) comes to our Countrey by his Mes-

sengers at *Onnondage*, and speaks of Peace, with the whole *House* quite hither : but War is in his heart, as you find by woful experience, but what shall we say ? it is the same as he did at *Cadarachqui*, and the *Sinnakes* Countrey. This is the *third time* that he has done so ; he has broken open the Jewel of our House on both ends, the one end at *Sinnondowanne*, and the other here, But we hope to be Revenged. There is one hundred of our young men out still, who will pursue them to their Doors at *Cannida ;* nay, the *French* shall not be able to cut a stick of Wood, we will lay so close Seige to them ; We do now gather the Dead together in order to their Interment. A manner of speaking amongst. [They do give a Belt of *Wampom*.

3. We are come here from our Castles with Tears in our Eyes to Bemoan the Murther committed by the perfideous *French* at *Shennechtady*, our young *Indians* are gone out in Pursuit of them, and while we are now busie in burying the Dead that were Murthered there, we may have bad news that our people that are gone out, may be kill'd also ; the same that is befallen you, may befal us : We do therefore come and bury our Brethren at *Shennechtady*. [They give a Belt of *Wampom*, according to their custome.

4. Great is the Mischief that is befallen us, it is come from the *Heavens* upon us, we are taught by our Fore-fathers, when any sad Accident or Disaster doth befal any of the Covenant, to go with all convenient speed to Bemoan their Death ; [They give a Belt of *Wampom*, which they call a Belt of *Vigilance*, that is, not to have too much thoughts on what is done that cannot be Remedied, but to be watchful for the future ; and they give *Eye-water* to make the Brethren *sharpsighted*.

5. We come to the house where we usually do Renew the *Covenant*, which House we find defiled with Blood, this is known to all the five Nations, and we are now come to wipe off the Blood and keep the House clean, and therefore pray that *Corlaer* and all they that

are in Office here in *Albany*, naming the Mayor whom they call *Peiter*, Mr. *Vessels*, and Mr. *Livingstone* may use all means and Direct all Affairs to be Revenged of the Enemy that hath done us this Evil [They give a Belt of *Wampom.*

6. Brethren : Do not be Discouraged, this is but a beginning of the· *War*, we are strong enough, the whole house have their .Eyes fixed upon you, and they only stay your motion, and will be ready to do whatever shall be Resolved upon by our Brethern, our Covenant is a firm Covenant it is a *Silver Chain* and cannot be broke, it must not be broke ; we are Resolute and will Continue the War, we will not leave off, if there were but Thirty Men of us left, we will proceed, therefore pray take good heart, do not pack up and go away, if the Enemy should hear that, it would much encourage them, we are of the Race of the *Bear*, and a *Bear* doth not yield as long as there is a drop of Blood in its body we must all be so ; [They give a Belt of *Wampom.*

7.—Brethren, Be Content, *Look up to the Heavens ;* from thence the Judgement is come now upon us, Be not Discouraged, the same hand that hath Chastized us can heal us ; The Sun which now hath been Cloudy, and sent us this Disaster, will shine again, and with its pleasent Beams comfort us, *Be Encouraged ;* [with many Repetitions. And they give a *Bear-skin.*

☞ 8. We were engaged in a Bloody ,War with the *French*, about three years ago, and were Encouraged to Proceed, and no sooner were we well Entred, and got several Prisoners, but a Cessation came, and *Corlaer* hindered us to proceed, and Demanded the Prisoners from us ; we were Obedient and did deliver them, and laid down the Hatchet, which if we might have gone forward, then the French would not have been in that Capacity to do so much mischief as they do ; But now we must dye; *such Obstructions will Ruine us ;* if we might have had our wills, we would have prevented their Planting, Sowing, and Reaping, and brought them low and mean ; Nevertheless let us be stedfast, and not take such measures again, let us go on briskly with the War. [They give a *Bear-skin*.

9. We Recommend the Brethern to keep good *Watch*, and if any Enemies come, take care that Messengers be more speedily sent to us then lately was done, we would not advise the Brethern quite to Desert *Sennechtady*, but to make a Fort there, the Enemy would be too glorious to see it quite Desolate, and the Town here is not well Fortified, the Stockades are so short, the Indians can jump over them like a Dog. [They give a *Bear-skin*.

☞ 10. This mischief is done at *Sennechtady*, and it cannot be helped, but as soon as any Enemy comes, let nothing hinder your speedy sending to us the News by Posts, and Fyring great Guns, that all may be Alarm'd; and our Advise is that you get all the River Indians who are under your Subjection to to come and live near unto you, to be ready on all occasions, and send word to *New-England* of all what's done here; undoubtedly they will awake and lend us their helping hand; let us not be Discouraged, *The French are not so many as People talk off ;* if we but mind our business, They can be subdued, with the assistance of our Neighbours of *New-England*, whose interest it is to drive on this War as much as ours, that it may be speedily ended.

We desire that the Brethern may Recommend the Smiths not to be too dear in Repairing our Arms, since Mony is so scarce, and we only go to *Warring* and not to *Hunting*, we shall take care to warn the the *Sinnakes* and the Nations living above us to be in Readiness; for we being one they hearken to us, and tell them of *New-England* that we shall take care that the upper Nations be Ready for our Security and Assistance, and 𝔏et them be 𝔦eady also with 𝔖hips and great 𝔊uns by 𝔚ater, and we will 𝔓lague him by 𝔏and: We are Resolved not to go out a Hunting, but to mind the War, for the *sooner* the *French* be fallen upon the *better*, before they get Men and Provisions from *France*, as their usual Custome is. They give a *Bear-Skin*

ANSWER upon the *Maquas Sachims Propositions;* *by the* Mayor, Aldermen, *and* Commonalty *of the City of* Albany, *and* Military Officers *of the said City and County: At the* City-Hall, Febr. 26*th,* 16$\frac{89}{90}$

Interpreted by Arnout, &c.

Brethren,

YOUR coming here according to the Custome of your Ancestors, to Condole the death of your *Brethren* Murthered at *Shennechtady* is very acceptable, whereby your Inclination toward us is Demonstrated; we must acknowledge that they did not keep so good Watch as they ought, considering what a false and deceitful Enemy they had to deal withal, but that which made them so secure, was, the great Trust which they Reposed in the Forty *Maquass* who came here, and Tendered their Service to go and be the Outwatch, and to spy the Enemy: To which end Powder and Lead was given them as they desired; we were about Hiring Christians to send thither, but were unhappily diverted by the said Company of *Maquass,* who who promised to have four Posts ready, two to go to their own Country, and two to come hither if any Enemy should appear. For the Brethren did assure us, that no *French* could come here without being Discovered; and then would all fall into our hands: We are likewise mindful, how that the five Nations last *Fall,* when the Gentlemen of *New-England* were here did Declare how they would Encompass the *French* of *Canada,* that they could not break out this Winter, without being Discovered and Fallen upon: We did likewise propose by our Messengers, *Arnout,* and *Robert Sanders* at the General Meeting of *Onnondage* to have Three or Four Hundred Men sent hither to be ready on all occasions, but see none.

Now Brethren, this Evil is done and cannot be called back again, and the only means to prevent the like for the future, is to keep good Watch, and to have good courage to oppose and resist the Enemy. We are no wayes Discomfited for this misfortune. It is the fortune of War, we do not fear to be even with the *French* in a short time; we have already sent Letters to all our Neighbours of *New-England, Virginia* and *Mary-Land,* the Subjects of the great King of *England,* and acquainted them of the *Evil* done here by the *French,* and how requisite it is, that Ships be fitted out with all convenient speed, to go to *Quebeck,* and to press the business the more, we do now send persons to *New-York* and *New-England,* a purpose to lay open the Case before them. And to perswade them to Rig out Vessels not only to hinder Succour coming from *France,* but to take *Quebeck* it self: as also to send more Men hither, that we may then send Men along with you to annoy the Enemy in their Country In the mean time we recommend the 𝔅rethren to send for *two hundred Men* from the upper Nations, to joyn with you, to keep the *French* in continual Alarm, and do them what mischief imaginable; and *Onnondages* and Sinnekes must go down the River of *Cadarachqui,* and meet one another about *Mont Royal,* and annoy the Enemy there: we shall in the mean while Fortifie the Town, and put our selves in a good posture of Defence, that we may not be Surprized, as they of Shennechtady were; and make all Preparations to oppose the Enemy.

The 𝔅rethren, see that we are in War with *France,* now that there is no time to speak of Peace. The *French* as you well observe have fallen on both ends of the Chain, but not broke it. Let us keep the Covenant so much the faster, which never has had the least crack since the very first the *Christians* came here: They strove to lull us all asleep, by their Messengers at *Onnondage,* speaking of Peace, and then they were upon the way hither to commit this Murther.

☞ The 𝔅rethren need not fear for a *Cessation* to hinder us to pursue the Enemy, for as we told you before, the KING that ordered *that,* was a *Papist,* and a great Friend of the *French ;* But our present Great KING will pursue the War to the outmost : Therefore we must all prepare for War. •It will therefore be very requisite that the 𝔅𝔯𝔢𝔱𝔥𝔯𝔢𝔫 for their better Security come and Plant this Summer at Shinnechtady upon the Land that cannot be cultivated this year, that we may be near to one another upon any occasion. Concerning the Proposition of the Shackkook Indians, 'tis concluded on some dayes ago, to propose to the Shackkook Indians the Planting on *Marte Gerritse* Island hard by the Town, and the River Indians that live below shall also come together to be ready on all occasions.

We must Insist and Recommend you to perswade them of *Oneyde* to send the *Priest* hither, for you have seen how dangerous it is to have such persons among you, who informs the Enemy of all your doings, and discovers all your Designs, we shall secure him that he Run not away, and when the Owner demands him, and these Troubles are over, shall be Delivered, for he can do more harm in *Oneyde* than an hundred men.

We think it Convenient that one or two of the *Sachims* stay here, and that a *Sachim* of each Nation be here to assist in the management of the Affairs of the War. There was given them six Belts of *Wampom*, some *Duffils*, Tobacco, and some Bags with Provision.

After the Proposition was answered, they gave a Shout according to their Custome, which signified *Amen*, that they would continue the War to the utmost.

After the said Answer was made, The *Maquas Sachems* said after they had Repeated our Answer. We are glad to see you are not Discouraged, A mistake can be made by the best and wisest of men, and we must see now to Pursue the War with all Vigour, we have an hundred men out in Pursuit of the Enemy still, who are good Skouts; in the mean time, we expect all the *Sachims* of the Upper Nations to Consult with us, who will come to Condole the Death of our *Brethern* Murthered at *Shennechtady*: You need not fear our being *Ready*, we are soon fitted out, our Ax is in our

hand. But take care for your selves to be in Readiness. The Ships that must do the principal work are
long a Fitting out and Rigging; we do not Design to
go out with a small Troop as Skouts, but as soon as
the Nations come together; we will go with a whole
Army to Ruine the Country. The Business. must be
soon brought to a Period; therefore send in all haste
to *New-England*, for we nor you cannot live long in
this Condition; we must order it so, that the *French* be
in a continual Fear and Alarm. and that is the way to
be in Peace here.

Concerning the *Shakook* Indians in our Opinion
they lye well where they are, as a good Watch, They are
our Children, we will take care that they do their Duty,
but as for the *Indians* that live below the Town, Them
we mean must be sent for up; and got to Plant and
live together, to be always in Readiness upon occasion.

This is a true Copy Examined

By **Robert Livingston.**

EXAMINATION of *three* French *Prisoners taken by*
the Maquase. *and brought to* Sennechtady, *who were*
Examined by Pieter Schuyler *Mayor of the City*
of Albany; Dom. Goduridus Delius, *and some*
other Gentlemen, that went from Albany *a purpose,*
and Report as follows : March 3d, 16$\frac{8}{9}\frac{9}{0}$.

1. THAT about the middle of *January*, they went
from *Mont-Royal*, being about Three Hundred
Men, *French* and Indians, to wit an hundred and
sixty *French*, among which onely nineteen Souldiers
taken out of divers Companies, the Rest all Boss-
lopers, them that frequent the Woods, and Inhabitants, and an hundred and forty Praying Indians and
others, with positive Orders to. Murder and Destroy all
People they met withal at *Shennchtady*, except such as
begg'd for quarters, as also to burn the Place, and take
with them those that they could carry along: after said
Company had Marched some days from *Canada*, some

French and *Indians* that were sick and Timorous, Returned; so that the Party were two hundred and fifty that did the Exploit at *Sheecnnhtady*, by the Indians called *Ochques*.

2. After Enquiry of the Particulars of the Murder, they Confessed, that four or five *French* had Murdered the Minister of the said Village called *Pieter Tossemaker*, first shooting him thorow the Leggs, and then hew'd him with their Swords most barbarously, and being asked if they had Express Orders to deal so Cruelly, said, that their Order was to do what was done.

3. Being enquired concerning the Prisoners they carried along with them, said, they were well Treated by the way, and within four or five days Journey of *Canada*, some of our Prisoners went with the Indians, and the Remainder with the *French*, but that we need not doubt of their good Entertainment at *Canada*, since they will be Delivered to the Jesuits to be instructed in their Religion.

4. That they had eat about twenty or thirty of the Horses they carried along with them, and intended to carry seven with them to *Canada*.

5. That nevertheless Provisions begun to grow scarce in their Army, and therefore two men were Dispatched upon Scates, who go Twenty five Leagues in a day to Cause Provisions be sent them from *Mont Royal*.

6. That the ten Prisoners, whereof these now Examined were three, were taken by our Indians about two of the Clock in the Afternoon, being at the same fire that the body of the Army went from in the Morning, attending some sick persons who could not March so fast as the Rest.   7.   That the manner of keeping their Scouts out a nights both in Coming and going was thirty men who Marched constantly Round the Army all night, about a Musket shot off, but near *Shennectady*, the number of the said Scouts was doubled.

8. That by the Tract they Trapann'd some *Maquase Squaws* near *Shennechtady*, whom they Compelled to give an account of the Condition of the Place,

and kept said Indian Women till they had committed the Massacre; when they were within some Miles of *Shennechtady*, the Officers had a Consultation about falling upon *Albany;* one *Monsieur de Tallie* who had been formerly here did Press hard to Attaque it, but because their Orders was Expresly for *Shennechtady* the Design on *Albany* was put by.

9. That they had lost but one only *French* man at *Shennechtady*, and one sore wounded.

The said Prisoners being Examined about the Affairs of Canada *do say,*

I. That last Summer eight or nine Ships arrived at *Quebek*, whereof two were Men of War, who brought store of Ammunition and Provisions, with which Ships the Earl of *Frontinak* came for Governour, and Monsieur *Callier* Governour of *Mont Royal*, and the Indian Prisoners, but brought no Souldiers, and that the Marquess de *Denonville* late Governour went away with said Ships.

II. That they expect for certain that Twelve Men of War will come this Summer with Two Thousand Men, and two Years Provisions for *Canada*.

3. The Governour *Frontenak* upon his Voyage to *Canada* met with a *French* Ship Loaden with Bisket, bound for the North-west Passage, carried the same along with him to *Canada*, and sent her Loading with great store of Pork and Meal come from *France* up to *Mont Royal*.

IV. That Provisions were not dearer at *Canada* now than formerly, a Minot of Meal being sold for a *French* Crown, adding that the Damage done by the Indians to their Corn in *Canada* was inconsiderable.

V. Governour *Frontenak* came to *Mont Royal* about the middle of *September*, which Place he hath Fortified with a Ditch two foot deep, and twelve foot wide, round about the Town, except at the River side, where he hath built of Stone right out where the Guard is kept.

VI. That he had brought twelve small Morterpeices and some small Canon from *France* with him, which Morter-peices a man can easily carry, one of the said Prisoners having try'd it himself.

VII. The Governour *Frontenak* had caus'd to be made one hundred and twenty *Batoes*, that is flat bottom'd Boats, fit to carry eight or nine men, with Provisions and Amunition; as also one hundred Bark Cannoes at *Mont Royal:* the first were all made, and the latter the greatest part ready: and that it was much discoursed among the *French* of light Ladders to storm the Fort at *Albany;* all which together with the Morter-pieces, are making ready to come early in the Spring with fifteen hundred men to Ataque Albany by the *French* called *Fort D'Orange.*

VIII. That Governour *Frontenak* went in the Moneth of *November* to *Quebeck*, and was design'd to return to *Mont Royal* in the Winter, or at longest early in the Spring, to accomplish their Design upon *Albany.*

IX. That for that purpose *Monsieur d' Lute* was to go as soon possible in the Spring, with fifty Souldiers to *Ottowawa*, to bring down the Indians to *Mont Royal.*

X. For the present, there are six Companies of Souldiers at *Mont Royal* of fifty men each, besides six or seven hundred *Burgers* and *Inhabitants.*

XI. The Kings Souldiers at *Canada* are computed to be fifteen or sixteen hundred men, and the said quanity of *Burgers* and *Inhabitants*, who are fit to carry Arms, besides their *Indians.*

XII. That said Souldiers are divided in the following Towns and Forts, Viz. *Quebek*, *Mont Royal*, *Chambly*, *Troy River*, *Sorel* and twenty-four Towns and Forts more.

XIII. They say that it was divulged at *Mont Royal*, that four hundred men were gone from *Quebek* under command of *Mons. Pirneusse*, and *Monsieur Courtimanche*, being all *Bosse-lopers* Inhabitants and Indians. (And no Souldiers) towards *Kinnebek* River, to take a certain *English Fort*, and that another Company, but not so numerous, under the Conduct of Mons.

Artel were gone towards the Province of *New York* to do mischief there.

XIV. That the *French* King was pleased to give Cadarachqui to Governor *Frontenak* as a Gift, who was very much displeased at his Arrival, when he heard that it was Deserted, and that Governour *de Denonville* had given Orders to demolish it, The Garrison that lay there, being eighty men, were come home, eight were drown'd most of the Ammunition being thrown in the Water; and among the rest four or five hundred small Arms, and have sunk the Canon about twenty Leagues from *Mont Royal.*

A true Copy, Examined by

Robert Livingston.

Memorandum, *The French Murther'd sixty Men, Women and Children at* Shennechtady, *and carried twenty-seven Men & Boys Prisoners to* Canada.

Boston *Printed by* S. Green. Sold by *Benjamin Harris* at the *London Coffee House,* 1690.

ARGUMENTS

Offer'd to the Right Honourable the

𝕷𝖔𝖗𝖉𝖘 𝕮𝖔𝖒𝖒𝖎𝖘𝖘𝖎𝖔𝖓𝖊𝖗𝖘

FOR

Trade & Plantation

Relating to Some Acts of Assembly past
at *New-York* in *America*.

👑👑👑👑👑👑
👑👑👑
👑👑👑👑👑👑

Printed in the Year 1701.

12

To the Right Honourable the Lords Commissioners for Trade & Plantations.

The humble Memorial of John Montague *of* Chancery-Lane, London, *Gent. on behalf of several hundreds of Land Owners and principal -Inhabitants of his Majesties Province of New York, touching some Acts (now before your Lordships) of the Assembly (or pretended Assembly) of that Province, beginning the 2d of March, 1698, and ending the 16th of May following.*

May it please your Lordships ;

HAVING received several Instruments from *New-York*, under the Hands of several Hundreds of the Gentlemen and others of that Province, to impower me to act for them against the said Acts, and in other Matters, I did on their behalfs present my humble Petition to your Lordships, praying to be heard by Council, against several of the said Acts; and have in answer thereto, received from Mr. *Popple* your Lordships Commands to lay before your Lordships in writing what I have to offer upon this Subject.

In obedience whereto, I shall with all humble Submission to your Lordships, attempt to say something against some of these Acts, in such a manner (tho' with much less advantage) as I can suppose Council would have done, had it been your Lordships pleasure first to have heard my Clyents by their Council.

And (*My Lords*) if the Consideration of my Duty to my Clyents, regard to the Trust I am favour'd with by so great a Number of People, and the apprehensions I have conceived of the weight of the Concern, shall occasion me to speak of things too high for me, rather than omit any thing I can in my small Capacity think of, that may be fit for Consideration upon this subject, I hope your Lordships will Pardon my so doing, together with the Prolixity thereby occasioned.

And I beseech your Lordships to believe, that nothing but the Considerations before-mention'd induced me thus to wander above my Sphere.

My Lords, I shall trouble your Lordships with particular Objections but against three of these Acts. And the first that I shall mention is that entitled, *An Act for committing* Ebenezer Willson *and* Samuel Burt (*Farmers of the Excise on the Island of* Nassaw) *for their contemptuous refusing to render an Account of what they farm'd the same for, to the respective Towns, Counties and Mannors on the said Island for the last year.*

This Act recites, That the Governour and Council had required the Farmers of the Excise to lay before the House of Representatives, upon Oath, the most plain and perfect Account they could give, of what they had let the Excise for, of the several Towns, Mannors and Jurisdictions within the Island of *Nassaw*, the last year of their Farm. And that Mr. *Burt* and Mr. *Willson*, without giving any sufficient Reason, in contempt of his Majesties Authority, wherewith (says the Act) the House, in the Quality they were then sitting, was invested, wilfully & stubbornly had done, and did refuse to give such Account as was required. And therefore enacts That Mr. *Burt* and Mr. *Willson* should be committed into safe Custody, without Bail or Mainprize, until they should exhibit under hands, upon Oath, the Account required, &c.

The Case (as I am inform'd, and as I presume will not be denyed) of these two Gentlemen was thus: They are Traders, and were Farmers of this Excise: They lost by the Farm, and were unwilling such loss should be made publick, lest it should prejudice their Credit, & so damnifie them in their Trade. The Governour sends for them, and [*extra judicially*] requires them to give an Account upon Oath (which Oath he likewise would have extrajudicially administred to them) of what they had made of their Farm. They refuse to take this Oath, & the Governour therefore was so rash as to commit them. After they had lain several days in Prison, then is this Act procur'd to be past.

Now, *My Lords*, with humble submission, either these Gentlemen were obliged by Law (antecedent to this Act) to give the Account required, or they were not. If they were obliged to it by Law antecedent to this Act, then there was no occasion for this Act, nor ought this Act to have been made; for they ought then to have been compell'd to do it by the Executive Power in the ordinary course of Justice; and the Legislative Power ought not to have been made Executive to compell them to it.

If these Gentlemen were not obliged by Law antecedent to this Act to give the Account required, Then, with humble submission, the Governour in committing them was guilty of a very arbitrary proceeding, and a great Violation of the Law; and then this Act is made to countenance or excuse an Illegal Act of the Governors; and with submission, the Governour's Commitment was illegal, even although they had been obliged to give such Account by Law antecedent to this Act; for in that case the Governour could not compell them thereto extrajudicially, but they would even in that case have been compellable thereto (only) in the ordinary course of Justice. And they were guilty of no manner of Offence in refusing to take the Oath the Governour thus arbitrarily and illegally tendered to them.

When the Excise was farm'd in *England*, there was, as I am inform'd, a Covenant on the part of the Farmers, to give an Account, like what was demanded in this case, which (if there needed any) is an argument they could not, without such Covenant, have been compell'd to it. And it would, with humble Submission, have been thought a very strange and arbitrary proceeding here in *England*, and a great Instance of Infringement of the *English Liberties*, for the King to have sent for the Farmers of the Excise and tendered them an Oath to give such Account, and upon their refusal immediately to have committed them, such a Commitment would, without doubt, have been illegal, and against the Letter and meaning of *Magna Charta ;* and therefore in his case neither the Governour, nor the House could (antecedent to the Act) be invested with any Authority to commit these Gentlemen, nor to require (especially in an extrajudicial manner) any Oath from them touching what they had made of their Farm. And yet this Act punishes them for an Offence, as such, antecedent to the Act, and does not first make it their Duty by enacting, That they should do it within a limitted time after the passing of the Act, & that in default thereof they should be committed for the breach of the Law after it was made, but enacts, *That they should be forth-with committed,* as having been guilty of an Offence before the Act made.

My Lords, therefore, with humble submission, to confirm this Law, will be either to countenance an illegal Act, and a violation of the Law by the Governour, in derogation of that Liberty whereto every *English Subject* is entituled, or else it will be to declare, That Mr. *Willson* & Mr. *Burt* were guilty of an Offence against the Law in refusing the Oath extrajudicially tendered to them before the making of this Act, when there was no Law to oblige them either to give the Account or take the Oath required ; and the very tendring the Oath to them was illegal.

The Complainers therefore against these Acts think their Liberties much concern'd in this matter, and humbly hope your Lordships will think so illegal and Arbitrary a Proceeding of the Governour's, as the tendring such an Oath extrajudicially, and afterwards committing these two Gentlemen only for refusing to take it, ought not afterwards to receive the Countenance, much less the Affirmance of the Legislative Power; & that your Lordships will so far discourage a Governour's acting arbitrarily and illegally and upon any slight occasion making use of the Legislative Power, as Executive in a particular case, to countenance his illegal Proceedings; or (as it may happen) to gratifie his Revenge, by making a Law to punish that as an Offence, which was not so before, nor at the time it was committed. They hope your Lordships will at least so far discountenance things of this Nature, as to advise his Majesty to reject this Act, which they apprehend to be a President of dangerous Consequences to the Laws and Liberties whereto they are very well assured your Lordships will, at all times, and upon all occasions, have a very tender regard.

My Lords, the next of these Acts that I shall beg leave to object to, is that entituled, *An Act for the vacating, breaking and annulling of several Grants of Land, &c.* Which is complain'd of not only as great Injustice to the Grantees and divers others, but also as a thing of dangerous Consequence, and that renders the Property of all Lands within this Province incertain and precarious, aud perfectly at the will of the Governour and fifteen, fourteen, or a less number of Men. But before I speak to the vacating of the Grants in Question by this Act, and divesting the Grantees of them, I must not omit to take notice of a Clause that is very strangely thrust into this Act, and more strangely into the Preamble of it, among the Recitals of the Grants there said to be Extravagant, in these words.

"That it having appear'd to the house of Represen-"tatives conven'd in general Assembly, That Mr. *Godfrey* "*Dellius* has been a principal Instrument in deluding the "*Mahaque Indians* and illegally and surreptitiously ob-"taining of said grant, that he ought to be, and is hereby "suspended from the Exercise of his ministerial function "in the City and County of *Albany.*

My Lords, What is here meant, by deluding, and
what by surreptitiously *obtaining this Grant,* is so uncertain that nothing can be more, had the Act specified
how and in what the *Indians* were *deluded,* and how
Mr. *Dellius* was *Instrumental* in that, what facts Mr.
Dellius did to *delude* the *Indians,* and what he did to
obtain this *Grant,* then his Majesty and your Lordships
might have been able thereby to judge whether Mr.
Dellius had been guilty of an Offence, of what nature
and Quality the Offence was, and what punishment it
ought to receive, and whether it were an Offence that
was worthy the consideration of and punishment by the
Legislative Power, But to attaint and punish a man by
the Legislative Power, and not to specifie and describe
plainly in the Act of attaint, the Offence for which he is
so punished, is, with submission, a Method altogether
strange and unusual, and very unbecoming the Justice
and Wisdom of a Legislative Power to use.   It is very
well known, that Mr. *Dellius* has been very Instrumental in converting the *Mohaques* and other *Indians* to
the *Christian* and *Protestant Religion,* and thereby
keeping them from the *French* and uniting them to the
English Interest; And (for ought appears by this Act)
that may be the deluding there meant.

The punishment is very severe, yet uncertain too ;
he is disgraced by an Attaint by the Legislative Power,
and is suspended from the Exercise of his Ministerial
Function in the City and County of *Albany,* where he
has been (with considerable Reputation) a Minister for
above fifteen years.   He is stript at once of his livelihood,
and no body knows (nor can learn by this Act) for how
long he is suspended, nor when or how he shall be restored.   Nor does it (as has been said) appear by this
Act what he has done to deserve so severe a punishment.
More might be said against this clause : But I shall
only, with submission, add at present, That at least your
Lordships will think That before his Majesty gives his
Authority for the inflicting so severe a Punishment on
a particular Person (especially a Minister) as the pub-

lickly disgracing him, and utterly stripping him of his Livelihood, his Majesty will be better satisfied of the crimes laid to his charge, than he can be by the incertain, general and ambiguous Terms used in this Act, for the reasons why he is thus punished.

My Lords, As to the principal part and design of this Act, to wit, the vacating Grants of Land and divesting the Owners of them, (for which no other reason is assign'd but that the Legislators are pleased to think them Extravagant, or at least to call them so) there seems to be so many things of weight to be objected to it, that the difficulty is not to find out Exceptions to, and Reasons against it, but rather which to begin with.

The Gentlemen who have attempted to be advocates for this Act have endeavoured to represent it as a thing done pursuant to the Lords Justices Instructions, and to be like an Act of Resumption of Crown Lands here in *England.*

As to the Lords Justices Instructions, They were to *break the Grants by legal means;* which term of [*Legal*] is a Relative Term, and must relate to the Law then in being, and not to a New Law after to be made; And therefore these Instructions cannot, with Submission, be construed to intend any thing but to vacate them by a proceeding in the Ordinary Course of Justice. And whose Representation from this Province, and Solicitation gave occasion to these Instructions, (or rather procured them,) is, I presume, not unknown to your Lordships.

My Lords, with Submission, This Act is not at all in the Circumstances or Reason of an Act of Resumption of Crown Lands in *England.* For *First,* All that have any Lands in this Province, have a Grant from the Crown of them, so that to disturb these Grants, is to disturb the Titles of the Lands of an whole Province. 2*dly,* Most of the Lands in Question, (and particularly those comprized in the Grants to Mr. *Dellius* and Coll. *Bayard,*) were by the Grantees purchased of the *Indians,* and afterwards Grants were taken of them from

the *Crown of England,* under small Quit-Rents, by way
of Acknowledgment, to fix the Tenure and Soveraignity
of them in this Crown, and put them under it's Protection; and so as to these Lands, the Revenues of the
Crown are not diminished by the Kings Grants, but the
Territories and Dominions of the Crown are inlarged
by the Subjects purchase.

My Lords, I will endeavour to reduce, at least, the
greatest part, I have to say to this Act, to these two
heads.

1st. *That it is Unreasonable and Unjust.*

2dly. *That it tends not only to the discouraging and
Interruption of all planting and improving of Lands
within this Province but even to the subversion of Government, and reducing things to disorder and Confusion.*

My Lords, with humble Submission, this Act is
Unjust and Unreasonable, and that for these Reasons.

1st. Because the Grantees are by this Act divested
of the Lands granted, and several of them have been at
considerable Charges in Buildings and Improvements,
and several of them have made Leases and Conveyances
of the granted Lands to others, who have made Improvements thereon; and yet by this Act there is no
manner of provision made to Reimburse the Grantees
the charges they have been at about the Lands it arbitrarily divests them of; nor any provision made for, or
care taken of those who have (upon the Credit of the
Grants in Question, and his Majesties Declaration,
*That they should be good against his Majesty, his Heirs
and Successors*) taken Leases or other Conveyances, and
made Improvements under these Grants. In case it
could be made out to be just for the Legislative Power
to take the Lands in Question away from the Grantees
(as for reasons which I shall mention hereafter I presume your Lordships will think it never can) yet certainly (with Submission) the Grantees and those that
have taken Leases & Conveyances under these Grants,
ought in all Reason and Justice at least to be satisfied
all Charges and Expences they have been at about these

Lands. It cannot (with humble Submission) but be thought a very strange proceeding in a Government, first, to grant these lands to particular Persons, & incourage them to be at Charge about them, and others and also to be at Expence about the Lands comprized in such Leases and Conveyances ; and afterwards (by an Act of the Legislative) arbitrarily to wrest these Lands out of the hands of the Grantees, and all claiming under them, without any manner of Consideration for the Charges they have been at about them. This, with humble Submission, is so manifest an Injustice, That it plainly seems (if there were no other) a sufficient reason for rejecting this Act.

But, 2*dly*, This Act is Unjust and Unreasonable, Because it seizes into the Kings hands, and divests several Persons of Lands, that were never the Possessions or Rights of the Crown, but purchased by these Persons so divested (or those under whom they claim) of the *Indians*. That this is the case at least of a very great (if not the far greatest) part of the Lands in Question, I presume the advocates for this Act will not deny; If they do, 'tis ready to be proved. Nor will it be deny'd I believe but the *Indians* had possession of at least a great part of the Lands in Question, till they sold them to the Persons who are divested of them by this Act. Nor that those Persons had Lycences from the Government to purchase them of the *Indians*. If the *Indians* had possession of them, then, with Submission, they had a Right to them by preoccupancy, by the Law of Nature; and by all other Laws, a Right by Possession against every one but he that could shew a better Right. The discovering and possessing these Lands, might give the English a Right against any others, but the Natives ; But that which gave them a Right before others (not being the Natives, *viz* Possession and Preoccupancy) gave the Natives a Right against them, until the Natives by free agreement should part with such their Right.

The advantage any Nation has over another, in

Might and Power, in true Religion, or in the Arts of Government, War or Improvements, or other Arts or Sciences, does not, (with humble Submission) give the Nation that has those Advantages, in ever so great a Degree, a Right to the possessions of another People, be they ever so Weak, and Unable to defend them, ever so Ignorant and Irreligious, ever so salvage and Barbarous. .Nor is it pretended that these Indians are in a state of War with *England*, for they have been treated with as Friends, and the granting Lycences by the Government to purchase Lands of them, admits them to have a Right to sell them ; which 'tis not to be doubted but they once had, and (with humble Submission) I do not see how they have lost it; unless their being Weak and Unable to defend themselves, or unskill'd in Religion, Policy and Arts, can alter matter of Right, upon the Principles of Natural Justice ; I shall therefore say no more at present as to this, until I have learn'd from the advocates for this Act, what Title the Crown had to the Lands purchased by Coll. *Bayard* and Mr. *Dellius*, and others respectively of the *Indians*, (and of which Lands they are divested by this Act) before they were so. purchased; Only that the Owners on such Lands by or under such purchases, do humbly insist and rely upon it, that by such purchases they have a full Right and Property in the Lands so purchased; And that I am inform'd that it was formerly thought for the Interest of the Crown of *England*, thas as much Lands as could, should be purchased from the *Indians* ; And also that all Incouragement was given to People to make such purchases, for that the Territories of the *Crown of England* are thereby inlarged.

But, 3*dly* This Act has the Misfortune to be most manifestly. Unjust and Unreasonable upon its own principles. . The Fundamental Principle upon which this Act proceeds, is, *That the Grants in Question are Extravagant*, but the Deduction it makes from that principle will by no means, in Justice or Reason, follow from it.

For, (for ought appears by this Act) all the Grants in Question, (except one of the two Grants to Mr. *Dellius*) were duly and legally made. But they are *Extravagant;* Admitting them to be so, then, with humble Submission, The proper and reasonable Measure is, not to take all the granted Lands from the Grantees, but such parts only, as would reduce the Extravagancy of the Grant to reasonable and moderate Limits: If a Grant be *Extravagant,* It is because more is granted than ought to have been, and then it will follow, that some part ought not to have been granted; But it will not from thence follow, that no part ought to have been granted, or that all ought to be taken from the Grantee.

Had the Act in taking notice of the Grant of Ground of fifty foot long to Mr. *Caleb Heathcote,* declared it to be *Extravagant,* because it granted him too much by Twenty five foot in length; and had divested him of twenty five foot of this ground, and left him the other twenty five. And in the last clause (which is introduc'd with these words, *To the intent it may not be in the Power of any of his Majesties Governours or Commanders in Chief, for the time being, hereafter to make any such Extravagant Grants.* And how little this Clause answers its own introductory words, I humbly submit to your Lordships Consideration) had enacted, That no body should hereafter have had Grants of Lands in this Province exceeding twenty five foot in length; This, with submission, would have made the Act much more coherent than now it is.

But, *My Lords,* with humble submission, to say, that because a Subject has too much, therefore all ought to be taken from him, deserves the Name of a gross Absurdity; and whether the former be not the very Principle this Act goes upon, and the latter the very deduction it makes from that Principle, is humbly submitted to your Lordships Consideration.

My Lords, The other Objection I humbly proposed to make to this Act, is, *That it tends not only to the Discouraging and Incorruption of all Improvements of*

Lands within this Province, but even to the subversion of Government, and reducing things to Disorder and Confusion.

I have already observed to your Lordships, That all Persons who have any Lands in this Province, have Grants from the Crown for them, although purchased from the *Indians*, which is to fix the Tenure and Soveraignity of such Lands (so purchased) in the Crown of *England*, and put them under its Protection.

I must now beg leave to observe two things more.

1st. By how few Persons the Acts of the Assembly of this Province may pass. The Assembly consists but of Twenty one Men, after the addition that the present Governour has made of Members to it, and so Eleven makes a Majority in a full House. And the Governour may displace all the Council, and take seven of his own chusing (and this Governour has done so, as I am informed) and of these seven, five or six may act, and so three or four, at the most, make a Majority in the Council.

2dly, That the Lands in question are taken away, by this Act, from the Grantees, because they are *Extravagant;* and yet here is no Rule or Measure (either expressed in the Act, or that can be collected from it) whereby it can be Known what is *Extravagant*, and what not, in the sence of these Legislators. A Grant of Lands of fifty Miles long is said to be *Extravagant*, and so is a Grant of a piece of Ground that is but fifty Foot long. A Grant in Fee is there said to be *extravagant*, and so is a Grant for a small Term of years, even so small as that of *seven years*, altho' it be for publick Use to support the Charge of a Church for the service of Almighty God ; so that upon the whole, that is *Extravagant* which a Governor and fourteen or fifteen Men (I mean the Majority of the Council and Assembly) shall please to call so.

My Lords, It is well known to your Lordships, that the Governors of this Province have been by their Commissions impowered to make Grants of Lands, under such moderate Quit-Rents and Acknowledgements, as the Governor (with the advice of his Council) should think fit or reasonable; and the King thereby declares. That such Grants shall be good and effectual against his Majesty, his Heirs and Successors.

This Declaration & Assurance was, without doubt, design'd to encourage People to accept these Grants, and Leases and Conveyances under them, and to settle, plant and improve the Lands granted, for he that builds on, or plants or improves Lands, does it with a prospect that he and his shall enjoy it; who then will settle, build on or improve Land, when his Property therein is altogether incertain and precarious? when a Governour and fourteen or fifteen Men may call the Grants of such Lands *Extravagant*, (though actually made according to the afore mentioned Power) and arbitrarily take them (with the Improvements) away from the Proprietors?

An Act therefore of the Legislative Power, that arbitrarily divests men of their Lands, for no other Reason, but that they have *too much*, (and without ascertaining what is too much in the sence of the Legislators) makes Property altogether incertain and precarious, and is the most effectual way to discourage and stop all manner of Improvements of Land, and not only so, but tends even to the Dissolution and Subversion of Government, and reducing things into Disorder and Confusion.

For, *My Lords*, with humble submission, it is a true Maxim, 𝕿𝖍𝖆𝖙 𝕴𝖓𝖙𝖊𝖗𝖊𝖘𝖙 𝕲𝖔𝖛𝖊𝖗𝖓𝖘 𝖙𝖍𝖊 𝖂𝖔𝖗𝖑𝖉. The great motive and inducement to People to unite themselves into Politick Societies, and to submit to Government, was the Preservation & Protection of their Properties, and rendering them more certain and secure than they could be in a state of Nature, without any publick Regimcnt. And this is the great Motive and Incouragement to People to contribute their endeavours for the Support and Defence of that Government, whereby they are protected in their Properties.

A settled Rule of Property, steadily observed, and

impartially applied, is the great Legament of Government; and when Property is made uncertain and precarious, this Legament is broken, and the Society in danger of running into Disorder and Confusion.

If Grants of Lands, in these Circumstances, shall be vacated, because a Governour and eleven, or a less number of Men (who if he does not chuse, he has at least a very great Influence in the choice of them) and three or four Men (absolutely of his own chusing) are pleased to call them *Extravagant* who can tell what they will call *Extravagant?* No man can be at any reasonable Certainty of his Title. At this Rate, a Governour and three or four Men, whom he may chuse himself, and eleven, or a less number of other Men (in whose choice he has at least a great Influence) may share and divide all the Lands of this Province among them & their Relations: 'Tis but saying, those that have them have *too much*, That their Grants are *Extravagant* & then (according to the excellent reason and justice of this Act) they may take them all from the present Owners, *Divest them of all;* and then the Governour has Power (with the consent of his Council) to grant them to whom he pleases: He may grant to his eleven Men in the Assembly, and three or four Men in the Council, such parts as [perhaps] they have privately bargain'd for before they gave their Votes, and the rest to others of his own Creatures, and [it may be] in trust for himself.

Should (therefore) this Act be confirm'd, it will put all the Province into Confusion. Who knows but the Governour, and his fourteen or fifteen Men in the Council & Assembly, will call any Grant *Extravagant*, when they or their Friends shall have a mind to have another Mans Estate, with the fruits of his Expence, Care and Labour, to wit, the Improvements made upon it? For if this Act be confirmed, the People of this Province may, with reason, fear, that this Assembly will, at the next meeting, take away some more of their Lands, with their Improvements; and another Assembly, more after that [for by the same Measures of this

Act, they are all now become Tenants at Will to their Governour & his fourteen or fifteen Men] And what an effect must such Apprehensions have? No Body will lend any Money upon a Mortgage of any of these Lands, nor accept long Leases or Conveyances, or make Improvements under these Grants [for the fate of those that have taken Leases and Conveyances, and made Improvements under the Grants in Question, will be too fresh in Memory] nor will any Body accept them in Settlements upon Marriage, because they know not but the Governour and his fourteen or fifteen Men, will some time or other, (and how soon they know not,) think the Lands too much for the Owners, and by their Legislative Power, arbitrarily divest the Owners of them; nor will any Body, for the same reason, make further Improvements on their own Lands, for improving them will advance their value, & that will occasion the Governour and his fourteen or fifteen men to call them *Extravagant*, and take them away.

My Lords, I beg leave upon this occasion, further, humbly to put your Lordships in mind of the dangerous Consequence of the *Legislative Power* acting as *Executive* in this Province.

It is the happiness of our *English Constitution*, that the *Legislative* and the *Executive Powers* act distinctly, in distinct Capacities, and by several. Agents. The former to make Rules and Laws, the latter to apply those Rules and Laws to particular cases. Where this is so, the individuals of the Legislative are cautious of making ill Rules or Laws, lest they should themselves suffer by them: And the latter stands in awe of punishment for mis-applying the Law in particular Cases. Hereby the true and great end of Government is answered, *viz.* None are without Check, and all sorts of Mankind are kept from injuring one the other.

But when the *Legislative Power* (who are too great to be punished) act as *Executive* in particular Cases, they are then without check, for they give no general Rules to fear the effects of themselves, and yet act without any prescribed Rules.

And when this is done in a Country where the Number of Men that compose the Legislative Power is so small, and where the Governour may have the choice of so great a part of them, & so great an Influence and Power towards getting his own Creatures to be return'd and sit in the other part, in a Country that is so remote from the Fountain of Justice [the place of their Princes Residence] To how great and how arbitrary Injustices and Oppressions the unhappy People of such a Country, where this is so practised, are liable, is not difficult to be conceived.

I beseech your Lordships to consider what two fatal strokes here are made by the two Acts I have here particularly mentioned the one at the Liberties, and the other at the Properties of the People of this Province, if the measures and methods of these two Acts be countenanced and practised, then are the Liberties and Properties of all the People of this Province wholly at the will of the Governour and fourteen or fifteen Men at the most. And if the Governour may displace the whole Council, and chuse another: then three or four of these fourteen or fifteen are of his own chusing. And if the Sheriffs (who are of his own chusing) shall be instrumental in undue Elections, and shall make false Returns of Members to serve in the Assembly, and those Members assembled stand by such undue Elections & false Returns, and are the Governours Creatures, Then will the *Liberties* and *Properties* of the People of this Province be at the will & pleasure of the Governour; for they will then be without Remedy, otherwise than by' complaining of such undue Elections in *England;* and in things of so great a Complication, and to be proved by so many Witnesses, as the facts about Elections are, it will be too chargeable to send Witnesses hither; and that Magistrates or Courts will not take the Depositions or Affidavits of Witnesses that are touching Elections, where the Governour favours the contrary side is, (as I am informed) found too true by very late Experience; & besides few dare appear as Witnesses against the frowns of a Governour; howbeit some Affidavits have been gotten and sent over, touching the undue Elections & Returns of several Members who served in this Assembly, that made these two Acts, which I shall beg leave to lay before your Lordships when I have them.

My Lords, With humble Submission, should an Act of Parliament be made in *England*, that should say such a one had an Estate of 50000*l.* a year, another 5000*l.* another 500*l.* and another 50*l. per ann* and that .these are *Extravagant Estates*, and for that reason divest the Owners of them; would not other Owners of Land have but too much reason to think themselves altogether insecure of their Properties, and to fear their Turns might be next? What a Discontent and Confusion such an Act would make in *England*, I humbly submit to your Lordships Considerations.

To shew further the Inconsistency of this Act with the Fundamental Principles and Ends of Government, and how unjust it is, and fit to be rejected, I will beg leave to cite the words of a very worthy and learned Author that but lately had the honour to sit at this Board.

"The Supream Power (saith he) cannot "take from any Man any part of his Prop- "erty without hiso wn consent; for the Pre- "servation of Property being the end of Government, "and that for which Men enter into Society, it necessarily "supposes and requires, that the People should have "Property, without which they must be supposed to lose "that by entering into Society, which was the end for "which they entered into it, too gross an Absurdity for "any Man to own. Men therefore in Society having Prop- "erty, they have such a Right to the Goods which by the "Law of the Community are theirs, that no body hath a "Right to take them, or any part of them from them, "without their own consent, without this they have no "Property at all. For I have truly no Property in that "which another can, by Right, take from me when he "pleases, against my Consent. Hence it is a Mistake to

Two Treatises of Government, fo. 273

" think that the Supream or Legislative Power of any
" Common Wealth can do what it will, and dispose of the
" Subjects Estate arbitrarily, or take any part of them at
" pleasure.

And again, afterwards, *fol.* 274. " But Government,
" into whatsoever hands it is put, being, as I have be-
" fore shewed, intrusted with this Condition, and for
" this end, that Men might have & secure their Proper-
" ties. The Prince or Senate (however it may have
" Power to make Laws for the regulating of Property
" between the Subjects one amongst another, yet) can
" never have a Power to take to themselves the whole or
" any part of the Subjects Property without their own
" consent ; for this would be, in effect, to leave them no
" Property at all.

My Lords, I will beg leave to mention one thing
that I have hinted at before, and that is, That in Commissions to Governours of this Province, there is this
Clause, *viz.* " And We do likewise give and grant unto
" you full Power and Authority, by and with the advice
" and consent of Our said Council, to agree with the
" Inhabitants of our Province and Territories aforesaid,
" for such Lands, Tenements and Hereditaments, as
" now are, or hereafter shall be in Our Power to dispose
" of, and them to grant unto any Person or Persons for
" such Terms, and under such moderate Quit-Rents,
" Services and Acknowledgements to be thereupon re-
" served unto Us, as you, by and with the Advice afore-
" said, shall think fit ; which said Grants are to pass
" and be sealed by our Seal of *New-York*, and (being
" entered upon Record by such Officer or Officers as you
" shall appoint thereunto) shall be good and effectual in
" Law against Us, Our Heirs and Successors.

My Lords, (with Submission) the Resolutions and
Declarations of a Prince, are the Fruit of great Wisdom, Advice and Deliberation, and ought to be steadily
pursued, and not lightly altered ; for that will be apt to
put too slight a value on them, and much lessen that esteem and credit they ought to have among the People,

and that relyance and dependance which 'tis necessary Subjects should have upon the Declaration of their Prince.

His Majesty might (if He had so pleased) have restrained this Power so granted to his Governours; but having not thought fit to do it, whether it be convenient to undo any thing afterwards that has been done pursuant thereunto, is humbly submitted to your Lordships Consideration.

His Majesty has, in a most solemn manner declared, under his great Seal, That the Grants made by his Governours, should be good and effectual against His Majesty, His Heirs and Successors; and his Subjects have believed and depended on such His Majesties Declaration, and in confidence of it have been at considerable Pains and Expences in treating with and purchasing Lands of the *Indians*, in suing for, and obtaining and passing these Grants, and in Improvements, & otherwise, about the granted Lands: And whether afterwards to confirm (or permit to remain in force) an Act that is made in manifest Contradiction to this Declaration, will not do the Publick more Mischief by far, than all the Lands in question are worth (*viz.* by discouraging Improvements of Lands, and by lessening the Esteem and Credit of his Majesties Declarations to his Subjects, and Powers granted to his Governours, and hindering that Relyance and Dependance upon them, which 'tis absolutely necessary his Majesties Subjects should have) is also humbly submitted to your Lordships consideration; as also, whether (if there were no other reason) this Consideration alone might not be a sufficient Motive for rejecting this Act.

But, *My Lords*, When your Lordships consider not only this, but that this Act proceeds upon such incertain Principles as have been mentioned, and is (even upon its own Principles) plainly and demonstrably Unjust and Unreasonable, in taking away all the Lands compriz'd in each Grant, from the Grantees; whereas it ought (even according to its own Principles) to have

taken away only a part, when it arbitrarily takes away
Lands from those who have honestly purchased them
from the *Indians,* and by such Purchases justly and
quietly enlarged the Dominions and Territories of the
Crown of England; and inflicts a most severe Punishment, an endless Suspension, on a Minister of the Gos-
pel, in an extraordinary manner, without setting out
what he has done to deserve it, so that any one can dis-
cern whether he hath been guilty of any Crime or not;
when (with submission) this Act is most plainly inconsistent with its own fundamental Principles, and contrary to the true fundamental Principles of Government.

When your Lordships consider it to be a thing done
by so few Persons, and upon such uncertainty of Reason, as may be applyed to any man's case, that has any
Lands within this Province, whose Lands may be taken
from him by the same, or the like small number of Persons, upon the same Principle, and in the same manner,
and that manner liable to so much Corruption, as has
been mentioned.

When your Lordships consider, That therefore this
Act (if permitted to remain in force) will discredit the
Titles of the Lands of an whole Province, discourage
all Improvements, spoil all Credit that might be raised
on the Lands by the Owners, and endanger a Confusion
& Disorder among the People of this Province, and
probably the Ruin of it.

The Complainers against this Act rest assured, That
your Lordships will (upon these Considerations) advise
his Majesty to reject this Act.

My Lords, The other of the said Acts that I must
beg leave to object to, is that, entitled, *An Act for
granting unto his Majesty the Sum of two Thousand
Pounds, fifteen hundred Pounds whereof to be allowed
to his Excellency* Richard *Earl of* Bellomont, *and five
hundred Pounds to Capt.* John Nanfan, *Lieut. Governor.*

And as for this Act, your Lordships have already
given such just & excellent Reason against such Pres-

ents (in general) that I will not trouble your Lordships with any about this Act, but what are particular.

And the Complainers against these Acts doubt not but your Lordships, upon consideration of your own excellent Reasons in general, and of the Undue Elections of the Representatives, (or at least some of them) that sate in this Assembly & voted for this Act and the two former, and of the ill Company this Act comes in (I mean, the other two Acts) will advise his Majesty to reject this Act, or at least to direct, That the Moneys thereby raised shall be applyed to the Publick Uses of the Province, and in case of future Taxes.

I cannot but believe my Lord *Bellomont* so just a Person, that if the Heat of his Pursuit would have permitted him to have stood still and considered, he would have been so far from promoting two such Acts as the two former are, as that he would himself have given the Negative Voice against them, and especially against that for vacating Grants, and still believe that his Excellency upon Re-consideration, will desire those Acts should be rejected.

And when his Excellency shall appear to have rectified these Mistakes, and some other that are thought to be such by the Complainers against these Acts, they will (I hope) be very willing to make his Excellency a generous Present; but till that be done, and a new House of Representatives fairly and duly elected and returned, they humbly hope that his Excellency and his Lieutenant shall rest contented with their Sallaries, and other Profits of their Government; and that all Moneys that is or shall be raised by Act of Assembly as a Present, shall remain in the Publick Treasury of the Province, for the publick Uses thereof.

My Lords, If the Advocates for these Acts shall undertake to defend them, I humbly desire they may also do it in writing, without Delay, and that I may have the favour of a Copy of it.

And if what I have offered be not sufficient Reasons for rejecting these Acts, I must still be an humble Suit-

or to your Lordships (on behalf of my Clyents) to hear them by their Council.

My Lords, I shall add no more at present, but humbly to beg your Lordships Pardon for troubling you so long, and for what failings I have been guilty of in this matter, humbly to beseech you to understand every thing I have presumed to say, to be with the greatest submission to your Lordships, and to take this opportunity of doing my self the Honour of subscribing,

Your LORDSHIPS

Most Obedient and most Humble Servant.

III.

MISCELLANEOUS DOCUMENTS.

LETTER ON SMITH'S HISTORY.

COLDENGHAM, July 5th 1759

DEAR SON: We may clearly see the the pernicious effects of liberty turned to licentiousness in New York, at the time of the Revolution. All the Governors of New York, even supposing them as bad as Mr. Smith represents them, did not produce half the mischief, in all the time of their Government, which was produced in one year by the suppression of legal Government. Blood shed, Rapine, confiscations, Arbitrary & tyrannic acts & animosities, which could not be stifled in many years, were the consequence. It is evident that K William & his Ministers thought the Revolution could not be obstructed, by continueing K James his officers in the exercise of their authority. This appears by the orders given for that purpose, & that they thought it most prudent to do so. They must have been very weak indeed, who could imagine, that the power of New York, tho' it had been united, could in the least promote or obstruct the Revolution in Great Brittain : & therefor, in my opinion, none in New York could claim any Merit on that occasion. They only pursued their own disorderly passions, without any real concern for the good of their country. This is too generally the case in all popular commotions, under the plausible outcry for Liberty. How cautious then ought every one to be in contributing anything towards the weakning of the legal powers of Government, or to do any thing which may give power to a disorderly Mob. A Mob can never be directed by reason ; but is hurried into the worst extremes, by prejudice and passion. The consequence generally turns to the destruction of those, who plumed them selves in their ability to incite the mob, which afterwards they are often no more able to govern, than to govern a whirl wind. Every attempt to put power in the mob ought to be crushed in the bud, especially in mixed governments. This was allwise don in the Roman republic, so long as they were able to preserve their liberty.

Our Ennemies never fail to take advantage of intestine divisions & confusion. It is probable this induced ʰe French at this time to attempt the Conquest of New ʸork. Mr. Smith has given an account of this, from Charlevoix; but he has omitted to inform us of an Instruction given to the Count de Frontinac, in case of success, which may be of use to the people to know. viz The French King ordered that all the Inhabitants should be driven out of the Country, Papists only excepted, who would swear allegiance to the King of France.

Mr. Smith tells us that Coll Slaughter, the first Governor of New York after the Revolution, was *utterly destitute of every qualification of government, licentious in his Morals, Avaritious & poor.* Who can read this Character without thinking that it is greatly exaggerated? If this be true, & characters which you will find afterwards, New York gained little by the Revolution. Colonel Slaughter may well be thought weak, in having been prevailed on, while in liquor, to order the execution of a person whom he had resolved to have reprieved till their Majesty's pleasure should be known, as I have been told he was resolved; but this is no proof of licentiousness of his Morals. Nor is there any thing in the History of New York to prove his Avarice. That he was poor is no proof of it.

By the first Act or Resolve of the first Assembly after the Revolution, a power is assumed of repealing Laws without the concurrence of the other branches of the Legislature, or a Judicial power of declaring them void. A Power which in no wise belonged to them: & which, if countenanced may be highly prejudicial both to the Crown & the Subject: & yet this usurped power has, in this instance, taken effect ever since. Do you think if a Governor had but attempted to usurp any such illegal power, that Mr. Smith would have passed it over without a note, as he does this in the Assembly.

As to the Claim of the People of New York as an inherent right to be represented in assembly, of which Mr. Smith takes notice page 75 they seem often to forget their Subordination, in the manner they make this Claim. I shall mention one remarkable difference between the Claim of the People of England, and the claim of the People in the Colonies. It is impossible that the Supreme Legislature, that the King Lords & Commons can be guilty of High Treason; but it cannot be doubted, that a Governor Council & Assembly may be guilty. It is an illegal usurpation in a subordinate power to claim the same Rights & Privileges with the Supreme. The admitting of it would at least be a Solecism in Politicks.

Mr. Smith's Character of Colonel Fletcher is that *He was by Profession a Soldier, a man of Strong passions, & inconsiderable talents, very active, & very avaricious.* I find several instances in the History of New York, which shew that Col. Fletcher pursued the Interest of his Country with zeal & activity : '& I discover no want of talents, unless it be, that he seems not to have Studied much the art of cajoling an assembly ; & this Mr. Smith might have excused, by his being bred a Soldier, had Mr. Smith any inclination to excuse any Governor. But I cannot discover the least instance of his Col. Fletcher avarice. Surely his thanking the Assembly & at the same time refuseing a present of £500 to himself & £500 more to be distributed among the officers & soldiers is not told as an instance of his Avarice: nor is his contributing largely to the building of Trinity Church an other instance.

As the greatest part of the province consisted of

Dutch Inhabitants all our Governors (Mr Smith says) as well in the Duke's time as after the Revolution, thought it good policy to incourage English preachers & School masters in this Colony; but he seems to differ in opinion, by calling Fletcher a Bigot, for being bent on such a *Project* as he terms it. There was not one Church of England nor one English School in the English Colony of New York But Col. Fletcher Built one Church & recommended to the assembly to provide for Ministers & School Masters *ergo* He was a Bigot. I do not think that I trespass on Candour when I suppose, that if an Independent Governor had been bent to bring over the whole Colony to his Principles Mr. Smith would have called it a Laudable zeal in him. The same kind of Warmth, which is Zeal for Independency, is Bigotry for the Church of England. Popular republican writers know the use of Epithets, with Superficial Readers, & never neglect the use of them.

While Col. Fletcher was Governor, the Inhabitants of New York carried on a Trade to Madagascar, while that Island was frequented by Pirates. Many likewise of the Pirates came & dispersed on Long Island & round Delaware Bay. They brought a great quantity of Gold with them. When I came first to America, in the year 1710, no payments were made without a considerable part in Chickeens or Arabian pieces, tho scarce one of them be now to be seen. Several of the now principal families, I have been told, took their first rise from their commerce with the Pirates, some of them by Gaming However it has been often remarked, that 'none of the Pirates made any use of their money to any real advantage to themselves, except one Jones, who settled on the South side of Long Island, whose son made a remarkable figure as Speaker of the Assembly, while Mr. Clinton was Governor: excepting this one, no remains of the others are to be discovered. That Col. Fletcher was really concerned in this commerce no where appears, so far as I know, or have heard. It would have been very difficult for him to have put a

stop to it with his utmost indeavour, where there are so
many harbours, under the inspection of no officer, &
where the temptations to concealment were so strong.

I intend to remark no farther on Mr. Smith's Character of any Governor, because what I have wrote I think
sufficient to shew how far his Characters are to be depended on. Notwithstanding of what I have observed,
it does not follow that he has willfully & maliciously
calumniated them. The force of early prejudice, from
a narrow education, a weak Judgement & a stubborn
temper of mind are sufficient to account for these &
many more absurdities in such kind of writers How
differently, at all times, do different Sects & parties
think & speak of the same actions. The truth often is
hid between them, & neither of them discover it. I
shall add a little story of Col. Fletcher, which I had
from Mr. Sharpass, who came to New York with him,
& retained the character of a very honest man to his
death. It will in part shew Col. Fletcher's character.

Col. Fletcher was Lieutenant Colonel of a Regiment,
which was ordered to Flanders. K William was scant-
ily supplied with money, & for that reason the Soldiers
were often unpaid, or paid only in part. This was the
case with this Regiment, when they were ordered to
march for imbarcation. On their march Col. Fletcher
with some of the officers, had gon forward to an inn,
when the Regiment mutinied, & refused to march farther, till their arrears were paid them. They formed
themselves in good order, with their Sergeants only at
their head; the commissioned officers being forced to
leave them. Col. Fletcher having notice of this, immediately returned, & after having harangued them &
reasoned with them for some time, he ordered them to
march; but not a man would stir a foot. On which
he rode off to the right of the Regiment, & pulling out
a pistol said, You right hand man march, or I will
shoot you through the head. The right hand man immediately moved his legs, and every man marched after
him, as the Colonel on horse back took the ground

which they left, & came close up to those, who according to their order were to march next, with his pistol in his hand: & thus put an end to the Mutiny.

I intend to make no farther remarks on Mr. Smith's History, till I come to the time in which I had opportunity to be well informed of the public transactions; only before I leave the subject I have been upon, I cannot forbear taking notice of that assumeing air which these Independents take upon them, in Judgeing & condemning others, & in setting up for Patriots. This they know gives them authority among the gaping mob, allwise pleased to hear their Superiors ill spoken of; but it lessens them more with men of sense & discretion, who love order & peace, & detest tumults and confusion. In place of argument, I think, it may be better to set the colony of New York, in its worst state of Government, while it was under the despotic rule of the Duke of York, in contrast with the Colony of the Massachusets Bay, while it was entirely under the Government of genuine independent republicans, that we may see how much reason these modern independents have to boast.

In New York a general liberty of conscience was allowed; not the least appearance of persecution on religious matters. In the Massachuset Bay none but Independents were allowed the common privileges; all others were persecuted, either driven out of the country or severely whipt, & some put to death.

In New York Mr Smith allows that Justice was speedily administer'd, the people remain'd easy & quiet in their possessions, & very few law suits any where, except in those parts which were peopled from New England. In the Massachusets Bay, on the contrary, it is known, that the people were exceedingly litigious, on every little difference at law. Offences were multiplied by Positive Laws, restraining the innocent freedom & pleasures or diversions usual among men. A man was whipt at Boston who accidentally meeting his wife in the street, after long absence, kissed her. By this unnecessary restraint of our natural freedom, Hypocrisy was unavoidably introduced among all ranks. By these unnatural restraints, a kind of Inthusiasm prevailed in Boston, which, if it had not been restrained by the Kings Authority, had gon near to have unpeopled the Country, by the numerous prosecutions & Executions on pretense of Witch Craft.

Lastly New York generally was at peace & in amity with the Indians and its neighbours; But New England was allmost perpetually at War with the Indians, & at variance with its neighbours.

In short we have instances in History of Kingdoms well governed, under absolute Monarchy; but it seems to me, that it is impossible that a people can be happy, under a Government formed on genuine independent principles: & this opinion is confirmed by what I have observed in New England, the only Country in the World, in which the Government was formed on these principles. Every prudent man will, as far as in his power, guard against the illegal usurpations of men in the administration; but at the same time, he will be no less carefull that legal authority be not so far depressed, as to introduce Licentiousness & public disorder. Tho this Maxim be evident to the meanest capacity, it is very little minded by popular declaimers.

I am come to a period, proper to put an end to this letter; but before I do it I shall mention two problems, which occurr'd to me, on reading Mr. Smith's History, the solution of which have given me some thought.

1. How comes it that the old genuine Independents, & Enthusiasts in general, have so little regard to Veracity? I think it not difficult to find the Solution of this. Enthusiasts are at perpetual variance with Nature; but Truth consists in a conformity with Nature: & therefor Enthusiasts are at continual variance with Truth. Generally, with some exceptions however, they, who have a byass to enthusiasm, have likewise a byass to Lyeing. They have still a stronger propensity to believe Lyes, & the more absurd or contrary to nature the more greedily they receive them.

14

2. What is the true Definition of a Bigot? We find
the Zealous men of all Sects & of all parties freely
bestowing this name on each other, it may be of
use therefor to discover, if we can, who are really
Bigots, & who not. I must answer this like a Doctor. It is a desease of the Brain, which, without distinction, often seizes the zealots of all Sects and Parties,
of whatever denomination they be: and the Pathog-
nomonic system, by which it may be distinguished from
all other deseases of the mind, is that they think it
right to tell any Lye, either in defence of or for promoting their Sect or Party. There are two distinct &
very different species of this Desease. One arises from
a preternatural formation of the Brain it self. These
when ever they obtain power become Tyrants: and all
Tyrants are Bigots. Indeed Tyranny & this species of
Bigotry are essentially the same, both agree in this general Maxim Every thing is Right which is necessary for
our purpose, whether it be by Calumny or Flattery,
Murder or Fawning, Robbery or Bribery, Perjury or
Praying &c. From what other principles could the
prosecutions & Executions on Witchcraft have arisen in
Boston. They think them fools who have any squeem-
ishness of Conscience in the use of the necessary means.
In the most common acceptation, Bigotry is only employed in speculative opinions, & Tyranny on our ex-
ternal actions; but, on due reflection, you will find that
they both proceed from the same principles, in different
persons, according to their different stations in life.
The other Species of Bigotry arises only from some disorder in the fluids of the Brain. These seldom go farther than to the free use of any kind of words, which
serve their purpose. The first sort is seldom cured, but
the other is frequently by accustoming the patient to
the use of free air, & change of company.

From what I have said I think a distinction may be
easily made, between Zeal & Bigotry. A proper degree of Warmth and Spirit is necessary to carry on any
great design; but then Zeal makes use only of Laud-

able means: Bigotry considers nothing farther than that the means are proper for its purpose. It is not however to be supposed that all Lyars are Bigots or Enthusiasts: no only such who lie in a certain & regular system. Irregular Lies arise only from sudden fits of disorder in the Imagination of weak minds, like Hysteric fits in Woemen. You see that I continue to write with that freedom which you my Son may expect from

Your affectionate father
Cadwallader Colden.

NOTE.

In the original drafts, from which this series of letters was printed in the *Collections for the Year* 1868, pp. 181–235, several of the dates were omitted. These are, in the order in which they are there printed, June 15th, 1759, p. 181; June 25th, 1759, p. 187; September 25th, 1759, p. 192; October 15th, 1759, p. 197; December 31st, 1759, p. 214; January 31st, 1760, p. 219; and February 21st, 1760, p. 226.

No date appears either in the original or the draft for the letter printed on pages 206–214; but the original enables us to supply the missing portions as indicated.

Page 206:—"*one half of the Sallary & of all the perquisites.* The adding of the word *of* before the words *all the perquisites* intirely removed the dispute; but at the same time altered the meaning, & I believe is contrary to the intention of the instruction; for by the word perquisite is intended a reasonable reward for a particular service, & certainly he that performs the service is intituled to the reward. This shews what the clerks of the great offices will sometimes take upon themselves to do. Whether the instructions to the Governors of New York continue to be made out as thus corrected by the clerk I know not.

" As soon as Mr. Burnet arrived in his Government, a dispute arose, whether the Assembly could be continued legally after the commission was determined by the authority of which it was called. To remove this objection it was answered, that the writ being in the King's name & under his seal, the death or removal of a Governor could not determine it, & the practice," etc.

Page 207 :—" This would have been too bald a reason, to be offered to the King, for removeing these gentlemen from his council of New York. The reason given was by proof of Col. Schuyler's having committed the custody of the King's seal to Mr. Philipse, & of Mr. Philipse's having received it into his custody. This was highly criminal in both, & they were gently used in having no farther notice taken of it, than by their removal from the Council. Mr. Burnet's motive to have them removed was to strengthen the interest of those gentlemen who had undertaken to serve him.

" I shall add nothing at present to the accounts, which Mr. Smith has given, of the methods taken by Mr. Burnet, to restrain the trade between New York and Canada, in goods fit for the Indian market, & of his indeavours to promote a direct trade with all the Indians to the westward of us; but I cannot pass over an egregious misrepresentation," etc.

PLOWDEN'S NEW ALBION.

————◆————

[P. R. O. LONDON COLONIAL PAPERS, VOL. VI., NO. 60.]

To the Kings most excellent Matie

The humble peticōn of Sr John Lawrence K^t: G. Barronett, Sir Edmund Plowden Kt: Sr Boyer Worsley K^t: John Trusler Roger Pack William Inwood Tho: Ryebread Charles Barret and George Noble, adventurers.

Sheweth

That whereas there is a remoate place wthin the confines of Virginia some 150 myles northwards from the Savages, & James Citty wthout the Bay of Chisapeak and a conuenient Isle there to be inhabited called Manitie, or long Isle in 39 degrees of lattitude, and within the bounds of Virginia abutting on the Ocean eastwards 18 myles and of the continent Westwards neere Dellawars Baye and not formerly granted, and are willing now att their only coste, and chardges to adventure, plant, and settle there 300 Inhabitants for the making of Wine, saulte and iron, fishing of sturgeon, & mullet, and for cattle and corne for the Coloney, and for the yearly building of shipping there with all materialls for yor Maties Service, All wch is to be done wthout any chardge to yor Matie att the only costs of the adventurers, and wth the haszard of yor said subiects liues and fortunes : Who humbly request only yor Maties Royall Proteccōn wth a fitting pattent and power to enable them to gouerne and order their planters, and servaunts and with a supply of victualls frō Ireland being much nearer, cheaper, and safer sailing then from hence.

Humbly beseeching yor most Excellent Matie to comand the L^d. Chauncelor of Ireland to make to yor subiects ye Adventurers a pattent vnd^r yor seale of Ireland of the saied Isle and 30 myles square of the coste next adjoyneing to be erected into a County Palatine called Syon to be held of yor Maties Crowne of Ireland wthout appeale or subieccōn to the Governour or company of Virginia and reserving ye 5th of all Royall mynes, and wth. the like title, dignity and priuiledges to Sr Edmund Plowden there as was graunted to Sr George Caluert K^t in Newfound land by yor Maties Royall father: And with ye vsual graunts and priuiledges to other Coloneys, and wth. power for ye supplyinge of the said Coloney by licence of the Lord Deputy President or Lords Justices to transpte thence corne, cattle and victualls, and condemned, or repriued malefactors, and Vacabonds at yor Maties price, and wages for necessary artificers.

And yor Subiects shall euer pray for yor Matie

Indorsed—Petition of John Lawrence & others.

THE COMMODITIES OF THE ISLAND CALLED MANATI ORE LONG ISLE WTH IN THE CONTINENT OF VIRGINIA.

[P. R. O., LONDON. COLONIAL PAPERS, VOL. VI. NO. 61.]

1. First thear grow naturally store of Black wilde vines wch make uerie good vergies or vinniger for to vse wth meate or to dresse sturgion but by the French mens Arte being boylde and ordred is good wine and remeanes for three moneths and no longer, But replanting the vines in 2 yeares it will then be excellent wine.

2. Ther is also great stoare of deere there and of three soartes, wch only by impaling the thickets ore forrests ore plashing trees a crosse are easely imparted.

3. There are verrie fayre turkeys fare greater than heere 500 in a flocke wth infinite store of berries chesnuts beechnuts and mast wch the feed on

4. Thears oacks of three seuerall soarts, wth ash and wallnut trees sweet red ceader and pines, fers and deale, and spruce for masts of shiping, and ashe all excellent hadge and infinite, pitch and tarr and masts and yeards for ships of 400 tunne, heere worth 30 and 40$^{£}$ a peece.

5. Whole groues of Wall nutt trees, to make Walle nutt oyle and milke, in Fraunce worth 20$^{£}$ a tunne and esteemed theare before other oyle ore milke.

6. Groues of mulberrie trees for silke wormes, wch in Ittalay are lett theare as howses are heere for rent, att vi^s the leaues of one tree by the yeare and lickewise are so lett in some pt of y^e pvince of Fr^{a}unce att y^e like rates.

7. Fitt places for to make bay salte in as low clay lands, as ye doe in Fraunce and sōner because hotter: ore white salte by boyling brine theare made by the sonne, and y^t in New England & Verginea to ye fishers is deerer solde then heere.

8. Ther are also fitt places to build and lanch ships and set vp sawing mills for timber and plancke and winsecote and for cabonets of sweete red ceader and barrell boarde for the Canaries ore Spaine ore Burdaux.

9. Ther are ponds of fresh watter 3 or 4 miles in compasse to set vp iron and water mills and sanday and clay cleefs likely for iron mines, and on ye continent northwards heigh rockey hills, wth christall sphare and glittering oare, and after great raines and washings the bring a third, wth some copper.

10. Theare is infinite store of Sturgion and mulliote verrie lardge: The mulliote is to be dryed and salted for Spaine, Canaries and Ittaley, and are treble the price of codfish ore poore John, and doe take them in netts by 500 att a draught in the sandey shoales: Whereas the Portugales 50 sayle att a tyme att Cape Blanque in Barbarie doe hooke them, being much lesse and not a quarter the gaine to be made by them, and the quantatie of Sturgion great store, of y^e Roes of w^{ch}, y^e make caviarie, and Potargo: wch bringeth redday golde and silver, and retorneth from the Straites, wines frutes and silks. And this is the Staple to imploy ships and sayl-

ors 4 moneths: As in sommer where each man bred to fish may erne 20$^£$ wages, 20$^£$ to the Honnor of the ship and 20$^£$ to the Victuler, as att thirds in the vsuall custome of y^e Westerne Fishers, and for making of greene fish dryde coad and traynde oyles is also 60 miles to the northwards a Bancke where ther is also good places to dry it as stages, much better then in Newfound lande, and is much bigger fish. The fishing begineth in Martch and endeth in Junne, and so is caught and sowlde before Newfound land fish is caught and att double the gaine & is worth 20 marks a vyage wch in Newfownd land is worth but 4$^£$ a share att the thirds.

11. The planters and coloney one moneth after cat-tell brought as cowes goats and hoggs doe digg and plant mayes wheate in Ap'ell and is reapt in August, ore planted in Junne and rept in October

12. Ther is infinite store of grownd nuts, and so much mast and walenuts as hoggs increase 20 for one in a yeare, and goats three for one without anney chardge.

13. There are deere breede 2 a peece, of wch y^e high-est are 16 handfulls and ther is also a race of bufaloes wch will be ridden and brought to draw and plowe and be milked.

14. The trade for hatchets kniues and nayles beads and toyes, wch the Savages for their Beauers, here worth 1$^£$ 2^s a waight, and otters and deere skinnes and for their Mayes wheat is worth ten for one by way of trucke.

15. Ther is infinite store of fowle and egs of all soarts of ponds of fresh fish, most excellent sea and shell fish in abondance and 1000 loade of oyster shells in a heape to make lyme of.

16. By letting out a pond 500 a$\bar{c}$ of meddoe and ara-ble lande is made in a weecke.

17. Irish Cowes of y^e English breede att 1$^£$ 10^s, in Aprell are best to be carried, wth y^e passengers goeing 50 in a ship, wth oate meale and wheat meale.

18. He that can lay out 20$^£$ for a mans armes bedding victuall and wages and passage wth a carpenter ore woodman may erne for it after in building shiping Bar-rell board Winscott and mast &c. 60$^£$ p ann$\bar{u}$.

19. A fisher in six moneths may make his wages worth 60$^£$ p ann.

20. For pitch and Tarr and hops and Woade and silke grace and fine flax, wch growes theare.

21. Ther is greene Tobacco and dryed wch you may haue theare by way of trucke wth the Savages.

22. The first yeares chardge will be to builde and to fortifie and to be provided of laborers and not of droanes and factious mutino^{r}s but good tradsmen is the gaine.

23. As for freedom and pleasure to haucke hunt fish and fowle theare is great varietie and also all deputies of fruits that Ittaley or the gardens of Spaine affordeth may be had out of those ritch grownds, for it is as hott as Spaine ore Ittaley and as full of pleasure and com-forte.

24. The winter for ye space of 2 moneths is as sharp as heere and stormes then, for by reason of the raine and the woods being so thicke the sonne enters not.

25. The spring waters thear are as good as small beere heere, but those that come from the woods are not so good, but alltogether naught.

26. By vnitie and societie of Partne^{r}s, securetie and hope of gaine growes if order and dissapline and intelligence wth the savages Verginea on the South New England on the North, the Dutch plantation 60 miles on the west be had.

27. So that 30 idle men as souldiers or gent be res-ident in a rownd stone towre and by tornes to trade wth the savages and to keep their ordinance and armes neate, so y^t 300 in one coloney of Tradesmen so y^t 100 of them be negro slaves condemnd men or apprentasies will free all danger if a gou^{r}nor for his watch & ward and trayn-inge and ammunition be carefull, and y^t 8 of ye plant-ers be in Councell wth their voyces wth the gou^{r}nor to see all planters and searvands, and all tennants y^t worke att halfe incoraged and well vsed, and y^t to woorke in sommer close att lande from tenne till two out of ye shade and abroad in the water for after it is hott and ye must rest.

28. The Partners are willing to mentaine ye gou^r-nor & 2 men to wayte on him & a Seward and a factor & his man theise to be att the chardge of ye Adventuro^{r}s and 25 soldiers and 25 marriners to trucke and trafficke by torne wth the Savages, and neuer above tenn of them abroad att once in a pinnace planqued against arrowes.

29. And lastly the feare of the Spanniard or forriners theare are litle, by reason the sowndings and coast to them is unknown unto aney, Besides the Verginnians being neer vs wher are 4000 inhabitants and the Barmodes 2000 the 2 Dutch foarts 2000 New Plimmouth and Salem 2300, All theise in three dayes sayle and some in one are allyed vnto vs to assist vs if need require against anny strangers, As for the Savages 10 peeces will affright 300 of them and put them to flight, having no other defence for themselves but bows and arrowes, and all naked people.

Indorsed—The Comodities of the Isle of Manati on the Continent of Virginia.

The King to the Lords Justices.

[Strafford's Letters and Dispatches. I. 72.]

Charles R.

Right trusty and wellbeloved Cousins and Counsellors, we greet you well. Whereas we have been inform'd by the humble Petition of our trusty and well beloved Subjects, Sir *John Laurence* Knight and Baronet, Sir *Edward Plowden*, Knt. and others, that there is a certain habitable and fruitful Island near the Continent of Virginia, named the Isle *Plowden* or *Long-Isle*, between 39 and 40 Degrees North Latitude, whereof neither we nor any our Royal Progenitors have hitherto made any Grant either of the whole or any Part thereof, which being by our People carefully Planted and inhabited, may prove of good Consequence to our Subjects and Kingdoms: And whereas the said Petitioners have made humble Suite to us for our Royal Grant of the said

Isle, and forty Leagues square of the adjoining Continent to be held of us as of our Crown of that our Realm
of *Ireland*, in the Nature of a County Palatine or Body-
Politick by the Name of *New Albion*, with other Privileges as by the said Petition (which herewith we send
unto you) you will understand, promising therein to settle five hundred Inhabitants for the planting and civilizing
thereof: Our Pleasure is, and we do hereby authorize
and require you upon the Receipt of these our Letters,
forthwith to cause a Grant of the said Isle called the
Isle *Plowden*, or the *Long-Isle* between 39 and 40 Degrees North Latitude, and of forty Leagues square of
the adjoining Continent, from us our Heirs and Successors to be made unto the Petitioners and their Heirs
forever, to be holden of us as of our Crown of *Ireland*,
by the name of *New Albion*, with such Privileges, Additions and Dignities to Sir *Edward Plowden* his Deputies and Assigns (as first Governor of the Premisses)
and so successively to every Governor that hereafter
shall be, as have heretofore been granted unto other
Governors of the Colonies; together with other usual
Grants and Privileges likewise accustomably given for
the governing and ordering their Planters and Subordinates. And lastly we do require you to take Order,
that by our said Grant our said Subjects inhabiting the
said Colony, be upon the Request of the Governors and
Principals from Time to Time furnished and supply'd
out of our said Kingdom of *Ireland* with Corn, Cattle,
and such other Necessaries as they shall have use of;
and also be furnished and have Power to carry Artificers and Labourers thence into the said Colony, which
being our Pleasure you are speedily to effect. And for
so doing these our Letters shall be, to you our Justices
now being, as also to our Deputy, Chief Governor, or
Chief Governors of that our Kingdom, that hereafter for
the time shall be, sufficient Warrant and Discharge.
Given at our Court at *Oatlands* the 24th day of July in
the eighth year of our Reign 1632.

By his Majesty's Commandment,

JOHN COKE.

The Petition of Sir Edward Plowden, &c.

Sheweth,

That near the Continent of *Virginia,* about sixty Leagues Northwards from *James* City without the Bay of *Chisapeake,* there is an habitable and fruitful Island named *Isle-Plowden,* otherwise *Long-Isle,* with other small Isles between 30 and 40 degrees of Latitude, about six Leagues from the Main near *De la Warre* Bay, whereof your Majesty nor any your Progenitors were ever possess'd of any Estate,. and which your Majesty never made any Grant of to any, these Petitioners at their own Coste and Charges are willing to venture therein the settling of five hundred Inhabitants for the Planting and Civilizing thereof to the Honour of Almighty God, and the Good of your Majesty.

Wherein first and principally the Petitioners humbly desire your Majesty's Royal Protection to be vouchsafed to them by Letters Patents under the Great Seal of your Majesty's Kingdom of *Ireland* to be effected by your Highness's Letters of Credence for that Purpose nder your Highness's Signet to the Lord Deputy, Lorde Chancellor, Lord's Justices, and Chief Officers there, or any of them for the Time being, for enabling the Petitioners, their Heirs and Successors forever, to have and enjoy the said Isles and forty Leagues square of the adjoining Continent as in the Nature of a County Palatine or Body Politick by the Name of *New Albion,* to be held of your Majesty's Crown of *Ireland,* exempted from all Appeal and Subjection to the Governor and Company of *Virginia,* and with such other Additions, Privileges and Dignities, therein to be given to Sir *E. Plowden,* Knt. his Deputies, Assigns, and Successors (as Governors of the Premisses) like as have been heretofore granted to Sir *George Calvert,* Knt, late Lord *Calvert* in Newfoundland together with the usual Grants and Privileges that other Colonies have for governing, and ordering. their Planters and Subordinates, and for supplying of Corn, Cattle and Necessaries from your Majesty's Kingdom of *Ireland*, with Power to take Artificers and Labourers there.

EXTRACTS FROM THE ENTRY BOOKS.

[P. R. O., LONDON. DOMESTIC INTERREGNUM, ENTRY BOOK VOL. XCII. P. 108.]

Extract. Die Jovis 21º Martii 16$\frac{4}{5}\frac{9}{0}$.

Lord President. Sr. Henric Mildmay. Lord Comr Whitlocke. Colonell Jones. Mr Scot. Sr Henrie Vane. Colonell Hutchinson. Earle of Salisburie. Lord Howard. Sr William Armyne. Mr Heveningham.

(7.) That the Petition of the Earle of New Albion relateing to the plantation there be referred to the consideration of the Committee of this Councell what they conceive fitt to be done therein.

[P. R. O., LONDON. DOMESTIC INTERREGNUM, ENTRY BOOK VOL. XCII. P. 159.]

Extract. Die Mercurii 3º Aprilis, 1650.

Lord President. Sr Henry Vane. Lo. Howard. Earle of Salisbury. Col. Jones. Sr James Harringtō. Col. Hutchinson. Col. Ludlowe. Mr Challenor. Lo. Visc: Lisle. Sr Wm. Armyne. Col. Morley. Ald. Pennington.

(9.) That it be referred to the Comittee for plantacōns or any three of them to conferre with the Earle of Albion, concerning the giveing good security to this Councell, that the men, armes & amunicōn, wch he hath now shipped in order to his voyage to New Albion, shall goe thither, and shall not be employed either there or elsewhere to the disservice of the publiqr

Lord Comr Lisle.
Lord Comr Whitlock.

[P. R. O., LONDON. DOMESTIC INTERREGNUM, ENTRY BOOK VOL. XCII. P. 441.]

Extract. Die Martis 11.º Junii 1650.

Lord President. Earle of Denbigh. Lord Howard. Lord Chiefe Baron Wilde. Colonell Purefoy. M.ʳ Martin. M.ʳ Challoner. S.ʳ Henry Mildmay. S.ʳ William Armyne. Lord Leiutenant of Ireland. S.ʳ Peter Wentworth. Colonell Stapeley. M.ʳ Holland. S.ʳ Henry Vane. M.ʳ Gourdon. Alderman Pennington.

(11.) That a passe bee granted for M.ʳ . . . . Batt and M.ʳ . . . . Danby themselves and seven score persons men woemen and children to goe to New Albion.

IV.

_____

GARDINER'S EAST HAMPTON, ETC.

I.

NOTES AND OBSERVATIONS ON THE TOWN OF EAST HAMPTON
AT THE EAST END OF LONG ISLAND WRITTEN BY JOHN
LYON GARDINER OF THE ISLE OF WIGHT IN APRIL 1798
AT THE REQUEST OF THE REV? SAMUEL MILLER OF
N: YORK.

Long Island is about 140 miles in length from the
Southwest end which lies near the mouth of Hudson's
river to Muntock point at the east or North east end
which lies a little to the east-ward of the mouth of
Conecticut River and about 50 miles distant from it.

The Island contains three Counties Kings Queens
& Suffolk the last extends from Muntock point Westerly about 100 miles. Suffolk County is divided into
two branches by a large Bay which extends south-
westerly as far as the River head where the Court house
stands. That part of the Island which lies on the North-
west side of this Bay contains the towns of River head
& Southold and terminates at Oyster pond point in the
latter town, this point is 30 miles from the Court-house.

The town of Southold was very extensive, but by an
act of the Legislature was lately divided into the two
towns of River head & Southold. To Southold belongs
Plumb Island separated from Oyster pond point by a
part of Long-Island sound called Plumb gut thro' this
passage the tide runs very rapid, it being about a mile
wide & the bottom very rocky. This Island contains

15

about 1000 acres of fertile land. Yet further eastward in the same township are two small Islands called the Gulls and Fishers Island containing about   acres of land & 9 miles in length. The east end of this Island is about 160 miles from N: York & is now the most eastern part of the State. From Plumb Island to Fishers Island the bottom is rocky & the water deep; from the rapidity of the tide thro' this passage up sound it is called the Race.

On the South East branch of Long Island lie the towns of Southampton & East-Hampton. This branch of the Island is the longest and terminates at Muntock point which is about 50 miles from the Court-house. The town of East Hampton is bounded South-easterly by the Atlantic Ocean, the shore on this side is a sand beach, free from rocks; the sea gains on the shore & it has been said by aged people that in some places the Sea now washes the shore where Indian corn has been planted by their fathers. The sand near the Sea shore is blown into hills on which nothing grows but a grass called the beach grass & a shrub bearing the beach Plumb. By this grass & the bushes the sand is in some measure prevented from being blown over the adjacent pasture & mowing fields.

Easterly the town terminates at Muntock point around which the tide runs very rapidly. The shores on this part of the town are rocky and large reefs run out into the Sea which abound with various species of fish; particularly, Codfish, sea-bass, striped-bass, blue fish, sheep's head &c. There are in the season of Fishing about 35 Sail of fishing smacks besides lite bottom boats employed near this point for the N York-markett. This is a source of Wealth to this industrious class of people; this fishery increases in proportion to the increase of Inhabitants in our Sea-ports. The fish are mostly caught with hook & line. On Muntock point upon a high clif near the point stands the light house built by John M Combs in the summer of 1796 at the expense of the United States, it is about 100 feet high from the foundation to the top of it. The stone with which it is built were transported from Connecticut River. It cost about 25,000 Dollars. In the summer season it affords a most beautiful Prospect; at a distance are to be seen Plumb Island, Gardiner's Island, Fisher's Island & the Continent from Conecticut River to Point Judith in the State of Rhode Island. Block Island is to be seen in a North east direction distant 7 leagues. The prospect on the land & the Sea is pleasing in the summer, but in the Winter it is a dreary & desolate place.

On the North & North west part the township is bounded by a body of water; part of which is called Gardiners Bay; Sag-harbour is formed by Long-Island & Shelter Island. The lower or N: East part of the large Bay which separates the South east from the North west branch of Long-Island is called Gardiners bay, there is a good depth of water in some parts of it & it is large enough for several hundred sail to ride secure. The upper part of the bay to the westward of Shelter Island is known by various names. Robins Island which contains about 400 acres of land lies in that part of it.

It was from that part of Gardiners Bay which lies between E: Hampton & Gardiners Island that Vice Admiral Arbuthnot lay with 11 ships of the line in the summer of 1780 & in the winter of 1781.

From this Bay he sent out four ships to watch the movements of the French fleet when the Culloden a fine 74 Gun ship was lost on Muntock & the Bedford was dismasted—this was in the winter of 1781. The other two ships went clear of Muntock point to sea & lived thro' the snow storm & gale of wind. Gardiners Island or the Isle of Wight lies on the North east side of Gardiners [Bay] & contains about 3000 acres of good land, its greatest length is from N W. to S: East & is about 7½ miles besides an Island called Ram Island which belongs to it & lies on the South part. The shape of the Island is irregular.

From its first settlement in 1639 it was a plantation by itself. As the Legislature in 1788 thought proper to annex it to the town of E: Hampton it will in these Notes be considered as a part of that township. This Island is distant from the town 10 miles & from the Long-Island shore about 3. By the Assessors of that town it is assess'd for about one sixth of the value of the township. The Shores on the Northside of E H: are rocky & indented with Bays, coves & creeks which lead into ponds that abound with shell & scale fish & are harbours for small Vessells.

The town is bounded Westerly by Southampton: the line between the two towns was in contention from the first settlement till 1695 when it was finally fixed where it now is by men mutually chosen by the two towns. It begins at the Sea shore on the South side & crosses the eastern branch of the Island to the Northside & leaves but a small part of the houses at Sag-harbour on the East: Hampton side. This line is about miles in length & was about 1664 fenced in order to keep the Southampton horses, &c. crossing over the bounds. This line is now much further to the Eastward than where it was fixed by the General Assembly of Connecticut about 1660 to whose decision it was refer'd. The Settlement of Sag-harbour is mostly in Southampton township & is a thriving place; It is exceeding well calculated for the whale & Cod fishery. A number of Vessells are now employed in this business, the larger Vessells are employed in the Whale fishery & sent to the Cape of Good Hope & on the Brazil coast; Col: Ben: Huntting & Capⁿ Steⁿ Howell have promoted this fishery. The smaller Vessells are sent to the Eastward for the Cod fishery. Some people used to this business have promoted it who moved here lately from the Sea coast of Massachusetts. If this business should increase Sag-harbour will probably be a township by itself. It was at this place that Col. Meigs of Conecticut with about 150 men in whale boats surprised & took 100 of the British in May 1777. Only

10 Men escaped. He hauled his boats over a narrow beach on the Southold side, crossed the Bay above Shelter Island and marched down upon the back of the British troops who were carousing & drinking, being the next Day to march for N York with large quantities of hay and grain exacted of the Inhabitants that had not moved off Long Island. This hay &c was burned by the Americans; it was demanded of the people to replace it; but by means of Dr. Buell & others who represented the case to Gov.ʳ Tryon it was not demanded. This expedition was well plan'd & executed. Col! Meigs received a Sword from Congress on account of it.

From the Western bounds of the town to Muntock point is 25 miles; the town is 20 Miles from the point, there are two small Villages one about 3 miles to the Westward of the Town & one as far Eastward. They contain about 30 houses each. They are known by the Original Indian names of Waynscutt and Am-eag-ansett. By the records it appears that East Hampton was at first called Maid-stone; this name does not appear after the year 1664 when they came under the Duke of York & soon after rec.ᵈ a Patent from Col: Richard Nicolls; by this Patent the town is called East: Hampton; tho' the records of the town prior to the year 1664 mention that name as the name of the Place. It was probably named East on account of its situation to the east of Southampton. By the records of the town it appears that some of the first settlers came from Stansted in the County of Kent in England, probably some of them might have come from Maid-stone in the same County. It is very evident from the records that some of the original 35 settlers & purchasers of the town removed from Lynn in Massachusetts and tradition informs us that they came from several of the towns on the Sea coast to the Eastward of Boston. These were probably natives of England as New-England had not been settled so long as to produce native immigrants when E: H was first settled. Those who were received by the Original Settlers " as accepted Inhabitants " might have been born in America. None were received into the town as Inhabitants but by a Vote; & some were forbid settling on account of their principles & laziness.

These were at first 35 purchasers the names of 13 of these are now entirely extinct in the town. The Christian & Sir names of many of the Original settlers are now found in the town, removed to the 4th. 5th & 6th. degree counting the first as one. Lands that were at first "allotted" have descended in the family & are after a space of 150 years occupied by one of the same family and name. When the town was first settled only a home lott at the South end of the town containing from 11 to 13 Acres was laid out; this was done upon both sides of the pond called the town pond, this was probably on account of the convenience of getting water for themselves and cattle before they dug wells. It is probable a brook might have discharged itself into the pond; which since the land is clear'd has disappeared. The next lands that was laid out to the owners were the salt marshes on various parts of the town; the last of the Woodland was allotted to the owners about 60 years ago. Excepting the Indian deed for the township there is nothing of an earlier date on record than the following

" At a General Court holden at East: Hampton March 7th 1650 It is ordered that Ralph Dayton is to gòe to Keneticut for to procure the evidence of our lands & for an acquittance for the payment of our lands & for a boddie of laws—it is alsoe ordered that any man have libertie to sett gunns for to kill Wolves, but not within half a mile of the town "—&c " & no man shall sett any gun but he shall look to it while the stars appear and to take the gun up by the sun rising and no man shall sell any Dog or bitch young or ould to any Indian upon the penaltie of paying of 30ˢ." Various town laws similar to the above are on record they are stiled orders. Many of them are relative to laying out vacant lands, making roads, destroying noxious animals

& in short laws that were necessary in a new settlement. The Indian Deed for the land is on record, it is from the four Indian Sachems Paggatacut of Munhansett; Wayandanck of Meantacutt; Momoweta of Corchake; Nowedonak of Shinacock; it is dated April 29th 1648 and conveys the land to the "East-ward of Southampton bounds to the Worshipful Theophilus Eaton Esquire Governor of the Colony of New Haven and the Worshipful Edward Hopkins, Governor of the Colony of Conecticut and their assotyats" "for & in consideration of 20 Coats, 24 looking glasses, 24 hoes, 24 hatchetts; 24 knives & One hundred Mugs already received by Us & reserve to our selves free liberty to fish in all the cricks and ponds and hunt up & down in the woods without molestation, giving the English Inhabitants noe just cause of Offence; likewise are to have the fynns and tails of all Whales cast up & desire they may be friendly dealt with in the other part; alsoe to fish for shells to make Wampum of and if the Indyans in huntting Deer shall chase them into the Water & the English shall kill them, the English shall have the bodie and the Sachem the Skin." The witnesses are Richard Woodhull, Thomas Stanton, Robt. Bond, Job Sayre & Chectanoo (by his mark) the Interpreter. There is recorded a receipt from Edward Hopkins to " Robt. Bond Inhabitant of E: H: for 34 : 4 : 8 being the amount of monies paid for the Purchase of the lands" & a certificate of the Delivery to said Bond of the writings of said Purchase & all the Interest that was thereby purchased, dated 16 April 1651. On a blank leaf of one of the old book of records are seen these words—Robert Bond deliver'd in to the Governour for the purchase of our lands for the towns Use the sum of 1 : 3 : 10. Robt. Bond for his expences going to the Mayne land in the towns service the sum is 1^l: 3^s: 6 . It appears that the purchase was made by these two Governors in trust & in behalf of the Original settlers of the town. The English and Natives appear to have lived on good terms ; the lands on the east end of Long Island as well as the neighbouring Islands Shelter Island, Gardiners Island, Plumb Island and Fishers Island were purchased of the Natives.

Some French writer I think Raynal speaks in praise of the Great Willm Penn for having sett an uncommon example in purchasing the soil of Pensylvania of the Native Indians & which if it had been followed by the settlers of New England and Virginia would have prevented some wars that took place. This Frenchman like many European writers who have never been in this country did not understand himself sufficiently on this subject. The fact was that the settlers of Virginia & New England purchased their lands of the natives before George Fox the founder of the Quaker's sect published their principles in England in Oliver Cromwells time & a long time before the celebrated Wm Penn settled in Pensylvania.

There is no doubt but the regular purchase & the Warrantee Deed from the four above mentioned Sachems in 1648 prevented Disputes between the natives & English. Some Indian writings on Record in E: Hampton speak of the friendship and amity of their neighbours the English about 1660.

Governor Winthrop in his Journal page & Governor Hutchinson in his history of Massachusetts page 88 mentioned that in 1640 a number of families removed from Lynn to the West end of Long-island & bought lands there of James Forett Agent to the Earl of Sterling but getting into some quarrell with the Dutch they removed to the East end and settled at Southampton & chose one Pierson for their Minister. Probably Southampton was settled before E: H:

Tradition informs us that before E: H: people built their first grist mill (which went with cattle) they went to Southampton to Mill & carried their grain on the back of a bull that belonged to the town (for the use of their cows). If this is true no doubt Southampton was settled first. Govr Hutchinson says that in 1644 Southampton by an act of the Commissioners of the

United Colonies was annexed to the Jurisdiction of Connecticut. One might suppose that E: H: might have been settled from Southampton but the method of pronunciation is quite different altho' the towns join. An E: H: man may be known from a Southampton man as well as a native of Kent in England may be distinguished from a Yorkshire man. The Original settlers of these towns probably came from different parts of England. Besides the names that prevail in one town are not met with in the other. The names of Pierson, Halsey, Howell, Toppin, Sandford, Cooper, White, Post, &c. are common in Southampton and confined there as are the names of Mulford, Osborn, Conkling, Baker, Parsons, Miller, Gardiner, Dayton, &c to East Hampton; the names of Hedges & Hand are met with in the eastern part of Southampton but originally from E: H: —Very little intercourse took place between the two towns before the Revolutionary War; since that visits & intermarriages are more frequent.

What time E: H: was first settled is not certainly known probably soon after Southampton. Neither of the towns was settled so early as Gardiners Island which was settled by Lion Gardiner in March 1639. David son of Lion Gardiner in a petition presented to Governor Dungan about 1683 mentions his father as the first Englishman that had settled in the Colony of N York. Southampton put itself under the jurisdiction of Connecticut in 1644. As Southold did under N: Haven in 1648 according to President Stiles history of the three Judges of King Charles 1st. E: H: was a Plantation or Commonwealth as it is stiled in their records that was independent of any other Government from the first settlement till about 1657. The Magistrates frequently asked advice in difficult cases of " the neighbour towns of Southampton & Southold " & sometimes of " the Gentlemen at Hartford." The three towns on the east end are stiled the 3 Plantations. The Government of the town of E: H: was purely Republican. Their laws were enacted by all the Citizens assembled in town meeting; this was stiled the General Court and a fine was inflicted on such as did not attend. In Dec.ʳ 9ᵗʰ 1653 By a Vote of the General Court "the Capital laws & the laws & orders that are noted in the bodie of laws that came from Conecticut shall stand in force among Us." Their Public Officers were few; three Magistrates who were called Townsmen were chosen annually. Their Oath of Office points out their duty; it is as follows: "You, —— ——— being chosen by this Court for the careful & comfortable carrying on the affairs of this town doe here swear by the name of the Great and Everliving God that You will faithfully & without respect of persons execute all such laws & orders as are or shall be made & established by this Court according to God according to the trust committed to You during this year for which you are chosen and until a new be chosen, if you remayn among Us So help you GOD." A Recorder & Constable were the only other public Officers chosen; their Oath points out their Duty and is *mutatis mutandis* similar to the above.

The Constable was always a reputable citizen & had great authority; he by law moderated the General Court. The Recorder or Secretary not only recorded all orders of the General Court, but the decisions of the Magistrates & by a Vote passed in 1656 the Depositions of Witnesses in their trialls at law for which he was allowed a stated price; as were the Magistrates & Constable. Their trials were sometimes with a Jury but mostly without. From 1650 to 1664 about the time they came under Govʳ Nicolls there are about 50, or 60 cases of law on record. These were mostly for small debts & for defamation. By law no one could recover more than 5£ for defamation.

In 165_ George Lee attorney to prosecuted "Lieutenant Lion Gardiner of the Isle of Wight in behalf of himself & the States of England for five hundred pounds Sterling" before the Magistrates in E: H: It appears from the very lengthy depositions

that a " Southampton man had hired a Dutchman to
bring a freight to that place from Manhadoes & that the
vessell was taken from the Dutchman & brought to the
Isle of Wight to the Lieftenant who retook her for the
Dutch owner " & was prosecuted by the original captors.
This affair was refer'd to the General Court at Hartford
by the E: H: Magistrates & both parties bound to appear there.   Lee obligated himself if he did not prosecute then the case should be drop'd ; this was likely the
case.   This is the most important case on record where
property was concern'd.

"The three Men were to meet the first second Day
of the Week of every month for the tryall of any cause
according to an order & to consider of those things that
may concern the publick good of the people & whosoever
of those three Men doe not attend the Day at 8 o'clock
in the morning shall be liable to pay 5 "

"John Mulford, Robert Bond & Thomas Baker are
chosen by this Court for the execution of those orders
comyted to their trust for this Year. Ralph Dayton
Cunstable & Benjamin Price Recorder ;" the above was
done at a General Court holden Octo^r 7. 1651.   The
first General Court was in March 1650.

"It was decreed Octo^r 5. 1652 that if any Man be
agrived with any thing that is done by the Men that
are in Authoritie that he shall have liberty to make his
appeal to the next General Court, or when the freemen
are assembled together for their Publique occasions."
Their town meetings were frequent & became burdensome
on the people, but being their own law makers they
made a multiplicity of them ; laws for regulating their
fences to fields that were pastured in common, for divisions of lands, making highways, building a mill, a meeting house &c took up much of their time.   The business
of killing whales was regulated by law & every one
obliged to take his turn to look out for them on the
shore.

Their houses were thatched and liable to take fire.   By
law every man was to be provided with a ladder that

reach'd to the top of his house & a man was appointed to see that the Chimneys were well plaster'd and swept. Severe laws were made against " selling any Indians Guns, swords, powder, lead, flints &c or any more than two Drams of strong water at one time." Many of the laws appear curious; but in general they are mild & the penaltie not very severe. There are only three or four cases of Corporal punishment & not one of capital.

In the Year 1653 the Indians were some trouble; powder & shot were sent for to the mouth of the Connecticut river & a watch by night of two & a ward by Day of one man was order'd to be kept by the Inhabitants in turn. "April 26. 1653 It is order'd that no Indian shall come to the town unless it be upon special occasion & none to come armed because that the Dutch hath hired Indians against the English and we not knowing Indians by face and because the Indians hath cast off their Sachem &c orders were given to shoot any Indian on third call or if they run away". "Every man was obliged to go armed to the meeting house every Lords Day under penaltie of 12 pence" and four assistants were added to the 3 townsmen.. It does not appear from the records that any battle was fought; probably the Indians who were then numerous had not learn'd the use of fire-arms. This was at the time Oliver Cromwell was at war with the Dutch Nation; & an opinion prevail'd thro' this Country that the Dutch at Manhadoes supplyed the Indians with arms; & urged them to destroy the English settlements. From the histories of those times it is evident something was design'd against the English by the Dutch & Indians. Oliver Cromwell about this time called on all the Colonies to assist in an expedition against the Dutch at Manhadoes; particularly N Haven and Connecticut who were nighest the Dutch. Major Sedgwick of Massachusetts was to have the command of the men that were to be sent from each Colony in a certain proportion. The following extract from E. H. records probably refers. to it. "June 29. 1654. Having considered the letters that come from Connecticut wherein men are required to assist the power of England against the Dutch we do think ourselves called to assist the said power." The expedition did not take place probably on account of Peace being made soon after between the two nations. Very little more is said about the Indians till the Great Indian War which threated all this Country in 1675 when the people were again on their guard, but it does not appear that any lives were lost. This was the most formidable combination of Indians that ever happen'd. Governour Andross sent an armed sloop to Gardiners Island to protect it against the Indians. The English and Indians were probably both on their guard against a surprise; but by 1675 the east end of Long Island had so many English settl'd that there was no great danger.

The five Nations joind this confederacy. "Octr 3^d 1654 It is order'd that there shall be a copie of the Connecticut Combination drawn forth as is convenient for Us & all men shall sett to their hands." This combination was signd Octr 24, 1654 by about 40 & is now on record signd by each on the book. All excepting 3 or 4 write a plain legible hand for those days. These sign by making their mark. " This Combination is to maintaine and preserve the libertie & puritie of the Gospell of our Lord Jesus which we now profess as alsoe the Discipline of the Church which according to the truth of the said Gospell is now practized among Us; As alsoe in our Civil Affairs to be guided & governed according to such laws & orders as shall be made according to God & which by Vote of the Major part shall be of force among Us, &c &c." This combination is similar to the One enter'd into in 163[8] by the 3 towns of Hartford Windsor & Wethersfield & is a copy of the preamble of that as recorded in Hazard's Collection of Papers page [437. Vol. I.] " March 19. 1657 It is order'd & by a Major Vote of the Inhabitants of this towne agreed upon that Thomas Baker & John Hand is to go unto Keniticut for to bring Us under their Government according unto the terms as Southampton is & alsoe to

carry up Goodwife Garlick that she may be delivered up
unto the Authoritie there for the triall of the cause of
Witchcraft which she is suspected for." It was afterwards agreed upon by the towne that Mr. Gardiner shall
be intrusted with the same power with Thomas Baker
& John Hand for coming under Government." In the
records it is interested it doubtless should be intrusted.
It is from the records evident that soon after this they
were under the Jurisdiction of that Colony or rather
composed a part of it altho' nothing is said of these men's
returning. Probably the General Court at Hartford
did not pay any attention to the latter part of the business on which Baker & Hand were sent: This poor
woman had a trial in E: H for witchcraft but nothing
was done, but refer'd to the General Court at Hartford.
At this Day it appears surprising that not only those
who settled in the American Wilderness should be so
infatuated about Witches & Witchcraft but that King
James 1st Lord C. Justice Holt & some of the first characters in the English nation should be so much carried
away with notions of this kind. If the affair of Witches
has made more noise in this Country than it has in some
Countries of Europe it is not owing to there having been
more executed for that supposed crime here; for I have
no doubt there have been during the same time as many
executed in England only as there have been in all New
England & Virginia. It was not confined to N. England but prevailed also in other parts. In Europe the
Execution of a few Individuals would be effaced from
the page of history by more important events that were
during the last century continually taking place; but in
this Country it was a singular affair & has been handed
down by our own writers & dwelt upon with wonder by
European writers who have endeavoured to account for it
from the Enthusiastic Ideas of the Inhabitants here.
Not considering that they acquired these Ideas in Europe from books published there by men of character
& information. It is to be hoped that this infatuation
is done away among the Citizens of both sides of the

Atlantic; but it is not doing justice for those of one side to suppose that this infatuation prevailed only on the other side. If King James Lord Holt & others of information who believed in Witchcraft are excusable certainly those persecuted exiles who fled to a savage wilderness are equally clear of blame. Perhaps the laws of Moses by which in many cases the first settlers were governed was a mean of urging them on in the belief of Witchcraft and its evils.

"Novr 29. 1662 It is jointly & fully agreed that Mr. T: Baker, Mr. Tho: James, Mr. Lion Gardiner, Mr. Robert Bond, Mr. John Mulford, Tho: Tomson & Tho: Chatfield shall go to Southampton the next second Day to compound a Difference between Us & Cap^n. John Scott, Esqr. & M^r. John Ogden about Montoquit & do hereby engage to ratifie & confirm what our Committee shall conclude upon and also we doe impower this our Committee to Joyne with Southampton & Southold about a Patten grant." Where they proposed to apply for a Pattent I do not know. N: York was then in the hands of the Dutch, it was either to King Charles 2nd or to the Government of Conecticut.

"Novr 23. 1663 a Committee was appointed to join Southampton & Southold committees & if they see cause to establish laws for settling Government among Us & what our Committee or a major part of them shall doe herein we engage ourselves to stand unto." It was doubtless in contemplation to have the three towns join in One government as other towns on the Continent had done. "Feby 23^d. 1663 It is agreed that Montauk shall pay fifty pounds of the 150 that is to purchase the pattent right: March 25 at a town meeting after long debate it was agreed to that the purchase of Pattent right should be borne by all the Inhabitants according to the land every man possesses." "April 26 1664 at a towne meeting the towne doth desire those Men that do goe to Hartford to debate together & with the neighbouring plantations for the things of mutual Government between Hartford & Us for our further settlement but to con-

clude of nothing as understanding that the Governour will come over or a Committee from the General Court."
"Dec. 21. 1664 The Inhabitants of this towne under-standing that we are off from Connecticut & the Magis-trates not willing to act further upon that account that we may not be without law and Government it is agreed that the former laws & Magistrates shall stand in force till we have further orders from York. It is agreed that the Constable of the shall be secured by the towne for not gathering the Rates."

The word *cast* appears to be wanting in the record. This resolve probably refers to the adjudication that was made at N York Dec. 1. 1664 by Gov. Nicolls & others on one part & Gov. Winthrop & others on the other that Long Island should not be under the Government of Conecticut but under his highness the Duke of York &c

There appears from this time to have been some al-teration in their Government. In April 1664, The Constable & Seven Overseers were chosen; no mention is made of townsmen. May 1. 1665. John Mulford took the Oath of Allegiance. This is the first time any such Oath is mentioned on record.

"Feb. 9. 1665. Tho: Tomson & Tho: Talmage are chosen to go to meet Southampton & Southold Commit-tees to consider of things for the Publique good, also to consider of the best Way whereby we might procure a redress of such grievances as are at present upon the plantations both with respect to the foundation of this Government—Viz—that we might have deputies to act in behalf of the several towns, as also concerning the laws themselves & their late amendments as they are called." The above extracts are made to show that about 1657 they came under the Government of Conec-ticut & that in 1664 being cast off from that Colony they came under the Duke of York.

In the records of the town is a manuscript book in a fair hand containing the laws that were in force under Gov. Nicolls which are refer'd to in the above resolve. These probably superseded those that were enacted by

the General Court of the town and those that were enacted at Hartford. I suppose these were what are stiled
the Dukes laws. As there may not now be so legible a
copy as this; I shall insert the title page. The laws are
too lengthy to extract, they are in Alphabetical order.
On the first page is written "Laus Deo—East Hampton
book of laws June 24. 1665." On the 2^d page "Lawes
Established by the Authoritie of his Majesties ———
Patents granted to his Royal Highness James Duke of
York & Albany; Bearing date the 12th Day of March
in the sixteenth Yeare of the Raigne of our Soveraign
Lord King Charles the 2^d:—Digested into One Volume
for the Publick Use of the Territorys in America under
the Government of his Royal Highness. Collected out
of the several laws now in force in his Majesties Amer-
ican Colonys & Plantations. Published March 1. Anno
Domini 1664 at a General meeting att Hampstead upon
Long Island by Virtue of a Commission from his Royal
Highness James Duke of York & Albany given to
——— Col^l. Richard Nicolls Deputy Governour bearing Date the second Day of April 1664."

Additions, Amendments & Explanations to these
laws were made by the Govr & confirmed at the General
Courts of Assises when convend. They are inserted in
this law book & directed "to the Justices of the Peace,
High Sheriff & all other officers both Military & Civill
in the East Riding of Yorkshire on Long Island" the
General Court of Assises I suppose consisted of Deputies
from each town occasionally called by the Governour.
No regular Assembly was convened till 1683. Perhaps
necessity obliged Col: Dungan to this—Smith in his
history says he saw the uneasiness of the people on the
east end of Long Island where he first landed. The
people being ruled in an Arbitrary manner by the Dukes
Governours who were (like himself) mostly Roman-
Catholics were disaffected to the Government. Smith
frequently mentions the Long Island representation
which was presented to the General Assembly at Hartford about the time of the Revolution in England when
16

they petitioned to come under their Jurisdiction, I have never seen a copy of this representation it possibly may contain some Usefull information. It is very evident that the Inhabitants of E: H: were uneasy under the Dukes Governours. These Governors were mostly in poor circumstances, they demanded large sums of money of the towns & of Individuals for the purchase of their Patents. These Patents were to be renewed frequently; the Quit rents were heavy & there are instances on the east end of Long-Island where they were for a Valuable consideration lower'd by One Governour & the arrearages demanded after a long course of Years by another. The people had no remedy but by applying to the King & a Voyage there was expensive. The Colony of Conecticut no doubt were willing to have Long-Island as a part of that Colony; but at that particular time were not willing to contest the affair with King Charles 2.ᵈ who was then lately restored to the throne or with his Brother James Duke of York & Albany afterwards King James 2.ᵈ. The Inhabitants on the East end of Long Island were not sufficiently numerous to establish a Government independent of the Dukes Governours. Some extracts from the records of E: H: will show under what grievances they laboured & what the political situation of things were then. The People appear to be more at ease under Col? Nicolls administration than they were till the revolution in 1688.

"May. 4. 1671, It was voted that M.ʳ Tho: James & M.ʳ Tho: Baker of this towne have full power to treate &c with the towns of Southampton & Southold or their agents concerning procuring a Charter, and what liberties & priviledges can be procured; either for the three towns in general or for this towne in particular, or to make agreements with any person now bound for England in order there to & what these our agents shall conclude upon, We engage ourselves to the performance of the same."

"June 24. 1672, It is agreed by the Voate of the town that the act of the Justices & Deputies assembled at Southold according to order from the Governour to consider for our safety in this time of Danger & the letter that was sent by them to the Governour of their Determination that they would contribute to the repairing of the fort att Yorke if they might have the priviledges that other of his majesties subjects in these parts have & doe enjoy, It is well approved of by this town & they are willing to answer their part in the charge according to their act if the priviledges may be obtained, but noe otherways."

" E: H: at a town meeting Nov.ᵗ 15. 1674. It was voated none contradicting the same that the endeavours still to continue under the Government of Coneticutt Colony & with all speede that can bee application be made to the authoritie & Court there with respect to the Message sent to us lately from N York."   "It was also voated that Mr. Tho: James of this town to be their Representee to mete with the Representees of S: hampton & Southold: there at S: old to conclude of a message to be sent to Conecticut, & to goe over thither if they shall see cause & the other two Ministers of the other two towns see cause to go over with them to act & conclude of all matters there which may conduce for the common good of the three plantations."   " E: H: Dec.ʳ 10. 1674 Voted that two men be chosen to act in behalfe of the town with respect to the present State of things among us. Voted that this Committee have full power to act with reference to the business of N York ; or not as they see cause to act together with the Committees of S: Hampton & Southold & as application hath already been made to Kenecticutt soe also shall all lawfull endeavours bee still put forth to the Utmost for our continuance under their Government.   Voted that Leift. Tho: Talmage & John Stratton Senr. Committee in & for the behalf of this towne to act as aforesaid & that We will stand by them both persons & Estates in all their lawfull actings with the Committees of the other two towns."   " E: H: Nov.ʳ 5. 1675.   Whereas the Governor hath order'd that all Indians shall be required to abide at their respective

plantations whereupon We the Cunstable & Overseers
have ordered that noe man in this town employ any
strange Indian to goe to sea a Whaling or to work on
the shore without consent of Justices &c"

"An action entered this 19 of April 1676 to be
tryed before the Cunstable & Overseers at E: H between John Stretton Jun.ʳ Plaintiff in an action of the
case against Steven Hand & Benj: Conkling Def.ᵗ concerning a Voayge toward N York with the colors and
Commissions to the Dutch." Probably this may refer
to a Demand made by the Dutch when they took N
York in 1673 & the Magistrates & Constables were
summon'd to N York to swear allegiance to the States
General & Prince of Orange.

"E: H: Sept.ʳ 24. 1683. At a legal town meeting
there Tho: Tallmage, Lef.ᵗ John Wheeler, Ensigne Samuel Mulford & Steven Hand were chosen to meete at
Southold upon Wednesday next to joine with the Committee of the other towns in chusing two Representatives
for this riding to meet at York according to order.

"The town have also desired & chosen M.ʳ Thomas
James to goe along with our men & to advise with them
in our concerns and have impowered the persons abovementioned to joine with the rest of the Riding to give
the Representatives instructions to stand up in the Assembly for the maintenance of our priviledges & English
liberties. And especially against any writ goeing in the
Dukes name but only in his Majesties whom we only
owne as our Soveraigne; alsoe in the Towns name to
certify Captain Young that they do not send these persons in obediance to his warrant but only because we
would neglect noe opportunity to assert our own liberties."

"E: H: Dec.ʳ 28. 1683 at a towne meeting warned,
—— —— were appointed to be prizers to value
houses lands & cattle in this towne & precincts for the
gift, that is to be given to the Governour according to
order." In June 1674 it appears by the records that a
Court was held. Present M.ʳ Sam.ᵗ Willis, Cap.ⁿ John

Allyn, Captain John Howell & M⁀ John Mulford. Several persons were fined for incontinence & fornication. Willis was probably Hartford, Allyn of N Haven, Howell of S: Hampton & Mulford of E̊ H. This was during the time of the suspension of the English Government; the Dutch having taken N York the preceding year. The following resolve on the same Day the Court sat may explain the business further. "At a town meeting held at E: H June 13. 1674 The Towne by their Vote agreed to joyne with their Neighbours of Southampton & Southold to petition his Majesty that they may be continued under the Government of Keneticut and priviledged with the priviledge of their Charter & they appointed M⁀ John Mulford, M⁀ T: Baker, T⁚ Talmage, T: Chatfield, J: Conkling & R: Dayton to sign the Petition in the behalf of the towne. The towne also by their Voate granted & agreed that they would give 150 £ their proportion of the same with S: hampton & S—old to procure the answer of their petition & confirmation according as is express'd in the bill the towne gave M⁀ Willis for the payment of the same & the afores ᵈ Committee whoe are appointed to signe the petition are alsoe appointed to signe the Bill in behalf of this town of E: Hampton."

The Duke of York soon after or about this time taking possession of the Colony it being delivered up by the Dutch by treaty & Sir Edmund Andross appointed his Governour it is probable that this attempt to come into the jurisdiction of Conecticut was again frustrated." By M⁀ Willis who I take to be a Gentleman from Hartford in office coming over it is not improbable but what this desire to be annexed to that Colony was agreeable to those in office there.

" The following resolves have reference to the Dutch it being soon after N York was taken by them in Aug. 73.

" E: Hampton Aug. 16. 1673, whereas We the inhabitants do understand that we are diserted of our present Government: and are in fear of some sudden & present Danger of being surprized or plundered.

1. We joyntly agree .. that the Military officers shall discipline & put Us in a posture of War for our defence & they are to take others into counsell &c .

2. That the present military laws shall be in force.

3. That if an Enemy doe assault Us, We desire that all lawfull means of treaty may be used; that they be not provoked to make spoile of Us, or what we *have*."

To the above extracts it may not be amiss to add a few more from the records of the town; these refer to the state of Public affairs in the Colony; chiefly to the affair of Cap.ⁿ Leisler's Usurpation of the Government which at that time divided the Citizens of this State into two parties more inveterate against each other than any two parties have been since. The Revolution —which took place in this country as well as in England about 1689 & the Death of Leisler after his condemnation under Governour Sloughter restored the colony to tranquillity. Perhaps a Representative Government which they began to enjoy just before this time agreeable to their requests promoted the peace & prosperity of the Colony.

"E: Hampton May 19, 1686. It is agreed by the Proprietors of the town assembled together; that whereas there is a warrant sent for four Men to appear at York to answer to what shall be laid against them & conceiving that it may have reference to Public affairs of this town or the Proprietors thereof they have agreed that those four mentioned in the Warrant are empowered to look out at whom & abroad for to get in readiness all the evidence they can for to strengthen themselves for the defending their right & Interest concerning our lands & the Proprietors have agreed that Lieft.^t John Wheeler & Steven Hand are to goe up to Keneticut to get what evidence may be had in reference to their protecting us in the time of the last Dutch War & to get what advice and help may be for the defending our Cause & Interest & the Proprietors are to be at the charge of it."

" April 27. 1689. The Inhabitants of this towne of

E: Hampton having this morning heard of strange changes & alterations of things in the Country ; & it being reported that some people are up in arms for their safety and preservation : This towne hath by a Major vote agreed that M.ʳ Samuel Mulford shall remayn in his place of being Justice for Civill power for the keeping the peace & Welfare of the town & likewise Captain John Wheeler & Lief.ᵗ Sam.ˡ Mulford shall remayne in the same place they were in formerly for to command the Militia as occasion may serve for the well being & defence of the Place & that untill further order. Alsoe Mr. Samuel Mulford & Cap.ᵗ John Wheeler are appointed by this towne to goe to Southold to meete with the Committee of the other towns of this County there to consider of things that may conduce to the Wellfare of these parts of the Country, in this Day of Calamitie.

"And this towne doth empower these Men above specified to act with the rest of the towns of this County as shall be thought most for our safety & this towne doth engage themselves to stand by them in the same."

"May 8.ᵗʰ 1689. This Towne of E: H: being assembled to-gether this Day upon occasion of tidings that is come from Yorke, understanding the people in those parts are much dissatisfied that the fort there is command'd by such as whose faithfulness may bee questioned in this exigencie of time & for help thereof. This town consider'd of the state of things as it now standeth & doe apprehend it needfull with our neighbour towns that some soldiers might goe up to Yorke from these parts to bee helpfull for to reduce that place that soe it might be better secured for the safety & Defence of the Country & for that end severall persons are now gone up ; as alsoe the Inhabitants of this towne perceiving that those that were in authority for Civill & Military affairs severall of them conceiving that they cannot act with safety now, by their late Commissions & the Inhabitants conceiving it dangerous if not destructive to be whollie left every one to his own will therefore they

have agreed by a Major Vote none openly opposing the
same that there be five men appointed by the town for
to act & determine of such things that may be for the
Welfare of the place, & that the five Men be ————
————, & the Inhabitants doe engage to stand by them
in these their actings and conclusions "

"E: H: June 18. 1689.   At a town Meeting warned
& assembled together it is agreed that Steven Hand &
Capt.ⁿ J: Wheeler are to goe to Southampton on the
20ᵗʰ of this Instant to meete with the Committee of the
County towns for to consider what may be done for the
good of the County in restoring this County to their
former liberties in respect of our coming under Kenec-
ticut Government & these two men are empower'd to
act & conclude with the rest of the Committee of the
towns for this end that soe we may be reduced to the
same state as wee were in, in the Year 1660 according
to the late act of Parliament.   And for the business of
Yorke we doe empower these two Men above mentioned
that they act with the rest of the Committee of this
County if they see cause."

"E: H. Sepr 9ᵗʰ 1689, Whereas not long since there
was a letter sent from N York by Cap.ⁿ Liesly to this
towne & Southampton that he the Cap.ⁿ aforesaid hath
some knowledge of some hundreds of Pounds of money
that is in the hands of two Men that are or were in
Authority at York which was paid by severall towns
& Counties of this Province as being of the late taxes
that was laid upon the Province by Governour Dungan
that then was: And Captain Liesly informeth Us that
if he had but orders from the towns or Counties about
it, & the sums of money that was paid by the towns &
their receits for the same he would do what he could
for the receiving & securing of the aforesaid money;
Whereupon Mr. Samuel Mulford with some of the
trustees of this towne considering of the premisses & the
town could not conveniently be called together at present did in behalf of the towne send to Captain Liesly
& impower him to receive & secure the same; the towne

doth this Day approve of what was done by Mr. Mulford & others."

"E H. Jany 23^d 16$\frac{8\ 9}{9\ 0}$. Whereas this towne hath received a letter from the towne of Southampton about the 22^d of this Instant whereby they give Us to understand that some intelligence in writing is come to them from Mr Leisler who is now Governour, or Commander 'in Chief of this Province who hath sent some order or commissions for Justices for the settling of some Government among Us & for that end they have sent to Us Desiring that our town would send two men on 24 Instant to mete with their Deputies & Southold to consider what may best conduce for the well being of these towns & County & the town doth appoint &c —— ——."

"E: Hampton Feby 16$\frac{8\ 9}{9\ 0}$. This Town being according to order given them assembled together to consider one with another what course may be taken for our reliefe in Delivering Us from this Arbitrarie power & government which We have so long groaned under and to that end it is agreed by a Major Vote of the Proprietors that a petition be drawn up to send for England; as alsoe some way may be taken to see if the rest of the towns of this County will Joyne to gether with Us to make our address to their Majesties of England for relief from this our long & heavy bondage. It was alsoe agreed the Day & time aforesaid by the Proprietors of this towne and that by a Major Vote none openly opposing the same that in case the County nor any part thereof doe see cause not to joyne with Us in this business; that then this towne in particular will Use what means We can to implore his Majesties Grace for our relief herein & that we may again be restored to the Colony of Keneticutt which formerly We did appertain unto"

"E: H: March 15. 16$\frac{8\ 9}{9\ 0}$ Whereas the Day before the Date hereof a Messenger from York came hither to inform Us from the Leif^t Gouernour Leisley of the Danger that seemeth to be approaching upon the Country & especially on this Province by the incursion of the French who hath made a very great *Massaker* in a remote part of the Country " &c

"E: H: May 3.ᵈ 1690—At a towne meeting warned it was then proposed that all those that were willing at this present juncture of time to yield themselves to Captain Leisler of N York in point of Government without any terms may express themselves by Voate—but this proposition none gave any Vote for it, but it was wholly carried in the negative. It was proposed that all that were willing to yield to the Government of N York upon terms—Viz—redress of Grievances & taking in with him the best Counsell he can may express it by a Voate; And all that are for things in matter of Government to rest as they are till we can have order from England; & in the mean time to doe the best they can to secure the Kings Interest express themselves by their Vote; these two last Votes were about equal "

July 30. 1685. Leiftenant John Wheeler & Ensigne S. Mulford were sent up to N York to meet with his Excellency Sir Edmund Andross Governour to present an address to him, they were to ask advice & assistance of the Worshipful Lief.ᵗ Co.ˡ Youngs. And in Feb.ʸ 1690/1 Upon Information of Governour Sloughters near arrivall at N York, Sam.ˡ Mulford was to take his Journey with all convenient speed to congratulate his honours happy arrival. In the towns behalf withal to make known the towns agrievances with petition for some redress.

The following is a copy of a loose paper found among the records of the town & as it refers to a remarkable event, it may be worth copying. " A Memorial & the Address of Stephen Bayley to the Inhabitants & trustees of the towne of E: Hampton April 2.ᵈ 1706—Gentlemen—Att a Committee held at the town of Southampton July 2.ᵈ 1689 by the representatives of E: Hampton Southold and Southampton then present Major John Howell, M.ʳ John Cambell & several others the trustees of Southampton, Cap.ⁿ John Wheeler, Stephen Hand for E Hampton & John Tuthill & Stephen Bayley for Southold which was in the time of the revolution & We being without any Government the result of said Committee was to petition the Gentlemen of Hartford to take these three Towns under their Protection accordingly there was a Petition drawn up & signed by six Men of said Committee & committed to the care of Us (Viz John Tuthill & Stephen Bayley) and obliged One of Us personally to deliver the same to the Gentlemen of Hartford & the Committee engaged that the charges should be defraid & I was 15 Days & brought the Return & wish you to allow me what is reasonable &c—Stephen Bayley."

The above are copied literally from the Records & serve to show the situation of Public affairs & the Republican spirit of those times. The people on the East end of Long Island did not approve of the Government under the Duke of York. After the Revolution in 1688 they probably enjoyed more liberty.

A Representation in a General Assembly was what they much desired & after 1688 enjoyed. If the Duke of York had granted this earlier it might have prevented some Uneasiness of the people & the frequent attempts made to be annex'd to the Colony of Conecticut. —There is nothing on record concerning such an event since the Petition made in July 1689. Probably encouragement was privately given them from Conecticut.—At least one would suppose the affair would not have been so frequently promoted unless they had reason to believe it would have been agreeable.

Very little is to be found on the records relative to Ecclesiastical affairs. The Original settlers of the town were what were then called Puritans. In their religious principles & Discipline answer'd nearly to the present independants or most rigid Congregationalist. Mr. Thomas James who was settled as early as 1651 was a man of information & was very usefull in the affairs of the town. He had 50£ per annum. In the same Year men were appointed to get thatch to cover a meeting house which was built 26 feet by 20 & stood where the old burying place now is. Before this house was built they held their meetings at a private house. Mr. James is buried on one side of the burying place & his head to the East contrary to the usual way. This was done, it is now said by his own order; that when he arose at the last day he might instantly face his people.

He is the only person buried in this way. Probably he is the same James mentioned in Mathers Magnalia. Nathaniel Huntting succeeded Mr. James, & the Rev^d. Doctor Samuell Buell who is now living in the 82^d year of his age succeeded him in 1745. These three Ministers have preached about 148 years.

Education engaged the attention of the original settlers of the town who in general appear from the records to have been men of good information. A School-master was hired annually by the town & upon a Dispute about 1680 whether he should receive his pay from the school or the town it was referred to the Governor & his determination was that each scholar shall pay 16/ & the remainder to be paid by the town. ·

Military affairs took up some part of the time of the first settlers of the Town. Every one capable of bearing arms was obliged to attend Divine service on the Lords Day armed. Six Days a Year they appear'd for traynings or reviews. At first their Officers were chosen by the company & confirmed by the Magistrates. They had no Captain at first; not until Governour Nicolls time. "In 1650 Every man that was fitt to bear arms was to be provided with a Gun, powder, shot, sword, worme & secure shot bag, Rest bolt & a fitt thing to carry powder in."

Their Guns were probably clumsy firelocks; their Rest bolts were to rest them on when they fired.

Match locks had then gone out of Use, flints are enumerated among the articles that were not to be sold the Indians. · It appears from ·the records that the business of killing Whales at the South side of the town

in the Atlantic Ocean was regularly followed by the
town & the profitts of the Whale divided among the
Inhabitants in proportion to their rights in the town as
Original Purchasers. Every one was obliged to assist
exeepting Mr. James & Mr. Lyon Gardiner who were
excused by the town on condition of paying so much
strong liquor. But as soon as their lands & stock required much attention; this business was carried on
with profitt by Individuals. A certain part of the Oyl
& bone was claimed for the Kings Use; this was a discouragement to the fishery. In 1716 Sam!. Mulford of
E H went to England to petition the King to give up
his tenth; he accomplished this business to the great
satisfaction of the Whalemen in Suffolk County. Mr.
Smith in his history of the State of N York says he
went with a view of getting the then Governour removed at the request of a party who were opposed to
the Governour. He did not obtain his end. He came
from N York and embarked with secrecy from the east
end of Long Island for Boston & then to England.
Probably he might be in fear of being stopd by the
opposite party if they got information of his business in
England.

Smith does not speak very favourably of this Mulford—a Representative from Suffolk County.

He was a man of an original genius of good judgement but of an odd turn, he was a native of E: Hampton & is the same person who is said to have been ex-
pelled the house for saying it was governed by the
Devil but readmitted on explaining his meaning which
was that the house was directed by the Albany members, they by Col: Schuyler, he by the Mohawk Indians,
and they by the Devil.

Nothing more than usual for all country towns has
taken place in E. Hampton for this century past. Remote from their Capitol, they have lived plain Agricul-
tural lives & generally happy, excepting a few years at
first few controversies in law happened. The magistrates have been respected & generally have discouraged

lawsuits. Since the Revolution in 1688 perhaps there have not been more than two lawsuits on an average per Annum. Since the first settlement of the town to this Day they have considered themselves as good Republican citizens. The original settlers of the town were not fond of titles; only five persons have the title of Mr. for thirty years. Goodman & Goodwife or Goody were the appellations they gave each other. Generally speaking the people are frugal, industrious & hospitable. Before the War offices of honor & profit were generally bestowed upon those that were of the Church of England or at least for a high toned Government. The Governour was directed in his appointments to office by some favourite of his in the County who was not always the most respectable person. This was too much the case in every County of the Province. The town of E. Hampton now contains about 1400 Inhabitants; this has been about the Usual number for a greater part of this Century. On the 1 of Jany. 1792 Doctor Buell preached to his people a half century sermon which has been published; he had in 50 years christened 1600 persons and there had died 989. People are continually removing to the new countries from this place; which accounts for the Difference between the births & deaths. The inhabitants being all of the Presbyterian religion attend his meeting; a regular record of the births or baptisms & Deaths is kept. The place is healthy and favorable to longevity. There are about —— die annually on an average. Several have reached their hundredth year. Excepting children who die in the Month, Consumptions, fevers & old age carry off the stage the greatest part of the Inhabitants. Consumptions probably do not abound so much here as in places remote from the Sea. The town being near the Ocean enjoys a cool air from it in the Summer & in the Winter it is not so cold as it is on the Continent adjacent. The snow lies but a short time. Thunder is not so frequent as it is back in the country; especially in the mountainous parts of the Country.

The soil is a loam with a little sand; & sand with a small quantity of loam. A greater part of the township is of a sandy soil; in a wet season it grows Indian corn well. Wheat is more liable to be killed with the severe cold of Winter when the snows is gone than it is to be blasted or mildewed. Rye will answer to soe later than Wheat and is often soed after a crop of Indian corn is taken off in October. Formerly farmers raised more grain per acre than they do now notwithstanding they now till their lands better and use fish and other manures more. Their lands were cropt too much at first, and using but little manure are now poor compared to what they were—formerly too they had better crops of corn and grain from their new cleared lands for then the wood was of little value for the New York & Rhode Island marketts was burned to ashes on the land. There is *communibus annis* about as much grain raised in the town as is consumed by its Inhabitants. Barley would answer well on their loamy lands. Very little is raised now; when the town was first settled a great deal of beer was made with Malt & with hops. But the crops now are Indian corn, flax wheat and oats. The more Philosophical farmers are continually making improvements in Agriculture but many of these improvements are lost from not being minuted down at the time. All the people of the town may be said to live by their Agriculture for the greater part of the Mechanics raise their own provisions. The business of tanning leather and making shoes is carried on by a considerable number; but not upon so large a plan as at Lynn in Massachusetts from which place E. H. was originally settled. There are very few fruit trees in the town; the Sea winds probably damage them but the experiment has not been fairly tried, they do not pay so much attention to the trees as they require & consequently the trees do not flourish. The Oak is the prevailing species of timber, pines grow on the sandy land. But the Woods on this part of Long Island is disappearing, thousands of cords are annually cut down in this county for sale.

If it were not for the vast forests of pine trees on Long Island it would be soon destitute of Wood.

. The farmers sometimes use oxen & sometimes horses for the draught & frequently both in the same team horses are more expensive but are a quicker team to work than oxen. Oxen will draw heavier loads when harnessed than when yoked. A singular custom prevails among a few farmers in this place. Cows are used in the yoke without spaying them. This custom prevails in some parts of Europe, but in most places they are spayed and are then said to make better cattle to work than Oxen. This custom began during the Revolutionary War ; the people in .the east end of Long Island who did not remove suffered a great deal from the British, besides being plundered from Connecticut, and having a heavy back tax to pay when the war ended. About the time that Sir Willm Erskine was stationed at the east end of Long Island ; Governor Tryon demanded of the people all their horses & Oxen that were fit for the British service, necessity obliged the farmers to get in their grain, hay wood &c with their cows for the want of oxen & horses which were continually liable to be called for, a few continue in the habit but it is only by a few small farmers and it is not thought to be a laudable plan. Beef & flaxseed are the principal articles for exportation among the farmers. Till within about thirty years Boston has been the place for a markett for this part of the Country—New York is now. The people are more properly Graziers than farmers, they raise large droves of cattle & sheep for sale ; but very little else except flaxseed & cord wood, the wood will soon be done unless it be preserved by Legislative authority. The Droves of cattle and flocks of sheep are during the Summer season pastured on Montock : which contains about 8,000 acres of good land. This land is owned by a number of persons ; and the pasturing of stock is according to shares that Individuals hold and is under good regulations which are carried into effect by three hired keepers of the stock. Besides a fatting field for 500 head of cattle there in this tract

of land —— sheep —— stock cattle and about ——
horses.

It is one of the largest tracts of land in the United
States that is pastured by ——. On this land there
are now living about —— persons who are the remains
of the Montock tribe of Indians, they have a right to
cultivate a large tract of this land; but their idle dispositions and savage manners prevent the most of them from
living comfortable altho' the soil is easily tilled & good.
Rum has reduced them from a very powerful tribe to a
few persons, they are continually disappearing. As
they say the pure old Indian blood does not run in all
their veins; it is corrupted by the black and white men,
fifty years ago there were ——. In the year 17—
Sir Willm Johnson spent six weeks with this tribe
his business was of a private nature. During the American War these Indians were friends to the British Government; they frequently detected Deserters from the
British troops at Southampton. To gain over these Indians as he had others might have been his business.
He doubtless foresaw the approaching contest.

There are now only four or five who speak the Indian
language; it is the same as the Nianticks of Lyme &
Moheags of Norwich on the adjacent continent. The
language is low and soft when compared to that of the
five nations. This language was probably spoken by all
the Long Island Indians.

Wayandance was the Sachem of this tribe when the
English first came to these parts, he was a friend to
them and died in 16—, and left his son the young
Sachem Wyonkombone in the care of his good friends
Lieftenant Lyon Gardiner and David Gardiner of the
Isle of Wight who were appointed Guardians to the
Young Prince. Wyonkombone died about 16—, & the
tribe elected another Sachem. Some Indian Deeds for
Montock on record in E. H., signed by the "Sachem
& his Counsellors" speak of the English about 16— "as
their very good friends and allies and having relieved
Us from the sore Distresses and Calamities which had

17

befallen Us by reason of the cruel opposition and Violence of our most deadly enemie Nimeecraft Sachem of
Narragansett whose crueltie hath proceeded so far as to
take away the lives of many of our dear friends &
relations &c &c." The Moheags &c of the Continent
were the same tribe as the Montocks; They speak the
same language with a little variation. When New England was first settled a war prevailed between the Narragansetts and the Block Island Indians on one part &
the tribes about the country where Groton, N. London,
Lyme &c. now are with the Long Island Indians their
friends on the other part. This War continued till
about 1675 when all the Indians laid aside their Wars
with each other to join the general combination to extir-
pate the English. The Indians by this time had become
used to firearms.

During the War between the Indians the Montock
tribe received a heavy blow from the Block Island Indians who were allies to the Narragansetts. The War-
riors of both tribes set out in their large War Canoes on
the same night to surprise and kill each other. Block
Island is about 21 miles to the Eastward of Montock
point. It was in the Summer Season and at the full of
the moon. They met each other about half way; the
Block Island Indians first saw the others at a distance
to the Westward in the Glade of the Moon while the
light of the moon which was in the same direction prevented their being seen by the Montock Indians. The
former faced about, returned and drew up their canoes
on the Island; the Montock Indians landed and fell into
the ambush that was laid for them; while one party was
killing the Montock Indians the other was staving their
canoes & killed such as attempted to fly to the water for
safety. The Montock Indians were nearly all killed a
few were protected by the English and brought away.
The Sachem was taken and carried to Narragansett, he
was made to walk on a large flatt rock that was heated
by building fires on it, he walked several times over it
singing his death song, but his feet being burned to the

Bones he fell and they finished the tragical scene as is usual for Savages. The Montock tribe soon after removed to the White people at E. H. town and lived several years.

They hold their lands of the White people that are proprietors of Montock by particular agreements, Altho' they sold their lands to the English 130 or 140 years ago in the most incontestable manner, they are not satisfied with the bargain that was made & the pay they received, they have a thousand acres of land to improve among them, their priviledges are more than they improve. If they ever sell their right it must by their agreements that they have made be sold to the Proprietors of Montock and no others. Many of these Indians get their living by whaling at sea, or from the shore at Montock. They are good Whalemen. On Montock there several ponds which abound with Fish, oysters &c. &c. One of these ponds is so deep that no bottom has been found with a line of — fathom. It is called the Money Pond from the report of the Pirate W^m. Kidd's having sunk two chests of money in it about 1699; when he was at the East end of Long Island. Near this Pond by the North side of the Island is a medicinal spring of water, it is exceeding cold and is continually boiling like a pott. If one might judge from the taste one would suppose it flowed from over a bed of Iron Ore. The valuable properties of this spring have never been ascertained from experiments; the Native Indians say that drinking the water is a remedy for common colds & good in consumptive complaints. It is within a few yards of the salt water at the shore.

The land on Montock is more hilly than in the other parts of the town. There are no flies to trouble the stock while grazing on the land. The use of this tract of land is a very great advantage to the Inhabitants of E. Hampton.

The licentiousness that prevailed during the war has had a tendency of making the people more lax in their morals & more profane perhaps.

The people are all Presbyterians and universally attend the Calvinistic meeting of D.ʳ Buell; Voltaire & Tom Paine have some admirers; but as they had not ingenuity & confidence enough to substitute a better system of Religious Principles than that of our Savior; they have not a great many admirers. Education engaged the attention of the Original settlers of the town, a free school was then established. The Gentlemen having received their education in England were men of information & endeavoured to educate their children as well as a new settled Country would permit. In 1784 the Academy was built by Individuals at the expense of 1000 £. It has been incorporated by the Regents of the University. It has the name of Clinton Academy, it is as flourishing as one would expect considering that now there are so many similar Institutions. But there may be many improvements made here as well as in other places in Manufactures, Agriculture, Learning and Religion which will no doubt in due time take place.

FINIS

II.

NOTES AND MEMORANDUMS CONCERNING GARDINERS ISLAND WRITTEN IN MAY 1798 BY JOHN LYON GARDINER THE PRESENT PROPRIETOR OF THAT ISLAND AT THE REQUEST OF THE REV.ᴰ SAMUEL MILLER OF N. YORK.

The Isle of Wight known now more Commonly by the name of Gardiners Island lies on the North East part of Gardiners Bay. A line drawn from Oyster pond point to Montock light house which would be nearly on East & West line will intersect the low sand beach which extends N W.ˡʸ from Gardiners three miles towards Plum Island. The end of this beach is called

Gardiners Point and the distance from it to Plum Island is six miles.

The length of Gardiners Island from S. E. to N. W. is 7½ miles, besides Ram Island which belongs to it on the South part. The Island containes about 3300 acres of very good soil including the beaches & four fish ponds. The shape of the Island is very irregular and the N. E. side is rocky, where the banks are high and steep. The land is caving away continually by frost, heavy rains & the sea beating against the banks. The family mansion is on the S. W. side of the Island : from it to the Long Island shore it is 3 miles & to the Fire place which is the usual landing is a S. W. course. The original Indian name was Manchannock pronounced by the neighboring Montock tribe of Indians Man-shon-o-noc which according to the information of George Pharaoh the Chief and the oldest of that tribe signifies the place where a great sickness had swept away a large number of people; it was observed to this Indian that it might have been the Small pox his answer was "No, it was a great while ago, before the English came among us." It was no doubt the same great sickness mentioned by Winthrop, Hutchinson and others in their accounts of the first settlement of this country and which was considered by our ancestors as an immediate interposition of Divine Providence in their favour. The small pox by inoculation was not introduced to England by Lady Montague till April 1721 & at Boston in the same month by the Rev.d Doctor C. Mather & Doctor Boylston so that it is not probable that the contagious disease which destroyed so many natives of this country about the beginning of the last Century was the small pox. It might have been the Venereal Disease received from some persons on voyages of discovery in the same manner as the natives of the Islands in the Southern Ocean have within a few years been afflicted with the same contagious Disorder, and which from the improper method of treatment has been so peculiarly mortal among them. Perhaps an unusual scarcity of proper food might have occasioned this destruction of Mankind. Whatever this Epidemic was it prevailed among the Indians on the East end of Long Island if we may credit the tradition of the natives of Montock.

Since the prevalence of the Yellow fever in N. York and Philadelphia we can easily conceive of its greater mortality among an ignorant people who derived no assistance from any who deserved the name of Physicians. Notwithstanding this sickness the Native Indians were numerous on this and the neighbouring Islands when the English first settled here. The soil was so easy to cultivate, that they could raise, corn, beans, pumpkins &c., without much labour; scale & shell fish could be procured at any time, besides these Islands doubtless afforded plenty of game. The Indians were probably numerous in proportion as they could procure the means of living. Eleazer Millar Esqʳ who died a few years ago aged 92 who was a very intelligent Gentleman & who was one of the Members of the Assembly for Suffolk County for a number of years; when a young man asked a very old Indian whether the Indians were numerous on the East end of Long Island when the English first came; placing his hand on the ground his answer was if you can count the spires of grass you could count the Indians that were living when I was a Boy. They were then probably destitute of anything to intoxicate themselves with, unless Tobacco answered this end, until the White people introduced Rum; this and other causes have been destroying them, so that they have now nearly disappeared. As soon as they got the taste of spirits they endeavoured to procure it more than provisions for themselves and families.

There are not at present any Indians living on this Island. The remains of them a few years ago joined the Montock tribe. This tribe is now become small & is a mixt breed of Indians; some White men (mere Vagabonds) having gendered with them, there are as the right Indians say but a few of them that have the pure old Indian blood in them. Very few of them can speak the Indian language. This language is the same as that that is now spoken by the Nianticks, the Moheags &c. of the adjacent continent. In a few years more it will be gone forever. When this country was first settled Hutchinson says that a war prevailed between the Pequods and their friends the Long Island Indians (who were a warlike and more than common savage like nation) on the one part and the Narragansetts who were a more mild tribe & engaged principally in the manufacture of Wampum. The Massachusetts on one side & the Connecticut people on the other urged them on till both tribes were much reduced, but they laid aside their enmity & entered the General combination about 1675 against all the White people. Governor Andros sent an armed sloop about this time to this Island to protect it; David Gardiner the second Proprietor being fearful that the Indians would put their threats in execution: who having acquired the use of Fire arms had become more formidable.

But it does not appear that any damage was done by them at this time. Lion Gardiner the first owner of the Island purchased it of the Indians as appears from an original grant from James Farrett Gentleman Deputy to the right Honourable the Earl of Sterling. The original grant is in the possession of the present Proprietor of this Island; it is dated 10th March 1639, and is on record in the town of East Hampton. As a curiosity it is copied & [annexed] to these memorandums.

Tradition among the Montock Indians informs Us that the Island was bought for a large black Dog, a Gun & Ammunition; some Rum, a few Dutch blankets, &c. These articles were in the estimation of the natives of incomparable value, they doubtless reserved to themselves the privilege of hunting, fishing & planting their Indian corn. Wiandance was probably the Great Sachem on the East end of Long Island in 1639 when Lion Gardiner settled on this Island. Wiandance died about 1660. He appointed Lion Gardiner and his son David Gardiner Guardians to the young Sachem Wionkombone. The Indian deeds on record in the town of East Hampton that are signed by Wionkombone & his mother the Seunksq Squa are mentioned to have been done with the consent of Lion & David Gardiner who sign the same as Guardians. This Wionkombone died about the time he was 22 (about 1661).

The word Seunksq in the Montock language signifies any thing that belongs to the Sachem or Royal family, as widow, children, &c. During the lives of Lion, David & John Gardiner the three first Proprietors of this Island, the Indians were considerable numerous & doubtless they all three understood the Indian language as the fourth owner did. They were hired then to plant & till the Indian corn; being thought good hands for that business. John Gardiner the 3ᵈ owner employed a good many of the Montock Indians to kill Whales for him in the Atlantic on the South side of Montock.

In Governour Winthrops Journal of transactions &c. page 91 the arrival of the first owner of this Island is mentioned in the following words: " Here arrived a small bark of 25 tons [November 28ᵗʰ 1635]

Nov. 28 1635.

sent by the Lords Say &c with one Gardiner an expert engineer or workbase and provisions of all sorts to begin a fort at the mouth of Connecticut. She came through many great tempests, yet through the Lords great Providence her passengers and goods all safe. Mʳ Winthrop had sent four days before a bark with carpenters and other Workmen to take possession of the place (for the Dutch intended to take it) and to raise some buildings." Under the name of the Lieutenant he is mentioned in this Journal see pages 109, 120 &c. On the records of the town of E. Hampton he is sometimes called the Lieutenant & sometimes by the name of Mister or Master. He lived in E. Hampton several years from about 1652 to 1657. He was chosen one of the three Magistrates or townsmen by the Inhabitants of that town for several years. By the records of the town it appears he was a man of some note & respectability there.

By the records of the town it appears that Jeremy Veale & Anthony Waters had this Island (which is called Manchannock) under their care, they are styled the Lieutenants farmers. This was for five or six years. Probably when David Gardiner the second owner returned from England about 1658 his father Lion Gardiner who lived till 1663 came again on here to reside. David married in June 1657 in the Parish of Margarett in Westminster. In a bible printed in England in the year 1599 in Queen Elizabeths reign which is now in the family & was probably brought out of England by Lion Gardiner is the following writing in a plain bold hand.

" In the Year of our Lord 1635 July 10th came I, Lion Gardiner and Mary my Wife from Worden a town in Holland where my Wife was born being the Daughter of one Derike Wilamson derocant her Mothers name Hachin bastians her Aunt sister of her Mother was the wife of Wouter Leonardson Old Burger Measter dwelling in the hofston ouer against the broeroer in the unicorns head, her brothers name was ——— Gearetson also old Burger Measter Wee came from Woerden to London and from thence to New England and dwelt At Say brooke forte four Years of which I was Commander, and there was born to me a Son in 1635 April the 29 the first born in that place : And in 1638 A Daughter was born to me called Mary ; August the 30th and then went to an Island of mine own which I bought of the Indians called by them Manchonake by us the Isle of Wight and there was born another Daughter named Elizabeth Sept 14, 1641 She being the first child born their of English parents."

His setting out from Woerden on 10 July according to his account might very well agree with Winthrops account of his arriving on 29 Novr 1635 but does not correspond with his son David being born at Saybrook 29 April 1635 the same year. Either Lion came over in 1634, or if in 1635 his son David was not born till 29 April 1636. I think there is a mistake for David could not be born in April 29, 1635 if Lion did not come from Woerden till July 1635 the same year.

This David was the first White child born at Saybrook & as this place was settled as soon or sooner than Hartford, Windsor & Weathersfield it is probable that he was the first white child born in the State of Connecticut. About the time of the Revolution in 1688, he went to the General Assembly of Connecticut on business for the people of the east end of Long Island and died it is said at Hartford: if so he was about 53 years old.

The remains of the fort at Saybrook which was built in 1634, or 1635 are yet to be seen & some of the old cannon which for several years served to keep the Indians in awe are now said to be buried under the meeting house in Saybrook. George Fenwick, Esq: succeeded Lion Gardiner in the command of the fort at Saybrook; he held the fort & lands in trust for Lords Say & Seal, &c. till Dec' 5, 1644 when he sold the title of the Lords to the Connecticut people. These Noble men & others finding that they were like to enjoy civil & religious liberty in Old England gave over the thoughts of removing to this Country. The fort at Saybrook with the buildings &c, took fire in the Winter of 1647 while under the command of Capt Mason & was of no further use in keeping the Indians in awe.

This G. Fenwick was afterward a Col! in the Parliament army & is probably the same who was one of the Judges of King Charles 1st. Whether Lion Gardiner who is styled the Lieutenant by Governour Winthrop in his Journal & by the records of E. Hampton derived this title from his being the second in Command at the fort (M: Winthrop being appointed Governour by the Lords) or from the circumstance of his being an officer in the Dutch service is not now known.

Governour Winthrop calls him an expert engineer

or work base.   A Base man then signified an engineer.*   It is now said that he was from Scotland.   He
probably went to Holland to seek his fortune as a
Soldier in the Wars of that country, or he might go for
the sake of enjoying that liberty which Charles the first
in endeavouring to establish Episcopacy in Scotland
about 1634 seemed determined to destroy.   It is said
that Col. James Gardiner who was killed in Scotland in
1745 was of the same family.   Lion Gardiner probably
died in 1663 & might have been a man in years; he
was probably buried in E. Hampton.   His oldest son
David it is said died at Hartford in 1688, was likely
buried there, aged about 53, *his* oldest son John died in
N. London 1738, by a fall from a young horse, aged 78
years & was buried there; *his* oldest son David died on
this island in 17—, aged — & was buried here.   His
oldest son John died in 1764 & was buried here aged
50 years.   *His* oldest son David died in 1774, aged 36
years, was buried here.   John Lyon Gardiner the
writer of these memorandums was born Nov. 8, 1770
& is the seventh owner of the Island in regular de-
scent being the sixth oldest son counting from Lion Gardiner.

The grant from James Farrett agent to Wm Alexander Earl of Sterling in 1639 is the oldest grant for
this Island the Patents were taken out from 1665 under
Governour Nicolls to 1714.   The Quit rent was five
pounds per Annum which has been paid from 1640 to
about 1789 excepting for a few years during the Revolutionary War which with the 14 years commutation
amounts to nearly 2000$ for Quitrents.   During the
last of the last century it was for a valuable consideration lowered from £5 to 5 . but in the beginning of this
Century the difference between 5£ & 5/ was demanded
by the then Governour.

In Governour Dongans time it was erected into a
manor & Lordship & till the Revolutionary war the
several proprietors by common custom had the title of

[* *Werkbaas* is a Dutch word which means workmaster.]

Lord. The present Proprietor is better pleased with the liberty both civil & religious which he enjoys in common with his Countrymen & fellow citizens than with any empty titles whatever.

In the town of Southold about 14 miles from this & nearly opposite Shelter Island is a small settlement known from time immemorial by the name of Sterling; it derives its name from the Earl of Sterling who had a grant from Charles 1st of all the Islands from Hudsons River to Cape Cod. He afterwards conveyed his title to these islands to James Duke of York & Albany. By the records of the town of East Hampton it appears that James Farrett Deputy to the right Honourable Earl of Sterling had purchased Shelter Island (Menhansett) of Unkenthie the Sachem & the said Farrett by Deed dated 18 May 1641 conveyed to Stephen Goodyear of N. Haven the said Island &c. & said Indian deed.

It does not appear that the original settlers of the town had any deed from this James Farrett, but it appears from writers in those times that he claimed the whole of Long Island from the Earl of Sterling. At the close of the last century & the beginning of this the Pirates were troublesome on the American Coast. Several of them visited this Island. Wm Kidd was here about 1698 he soon after was taken in the town of Boston, sent to England and hung for murder. While he was at this Island he took what provisions &c. &c. he pleased. He left on here a considerable quantity of treasure, the place where he left it is yet pointed out. He left it in the care of John Gardiner the 3d. Proprietor to whom he showed the place where he put it & told him if he never called for it he was welcome to it; if he ever called for it & it was missing he would take his head or his sons. When Kidd delivered himself up at Boston by his papers it was known what he left on this Island and an express was sent down from the Earl of Belmont who was Governour of this Colony & of Massachusetts for John Gardiner to carry to Boston the property Kid left here. He went agreeable to orders & delivered up the property to the Commissioners that were appointed to receive & secure the Treasure, Goods & Merchandize imported by Captn. Willm Kidd anno 1699.

From a Manuscript account now in the possession of John Lyon Gardiner of the Isle of Wight dated July 1699 it appears that Samuel Sewall, Nathan^l Byfield Jeremiah Dummer & Andrew Belcher were appointed to receive and secure the treasure &c. imported in the sloop Antonio Cap^n. Wm Kidd late Commander after mentioning various articles of treasures such as Gold, Silver, precious Stones, Silver Candlesticks, pieces of Silk &c. &c. received of Duncan Campbell &c &c. it goes on to mention sundries received of Mr John Gardiner on 17 July 1699. Viz. $747\frac{3}{4}$ ounces of Gold Bars and gold dust, $817\frac{1}{2}$ ounces of Silver & $4\frac{7}{8}$ ounces of precious Stones, $12\frac{1}{2}$ ounces of unpolished stones one piece of Cristal & beazer Stones &c.

This was said to be demanded for the Kings use. When Kid left the property here it was probable he intended to call for it & he might then have paid for the property he took from here.   Altho Mr John Gardiner was under the necessity of keeping it a perfect secret for fear of Kid's putting his threat in force; yet he was probably glad to be relieved of a treasure which doubtless afforded some anxiety on many accounts.   Perhaps the King was no better on account of this treasure being delivered up; than if it had remained to this time in the bog or swamp where Kid put it. The place has been visited several times by Pirates; about 100 years ago one of them cut with their swords the hands of the then owner John Gardiner very badly.

A person was sent off from E. Hampton to the Governour at N. Y. who had a ship sent down but the Pirate. had sailed the Day before having received information of the ship that was coming by means of an Indian from Montock.   This about 1725. ; People who are credulous and anxious to get rich soon are to this year searching for treasure on this Island that they vainly imagine to be still hid here. Receipts as they are styled are forged & sold by some idle fellow for a small sum.

In August 1775. This place was plundered of 70 head of fatt cattle 1200 sheep &c. &c. by General Gage's order and were carried to Boston by a large number of vessels under convoy for the use of the British army in that place. They landed several hundred armed men here and took what they pleased. Necessity obliged these British Officers and soldiers to turn Sheep-stealers.

About the Summer of 1778 it was robed of considerable property by two British Refugee sloops under the protection of a Frigate. In 1780 much damage was done to the timber &c by Admiral Arbuthnot's fleet. After the fatt stock was taken to Boston in '75 all the remainder of the stock was taken off by order of the County Committee & sold for Continental money. Near the close of the War the Island was plundered by small armed boats from Connecticut. Nothing but a few horses were kept on the Island during the War & part of these the British army under Sir Wm Erskine demanded. When the peace of 1783 took place this Island which did in 1775 Rent for 1000£ was gone to Decay. The buildings, fences, stock of cattle, sheep &c were gone and the Gentleman who had the care of the Estate was under the necessity of borrowing money to to pay a very heavy back tax. The Gentleman who then had care of it had his own estate exempt on account of his being in the State of Connecticut during the War. The owner of the Island was an infant under age. Col. David Mulford one of the Executors died in 1778 with the small pox which he took in N. York while endeavouring to get some pay for the stock Col! Willard took away in 1775 to Boston. Col! Gardiner died in 1782.

The soil of this Island is good & is very natural for Wheat & White clover. The timber is of various kinds mostly large White oak timber. The land is well watered with brooks, springs & ponds a considerable quantity of Iron bog ore & various kinds of clay may be procured. Beef, Cheese, Wheat & Wool are the staple articles. The Island is under the direction of the owner with an overseer. In the summer season it supports 400 head of horned cattle, 100 horses 2500 sheep including calves colts & lambs. There is a Dairy from 60 or 70 cows.

Till within thirty years Boston was the place of Markett for this Island & this part of Long Island. N. York is now the market. Fish of various kinds may be procured at almost any time. For fertility of soil & for various advantages it is not perhaps exceeded by many farms in the United States.

FINIS.

COPY OF JAMES FARRETT'S GRANT TO LION GARDINER.

Know all men whom this present writing may concern, that I James Farrett of Long Island Gent. Deputy to the Right Honourable the Earle of Sterling, Secretary for the Kingdom of Scotland, Doe by these presents in the name and behalf of the said Earle of Sterling and in my own name also as his Deputy as it doth or may concern myself, Give & grant free leave & liberty to Lion Gardiner. his heirs executors & assigns to enjoy that Island which he hath now in possession, Called by the Indians Manchonack, by the English the Isle of Wight, I say to enjoy both now and forever. Which Island hath been purchased before my coming from the Ancient Inhabitants the Indians Nevertheless though the said Lion Gardiner had his Possession first from the Indians before my coming, yet is he now contented to hold the tenor & title of the Possession of the aforesaid Island from the Earle of Sterling or his successors whomsoever, who hath a grant from the King of England under the great seal of the aforesaid Kingdom. Bee it known therefore that I the said James Farrett Doe give & hath given free liberty & power to the said Lion Gardiner his heirs Executors & Assigns & their successors forever to enjoy the possession of the aforesaid Island : to build & plant thereon as best liketh them and to dispose thereof as they think fitt. And also to make Execute & put in practice such Laws for

Church & Civil Government as are according to God the King and the practice of the Country without giving any account thereof to any whomsoever.

And the aforesaid Right & title both of Land and Government to Remain with & to them & their successors forever without any trouble or Molestation from the said Earle or any his Successors for now & ever. And forasmuch as it hath pleased our Royal King to give the Patton of Long Island to the aforesaid Earle of Sterling in consideration whereof it is agreed upon that the trade with the Indyons shall remain with the said Earle & his successors to dispose upon from time to time & at all times as best liketh him. Notwithstanding the said Lyon Gardiner to trade with the Indyons for Corne or any kinde of Vituals for the Use of the Plantation & no farther. And if the said Lion Gardiner shall trade in Wampum from the Indyons hee shall pay for every fadome twenty shillings; And also the said Lion Gardiner and his successors shall pay to the said Earle or his Deputies a yearly acknowledgement being the sum of five pounds (being Lawfully Demanded) of Lawful money of England or such commoditys as at that time shall passe for money in the country; & the first payment to begin upon the last of October 1643, the three former years being advanced for the use of the said James Farrett

In Witness whereof the party Have put his hand and seal the tenth Day of March 1639.

Sealed & Delivered in the presence of	JAMES FARRETT.
FFULKE DAVIS	Seal O
BENJAMIN PINE.	Seal O

NOTE.

WITCHCRAFT IN NEW YORK.

THE remarks of the writer of the foregoing *Notes and Observations* in connection with the case of Goodwife Garlick (*ante*, pp. 238, 239), however judicious in general, seem to require some additions by way of correction. Elizabeth Garlick, wife of Joshua Garlick of East Hampton, was brought before the magistrates of that town, on suspicion of witchcraft ; and the examination resulted in the order of March 19, 1657-8, to send her for trial to Connecticut, whose jurisdiction was at the same time fully recognized. Her trial took place before a Court of Magistrates, called for the purpose, in Hartford, on the 5th of May, 1658, and resulted in her acquittal. Gov. John Winthrop presided in the Court. An account of the proceedings can be found in the *Historical Magazine*, vol. vi. 53 ; and a letter printed in the *Colonial Records of Connecticut*, 1636–1665, Appx. v. p. 572, from the copy on file among the archives of that State, in the handwriting of Governor Winthrop, may complete the record of the case.

Another case is said to have occurred in 1660, when Mary Wright, of Oyster Bay, being suspected of witchcraft, was sent to Massachusetts, where, upon trial, she was acquitted of that charge, but convicted of being a Quaker, and banished. Hutchinson's account of this affair (*History of Mass.* : i. 202) furnishes no notice of the alleged witchcraft ; and her answers to the Court upon examination, as well as the punishment, indicate that she was in Massachusetts of her own accord, to give her testimony against the rulers there for their cruelty in putting Mary Dyer to death. She was one of those discharged with Wenlock Christopherson in June, 1661, and driven out of that jurisdiction. (Bishop : *N. E. Judged*, 165, part ii. 35.)

In 1665, Ralph Hall and his wife were accused of witchcraft at Brookhaven, and the cause was tried before the Court of Assizes at New York, terminating in their acquittal. The proceedings were printed by Mr. Yates in the appendix to his edition of Smith's *History of New York*, and again in the *Documentary History of New York*, vol. iv. vii. by Dr. O'Callaghan.

18

In 1670, one Katharine Harrison, of Wethersfield in Connecticut, had been indicted, tried by a jury, and found guilty of witchcraft. ⋅ But the Court refused to sentence her to death or further imprisonment, and discharged her upon payment of her just fees ; at the same time " willing her to minde the fulfilment of removeing from Weathersfield, which is that will tende most to her owne safety and the contentment of the people who are her neighbours." Thus banished from Connecticut, she came to settle in Westchester. She was immediately complained of, and presently ordered to remove, with an admonition to return to her former place of abode. Various proceedings, however, followed, upon which she was bound over to appear at the Assizes upon suspicion of witchcraft ; where she was promptly released from her obligation, with " liberty to remain in the towne of Westchester where she now resides, or anywhere else in the Government during her pleasure." *Colonial Records of Connecticut*, 1665-77 : 132. *Documentary History of New York*, vol. iv. vii.

All these proceedings were taken at common law, or under the English Statute of James I. No law against witchcraft has been found on the statute-book of New York. At the same time, there is no room for doubt that the principal clergymen then in the colony were firm believers in witchcraft, and it may fairly be presumed that far the greater portion of the community shared in their faith. Yet we are informed by Cotton Mather that the opinions of the Dutch and French Ministers of New York, furnished to Sir William Phips while the storm of delusion on the subject was raging in Massachusetts, contributed to destroy the authority of " the spectral testimony," then too much in credit there. Some interesting particulars respecting their intervention were found among the papers of the Rev. JOHN MILLER who was Chaplain to the King's forces at New York in 1692-95. Sir William Phips having become very uneasy upon the convictions and executions which had taken place within his jurisdiction, applied to the New York Ministers through Chief Justice Dudley, for their opinions and advice. Seven questions were presented for consideration, and either directly or through the other ministers, Mr. Miller's opinions also were desired.

" *Question* 1. Is it a fact that there have been witches from the beginning of the world to the present time ?

" 2. What is the true definition of a witch, and in what does his power (*formalis ratio*) consist ?

" 3. Does God justly permit the Devil to show and represent to those who are bewitched the images of innocent persons as if they were the authors of the witchcraft ?

" 4. Is previous malice and cursing to be necessarily proved in order to convict a witch ?

" 5. Is any one whose figure appears to the person bewitched, and is by him accused as the author of the witchcraft, to be adjudged guilty, and convicted of the witchcraft ?

" 6. Is the accusation alone of the party supposed to be bewitched, sufficient to prove a man who lives piously, justly, and soberly, guilty ? ·

" 7. If the person bewitched, after suffering various and heavy torments, after the paroxysm is over, appears of a strong and firm habit of body, without receiving any other damage, is it not a cause for suspicion of delusion or diabolical possession ?

In answer to the First Question, Mr. Miller asserted his belief in the actual existence of Witchcraft from the beginning of the world, taking his authority from Scripture and a variety of heathen authors.

" 2· Witchcraft is the art of torturing and destroying men, and it is an art, because it practises certain forms of incantation, uses composition from herbs, &c. : it is performed by the assistance of the Devil, otherwise it is not Witchcraft : the coöperation of the Devil is the *ratio formalis.*

" 3. The hearts of men are unknown to us ; we cannot say whether those whom we suppose to be innocent are really so ; and perhaps God permits their representation (in vision to the enchanted) that he may punish their sins, by the subsequent disgrace and punishment which they endure.

" 4. If previous malice, &c., can be proved, it will confirm the Witchcraft proved otherwise by all or the principal circumstances mentioned in the *English* statute ; but they are not necessarily to be proved, because legal proof of the circumstances expressed in the statute will suffice for the condemnation of the Witch.

" 5, 6. Men, whether they live soberly or impiously, are scarce on that account to be publickly accused, much less found guilty, because the minds of men, especially of the ignorant or depraved, can easily be and frequently are deceived by the Devil.

" 7. Since whatever the Devil himself does, or men do by his coöperation, tends to the ruin of those who are tortured, and since I understand some to be in this manner tortured, who, after the paroxysm, are cheerful, healthful and merry, I suppose them not to be maliciously enchanted by any sorcerer, but deluded by the Devil to promote the misery of mankind."

The only account we have of the opinions of the Dutch and French Ministers is that of Mather, who states that " they gave it in under their hands that if we believe no *venefick witch-craft*, we must renounce the Scripture of God, and the consent of almost all the world ; but that yet the *apparition* of a person afflicting another, is a very insufficient proof of a *witch;* nor is it inconsistent with the holy and righteous government of God over men, to permit the affliction of the neighbours, by devils in the *shape* of good men ; and that a good name, obtained by a *good life*, shall not be lost by *meer spectral accusations."*

To the record of this beneficent intervention it may not be improper to add a reference to the fact that several of these victims of persecution in Massachusetts sought and found refuge and protection in New York, until the danger was past. The historian of the Witchcraft Delusion, the Rev. Charles W. Upham, D.D., says : " The fact that when Massachusetts was suffering from a fierce and bloody, but brief, persecution by its own Government, New York opened so kind and secure a shelter for those fortunate enough to escape to it, ought to be forever held in grateful remembrance by the people of the old Bay State, and constitutes a part of the history of the Empire State of which she may well be proud." *Historical Magazine*, 2d Series, vi. 215.

V.

NEW YORK AND THE N. H. GRANTS.

COLLECTION OF EVIDENCE

IN VINDICATION OF THE

TERRITORIAL RIGHTS AND JURISDICTION

OF THE

STATE OF NEW YORK

AGAINST THE CLAIMS OF THE COMMONWEALTH

OF

MASSACHUSETTS AND NEW HAMPSHIRE

AND THE

PEOPLE OF THE *GRANTS*

WHO ARE COMMONLY CALLED

VERMONTERS.

COLLECTION OF EVIDENCE, Etc.

———◆———

N.° 1. At a Council held at Fort George in the City of New York the 3.ᵈ day of April 1750

Present

His Excellency the Hon.ᵇˡ George Clinton Cap.ᵗ Gen.ˡ &c

M.ʳ Colden	M.ʳ Murray
M.ʳ Kennedy	M.ʳ Rutherford
M.ʳ Chief Justice	M.ʳ Holland

His Excellency communicated to the Board a letter from the Hon.ᵇˡ Benning Wentworth Esq.ʳ Governor of New Hampshire dated the 17ᵗʰ November last acquainting his Excellency that he has it in Command from his Majesty to make Grants of the unimproved lands in New Hampshire Government and therefore desiring information how far North of Albany this Province extends and how many miles to the Eastward of Hudson's River to the Northward of the Massachusetts line that he may govern himself accordingly—also an extract of his Majesty's letters patent to Governor Wentworth respecting the boundaries of New Hampshire—and his Excellency having required the advice of the Board thereupon the Council humbly advise his Excellency to acquaint Governor Wentworth in answer to his said letter. That this Province is bounded Eastward by Connecticut River. The letters patent from King Charles the 2.ᵈ to the Duke of York expressly granting " All the lands from the west side of Connecticut River to the East side of Delaware bay."

N.° 2.   Portsmouth Novembᵉ 17ᵗʰ 1749.

Sir:—I have it in Command from his Majesty to make Grants of the unimproved lands within my Government, to such of the Inhabitants and others as shall apply for Grants for the same, as will oblige themselves to settle and improve, agreeable to his Majesty's Instructions.

The war hitherto has prevented me from making so great a progress as I hoped for, on my first appointment; but as there is a prospect of a lasting peace with the Indians, in which your Excellency has a great share, people are daily applying for Grants of lands in all quarters of this Government, and particularly some for Townships to be laid out in the Western part thereof, which will fall in the Neighbourhood of your Government.

I think it my duty to apprize you thereof, and to transmit to your Excellency the description of New Hampshire, as the King has determined it in my commission, which after you have considered I shall be glad you will be pleased to give me your sentiments in what manner it will affect the grants made by you or preceeding Governors, it being my intention to avoid as much as I can, consistent with his majesty's instructions, interferring with your Government.

In consequence of his Majesty's determination of the boundary's between New Hampshire and the Massachusetts, a surveyor and proper *Chainmen* was appointed to run the western line, from three miles north of Pautucket Falls, and the Surveyor upon oath has declaired that it strikes Hudson's River about eighty poles between, where Mohawk's River comes into Hudson's River, which I presume is north of the City of Albany, for which reason it will be necessary for me to be informed how far North of Albany the Government of New

York extends by his Majesty's commission to your Excellency, and how many miles to the Eastward of Hudson's River, to the Northward of the Massachusetts line, that I may govern myself accordingly. And if in the execution of the Kings commands, with respect to the lands, I can oblige any of your Excellency's friends I am allways at your service

I am with the greatest respect Sir your Excellency's

Most obedient humble Servant

B. WENTWORTH

A true Copy Exam.ᵈ

By Gw. BANYAR, P. Secrʸ

N.° 3. George the Second by the grace of God, of Great Britain France and Ireland King defender of the Faith &.ᶜ

To our trusty and well beloved Benning Wentworth Esqʳ Greeting Know you that we reposing especial Trust and Confidence in the prudence Courage and Loyalty of you the said Benning Wentworth out of our especial Grace, certain knowledge and mere Motion, have thought fit, to constitute and appoint and by these presents do constitute and appoint you the said Benning Wentworth to be our Governor and Commander in chief of our province of New Hampshire, within our dominions of New England in America, bounded on the south side, by a similar curve line pursuing the Course of Merrimac River, at three miles distance, on the north side thereof, beginning at the Atlantic Ocean and ending at a point due north of a place called Pautucket Falls, and by a straight line drawn from thence due west cross the said river till it meets with our other Governments, and bounded on the south side by a line passing up through the Mouth of Piscataqua Harbor, and up the Middle of the River, to the River of Newichwannock, part of which is now called Salmon Falls, and though the middle of the same to the Furthest Head thereof, and from thence North two degrees Westerly, untill one hundred and twenty miles be finished from the Mouth of

Piscataqua Harbor aforesaid, or untill it meets with our other Governments.

His Majesty's discription of the Province of New Hampshire, as it stands in his Excellency's commission. Given at Whitehall July the 3ᵈ in the fifteenth year of his Majesty's Reign.

Attest.ᵈ

THEODORE ATKINSON Secry.

Province of New Hampshire
  Portsmᵗ Nov. 17 1749
 New York A true Copy Examᵈ by

Gw. BANYAR P. S.

Nº 4. At a Council held at Fort George in the City of
   New York the 5ᵗʰ day of June 1750
Present
   His Excellency the Honᵇˡ George Clinton
Capᵗ Genˡ &c
  Mᵣ Colden   Mᵣ Chief Justice
  Mᵣ Kennedy   Mᵣ Murray

His Excellency communicated a letter from Governor Wentworth of the 25ᵗʰ April last in answer to his Excelʸ of the 9ᵗʰ of the same month desiring to be informed by what authority Connecticut and the Massachusetts Governments claim so far to the westward as they have settled and acquainting his Excellency that before the receit of his said letter he had by the advice of the Council granted a Township due North of the Massachusetts line of the Contents of six miles square and by measurement twenty four miles East of the City of Albany.

The Council humbly advised his Excellency to acquaint Governor Wentworth in answer to the said letter. That the claim of the Government of Connecticut is founded upon an agreement with this Government in or about the year 1684 afterwards confirmed by King William. But as to the Massachusetts settlements so far to the westward it is presumed they were first made by intrusion and since continued thro' the neglect of this Government. And that it is probable the lands within the Townships he hath lately granted or some part of them have been already granted in this Government.

Nᵒ. 5.   Portsmouth April 25ᵗʰ 1750.

Sir:—I have the honor of your Excellency's letter of the 9ᵗʰ instant before me, in which you are pleased to give me, the opinion of his Majesty's Council of your Government, that Connecticut River is the Eastern boundary of New York Government which would have been entirely satisfactory to me, on the subject of my letter, had not the two Charter Governments of Connecticut and Massachusetts Bay extended their boundaries many miles to westward of the said river; and it being the opinion of his majesty's Council of this Government, whose advice I am to take on these occasions, that New Hampshire had an equal right to claim the same extent of Western boundaries with those Charter Governments— I had in consequence of their advice before your letter came to my hands, granted one Township due North of the Massachusetts line, of the contents of six miles square, and by measurement twenty four miles East of the City of Albany presuming that this Government was bounded by the same North and South line with Connecticut and Massachusetts bay, before it met with his Majesty's other Governments.

Altho' I am prohibited by his Majesty's Commission to interfere with his other Governments, yet it is presumed, that I should strictly adhere to the limits precribed therein, and I assure you I am very far from desiring to make the least incroachment or set on foot any disputes on these points. It will therefore give me great satisfaction, if at your leisure you can inform me by what authority Connecticut and the Massachusetts Governments claim'd so far to the westward as they have settled, and in the mean time I shall desist from making any further grants on the Western Frontier of my Government, that may have the least probability of interfering with your Government.

I am your Excellency's

Most Obedient humble Serv.[t]

B WENTWORTH

A true Copy Exam[d] by

Gw BANYAR D. Secry.

N[o] 6.   New York June the 6 1750.

Sir :—I have received your letter of 25th April last, in answer to mine of the 9th of the same month respecting the Eastern boundary of this Government wherein you desire to be informed by what authority Connecticut and the Massachusetts Governments claim so far to the westward as they have settled. As to Connecticut their claim is founded upon an agreement with this Government in or about the year 1684 afterwards confirmed by King William. In consequence of which the lines between the two Governments were run and the boundaries marked in the year 1725 as appears by the Commissioners and Surveyors proceedings of record here. But it is presumed the Massachusetts Government at first possessed themselves of those lands by intrusion and thro' the negligence of this Government have hitherto continued their possessions the lands not being private property.

From the information I have there is reason to apprehend that the lands within the Township you have lately granted or part of them have been granted here.

And as my answer to your letter might probably have furnished you with objections against any grant which might interfere with this province— I am surprized you did not wait till it came to hand before you proceeded therein. If it is still in your power to recall the Grant your doing so will be but a piece of justice to this Government, otherwise I shall think myself obliged to send a representation of the matter to be laid before his Majesty.

Nº 7. At a Council held at Fort George in the City of
New York the 24ᵗʰ July 1750
Present

His Excellency the Honˡᵉ George Clinton
Capⁿ Genˡ &c

Mʳ Colden	Mʳ Murray
Mʳ Kennedy	Mʳ Rutherford
Mʳ Chief Justice	Mʳ Holland

His Excellency communicated to the Board a letter
from his Excellency Governor Wentworth of the 22ᵈ
June last advising that he had communicated his Excellᶜʸ.
letter of the 6ᵗʰ ultº to his Majesty's Council of New
Hampshire who were unanimously of opinion not to
commence a dispute with this Government respecting
the extent of Western boundary to New Hampshire
untill his Majesty's pleasure should be further known.
And accordingly the Council had advised that he should
on the part of New Hampshire make a representation
of the matter to his Majesty relying that his Excellᶜʸ will
do the same on the part of New York.

The Council humbly advised his Excellency to make
a representation of the matter to his majesty on the
part of this province, and to acquaint Governor Wentworth with such his intentions. And that it will be
for the mutual advantage of both Governments, if they
exchange copies of each others representation to his
Majesty on this head.

Nº 8. Portsmouth June 22ᵈ 1750.

Sir:—As soon as your letter of the 6ᵗʰ instant came
to hand I thought it proper to have the sense of his majestys council thereon, who were unanimously of opinion,
not to commence a dispute with your Excellency's
Government, respecting the extent of Western Boundary to New Hampshire, untill his Majestys Pleasure
should be further known, accordingly the council have
advised, that I should on the part of New Hampshire,
make a representation of the matter to his Majesty,—re-

lying that your Excellency will do the same on the part
of New York, & *that whatever shall be determined thereon, this Government shall esteem their duty to acquiesce
in without any further dispute*, which I am hopeing will
be satisfactory on that point.

When I first wrote you on this subject, I thought I
had given sufficient time to receive an answer to my
letter, before I had fixed the Day for passing the
Grant referred to in your letter, and as the persons concerned therein lived at a great distance, it was inconvenient for them to be Delayed beyond the appointed
time, I was not apprehensive any difficulty could arise
by confineing myself to the Western Boundaries of the
two charter Governments, accordingly I passed the Patent about ten Days before your favour of the 6th Jan^y
1749 came to hand.

*There is no possibility of vacateing the Grant as you
desire, but if it falls by his Majestys Determination in
the Government of the State of New York, it will be void
of course.*

I should be Glad the method I have proposed may
be agreeable to your Province, and if submitting this
affair to his Majesty meets with your approbation, I
shall upon receiveing an answer lose no time in transmitting what concerns this Province to the Proper Officers.

I am with the Greatest respect Sir Your Excellencys
most Obedient humble Servant

B. WENTWORTH

His Excellency Gov. Clinton
New York a true Copy Exm^d with the original
p .Gw. BANYAR, *Dep. Sec.*

N° 9.   New York 25th July 1750

Sir :—I have taken the sentiments of his majestys
council, on your excellencys letter of the 22^d Ult^o respecting the extent of the Western Boundary of your Government, who think it highly expedient I should lay
before his Majesty, a representation of the matter on the
part of this province, and as you purpose to do the like

on the part of New Hampshire, they are of opinion it will be for the mutual advantage of Both Governments, if we exchange Copies of each others representations on this head, if you approve of it I will send you a copy of mine accordingly.

I am

His Excellency Gov Wentworth

N.º 10. At a Council held at fort George in the City of New York 19th day Sep^t 1750

Present

His Excell^y The Honb^{le} George Clinton Capt Genl &c

Mr Colden   Mr Chief Justice
Mr Rutherford   Mr Kennedy
Mr Murray   Mr Holland

His Excellency communicated a letter from Go^r Wentworth of the 2^d Ins^t signifying that upon laying his Excellencys letter of 25th July last before his Majesty's Council of New Hampshire, it was advised, that exchanges of the representations to be made to his Majesty, for determineing the Boundaries between the two Governments, might contribute to the speedy Settlement thereof, and that he will transmit an authentic Copy of his, to his Excellency when completed.

N.º 11.   Portsmouth Sep^t 2^d 1750

Sir:—Upon my laying your favour of the 25th July before his Majesty's council, it was advised, that agreeable to your proposal, that exchanges of the representations, made by your Excellency and myself, for determineing the Boundaries between his two Governments, might contribute to the speedy settlement thereof, and without any expence on either side, I shall therefore as soon as mine is perfected transmit you an authentic Copy thereof, and I shall endeavour to make

19

it as short and plain, as the nature and circumstances of the matter will admit.

I am with Great Truth Sir Your Excellencys
most Obedient Humble Servant
B. WENTWORTH

His Excellency Go.ʳ Clinton
New York a true Copy Exam.ᵈ
p Gw. BANYAR Dep. Sec.ʸ

Nº 12. At a Council held at Fort George in the City of New York on the 6ᵗʰ day of December 1753
Present
The Honbˡᵉ James Delancey Esqʳ Lieuᵗ Gov.ʳ
&c

Mʳ Alexander	Mʳ Holland
Mʳ Kennedy	Mʳ Chambers
Mʳ Murray	Mʳ Smith

A Representation to his Honor the Governor from the Committee and Commissioners appointed to examine into the Eastern Boundaries of this Colony dated the 14ᵗʰ ultº containing Remarks and observations on the Letter from Governor Wentworth of the 23ᵈ March 1750|1 to the board of Trade proposing a division Line between New York and New Hampshire was read, and approved of by this Board, and the Council advised his Honor to Transmit the same and the papers delivered therewith to the Right Honorable the Lords Commissioners for Trade and Plantations.*

Nº 13. At a council held at Fort George New York on Tuesday the 7ᵗʰ Day of August 1764
Present
The Honbˡᵉ Cadwallader Colden Esqʳ Lᵗ Gov.ʳ

Mʳ Horsmanden	Mʳ Delancey
Mʳ Smith	Mʳ Reade
Mʳ Watts	

[* Compare document No. 178, *post.*]

His Honor the Lieutenant Governor laid before the council a letter without date recv.^{d} the last Post from Harmanus Wendell Esq^r_i high Sheriff of the City and County of Albany, advising, that he had in Pursuance of his Honor the Lieu.^{t} Governors Proclamation of the 28th Dec.^{br} last, apprehended Samuel Ashley, Saml Robertson, John Herfort, and Isaac Charles, and shall detain them in Custody untill they give Bail, haveing lately turned forceably Peter Vasand, Bastian Deal, out of the possession of Lands held by them for the space of thirty years within this Province, under Pretence that Land lay Within the Province of New Hampshire.

N° 14. At a Council held at Fort George in New York on Friday 6th day of June 1766
Present
His Excellency Sir Henry Moore Bart. Capt Genl &c
Mr Smith   Mr Morris
Mr Watts   Mr Reade
Mr Delancey

The Board haveing Sundry petitions under Consideration, for lands lying on the West Side of Connecticut River, which were formerly granted by letters Patent under the Seal of the Province of New Hampshire, but were then actually and do now, by his Majesty's order in Council of July 20th 1764 appear to be within the limits of this Province, it is ordered by His Excellency the Governor by the advice of his Council that all persons holding or Claiming lands under such Grants do as soon as may be, appear by themselves or. Their Attorneys and produce the same together with all deeds conveyances and other instruments by which they derive any title or claims to the said lands before His Excellency in Council, and that the Claims of such persons or person who shall not appear and support the same as aforesaid, within the space of 3 Months from the Date hereof, be rejected, and the Petitions already preferred for the Said lands forthwith proceeded upon, also that notice be given, by Publishing this Order Three Weeks, in one or more of the Public News Papers published in this City.

N.º 15. At a Council held at Fort George in the City of New York on Wednesday the 22ᵈ Day of May 1765.
Present
          The Honorable Cadwallader Colden Esqʳ Liuᵗ Governor &c.
          · Mʳ Horsmanden   Mʳ Reade
          Mʳ Smith   Mʳ Morris
          Mʳ Watts

The council taking into consideration the case of those persons who are actually settled under the Grants of the Government of New Hampshire on lands Westward of Connecticut River, and eastward of Hudsons River, which by his Majestys order in Council of the 20ᵗʰ ·July last, are declared to be within the Jurisdiction of this Province, and that the dispossessing such persons might be ruinous to themselves, and their Families, Are of opinion, and it is accordingly ordered by his Honor the Lieuᵗ Governor with the advice of the Council, that the Surveyor General do not untill further order, make returns on any warrant of survey already or which may hereafter come to his hands, of any Lands so actually possessed under such grants, unless for the Persons in actual Possession thereof, as aforesaid, and that a copy hereof, be served on the said Surveyor General.

N.º 16. At a council held at Fort George in the City of New York on Tuesday 22ᵈ day of Octobʳ 1765
Present
          The Honbˡᵉ Cadwallader Colden Esqʳ Lieuᵗ Govʳ &c

M.ʳ Horsmanden   M.ʳ Delancey
M.ʳ Smith   M.ʳ Reade
M.ʳ Morris   M.ʳ Watts

The Petition of Thomas Chandler and others, was presented to the Board and read, setting forth the reasons why they humbly conceive a new County is become necessary, to be erected in The North Eastern Parts of the Province, and praying that the same may taken into consideration, and that the Petitioners may be dismissed to their several homes, with protection of Law.

Ordered that said Petition be refered to the Committee to whom the two former Petitions on the same subject are referred, and that the Committee meet to proceed thereon at Six o'clock this Evening.

N.º 17. At a Council held at Fort George in the City of New York on Wednesday the 28.ᵗʰ Day of February 1770

Present

The Honb.ˡᵉ Cadwallader Colden Esqʳ Lu.ᵗ Gov.ʳ

M.ʳ Watts   M.ʳ Smith
M.ʳ Delancey   M.ʳ Cruger
M.ʳ Reade   M.ʳ Wallace
M.ʳ Morris   M.ʳ White

The Petition of the Proprietors, or Inhabitants of the lands, on the west side of Connecticut River, to the number of one hundred and twenty Persons in the whole, was presented to the Board and Read, setting forth among other things, that there is a vast and valuable country between Connecticut River and Lake Champlain, extending from the county of Cumberland on the South, to the latitude of forty five north, capable of subsisting many Inhabitants, to the great Increase & Strength of the Empire in General, and the Province of New York in Particular. That the Establishment of the County of Cumberland as it conduced to the improvement of good order, has greatly conduced to the Increase of that district, which is daily advanceing, and will soon become an important and flourishing Country. That such of the Petitioners as live to the northward of Cumberland, are exposed to Rapine and Plunder from a Sett of Lawless wretches of Banditti, Felons & Criminals who fly thither from other places, and it is impossible to obtain Justice while they remain a part of the County of Albany, as the magistrates can have no Eye on those distant Parts, nor can your petitioners procure Officers to come thither nor they in their Present State go to them, that there are Seven hundred Souls to the northward of the county of Cumberland, and such is the situation and Quality of the country, and Land, that by proper encouragement, and the help of the overflowings of the neighbouring Colonys, the whole .Country may in a few years be under actual cultivation, and therefore the Petitioners humbly Pray, That a new County may be constituted to the northward of the said County of Cumberland.

On reading and due consideration whereof, his honor the Lieu⸱ Governor, with the advice and consent of the council, orders that his majesty's attorney General of this Province, do forthwith prepare and lay before his honor the Lieu⸱ Gov⸱ in Council the Draft of an ordinance erecting into a separate County by the name of Gloucester with such powers as are necessary, for the due administration of Justice within the Same, all that certain Tract and district of land, situate, laying, and adjoining to the county of Cumberland, on the north, beginning at the northeast corner of said county of Cumberland, thence running north as the needle points fifty Miles, thence East to Connecticut river, thence along the West Branch of the Same River as it runs to the northeast Corner of the said county of Cumberland, on the said River, and thence along the north bounds of the County of Cumberland to the place of Beginning, and that the Township of Kingsland, be by the said ordinance, declared, and appointed, the county Town.

N? 18. At a council held at Fort George New. York on Friday the 11ᵗʰ Day of July 1766
Present.

His Excellency Sir Henry Moore Barᵗ Capᵗ Genᶦ &c

Mʳ Horsmanden   Mʳ Reade
Mʳ Watts   Mʳ Morris
Mʳ Delancey

The Draft of an Ordinance for establishing a Court of Common Pleas, and a court of General sessions of the Peace in the county of Cumberland in the Province of New York, was read at the Board, and being approved of, it is ordered by his Excellency with the advice of the council, that the same be engrossed, and passed the seal.

His Excellency then laid before the Board a list of those persons proposed to be appointed Judges and assistant Justices, of the Court of Common Pleas, also a list of persons names intended to be inserted in the Commission of the Peace, for the said court of Cumberland, which were read, and being approved of, Commissions were ordered to be issued accordingly.

N? 19. At a council held at Fort George in the City of New York on Wednesday the thirteenth Day of Nov. 1771
Present

His Excellency William Tryon Esqʳ Capᵗ Genᶦ

Mʳ Horsmanden   Mʳ Smith
Mʳ Watts   Mʳ Cruger
Mʳ Delancey   Mʳ Wallace
Mʳ Apthorp   Mʳ White
Mʳ Morris   Mʳ Axtell

His Excellency was pleased to communicate a Letter of the 19ᵗʰ day of October last from Benning Wentworth Esquire Governor of the Province of New Hampshire in answer to a Letter from his Excellency the Governor of this Province complaining of an Ex parte survey of the River Connecticut lately made by the Government of New Hampshire, also informing Governor Wentworth of the Riotous behaviour of Persons within this Province claiming Lands under Grants of New Hampshire, and that the Riotous spirit of those People seems to be greatly Owing to the assurance they pretend to have received from Governor Wentworth, that the Line will be altered so as to Include the said claimants within the Jurisdiction of his Government—In which Letter Governor Wentworth utterly disclaims any such or the like assurances, and declares he had invariably recommended implicit obedience to the Laws, and upon all occasions utterly disavowed all connection with those People, and observes he thought it unnecessary to consult this Government previous to the late Survey of Connecticut River, *as that River is comprehended within the Limits of his own Government.*

The Board takeing into consideration the dangerous tendency of the disturbances at present prevailing in that part of the Country, and that Govr Wentworth had not thought proper by public act of his Government to disown the assurances, the Rioters pretend to have received from his Government, humbly advise his Excellency, and it is accordingly ordered by his Excellency the Govr, by advice of the Council, that a Proclamation be prepared notifying the declaration of Govr Wentworth on this subject contained in his letters abovementioned, Stateing the Claims of this Province to the Lands westward of Connecticut River, strictly enjoining the Inhabitants of those lands to yield obedience to the Laws within this Government, and Strictly enjoining the Magistrates and other civil officers to be vigilant in their Duty, and attentive to preservation of Public Peace, and to transmit the names of All offenders herein, that such means may be taken for their punishment as the nature of their Crimes may require, and that the Draft of such Proclamation when prepared, be laid before His Excellency, for the approbation of the Board.

N°. 20. At a Council held at Fort George New York on Wednesday the twenty ninth day of January 1772
Present

The Honb^l. William Tryon Esqr. Capt. Genl. &c

M^r. Horsmanden	M^r. Smith
M^r. Watts	M^r. Cruger
M^r. Delancey	M^r. White
M^r. Apthorpe	M^r. Axtell.

His Excellency Communicated a letter of the 8^t. Inst. from Go^r. Wentworth of New Hampshire, with the Copy of a minute of the council of that Province of the same date, which were read and the letter except the last paragraph on a private subject, with the minutes a length, ordered to be entered at length in the minutes which follow in these words

New Hampshire Jany 8th 1772

Sir:—By the enclosed Copy of the Journals of his Majesty's council of this province, upon communicating to them your Excellency's letters to me dated Fort George New York Octr. 2^d. 1771 together with your proclamation enclosed in the latter, and my answer to the first letter, It will appear I cannot issue any public act Relative to those violences recited in your Excellency's Letters, and Proclamation, as done in the Province of New York, unless in express contrariety to the advice officially required, and given me on this occasion. Notwithstanding I must herein be denied the satisfaction of executeing your Excellency's request in these Matters, it gives me great pleasure to hear that there has not been any disturbance on the Banks of Connecticut River, where the Inhabitants of New York have Daily Intercourse with those of this Government, but on the contrary, that the reported evils are confined to a small district, remote from our Boundary Line, and more immediately connected with Hudsons River, and the Colony's of Connecticut, and Mass.^{ts} Bay, from whence they originally Migrated.

It is beond a Doubt that violence, and Illegal opposition to Government, is the aversion of this Province, from their exemplary conduct especially for five years past every contrary assurance or pretence, must be groundless, and proceed from artfull wicked men, injurious to the Interest and diametrically opposite to the Public, and private Opinion, and desire, of This Province.

Sir yours &c.

J. WENTWORTH.

Province of New Hampshire

At a council held at Portsmouth By his Excellency's summons on Thursday the Eight day of January 1772

Present

His Excellency John Wentworth Governor &c
The Council

Theodore Atkinson		Daniel Peirce	
Daniel Warner		George Jaffrey	
Peter Livius	Esq^{rs}	Daniel Rogers	Esq^{rs}
Jonathan Warner		Peter Gilman	
Daniel Rindge		Thos W. Waldron	

His Excellency the Govr haveing laid before the council two letters for their advice, From His Excellency Govr Tryon of New York dated Octr 1771 and Decemb.^{r} 23.^{d} 1771, the latter encloseing a proclamation also his Excellencys answer to the first letter

The Premises being Read it is considered, that by his Majesty's order in Council of the 20th July 1764. the Western Bank of Connecticut River, was then commanded to be the Western Bounds of this Province, and this Government has been and is entirely obedient thereunto, therefore the said Proclamation relating wholly to matters and things without the Boundaries of this Province, and it advised that the Publication thereof by authority of this Province, would be extra provincial, therefore in our opinion improper, and that his Excellency is further advised, not to Issue any Proclamation relating to the Premises—Secondly that it is not expedient for this Government in any wise to Interfere with, or concern in running the lines between his Majestys Provinces of New York, and Canada, which (by his Excellency, Gov. Tryons Letter of the 23.ᵈ December 1771) is already began by commissioners appointed for that service, agreeably to his Majesty's instruction's, wherin it does not appear that this Province is referred to or mentioned

A true Copy from the Minutes of Council

attest.   Gᴇᴏ Kɪɴɢ Dep.ʸ Sect.ʸ

N.° 21.   At a Council held at Fort George in the City of New York on Thursday 12ᵗʰ Day Dec.ʳ 1769

Present

The Hon.ˡᵉ Cadwallader Colden Esq.ʳ L.ᵗ Go.ᵛ &c

M.ʳ Watts	M.ʳ Smith
M.ʳ Delancey	M.ʳ Cruger
M.ʳ Reade	M.ʳ Wallace
M.ʳ Morris	M.ʳ White

Upon Reading this Day at the Board the petition of Abraham Ten Broeck in behalf of himself, and others, interested in A Tract of Land in the County of Albany called Wallumschack, setting forth that the commissioners and surveyors lately employed To make Partition of said tract, pursuant to the directions of the Act of Assembly in that case, made and provided, has been notoriously opposed by sundry persons and prevented by their Threats from executing the trust reposed in them, And Praying the order of this government thereupon, and also on reading four depositions therewith presented and now filed, it is ordered by his Honor the

Lieu^t Govr. with the advice of the Council, that a proclamation be Issued for apprehending and secureing in safe custody, the principals and ringleaders among the said Rioters, that they may be dealt with according to Law, and directing the Sheriff to raise and take to his assistance the Posse Comitatus or power of the county, and the Magistrates, Officers, and Ministers, of Justice, to give their aid not only in apprehending the offenders, but in preventing and suppressing all future Riots, and disturbances of the like dangerous Tendency.

N° 22. At a Council held at Fort George in the City of New York on Wednesday the thirty first day of October 1770

Present

His Excellency the right Honb^l John Earl of Dunmore Capt. Genl &c

Mr Horsmanden	Mr Smith
Mr Watts	Mr Cruger
Mr Delancey	Mr Wallace
Mr Reade	Mr White
Mr Morris	

Upon reading this day at the board the Petition of Abraham Ten Broeck In behalf of himself and the other Proprietors of the Patent of Wallumshack, setting forth that the Proclamation of Dec^{br} 12th 1769 for the apprehending certain Rioters therein named hath hitherto been attended with no effect, that the Petitioners finding a Claim was set up under New Hampshire to those lands, and willing to evince the legality of their titles in a course of Law, caused an ejectment to be prosecuted against one of these New Hampshire claimants, which was brought to Trial at the last Summer assize at Albany, with three other causes under similar circumstances and three different Verdicts being given by special Juries in favour of the New York Titles, and the Defendants in the other action makeing default from a conviction that his claim could not be supported, The

Petitioners hoped the Riotous spirit whch had so long prevailed to the great injury of that part of the country would wholly have been suppressed, and thereupon directed the Commissioners to resume and complete the Partition of Certain lands in the said Patent, But that the commissioners were again opposed by a riotous and tumultuous Body, who armed themselves with clubs and warned them to desist from their Business, threatning them with Violence so that seeing themselves in Danger, they did not think it safe to proceed further, and that your Petitioners are informed the reason they assign for this second act of violence, was an assurance from their friends in New Hampshire that his Lordship was instructed to protect them in their Usurpation, and to use measures to repeal the Petitioners said letters Patents, and reffering for the truth of the Facts to the affidavit with the said Petition presented, and to those laid before the government on their former complaints, the Petitioners humbly pray his Lordships interposition, and that such effectual methods may be taken for secureing the course of Justice, and the Public peace, and bringing the offenders to Condign punishment as shall be thought expedient.

On reading whereof, and affidavit of John Bleecker, Peter Lansing, Thomas Hun, and Manning Vischer, His Lordship was pleased to declare he had the highest reason to think it is his Majesty's fixed resolution, to adhere to his Royal Decision of July 20th 1764, and leave this government in the Fullest enjoyment of its ancient Rights as Thereby Bounded by Connecticut River and then His Lordship required the advice of the Council, as to the steps necessary to be taken on this Occasion.

On Due consideration of the matter, the Council humbly advised his Lordship to Issue a proclamation for Apprehending Simeon Hathaway, Moses Scott Jonathan Fisk, and Silas Robinson, principal authors and actors in the said Riot and breach of the peace, and to Insert therein the above mentioned Declaration, which may have a further tendency to prevent disorders ariseing from an opinion, that his Majesty's order of July 20th 1764 will be Rescinded.

N° 23. At a Council held a Fort George in the City of New. York on thursday the fifth day of November 1771

Present

His Excellency William Tryon Esqr Capt Genl &c

Mr Horsmanden	Mr Smith
Mr Watts	Mr Cruger
Mr Delancey	Mr Wallace
Mr Apthorp	Mr White
Mr Morris	Mr Axtell

The Affidavits of Robert Yates and sundry other persons summoned as the Posse, by the Sheriff of Albany, to assist him in the service of a writ of Possession on James Brackenbrige, liveing on the Patent of Wallumshack were laid before the Board and Read, whereby it appears that the Sheriff and his Posse did in the month of July last proceed to the premises in Order to to give Possession as required by the Writ, but were opposed and prevented by a large Body of Men (from executing their purpose) assembled in arms, which Affidavits were ordered to lay for the consideration of the Board.

N° 24. At a council held at Fort George in the City of New York on Wednesday, the twenty first Day of August 1771

Present

His Excellency William Tryon Esqr Capt Genl &c

Mr Watts	Mr Cruger
Mr Delancey	Mr Wallace
Mr Morris	Mr White
Mr Smith	Mr Axtell.

Upon Reading this Day at the Board the Petition of Donald M⁰ Intyre, and six other Persons, setting forth that the Petitioners were on the 11th of June last forcibly turned out of Possession of the lands they had settled and improved, near Argyle Town, by one Cockran and fourteen armed men, and praying relief—The Council humbly advised His Excellency to recommend this Matter to His Majestys Justices of the Peace resideing in that part of the Country, or to any two or more of them, and the said Justices do after full inquiry into the Facts and proof of the force, give the petitioners the relief directed by the Statutes of Forcible entry or such other redress as the case shall appear to them to require, Transmitting to His Excellency as soon as may be, an acknowledgement of their proceedings with such examinations as shall be taken before them.

N⁰ 25. At a Council held at Fort George in the City of New York on Wednesday the third day of July 1771
Present
   His Excellency The Right Honb John Earl of Dunmore Captain Genl &c.
    Mr Horsmanden   Mr Delancey
    Mr Watts   Mr Cruger
    Mr Smith   Mr White

A Letter dated the 30th May last from John Monroe Esqr one of his Majesty's Justices of the Peace for the County of Albany, was laid before the Board, together with the copies of sundry Affidavits taken before him relative to the behavior of sundry Riotous, and disorderly Persons in the neighbourhood of the said Justice, on reading whereof the council advised, and it is accordingly ordered by his Excellency the Govr, that the deputy secretary do write to the Sheriff of Albany encloseing him Copies of the Said affidavits, and signifying his Excellencys directions that he should apply to Mr Justice Monroe for a warrant or warrants for apprehending the Rioters, and that he shall exert himself in takeing them, that they may be brought to Justice.

N.º 26. At a Council held at Fort George in the City of New York on Wednesday the twenty seventh Day of November 1771

Present

.   · His Excellency William Tryon Esq.ʳ Cap.ᵗ Gen.ˡ &c

M.ʳ Watts   M.ʳ Smith   M.ʳ White
M.ʳ Delancey   M.ʳ Cruger

His Excellency Communicated to the Board a letter of the 12.ᵗʰ Ins.ᵗ from Allexander M.ᶜ Naghten Esq.ʳ one of his Majestys Justices of the Peace for the County of Albany, advising that he had in pursuance of his Excellencys instructions by the advice of this Board on the 21.ˢᵗ August last inquired into the Riotous conduct of those persons who had forceably dispossessed Donald M.ᶜ Intyre and others settled on the Lands Eastward of Hudsons River under grants of this Province and he had Issued a warrant for apprehending Robert Cockran and three other Persons known by the sirnames of Allen, Baker and Sevil, charged with pulling down and Burning the House of Charles Hucheson and with Burning the House of John Reid, but that he apprehended the number of the New Hampshire Rioters and their situation in the Mountain was such that no sheriff or Constable would apprehend them, and it would be highly necessary for the Public peace and for the relief of the Sufferers, to offer a reward for Apprehending the Offenders. Whereupon it is ordered by his Excellency the Gov.ʳ with the advice of the council, that a Proclamation Issue for apprehending the said Cockran, Allen, Baker, and Sevil, and the other five Persons charged with the Felony, and Riots, lately committed by them, and offering a Reward of Twenty Pounds to be paid to the Person who shall apprehend and secure each and either of the said Offenders, that they may be proceeded against as the Law Directs.

N°. 27. At a council held at. Fort George in the City of New York on Wednesday the 11ᵗʰ. Day of December 1771
Present
    His Excellency William Tryon Esqʳ Capᵗ Genˡ &c

Mʳ Horsmanden	Mʳ Morris	Mʳ White
Mʳ Delancey	Mʳ Smith	Mʳ Axtell
Mʳ Apthorpe	Mʳ Cruger	

His Excellency laid before the Board a letter of the 6ᵗʰ Ultᵒ from John Monroe Esqʳ one of his Majesty's Justices of the Peace for the County of Albany, enclosing the copy of an affidavit sworn the 2ᵈ of that month, before himself by John Todd charging Robert Cockran with having on the 28ᵗʰ October last in conjunction with a number of other Rioters forcibly and with violence turned him and his Brother Robert Todd out of Possession of the Lands they had settled within Lieutenant Farrants Patent which by the confession of the New Hampshire claimants themselves is distant from Hudsons River only fourteen miles and three quarters. The draft of a Proclamation prepared in pursuance of the order of the 13ᵗʰ ultᵒ was laid before the Board and Read, Reciting the late Riots and Disorders committed by Persons and claiming the Lands they possess under grants of New Hampshire and Governor Wentworths Letters of the 19ᵗʰ of October last disclaiming of his having given to these People the assurances they pretend to have received from him Stating the Title of this Province to the Lands westward of Connecticut River and the Transactions between the two Provinces from the first commencement of the controversy respecting the limits in 1749 enjoining the Settlers there to yield Obedience unto the Laws within this Government, and directing the magistrates and civil officers to exert
20

themselves in Maintaining Publick Peace and return
the names of all Offenders therein that they may be proceeded against as the Nature of their crimes require, and
the draft having been duly considered and Amendments
made thereto the same was approved of and the Council
Humbly advised his Excellency to issue his Proclamation accordingly.

N.º 28. At a council held at Fort George in City of
    New York on Friday the twenty eight Day of
    February 1772
Present
      The Honbᴸ William Tryon Capᵗ Genᴸ &c
  Mʳ Delancey   Mʳ Cruger
  Mʳ Morris   Mʳ Wallace   Mʳ Axtell
  Mʳ Smith   Mʳ White

    His Excellency communicated to the Board a letter
from Joseph Lord Esqʳ one of the Judges of the Superior
Court of Common Pleas for the county of Cumberland,
informing his Excellency of a great Riot on the 27ᵗʰ
of that month, in the Township of Putney, perpetrated
by a party of seventy or eighty Persons who came from
the New Hampshire side of the River, and forcibly
broke open the House of Jonas Morse and took out of
his Custody certain goods taken in execution and de-
posited with him. Also another letter of the 16ᵗʰ Inst
from the said Joseph Lord, acquainting his Excellʸ, that
himself, and Thomas Chandler Junʳ and William Esqʳˢ
Justices of the peace for the same county, had met and
were proceeding to take examinations, and to make the
fullest inquiry into the Facts, in Order to Punish the
offenders as far as in their power, And that five of the
Principal Rioters came and submitted themselves to
Justice, before any Warrants issued against them, and
had satisfied the Judgement on Which the Fieri Facias
Issued against in virtue of which the goods were taken
which the Rioters had taken from the custody of the
Officer, and made full satisfaction also to every party

Injured. That he cannot find any Gentlemen, Magistrates, or Officers, were encouragers or abettors in this Riot, on the contrary Mess.ʳˢ Bellows and Olcott two Justices in the Government of New Hampshire had exerted themselves on the occasion and Issued their Warrants and bound over near thirty of the Rioters to answer for Their Misdemeanor.

On Reading whereof it is ordered by Excellency the Go.ʳ with the Advice of the council, that the Deputy Clerk of this Board do by letter to the said Joseph Lord Esq.ʳ signify the approbation of His Excellency and the Council, of his conduct and of the other Magistrates, in bringing the Persons Guilty of the above mentioned Riot to a submission and acknowledgement of their Crimes, to recommend their persisting and preserving a due obedience to the Laws to prevent as much as in their Power all future Riots, and to exert themselves in bringing all offenders herein to a speedy and Exemplary Punishment.

N.º 29. At a Council held at Fort George in the City of New York on the 26 day of March 1772
Present

      His Excellency William Tryon Esq.ʳ Cap.ᵗ Gen.ˡ

M.ʳ Watts	M.ʳ Smith
M.ʳ Delancey	M.ʳ Cruger
M.ʳ Morris	M.ʳ Axtell

His Excellency communicated to the Board a letter from Henry Ten Broek Esq.ʳ sheriff of Albany of the 2 March, acknowledging the receipt of the Proclamation of the ninth of December for apprehending certain Rioters therein named, and acquainting his Excellency that three of them viz, Baker, Allen and Sevil, are retired to the neighbouring Government, that he has not been able to apprehend any of the rest and that from the conduct and behaviour of those who were at home tho not particularly mentioned or concerned in the Riot he finds the Greatest appearance of a determined resolution not to submit to this Government and this he found particularly verified in the Conduct of two or three who were armed with guns and Clubs in which manner they came to the House of one Harman near the Indian River where he then was and from their Conduct it Plainly appeared what they Intended.

N.º 30. At a council held at Fort George in the City of New York on Wednesday the fifteenth day of April 1772

Present

His Excellency William Tryon Esq.ʳ Cap.ᵗ Gen.ˡ &c·

M.ʳ Horsmanden	M.ʳ Cruger
M.ʳ Watts	M.ʳ Wallace
M.ʳ Apthorpe	M.ʳ White
M.ʳ Morris	M.ʳ Axtell.

His Excellency also communicated to the Board two letters he had recv.ᵈ from John Monroe Esq.ʳ one of his Majesty's Justices of the Peace for the county of Albany, one dated the twenty third of March, acquainting his Excellency that he had proceeded against one of the worst men among the Rioters, and should have had him secured in Goal, had he had the assistance of ten men that would have taken arms, and obeyed his orders, but that they all ran into the woods when they should have resisted, that two constables behaved well during the whole time, and that he has transmitted a full account of his proceedings to the Attorney Gen.ˡ who will wait on his Excellency with it. That he is greatly distressed haveing no other assistance than his own Servants to defend his Person and property, and his house surrounded every night fireing their Guns &c, and that he has reason to be thankfull to Divine providence for their preservation, as had they not acted with spirit and resolution they should have been all kill'd on the Spot, for haveing got but a small hole in the Door one of the Rioters run his Pistol through it and snapt it at his breast, after they got into the house he flashed it at his servant who was going up stairs after him, and fired at the constable who took him, and he hopes his Excellency will loose no time to afford him such relief as the nature of the case may require, and the other of the said letters dated the sixth Ins.ᵗ, in which the said Mᵣ Justice Monroe informs His Excellency The Rioters are in that part of the country enlisting men Daily, and 15£ Bounty to every man who Joins with them, and thus strike terror in the whole Country and that have too many friends owing to self Interest that he is affraid of the consequences every moment as he cannot one Justice or one Officer that will act or say against them, that he is almost wore out with watching, and that nothing saves him but the Figure he makes about his House with arms &c.

Nᵒ 31. At a council held at Fort George in the City of New York on Saturday the Ninth Day of May 1772
Present

  His Excellency William Tryon Capᵗ Genˡ &c
  Mᵣ Watts   Mᵣ Delancey
  Mᵣ Morris   Mᵣ Wallace
  Mᵣ Cruger

Horace Wilcox of Bennington in the County of Albany attending without was called in and examined touching the Riots and Disorders in that part of the Country, declared that he lived on the Patent of Wallumschack about seventeen miles from Hudsons River and that he understood the present Riotous disposition of the People there, to proceed from their claims to the soil under the grants of New Hampshire, that many he was of opinion would be willing to purchase Titles under this Government to the Lands they have improved but are deterred by the Majority, who are of a contrary opinion and seem determined to hold their possession by force and that among their principal leaders are James Brackenbridge, Jedediah Dusey and Stephen Fades.

Nº 32. At a Council held at Fort George in the City
   of New York on Tuesday the nineteenth day of
   May 1772
Present

> His Excellency William Tryon Capt Genl
> Mr Horsmanden   Mr Delancey
> Mr Watts   Mr Wallace
> Mr Cruger

His Excellency communicated to the Board a letter
to him from Mr Justice Monroe of the 3d Inst with a
letter from Ebenezar Cole to Mr Monroe of the second
Inst, whereby it appears the Rioters had brought two
pieces of Cannon and a Mortar Piece from the small fort
at East Hosack with Powder and Ball, and were making
great preparations for their defence, giving out that a
Body of Regulars were on their March against them,
and that Remember Baker and his Party went the Day
before to the House of Bliss Willoughby, and cut him
in a barbarous Manner.

His Excellency then communicated to the board the
Draft of a letter he had wrote and intended to forward
to some of said Rioters in pursuance of a Resolution of
this Board at their last Meeting, which being read and
approved of was ordered to be forwarded by letter from
the deputy Clerk of this Council to the Sheriff of Albany, with directions to him to deliver it with his Own
Hands to Mr Dewey, or in case of his absence to any
principal Inhabitant at Bennington.

Nº 33. At a Council held at Fort George in the City of
   New York on Tuesday the 26th Day of May 1772
Present

> His Excellency William Tryon Capt Genl
> Mr Horsmanden   Mr Cruger
> Mr Watts   Mr Wallace
> Mr Delancey   Mr White
> Mr Apthorpe

His Excellency acquainted the Board that Ebenezar Cole, Bliss Willoughby, and Jonathan Wheaten who lately resided near Bennington, had represented to him that they had been forced by the Rioters in that part of the country to leave their habitations and were come hither to lay their situation before this Govn.ᵗ, and the said persons attended without with Mʳ Justice Monroe they were called in separately and examined touching the State of that part of the country, and thereupon it was ordered that their examinations be taken and reduced to writing to be sworn to before this board on Friday next, and that the examination or Deposition of Lieutenant Hugh Fraser be also taken, and laid before the Board.

Nº 34. At a Council held at Fort George in the City of New York on Friday the twenty ninth Day of May 1772
Present
  His Excellency William Tryon Capᵗ Genᝋ &c.
  Mʳ Horsmanden   Mʳ Cruger
  Mʳ Watts   Mʳ Wallace
  Mʳ Delancey   Mʳ White
  Mʳ Apthorp   Mʳ Axtell

The examinations of John Munro Ebenezar Cole Bliss Willoughby and Jonathan Wheate being reduced to writing, they were severally called in and their respective depositions read to them, which they signed and which they swore to before the Board, and they then withdrew.

Doctor of New Perth attending without was called in and examined touching the State of that Part of the country and then Withdrew.

Then the Depositions aforesaid together with the Deposition of Lieuᵗ Hugh Fraser, and several Affidavits taken before Mʳ Justice Monroe were read and the board having spent some time in the consideration thereof, the further consideration of the state of that Part of the country was postponed untill the next, or some future meeting of the Board.

N.° 35. At a council held at Fort George in the City of
   New York on Wednesday the third of June 1772
Present
           His Excellency William Tryon Esq.ʳ Cap.ᵗ
Gen.ˡ &c
       M.ʳ Horsemanden   M.ʳ Cruger
       M.ʳ Watts   M.ʳ White
       M.ʳ Smith   M.ʳ Axtell

   His Excellency communicated to the Board a letter
of the 22.ᵈ Ult.ᵒ from Benjamin Spencer Esq.ʳ one of his
Majesty's Justices of the Peace for the County of Albany, informing his Excellency of the Riotous Spirit
which now prevails among the People seated under
Title derived from the Province of New Hampshire, that
the Inhabitants of Durham the place of his own Residence are daily threatened to be driven off their Possessions, the House he lives in to be Burned, and he is
Obliged to confine himself at Home, as he cannot with
safety go from thence to transact his Business, also a
deposition therein inclosed of Josua Pringle taken before M.ʳ Justice Spencer and the same being read the
said Josua Pringle who attended without was called
in and being examined at the Board his deposition
was taken and sworn to before M.ʳ Chief Justice Horsmanden.

N.° 36. At a council held at Fort George in the City of
   New York on Thursday the twenty fifth day of
   June 1772
Present
           His Excellency William Tryon Esq.ʳ Cap.ᵗ
Gen.ˡ &c
       M.ʳ Horsmanden   M.ʳ Smith
       M.ʳ Watts   M.ʳ Cruger
       M.ʳ Apthorpe   M.ʳ Wallace
       M.ʳ Delancey   M.ʳ White
       M.ʳ Morris   M.ʳ Axtell

His Excellency communicated a letter from Major Philip Skene of the 17th Inst acquainting his Excellency that some of the People from the meeting of the Inhabitants of Bennington and the adjacent Towns had been with him, and from their information he finds that they do not follow his advice as they promised to do, that they are divided among themselves, those of the best character do not choose to go to New York lest as they say they should be guilty of a breach of Trust and have it out of their power to apply for terms of settlement under New York Jurisdiction, That Mr Brackenbridge has been through New England to New Hampshire, and declines going to New York though he has his Excelly Protection to go, alledging that a civil matter would take hold of him, that he (Major Skene) to induce Brackenbridge to go to New York had Pledged his own faith and Security but to no purpose —That New Hampshire has taken upon them to recommend their case Home, Mr. Brackenbridge having applied to the Assembly of that Government and that the country in Genl rest upon this answer, hoping a change in their favour, which designing men among them persuade them will will take place.

A memorial of Benjamin Spencer Jacob Marsh Ebenezar Cole Bliss Willoughby and Joseph Pringle, in behalf of themselves and other freeholders & Inhabitants of the Counties of Albany and Charlotte, was laid before the Board read setting forth the Distresses of the People in that Part of the Country arising from the Riotous proceedings of Inhabitants of Bennington and that Vicinity, and Praying His Excellency would take into consideration their distressed situation and grant them all that Relief, countenance, aid, and Protection in his Power, which as faithful and obedient subjects they have Just reason to expect from the Justice and Wisdom of Government.

Ordered that the consideration of the said Petition be Deferred untill the next meeting of the Board.

N? 37. At a council held at Fort George in the City of New York on Monday the twenty ninth Day of June 1772.
Present
          His Excellency William Tryon Esq' Cap.
Gen!

M.ʳ Horsmanden	M.ʳ Smith
M.ʳ Watts	M.ʳ Cruger
M.ʳ Apthorpe	M.ʳ Wallace
M.ʳ Delancey	M.ʳ White
M.ʳ Morris	M.ʳ Axtell

The parties directed on Saturday last to attend the Board this Day were called in To wit, Stephen Fay, and Jonas Fay in Behalf of Inhabitants of Bennington and the adjacent Towns, and Benjamin Spencer, Jacob Marsh Ebenezar Cole, and Bliss Willoughby, Joseph Pringle, who by their memorial read at the Board the 25ᵗʰ Ins.ᵗ praying relief and protection of Government against the Riotous, and disorderly behavior of the said Inhabitants, and the said memorialists have severally repeated the substance of their charges against the said Inhabitants as contained in the several Depositions to which they refer in their Memorial, and that the said Stephen Fay and Jonas Fay, having been heard in answer thereto, were also fully heard as to what they had further to offer in behalf of their constituents, and the Parties being withdrawn it is ordered by His Excellency the Go.ʳ with the advice of the Council that the letter from the Inhabitants of Bennington and other adjacent Towns, dated the nineteenth of June Ins.ᵗ the memorial aforesaid, and the Depositions of John Munro Ebenezar Cole, Bliss Willoughby, Jonathan Wheaton, Hugh Fraser, Joseph Pringle, Benjamin Spencer, Jacob Marsh & Hugh Monro together with all other papers which have been read at this Board relative to the disorders and disturbances in that part of the country be referred to the Gentlemen of the council or any five of them, and that they make report thereupon on Wednesday next.

N.º 38. At a council held at Fort George in the City
of New York on Wednesday the first day of July
1772
Present

His Excellency William Tryon Cap.ᵗ Gen.ˡ &c
Mʳ Horsmanden   Mʳ Cruger
Mʳ Watts   Mʳ Wallace
Mʳ Delancey   Mʳ White
Mʳ Morris   Mʳ Axtell
Mʳ Smith

Mʳ Smith from the Committee to whom by order of
the 29ᵗʰ June were referred the Letter of the nineteenth
June last from the Inhabitants of Bennington and that
vicinity and several other Papers mentioned in the said
order relative to the disorders and Disturbances at
Bennington, and the Towns adjacent thereto, presented
to his Excellency the report of the said committee thereupon which being read was on the question put agreed
to and approved of, and Stephen Fay and Jonas Fay
with the other persons who attended at the Board on
the twenty ninth of June were called in, and the report
Read in their presence, and then being withdrawn, It is
ordered that the said report be entered on the minutes
and the council humbly advise His Excellency to deliver
to the Parties an extract of so much of the said report
as relates to the conditions to be observed by the Parties on both sides.

N.º 39. At a Council held at Fort George in the City
of New York on Tuesday the 8ᵗʰ of September
1772.
Present

His Excellency William Tryon Cap.ᵗ Genl. &c.
Mʳ Horsmanden
Mʳ Watts   Mʳ Smith
Mʳ Delancey   Mʳ Cruger
Mʳ Apthorp   Mʳ White
Mʳ Morris   Mʳ Axtell

His Excellency communicated three letters he had recv.^d from John Munroe Esqr one of His Majesty's Justices of the peace for the county of Albany, dated the 10.th 17.th and 25.th August last also a letter of the 20.th of the same month from Ebenezar Cole and Bliss Willoughby respecting the conduct and behavior of the Inhabitants of Bennington and the adjacent Towns since the hearing before his Excellency in Council and the opinion before this Board on the Petition of said Inhabitants on the first Day of July Last, Which letters were read, and with the papers referred to therein ordered to be filed.

N.º 40. At a Council held in the City of New. York on Tuesday the twenty ninth Day of Sep.^t 1772
Present
  His Excellency William Tryon Esqr Captain General &c

Mr Horsmanden	Mr Smith
Mr Watts	Mr Cruger
Mr Delancey	Mr Wallace
Mr Apthorpe	Mr White

His Excellency laid before the Board a Letter from Gloucester county of the 22.^d August last giving information of the concertion of measures both in Massachusetts Bay and New Hampshire for exciting Petitions to his Majesty for extending the Jurisdiction of New Hampshire to the westward of Connecticut River for confirming the grants of that Colony within this Government, and for vacating the Patents under the Great Seal of this Province in the District adjudged to belong to it By the Royal Decision of July 1764. And His Excellency requiring the Opinion of the council as to that intelligence and on the Letter communicated to, and read at this Board on the 8.th Ins.^t from the Inhabitants of Bennington and the adjacent Towns, justifying their late conduct in dispossessing certain persons settled near Otter Creek on lands granted and held under this province— The council observed that these Riotous and disorderly persons at first confined their claims to the lands they then Possessed by the grants of New Hampshire, and were but few in number at the Time His Majesty's order was Published declaring the Western Banks of Connecticut River as the limits between his two Provinces, that their present Claims include not only all those who have since seated themselves in that part of the Country but that their conduct plainly evinces their intention to suffer no person quietly to enjoy by Titles from this Province any Lands comprized within the Grants of New Hampshire Westward of the Green Mountains. Although only a very small portion of that extensive Territory is even pretended to be occupied by Claimants under New Hampshire— That His Excellency in pursuance of the Report of the Committee of this Board of the 1ˢ July last has already offered them Terms much more favourable than considering the violence of their past conduct they had any reason to expect, (to wit) to suspend until his Majesty's pleasure shall be known all prosecutions in Behalf of the Crown on account of the crimes with which they stand charged, and to recommend it to the owners of the contested Lands under Grants of this Province to put a stop during the same period to all civil Suits concerning the lands in Question, and to agree with the settlers for the purchase thereof on moderate Terms exacting no other condition on their part than their future peaceable and quiet behavior, that instead of embracing so favourable an offer with Gratitude they have perpetrated fresh acts of Violence, and rendered themselves still more obnoxious and inexcusable— That there is to much reason to apprehend that so pernicious an example if not speedily checked and punished must be attended with the worst consequences by bringing the authority of Government into Contempt and obstructing the course of Justice, and that the Board consider the letter from Bennington as highly insolent and deserving of sharp reprehension, and the

insinuation that the settlements were to proceed under
the New Hampshire Grants and to be stayed under
those of New York as utterly without foundation. The
Council further observed to his Excellency that every
under act of executory Government to restrain the Patentees of this Colony from improving their Estates
would be unauthoritative, and flatly repugnant to the
Law as well as against the conditions and terms expressed in their Patents and directed by the royal instruction—and that the Board therefore foresee that
the endeavors of the Hampshire Grantees to increase
the number of their possessions upon the controverted
Lands must speedily create confusion and Bloodshed—
That it is beyond the Power of the Civil Magistrates to
put a stop to this growing evil, which in the opinion of the
Board cannot effectually be suppressed without the aid
of the Regular forces. That every material information
Touching this contest has been transmitted and now lies
for his Majesty's consideration. And as the circumstances of the colony absolutely require it the Board
are unanimously of opinion that his Excell.ᵧ do urge
to His Majesty's Ministers the necessity of a speedy signifying of his Majesty's Pleasure, and at the same time
intimate that from the number and extent of the Grants
under this Province to reduced Officers and Soldiers and
others as well as those who had Grants under New
Hampshire and others associated with them in the
Counties of Cumberland Gloucester and Charlotte and
the numerous settlements that have been made under
these Patents and under ancient Grants in the County of
Albany the revocation of the Royal Decision 1764 and
the subjecting of the Country Westward of Connecticut
River To the Jurisdiction of New Hampshire, appears
to this Board to be a Measure unfriendly to the Rights
of the Crown, dangerous to the Patentees holding under
the Great Seal of this province, introductive of endless
contentions among the Inhabitants and subversive to
the growth and cultivation of the country, which but for
the Disturbances in Bennington and the neighbourhood

of that Town would be now in a peaceable and Flourishing Condition.

No 41. An Act to appoint commissioners to settle a Line or Lines of Jurisdiction between this Colony and the Province of Massachusetts Bay.

Be it Enacted by His Excellency the Governor with the Council and the General Assembly and it is hereby enacted by Authority of the same that The Honbl John Watts The Honl William Smith, The Honbl Robt R. Livingston and William Nicoll Esquires shall be commissioners on the Part of this colony who shall be commissioned by the Govr or Commander in Chief for the time being and who shall have full power and are here by authorised to meet with the commissaries who are or may be appointed in in like manner authorised and empowered by the Govr Council and General Court or Assembly of the Massachusetts Bay, at such time or times place or places as shall be agreed upon and determined by the Governors or Commanders in Chief for the time being of this Colony and the province of the Massachusetts Bay then and there to agree upon a line or lines of Future Jurisdiction between the said province of the Massachusetts Bay and this Colony, on the Easterly part of this Colony to begin at the southern corner of the Province of New Hampshire, on the West Bank of Connecticut River, and from Thence in such manner and by such line or lines as shall be found Eligible, with Due regards to the Rights of this Colony to the Colony of Connecticut, the Governor or Commander in Chief of this Colony for the time being and the Govr of the said Province being present and such line or lines so agreed upon and approved of And consented to by the said Governor or Commander in Chief of this Colony, and the Goverr of the Province of the Massachusetts Bay for the time Being shall be presented by the said Governors respectively to His Majesty for his Royal approbation, and being Ratified and confirmed by His Majesty shall at all times thereafter be

the Line or Lines of Jurisdiction between this Colony
and the Province of the Massachusetts Bay the True
and Real extent or Boundary of this Colony by the
Royal Grants or any Law, Act, Declaration or Ordinance to the contrary thereof in any wise notwithstanding.

And Be it Further Enacted by the same authority
that after such Line or Lines shall be so agreed upon
approved ratified and confirmed the Commissaries appointed by this Act are hereby authorised and empowered to employ a surveyor or surveyors, chain bearers,
and such and so many other persons as may be found
necessary to perform the Executive Part in Running
marking and ascertaining the said line or Lines in conjunction with such as may be appointed on the part of
the said Province of The Massachusetts Bay for that
purpose.

And to the Intent that the good ends of this act
may not be defeated by the Death sickness or unavoid-
able absence of either of the commissaries above
named—

Be it Enacted by the same authority that in case any
such accident happening to any of the commissaries the
major part of said commissaries or the survivors, and
survivor of them, shall and may execute and perform
all such acts as they may conceive necessary and expedient for settling the said Line or Lines of Jurisdiction between this colony, and the Province above-men-
tioned, and that as fully to all intents and purposes
aforementioned, as all the commissaries could or might
execute and perform the same

City of New York 8th March 1773.

I assent to this Bill enacting the same and order
it to be enrolled

W$^{M.}$ TRYON

(Note) The above assent
should have been entered
after the passing by the

City of New York the 26
Day February 1773 in the
thirteenth year of his Ma-

council as the date of the Order of Transactions will shew, but the form through which it passed the Council are indorsed and the passing by the Go.ʳ is at the foot of the Bill which occasioned the mistake in copying.

jesty's. Reign — General Assembly for the Colony of New York, this Bill having been read three times Resolved That the Bill do Pass

JOHN CRUGER Speaker

Assembly chamber City of New York Die Veneris the 26ᵗʰ Day of February 1773 this Bill being passed, Ordered that Coⁱ Ten Broek and Coloⁱ Wells do carry this Bill To the council and desire their Concurrence thereto

By Order of the General Assembly
EDMᴰ SEAMAN Clk

Council Chamber City of New York 26ᵗʰ Febrʸ 1773 this Bill was then read the first time and Ordered a second reading March 2ᵈ Read the Second time and ordered to be committed, Reported without Amendment and ordered a third reading. March 3ᵈ Read the third time and passed

Gw. BANYAR, Dep Sec.

Nᵒ 42. [Seal] George the, third, by the grace of God of Great Britain France and Ireland, King defender of the faith, &c.

To all to whom these presents shall come or may concern Greeting—Know Ye that among the records remaining in our Secretary's office of our province of Massachusetts Bay in New England, we have inspected a certain Act of the Governor Councill and general Assembly of our said province there enrolled passed the twenty fifth day of April in the year of our Lord one thousand seven hundred and seventy two and in the twelfth year of our reign, the tenor whereof follows in these words, An Act to appoint Commissaries

21

to settle a line of Jurisdiction between this Province and the province of New York, Be it Enacted by the Go.ᵛ Council and House of Representatives that William Brattle, Joseph Hawley, John Hancock Esquires, shall be Commissaries on the Part of this Province who shall be commissionated by the Governor, and who shall have full powers and who are hereby authorized to meet with Commissaries who are or may be appointed and in the like manner authorised and empowered by the Go.ᵛ Council and General Assembly of the Province of New York at such Time or Times Place or Places as shall be agreed upon by the Gov.ᵗ of this Province, and the Governor of the Province of New York, then and there to agree upon a line of Future Jurisdiction betwen the said Provinces on the Easterly part of the said province of New York, and from the South to the North Boundaries of this Province, the Governors aforesaid being present and such Line agreed upon approved of and consented shall be presented by the Governors respectively to His Majesty for His Royal approbation, and being Ratified and Confirmed by His Majesty shall at all Times hereafter be the Line of Jurisdiction between This Province, and the Province of New York, in all and every part or Place where the said Province of New York on its Eastern Boundary shall adjoin on this Province, the True and Real extent or Boundary of this Province By the Royal Charter being in any wise to the Contrary notwithstanding. And be it Further Enacted that after such line shall be so agreed upon and approved of ratified and Confirmed the commissaries appointed by this Act are hereby authorised and empowered to employ a Surveyor or Surveyors Chainbearers and such and so many other persons that may be found necessary to perform the executive part, to run mark and ascertain the said Line in conjunction with such as may be appointed by the Province of New York, for that purpose. All which we have caused to be exemplified by these presents, In Testimony wherof we have caused these our letters to be made Patent and the great. Seal of our Province of Massachusetts Bay in New England to be threunto affixed witness our trusty and well beloved Thomas Hutchinson Esquire our Captain General and Govornor in Chief in and over our Province of Massachusetts Bay in New England and Vice Admiral of the same, at the Council Chamber in Boston the fifth Day of May in the year of our Lord one Thousand seven hundred seventy three and of our Reign the Thirteenth.

By His Excellency's Command

THOMAS FLUCKER Secr.ʸ

N.º 43. (Seal) Thomas Hutchinson Esquire Captain Genˡ and Governor in Chief in and over his Majesty's Province of Massachusetts Bay in New England and vice Admiral of the same—

To William Brattle, Joseph Hawley and John Hancock Esquires Greeting

Whereas the great and general court or Assembly of the Province of the Massachusetts Bay above said did at their Session, begun and held at Cambridge in April last make choice of William Brattle Joseph Hawley and John Hancock Esqˢ. as commissaries on the Part of said province to act in conjunction with such persons as may be appointed by the Government of New York, for settling the Boundary Line between the two provinces, and did desire I would commissionate them for that purpose aforesaid—

I do therefore commissionate by these Presents and empower you the said William Brattle, Joseph Hawley, and John Hancock Esqˢ. on the part of this Government, to meet, and act in conjunction, with such persons as may be appointed by the Government of New York in settling the Boundary line as aforesaid between the Two Provinces.

In. Testimony whereof I have caused the public Seal of the province of Massachusetts Bay aforesaid to be hereunto affixed. Dated at Boston the twenty ninth

Day of April 1773 in the Thirteenth year of His Majesty's Reign

By His Excellency's Command

Jn⁰. Cotton Dep.ᵗ Sec.ʸ

N⁰. 44. This Agreement indented made the eighteenth Day of May in the thirteenth year of the Reign of His Most Gracious Majesty George the Third King of Great Britain France and Ireland Defender of the Faith &c and in the year of our Lord one Thousand seven hundred and seventy three, Between John Watts, William Smith, Robert R Livingston and William Nicoll Esquires duly authorised to make such agreement by virtue of a Law of the Province of New York on the one Part and William Brattle, Joseph Hawley, & John Hancock Esquires thereunto also duly authorised by virtue of a Law of the Province of Massachusetts Bay on the other Part Witnesseth, that the Commissaries aforesaid being met at Hartford in the Colony of Connecticut for the settlement of a partition Line of Jurisdiction between the said provinces of New York and the Massachusetts Bay on the Easterly part of the said province of New York, and from the South to the North Boundaries of the said Massachusetts Bay, in Pursuance of the said Laws and Certain Commissions respectively Issued to the commissaries above named by the Governors of the Provinces aforesaid and in compliance of the Royal recommendation heretofore signified to Sir Henry Moore, Br.ᵗ and to Francis Bernard Esq.ʳ the then Gove.ʳˢ of the Said provinces by Letters from the Right Honorable the Earl of Shelburne late one of His Majesty's Principal Secretary's of State and after having had divers conferences relative to the aforesaid Boundary of the said provinces they the said commissaries do thereupon unanimously agree that the Following *Line, that is to say a line beginning* at a place fixed upon by the two Governments of New York and Connecticut in or about the year or our Lord One Thousand seven Hundred and thirty one for the northwest corner of a tract of Land commonly called Oblong or Equivalent Land and running from the said corner north twenty one Degrees Ten Minutes and thirty seconds East as the Magnet needle now points to the North Line of the Massachusetts Bay shall at all times hereafter be the Line of Jurisdiction between the said province of the Massachusetts Bay and the said Province of New York in all and every part and place where the said province of New York on its Eastern Boundary shall adjoin on the said Province of the Massachusetts Bay. In Testimony whereof the commissaries aforesaid have hereunto Set their Hands and seals the Day and year first abovementioned.

Wm BRATTLE (seal)   J^{no} WATTS (seal)
JOHN HAWLEY (seal)   Wm SMITH (seal)
J^{no} HANCOCK (seal)   Wm NICOLL (seal)
Sealed and Delivered   R. R. LIVINGSTON (seal)
   in the Presence of
ELIPH^t DYER
W^m SAM^l JOHNSON

We the Governors of the Provinces aforesaid having been present at the execution of the agreement aforesaid in Testimony of our consent thereto and of our approbation thereof have hereunto set our hands and seals, at Hartford aforesaid this Eighteenth Day of May in the year of our Lord one Thousand seven hundred and seventy three, and the Thirteenth year of His Majestys Reign.

Sealed and Delivered   Wm TRYON (seal)
   in the presence of   T. HUTCHINSON (seal)
ELIPH^t DYER
W^m SAM^l JOHNSON

N° 45. The Report of William Nicoll, Appointed to superintend the running out and marking the Boundary Line between the Colony of New York and Massachusetts Bay, and of Gerard Bancker surveyor appointed to Run and Mark the same, in

Conjunction with such persons as should be authorised for that purpose on the Part of the Massachusetts Bay.

Monday the 11th of October being the Day appointed by His Excellency Go.r Tryon and Governor Hutchinson for meeting to Run the Line we accordingly
attended at the North West Corner of the Oblong, the
Massachusetts Gentlemen were not there, but that evening Major Hawley sent word, that he was to lodge
about six miles north of it, and would meet us on the
spot the next morning, we accordingly met the next
morning at the Monument put up for the North West
corner of the Oblong, which was shown by Cornelius
Brower of New York Government and Jacob Spoor of
Massachusetts Bay, who severally declared on Oath that
they were present at the Erecting of it about the year
1731 it was a small heap of stones and a stake marked
on the south and west sides $\stackrel{\circ}{\times}$ we enlarged the heap
of stones, and put up a Red Cedar post with the old
stake and marked it $\stackrel{Y}{GB}\stackrel{M}{\times}$. Major Hawley brought
with him David Ingersol and Elijah Dwight Esquires
two Justices who swore the surveyors, Miller and
Bancker, as well as the chainbearers, to perform the
service without any fraud, deceit, or sinister views whatever—this being done, we produced our Commissions.
Major Hawley in return shewed us a copy of a Minute
of Council of the 17th June Signed by His Excellency
Governor Hutchinson, in which after thanking their
commissaries for settling the Line, they appoint Major
Hawley to see it run and Marked and empower the
Governor to appoint a surveyor and the necessary assistants, and a letter from the Governor to Major Hawley
acquainting him that he had appointed M.r Miller to
Survey and Run the Line.

The surveying instruments were then produced and
on comparing them it was found that the Massachusetts
Instrument would Run the Line considerably more East
than our instrument where upon Major Hawley proposed that the Mean difference of the two Instruments

should be taken and used, which was agreed to. The
Massachusetts Gentlemen chose their Instrument should
be used, we consented and that afternoon went about
25 Chains the next Morning they chose to go Back to
the Oblong corner and examine the course that had been
Run, in doing which we discovered a defect in their Instrument for which they agreed that ours should be
used in preference to it. The survey went on with our
Instrument for about six miles but finding the needle
frequently affected by minerals the Massachusetts gentlemen expressed a doubt whether we had continued on
the true course, it was here tryed on low land, where
we did not apprehend there was any attraction and after
correcting a back monument or two and satisfying both
sides, it was agreed to run by stakes and back sights
only as we found the needle so often affected as not to
be depended upon, for this purpose we used the Teles-
cope of their Instrument, went on a·far as the Kinderhook Road which is about eleven Miles from our beginning. It then occurred to them that a Line run thus by
stakes would incline more Easterly than a line run by
the needle, as the needle by an increase of the variation in
going on would form a curve line inclining westerly, but
after considering the Difference that this would make,
it was agreed that a Strait line should be continued, by
stakes, and that our method of running the Line should
be particularly described in the Report that was Intended to be made on Finishing the Business. Upon
this Major Hawley finding the survey going on to his
satisfaction left and went home for six days but on the
second day after his return when we had Gone about
twenty Miles from the Oblong corner he Objected to the
Line as it had been run, alledging the Course we had
run was too much East, and the Line run by stakes, was
not the Line intended by the Hartford agreement, and
insisted on altering the course from the Beginning. He
was put in mind that the difference between a Line run
by stakes and one run by the needle had before been
considered, and ought not to be raised as an objection,

but to no purpose.　M.̣ Nicoll urged him to continue the Line in the manner it had been run thus far, and to report it to the commissaries of both governments, particularly describing the manner of running it, on which they might hereafter determine, as the final Settlement of the Line after the Royal approbation to the Hartford agreement was obtained, is left to them, but this was refused.　It was then offered to him to begin at the Kinderhook Road about eleven miles from our beginning (where we had proved our course was right by trying it with the compass which M.̣ Yates used in makking the survey of Hudsons River, which was laid before the Commissaries at Hartford) and endeavour to ascertain what a Line run by stakes differed from a Line run by the needle, and from thence forward make the offsetts from our Monument agreeable to their plan, but this was also refused and he would not agree to go on any further unless we would alter the course and compute the offsetts from the beginning and here the business stopped.

W.ᴹ NICOLL
GERARD BANCKER.

New York 5.ᵗʰ Nov.ʳ 1773

N.º 46.　Governor Stuyvesants answer to the Letter of Summons [from the English Commissioners in 1664.]

My Lords:—Your 1.ˢᵗ Lre unsigned of $\frac{20}{30}$ Aug.ᵗ together with that of this day signed according to fform being the 1.ˢᵗ September, have beene safely delivered into o.̣ hands by yo.ʳ deputyes unto which wee shall say！

That the rights of His Ma.ᵗⁱᵉ of England unto any Part of America hereabout, amongst the rest unto y.ᵉ colonyes of Virginia, Maryland, or others in New England, whether disputable or not, is that w.ʰ for the pr.ᵉˢent, wee have no designe to debate upon—But that his Ma.ᵗⁱᵉ hath an indisputable right to all the Lands in the north part of America, is that w.ʰ the Kings of ffrance and Spaine will disallow, as we absolutely do, by vertue

of a commission given to me by my Lords the high and
Mighty States Gen.ᵃˡˡ to be Govern.ʳ Gen.ᵃˡˡ over New
Holland, The Isles of Curaco, Bonaire, Aruba, with
theire apurtenances and dependances bearing date 26.ᵗʰ
of July 1646 as also by vertue of a Grant and Commission given by my said Lords the High and Mighty
States Gen.ᵃˡˡ to the West India Company in the yeare
1621 with as much power and as Authentique, as his
Majestie of England hath given or can give to any
Colony in America, as more fully appeares by the Patent
and Commission of the said Lords the States Gen.ᵃˡˡ by
them signed, registred, and sealed w.ᵗʰ their Great Seal,
which were shewed to yo.ʳ Deputy'es, Coll George Cartwright, Cap.ᵗ Rob.ᵗ Needham, Cap.ᵗ Edward Groves, and
M.ʳ Thomas Delaval, by w.ᶜʰ commission and Patent together (To deale frankly w.ᵗʰ you) and by divers Lres
Signed and sealed by our said Lords the States Gen.ᵃˡˡ
directed to several persons both English, and Dutch.
Inhabitants of the Towns, and Villages, on Long Island,
(which without doubt have been produced before y.ᵒ by
those Inhabitants) by which they are declared and acknowledged to be their subjects, w.ᵗʰ express command
that they continue Faithfull unto them, under penalty
of Incurring their utmost displeasure w.ᶜʰ makes it appear more cleare than the Sun at noon Day! That
yo.ʳ first Foundation Viz (That the Right and Title of
His Ma.ᵗⁱᵉ of Great Brittiane To these parts of America
is unquestionable) is absolutely to be denied.

Moreover it is without dispute and acknowledged
by all y.ᵉ world, that our predecess.ʳˢ by vertue of the
commission, and Patent, of the said lords the States
Gen.ᵃˡˡ have without controul and peaceably, (the contrary
never coming to our knowledge) enjoyed ffort Orange
about 48, or 50 years, the Manhattans about 41, or 42
yeares the South River 40 yeares & y.ᵉ ffresh water
River about 36 yea.ʳˢ. Touching the second subject of
yo.ʳ lre (Viz: his Ma.ᵗⁱᵉ hath commanded me in his
name to require a surrender of all such fforts, Townes,
or places of strength, w.ʰ now are possessed by the

Dutch under yo. command,) We shall answer, That wee are so confident of the discretion and equity of his Matie of Great Brittaine, that in case His Matie were informed of the Truth, w^h. is that the Dutch came not into these provinces by any violence but by vertue of Commission from My Lords the States Gen^{all} first of all in the years 1614, 1615, and 1616, up the North River neare ffort Orange, where to hinder the Invasions, and massacres commonly committed by the Salvages They Built a Little Fort, and after in the year 1622 and even to this present time by vertue of Commission and Grants to ye Governors of the West India Company, and moreover in the yeare 1656 a Grant to the Burgomasters of Amsterdam of the South River, insomuch that by vertue of the abovesaid Commission from the High and Mighty States Gen^{all}, given to ye per^s interested as afores^d. and others, These Provinces have been governed and consequently enjoyed, as also in regard of their first discovery uninterrupted possession and purchase of the Lands of the Princes, natives of the country, and private Persons (Though Gentiles) Wee make no dou^t that if His said M^{atie} of Great Brittaine were well informed of these passages, he would be too Judicious to Grant such an Order, principally in a time when there is so Straight a friendship and confederacy between our said Lords and Sup^{rs} to trouble us in the demanding and summons of the Places & ffortresses wch were put into our Hands wth order to maintaine them in the name of the said Lords the States Gen^{all}, as was made appeare to yor deputyes under the names and seals of the said High and Mighty States Gen^{all} dated the twenty eight July 1646.

Besides what has beene mentioned there is Little probability that his said Matie of England (in regard the articles of Peace are printed and were recommended to us to regard seriously and exactly) by a lre written to us by our S^d Lords ye States Gen^{all} and to cause them to be observed religiously in this Country) would give order touching so dangerous a designe, being also so apparent, that none other than my said Lords the States Gen^{all} have any right to these provinces and consequently ought to command and maintaine their Subjects wee ye Governor Gen^{all} are obliged to maintaine their rights, and to repell, and take revenge of all threatnings, injustice, attempts, or any force whatsoever, that shall be committed against their Faithfull Subjects, and Inhabitants it being a very considerable thing to affront so mighty a State, although it were not against an ally and confederate.

Consequently if his said Matie (as it is fit) were well informed of all that could be spoken on this subject, hee would not approve of what expressions are mentioned in yor lre which are that you are commanded by his Matie to demand in his name such places and ffort^{ts} as are in ye possession of the Dutch under my Government, which as it appears by my commission beforementioned was given me by my Lords the High and Mighty States Gen^{all} And there is lesse ground in the express demand of my Government since all the the world knows that about three years agone, some English ffriggots being on ye Coast of Africa, upon a pretended commission they did demand certaine places under the Government of our s^d Lords the States Gen^{all} as Cape Vert, River of Gambo, and all other places in Guyny to them belonging, upon which our said Lords the States Gen^{all} by vertue of the articles of Peace, having made appeare the said attempt to his Matie of England, they recv^d a favourable answer, His said Majesty disallowing all such acts of Hostility as might have been done, and besides gave orders that restitution should be made to the East India Company of whatsoever had been pillaged in the said River of Gambo, and likewise restored them to their Trade. Which makes us think it necessary that a more express order should appeare unto us, as a sufficient warrant for us towards my Lords the High and Mighty States Gen^{all} since by vertue of our said commission wee do in these provinces represent them; as belonging to them and not to the King of Great Brittaine, except his said Matie upon better grounds make it appear to our s^d. Lords the States Gen^{all} against wch they may defend themselves as they shall think fit.

To conclude, wee cannot but declare unto you though the Governo^{rs} and Com^{rs} of his Matie have·divers times quarrelled with us, about the bounds of the Jurisdiction of the High and Mighty the States Gen^{all} in these parts, yet they never questioned their Jurisdiction in itself, on the contrary in the yeare 1650 at Hartford, and the last yeare at Boston they treated with us on this subject wch is a sufficient prooff that his Majesty hath never been well informed of the Equity of oure cause, Insomuch as we cannot imagine in regard of the articles of peace betweene the Crown of England and ye States Gen^{all} (under whom there are so many subjects in America as well as in Europe) that his s^d ma^{tie} of Greate Brittaine would give a commission to molest and endamage the subjects of my said Lords the States Gen^{all} especially such as ever since [for] 50, 40 and ye latest 36 years have quietly enjoyed their Lands, Countryes, fforts, and Inheritances. And lesse that his subjects would attempt any acts of Hostility or violence against them, and in Case that you will act by Force of Arms, We protest and Declare in the name of our said Lords the States Gen^{all}, and before God and man, that you will act an unjust violence and a breach of the articles of peace, so solemnly sworn, agreed upon, and Ratified by His Majesty of England, and my Lords the St^{es} Gen^{all} and ye rather to prevent the shedding of Blood, in the Month of February last, wee treated with Capt John Scott (who reported he had a commission from His s^d Matie) touching ye Limits of Long Island, and concluded for the space of a yeare, that in the meane time the business might be treated on, between ye the King of Greate Brittaine, and my Lords the High and Mighty States Gen^{all} and again at p'sent for the hindrance and prevention of all differences, and the spilling of Innocent Blood not only in these p^{ts} but in Europe, We offer unto you a Treaty by our Deputyes Mr Corn^{lis} Van Ruyven, Secretary and

Receiver of New Holland, Cornelius Steenwich Burgom.
M. Samuel Megapolensis Doctor of Physick, and M.
James Cousseau heretofore Sherriffe.

As touching the threats in your conclusion wee have
nothing to answer, only that we Feare nothing but what
God (who is Just as mercifull) shall lay upon us, all
things being in his Gracious disposal, and we may as
well be preserved by him with small Forces, as with a
greate Army wch makes us to wish yo^u all happynesse
and prosperity and recommend you to his Protection.

My Lords Yo^r thrice humble and affectionate
Servant and Friend
(Signed) P. STUYVESANT.

Ffort Amsterdam
2^d Sep^t New Stile
1664

N°. 47. These articles following were consented to by
the persons here under subscribed at the Go^{vs} Bow-
ery August 27th old stile 1664.

1. We consent that the States Gen^{all} or the West
India Company shall freely enjoy all ffarms and
Houses (except such as are in the fforts) and that within Six monthes, they shall have free Liberty, to transport
all such arms and ammunition as now doe belong to
them, or else they shall be paid for them.

2. All Publique Houses shall continue for the uses
which they are for.

3. All people shall still continue Free Denizens and
enjoy their Lands, Houses, Goods, Shipps, wheresoever
they are within this Country and dispose of them as
they Please.

4. If any Inhabitant have a mind to remove himself he shall have a yeare and six weeks from this Day
to remove himself Wife, children, Servants, Goods and
to Dispose of His Lands here.

5. If any Officer of State or public Minister of
State have a mind to go for England, they shall be
transported fraught free in His Majesties ffriggots when
these ffriggots shall returne thither.

6. It is consented to, that any People may freely come from the Netherlands, and plant in this country, and that Dutch Vessells may freely come hither and any of y⁰ Dutch may freely return home, or send any sort of Merchandize home in vessels of their own country.

7. All Shipps from the Netherlands or any other place, and Goods therein shall be received here, & sent hence after the manner which formerly they were, before our coming hither, for six months next ensueing.

8. The Dutch here shall enjoy the Liberty of their consciences in Divine Worship and church Discipline.

9. No Dutch man here nor Dutch shipp here shall upon any occasion be pressed to serve in Warr against any nation whatsoever.

10. That the Townsmen of the Manhattoes shall not have any Souldier quartered upon them, without being satisfied, and paid for them by their Officers, and that at this present if the ffort be not capable of lodgeing all the Souldiers, then the Burgomasters by their Officers, shall appoint some Houses capable to receive them.

11. The Dutch here shall enjoy their own customs concerning their Inheritances.

12. All Publique writings and records wᶜʰ concern yᵉ Inheritances of any people or yᵉ Reglmᵗ of y⁰ Church or poor, or Orphans, shall·be carefully kept by those in whose hands now they are, and such writings as particularly concerne the States Genᵃˡˡ may at any time be sent to them.

13. No Judgement that has passed any Judicature here, shall be called in question, but if any conceive that he hath not had Justice done him, if he apply himself to the States General, the other party shall be bound to answer for yᵉ supposed Injury.

14. If any Dutch living here shall at any time desire to travaile or traffique into England, or any place, or plantation in Obedience to His ᴹaᵗⁱᵉ of England or wᵗʰ the Indians hee shall (upon his request to the Governor) have a certificate that hee is a free Denizen of this place and Liberty to doe soe.

15. If it doe appeare that there is a publique Engagement of Debt by the Town of the Manhatoes, and a way agreed on for the Satisfying of that engagement, it is agreed that ye same way proposed shall goe on, and that ye Engagement shall be satisfyed.

16. All inferior civil Officers and Magistrates shall continue as now they are, (if they please) till the customary time of new Elections, and then new ones to be chosen by themselves, provided that such new chosen magistrates shall take the oath of allegiance to His Majesty of England before they enter upon their Office.

17. All differences of contracts and Bargains made before this Day by any in this country, shall be determined according to the manner of the Dutch.

18. If it do appear that the West India Company of Amsterdam doe really owe any sums of Money to any persons here, it is agreed that Recognition, and other dutyes payable by shipps going for the Netherlands, be continued for six months Longer.

19. The Officers, Military, and Souldiers shall march out with their arms, Drums beating, and colours flying and lighted matches; and if any of them will plant they shall have 50 Acres of land set out for them, if any of them will serve any as servants they shall continue with all safety, and become Free denizens afterwards.

20. If at any time hereafter the King of Greate Brittaine and the States of the Netherlands doe agree that this Place and country be redelivered into the hands of the said States whensoever his Majesty will send his commands to redeliver it shall immediately be Done.

21. That the Town of Manhatans, shall choose Deputyes, and those Deputyes shall have free voices in all Publique affaires, as much as any other Deputyes.

22. Those who have any Property in any houses in ye ffort of Aurania shall (if they please) slight the Fortifications there and then enjoy all their Houses as all people do where there is no ffort.

23. If there be any Souldiers that will goe into Hol-

land and if the Company of West India in Amsterdam or any private persons here will transport them into Holland, then they shall have a safe Passport from Col Richard Nicolls Deputye Gov.⁻ unto his Royall Highnesse, and the other Com.ʳˢ to defend the shipps that shall transport such souldiers, and all the Goods in them from any surprisall or acts of Hostility to be done by any of His Ma.ᵗᵉˢ Shipps or Subjects. [24]. That the Copies of the Kings Grant to his Royal Highnesse, and the Copy of His Royal Highnesse's Commission to Coll. Richard Nicolls, testified by two commissioners more and Mʳ Winthrop to be true Copies, shall be delivered to yᵉ honb.! Mʳ Stuyvesant the p.⁻ Governor, on Monday next by Eight of the clock in the morning at yᵉ. old Miln, and these articles, consented to, and signed by Coll. Richard Nicolls Deputye Govʳ to his Royall Highness, and that within two hours after, the Fort and Town called New Amsterdam upon the Isle of Manhatoes, shall be delivered into yᵉ hands of the sᵈ Coll. Rich.ᵈ Nicolls by the service of such as shall be by him thereunto deputed by His Hand & Seale.

JOHN DE DECKER	ROBERT CARR
NICH. VERLEETT	GEO. CARTWRIGHT
SAM. MEGAPOLENSIS	JOHN WINTHROP
CORNELIUS STEENWICK	SAM. WYLLYS
OLOFFE S. VAN KORTLANT	THOMAS CLARK
JAMES COUSSEAU	JOHN PINCHON

I doe consent to these articles

RICHARD NICOLLS.

No. 48. Articles made and agreed upon the 24ᵗʰ day Sep.ᵗ 1664 in Fort Albany Betweene Ohgehaudo, Shanarage, Soacheneghton, Sachamackas, of the Maquas, Annawweed, Conkeeherat, Tewasserany Aschannoondak, Sachamackas of the Synicks, on the one part, and Coll. George Cartwright in behalf of Coll. Richard Nicolls, Governor under his Royal Highnesse the Duke of Yorke of all the Territorys in America as Followeth : viz.

1. Imprimis. It is agreed that the Indyan Princes above named and their subjects, shall have all such wares and commodities from the English for the future as heretofore they had from the Dutch.

2. That if any English, Dutch or Indyans (under protection of English) doe any wrong, injury, or violence to any of the said Indyan Princes, or their subjects in any sort whatever, if they complain to the Governors in New York, or to the Offi^r in Chief at Albany, if the person so offending can be discovered, that person shall receive condigne punnishment, and all due satisfaction shall be given, and the like shall be done for all other English Plantations.

3. That if any Indian belonging to any of the Sachims aforesaid, doe any wrong, Injury, or Damage to the English, Dutch, or Indyans (under the Protection of of the English) If complaint be made to the Sachims and the person be discovered who did the Injury, then that Person so offending shall bee punnished, and all just satisfaction given to any of his Ma^{tles} Subjects in any Colony, (or other English Plantation in America)

4. The Indyans at Wamping and Espachomy and all below to the Manhatans, as also all such as have sub-mitted themselves under the Protection of his Ma^{tle} are included in these articles of agreement and Peace. In confirmation whereof, the Partyes above mentioned have hereunto sett their Hands the day and yeare above written

GEORGE CARTWRIGHT.

Signed and deliver-
ed in the pres-
ence of
THO^S. WILLETT
JOHN MANNING
TH^O. BREEDON
DAN^L. BROADHEAD
-&-&- {SMITH JOHN
his marke
STEPHEN an

These articles following were likewise proposed by the same Indyan Princes, and consented to by Coll. Ge̊ Cartwright in Behalfe of Coll. Nicolls the 25ᵗʰ day of September 1664.

1. That the English do not assist the three nations of the Ondiahes, Pinnehoocks, Pecamtehookes who murdered one of the the Princes of the Maques, when hee brought ransom and Presents to them upon a treaty of Peace.

2. That the English do make Peace for the Indians with the Nations downe the River.

3. That they may have free trade as formerly.

4. That they may be lodged in houses as formerly.

5. That if they be beaten by the three nations above mentioned, they may receive accommodation from the English.

Nᵒ 49.   Monday June 22ⁿᵈ 1741
Present
            The Honblᵉ Cadwallader Colden Esqʳ Presᵗ
                    Archibald Kennedy ⎫
                    James De Lancey   ⎪
                    William Skene   ⎬ Esqʳˢ
                    William Sherriff ⎪
                    Evaˢ James Phillipps ⎪
                    Otho Hamilton   ⎭

The Court Opened

The Committee for the Province produced the Original Charter for the province of the Massachusetts Bay under the Great Seal, and the Court ordered that a Copy thereof be transcribed & examined by two of the Clerks and attested by them, which was accordingly done and is as follows—

William & Mary by the Grace of God King and Queen of England, Scotland, France, and Ireland, Defenders of the Faith &cᵃ To all to whom these Presents shall come, Greeting. Whereas His late Majesty King James the first our Royal predecessor, by his Letters Patents under the Great Seal of England, bearing Date at Westminster the third day of November in the Eighteenth year of his Reign did give and Grant unto the Council established at Plymouth in the County of Devon for the planting Ruling ordering and Governing of New England in America, and to their successors and assigns, All that part of America lying and Being in breadth from Forty Degrees of Northerly Latitude from the Equinoctial Line, to ye Forty Eighth Degree of the said northerly Latitude inclusively and in Length of and within all the Breadth aforesaid through out all the Lands from *Sea to Sea* together also with all the Lands, Soils, Grounds, Havens, Ports, Rivers, Waters, Fishings Mines & Minerals as well Royal Mines of Gold and Silver, as other mines and Minerals Precious Stones, Quarries & all & singular other commodities, Jurisdictions, Royalties, Priviledges, Franchises and preheminences, both within the said Tract of Land upon the Main & also within the Islands and Seas adjoining, *Provided Always* that the said Lands Islands or any of the Premises by the said Letters Patents intended or meant to be granted were not then actually Possessed or Inhabited by any other christian Prince or State, or within the Bounds Limits or Territorys of the Southern Colony, then before Granted by the Said late King James the first to be planted by Divers of his Subjects in the South parts To Have and To Hold possess and Enjoy all and Singular the aforesaid Continent, Lands, Territories, Islands, Hereditaments & Precincts, Seas, Waters, Fishings with all & all manner of their Comodities, Royalties, Liberties, Preheminences & Profits that should from thenceforth arise from thence with all and Singular their apurtenances and every part and parcel thereof unto the Said Council and their successors & Assigns for ever to the sole use and benefit of the said Council and their successors and assigns forever: To be holden of His said Late Majesty King James His Heirs and Successors, as of his Mannor of East Greenwich in the County of Kent, in free and common Sockage & not in Capite, nor by Knights

Service Yielding and Paying therefore to the said late King, His Heirs and successors the fifth part of the ore of Gold and Silver, which should from time to time, & at all times thereafter happen to be found gotten had and obtained in, at, or within any of the said Lands, Limits, Territories or precincts, or in or within any part, or parcel thereof for or in respect of all & all manner of Duties, Demands and Services whatsoever to be done made or paid to the said late King James the first, His Heirs and Successors (as in and by the Said Letters Patents, amongst sundry other clauses Powers, Priviledges, and Grants, therein contained more at large appeareth:) And Whereas the said Council established at Plymouth in the County of Devon for the planting ruling, ordering and Governing of New England in America did by their Deed indented under their common Seal bearing date the nineteenth day of of March in the third year of the Reign of our Royal Grandfather King Charles the first of ever Blessed memory, Give, Grant, Bargain Sell Infeoff, alien and confirm To Sir Henry Roswell Sir John Young, Knights, Thomas Southcott, John Humphreys, John Endicott & Simon Whetcombe Their Heirs and assigns & their associates for ever, all that part of New England in America aforesaid which lyes and extends between a great River there commonly called Monomack alias Merimack & a certain other River there called Charles River being in a bottom of a certain Bay, there commonly called Massachusetts Bay alias Mattachusetts alias Massatusetts & also all and singular those Lands & Hereditaments whatsoever lying within the space of three English miles on the South part of the said Charles River or of any and every part thereof and also all and singular the Lands & Hereditaments whatsoever lying and being within the space of three English Miles to the Southward of the Southermost part of the Said Bay called the Massachusetts alias Mattachusetts alias Massatusetts and all those Lands and Hereditaments whatsoever which Lye and be within the space of three

English miles to the northward of the said River
called Monomack alias Merimack or to the northward
of any and every part thereof & all Lands & Hered-
itaments whatsoever lying within the Limits aforesaid,
North and South in Latitude, and in Breadth and in
Length and Longitude of and within all the Breadth
aforesaid, Throughout the main Lands there *From the
Atlantic and Western Sea and Ocean on the East Part
to the South Sea on the West Part,* and all Lands &
Grounds place and places, Soil, Woods, and Wood
Grounds Havens, ports, Rivers, Waters, Fishings and
Hereditaments whatsoever lying within the said Bounds
& Limits & every part and parcel thereof, and also
all Islands lying in America aforesaid, in the said
Seas or either of them on the Western or Eastern Coasts
or parts of the said Tracts of Land by the said Indenture mentioned to be given and granted Bargained Sold
Enfeoffed, alien'd and confirmed, or any of them & also
all mines & minerals, as well Royal mines of Gold &
Silver as other mines & minerals whatsoever in the said
Lands & Premises or any part thereof and all Jurisdictions, Rights, Royalties, Libertys, Freedoms, Immunities, Priviledges, Franchises, Preheminences &
commodities whatsoever which they the said council
established at Plymouth in the county of Devon for the
planting, Ruling, ordering, & Governing of New England in America then had or might use exercise or
Enjoy in or within the said Lands or Premises by the
same Indenture mentioned to be given granted Bargained Sold Enfeoffed and confirmed in or within any
part or parcel thereof: To have and to hold the said
part of New England in America, which lies and extends, and is abutted as aforesaid, and every part and
parcel thereof; and all the said Islands, Rivers, Ports,
Havens, Waters, Fishings, Mines, Minerals, Jurisdictions, Franchises, Royalties, Libertys, Priviledges Commodities, Hereditaments & Premises whatsoever with
the appurtenances unto the s.ᵈ Sir Henry Roswell,
Sir John Young, Thoˢ. Southcott, John Humphreys,

John Endicott and Simon Whetcombe, their Heirs
and assigns & their associates for Ever, to the only
proper and absolute use and behoofe of the s.^d Sir
Henry Roswell, Sir John Young, Thomas Southcott,
John Humphreys, John Endicott & Simon Whetcombe, Their Heirs and assigns and their associates for evermore, To be holden of our said Royal
Grandfather King Charles the first, His Heirs &
successors as of his Mannor of East Greenwich in the
County of Kent in Free and common Sockage and not
in Capite nor by Knights service, yielding and paying
therefore unto our said Royal Grandfather, his Heirs
and successors the fifth part of the ore of Gold and
Silver which sh.^d from time to time and at all times
hereafter happen to be found gotten, had and obtained
in any of the said Lands within the said Limits or in
or within any part thereof, for and in satisfaction of all
manner of Duties, Demands, and Services whatsoever
to be done made or paid to our s.^d Royal Grandfather,
His Heirs or successors (as in & by said recited Indenture may more at large appear.)   And Whereas our
s.^d Royal Grandfather in and by his Letters Patents under
the Great Seal of England bearing date at Westminster
the fourth day of March in the Fourth year of his Reign
for the consideration therein mentioned did grant and
Confirm unto the said Sir Henry Roswell Sir John
Young, Thos Southcott, John Humphreys, John Endi-
cott & Simon Whetcombe and their associates after
named Viz Sir Richard Saltonstall Knight, Isaac John-
ston, Samuel Aldersey, John Ven, Matthew Craddock,
George Harwood Increase Nowell, Richard Perry,
Richard Bellingham, Nathaniel Wright, Samuel Vassall,
Theophilus Eaton, Thomas Goffe, Thomas Adams, John
Brown, Samuel Brown, Thomas Hutchins, William
Vassall, William Pincheon & George Foxcroft their
Heirs & Assigns all the said part of New England in
America lying and Extending between the Bounds &
Limits in the said Indenture expressed, & all Lands
and Grounds, place & places, Soils Woods and Wood

Grounds, Havens, Ports, Rivers, Waters, Mines, Minerals, Jurisdictions, Rights, Royalties, Liberties, Freedoms, Immunities, Priviledges, Franchises, Preheminences & Hereditaments whatsoever bargained Sold Enfeoffed and confirmed or mentioned or intended to be given granted Bargained Sold Enfeoffed, aliened & Confirmed to them the said Sir Henry Roswell, Sir John Young, Thomas Southcott, John Humphreys, John Endicott and Simon Whetcombe, their Heirs and assigns & to their Associates forever by the said recited Indenture, To Have and To Hold the said part of New England in America and other the premises thereby mentioned to be granted and confirmed & every part and parcel thereof with the Appurtenances to the said Sr Henry Roswell, Sir John Young, Sr Richard Saltonstall, Thomas Southcott, John Humphreys, John Endicott, Simon Whetcombe, Isaac Johnston, Samuel Aldersey, John Ven, Matthew Craddock, George Harwood, Increase Nowell, Richard Perry, Richard Bellingham, Nathaniel Wright, Samuel Vassall, Theophilus Eaton, Thomas Goffe, Thomas Adams, John Brown, Samuel Brown, Thomas Hutchins, William Vassall, William Pincheon and George Foxcroft, their Heirs and Assigns for ever to their only proper and Absolute use and Behoof forever more: To Be Holden of our Said Royal Grandfather his Heirs and successors as of his Manor of East Greenwich aforesaid in free and Common Sockage, and not in capite nor by Knights Service, and also yielding and paying therefore to our said Royal Grandfather his Heirs and successors the fifth part only of all the ore of Gold and Silver which from time to time and at all times after should be there gotten had or obtained, for all services Exactions, and Demands whatsoever, according to the Tenor and reservation in the said recited Indenture Expressed, and Furtther, our said Royal Grandfather by the said Letters Patents Did *Give* and *Grant* unto the said Sir Henry Roswell, Sir John Young, Sir Richard Saltonstall, Thomas Southcott, John

Humphreys, John Endicott, Simon Whetcombe, Isaac Johnston, Samuel Aldersey, John Ven, Matthew Craddock, George Harwood, Increase Nowell, Richard Perry, Richard Bellingham, Nathaniel Wright, Samuel Vassall, Theophilus Eaton, Thomas Goffe, Thomas Adams, John Brown, Samuel Brown, Thomas Hutchins, William Vassall, William Pincheon & George Foxcroft, their Heirs and assigns all that said part of New England in America which lyes & extends between a Great River there commonly called Monomack alias Merimack River, and a certain other River there called Charles River, being in the bottom of a certain Bay there commonly called Massachusetts alias Mattachusetts alias Massatusetts Bay and also all & singular those Lànds & Hereditaments whatsoever lying within the space of three English Miles on the South part of the said River, called Charles River or of any or every Part thereof & also all and singular the Lands and Hereditaments whatsoever lying & being within the space of three English Miles to the Southward of the Southermost part of the said Bay and also all those Lands and Hereditaments whatsoever which lye and be within the space of three English Miles to the Northward of the said River called Monomack alias Merimack or to the Northward of any and every part thereof & all Lands and Hereditaments whatsoever lying within the Limits aforesaid, North and South in Latitude & in Breadth & in Length and Longitude of & within all the Breadth aforesaid Throughout the Main Lands there *From the Atlantic or Western Sea & Ocean, on the East part To the South Sea on the West part*, & all Lands, Grounds, Place and Places, Soils, Woods, and Wood-Lands, Havens, Ports, and Rivers, Waters & Hereditaments whatsoever lying within the said Bounds & Limits and Every part and parcel thereof, and also all Islands in America aforesaid in The said Seas or either of them on the Western or Eastern Coasts, or parts of the said tracts of Lands thereby mentioned to be given & Granted or any of them, and all mines &

Minerals, as well Royal Mines of Gold and Silver as other Mines and Minerals whatsoever in the said Lands & premises or any part thereof & Free Liberty of Fishing in or within any of the Rivers or Waters within the Bounds and Limits aforesaid, & the Seas thereunto adjoining and all Fishes, Royal Fishes, Whales, Balene, Sturgeon, and other Fishes of what Kind or nature soever that should at any time thereafter be taken in or within the said Seas or Waters or any of them, By the said Sir Henry Roswell, Sir John Young, Sir Richard Saltonstall, Thomas Southcott, John Humphreys, John Endicott, Simon Whetcomb, Isaac Johnson, Samuel Aldersey, John Ven, Matthew Craddock, George Harwood, Increase Nowell, Richard Perry, Richard Bellingham, Nathaniel Wright, Samuel Vassall, Theophilus Eaton, Thomas Goffe, Thomas Adams, John Brown, Samuel Brown, Thomas Hutchins, William Vassall, William Pincheon & George Foxcroft their Heirs and Assigns or by any other person or persons whatsoever there Inhabiting by them or any of them to be appointed To Fish therein. Provided always that if the said Lands and Islands or any the premises beforementioned intended and meant to be granted by the said Letters patents last mentioned were at the time of Granting the said former letters Patents last mentioned dated the third day of November in the Eighteenth year of the Reign of His Late Majesty King James The first, actually possessed or Inhabited by any other Christian Prince or State, or were within the Bounds or Limits or Territorys of the said Southern Colony then before granted by the said King to be planted by Divers of his loving Subjects in the South part of America, That then the said Grant of our said Royal Grandfather should not extend to any such parts or parcels thereof so formerly inhabited or lyeing within the Bounds of the Southern plantation as aforesaid, But as to those parts or parcels so possessed or Inhabited by any such christian prince or State or being within the Boundaries aforesaid, should be utterly void: To Have and To Hold possess and enjoy the said parts of New England in America which lye extend and are abutted as aforesaid, and every part and Parcel thereof, & all the Islands Rivers ports Havens, Waters, Fishings, Fishes Mines, Minerals, Jurisdictions, Franchises, Royalties, Liberties, Priviledges, Commodities, & Premises whatsoever with the appurtenances unto the said Sir Henry Roswell, Sir John Young Sir Richard Saltonstall, Thomas Southcott, John Endicott, John Humphries, Simon Whetcombe, Isaac Johnson, Samuel Aldersey, John Ven, Matthew Craddock, George Harwood, Increase Nowell, Richard Perry, Richard Bellingham, Nathaniel Wright, Samuel Vassall, Theophilus Eaton, Thomas Goffe, Thomas Adams, John Brown Samuel Brown, Thomas Hutchins, William Vassall, William Pincheon & George Foxcroft, their Heirs and Assigns forever: To the only proper use & behoof of the said Sir Henry Roswell, Sir John Young, Sir Richard Saltonstall, Thomas Southcott, John Humphries, John Endicott, Simon Whetcombe, Isaac Johnson, Samuel Aldersey, John Ven, Matthew Craddock, George Harwood and Increase Nowell, Rich.d Perry, Richard Bellingham, Nathaniel Wright, Samuel Vassall, Theophilus Eaton, Thomas Goffe, Thomas Adams, John Brown, Samuel Brown Thomas Hutchins William Vassall, William Pincheon, George Foxcroft, their Heirs and Asssigns Forevermore. To be holden of our said Royal Grandfather his Heirs and Successors as of his Mannor of East Greenwich in the County of Kent within the Realm of England in free & common Sockage, and not in Capite, nor by Kng.ts Service. And also yielding and Paying therefore to our s.d Royal Grandfather his Heirs and Successors, the fifth Part only of all the Ore of Gold and Silver which from time to time, and at all times thereafter should be gotten had and Obtained for all services Exactions and Demands, whatsoever, Provided Always, and his Majestys express will and meaning was that only one fifth part of all the Gold and Silver Ore above mentioned in the whole and no more should be answered reserved & payable to our s.d Royal

Grandfather his Heirs and successors, by colour and Virtue of the said last mentioned Letters Patents, The double reservations or Recitals aforesaid or anything therein contained notwithstanding, and to the End that the Affairs and Business which from time to time happen to arise concerning the said Lands, And the Plantations of the same might be the better managed & ordered and for the good Government thereof our s^d Royal Grandfather King Charles the 1st did by his letters patents, create and make the s^d Sir Henry Roswell, Sir John Young, Sir Richard Saltonstall, Thomas Southcott, John Humphreys, John Endicott, Simon Whetcombe, Isaac Johnson, Samuel Aldersey, John Ven, Matthew Craddock, George Harwood Increase Nowell, Richard Perry, Richard Bellingham, Nathaniel Wright, Samuel Vassall, Theophilus Eaton, Thomas Goffe, Thomas Adams, John Brown, Samuel Brown Thomas Hutchins William Vassall, William Pincheon, George Foxcroft, & all such others as should thereafter be admitted and be made Free of the company & society therein aftermentioned one Body Politique & corporate in Fact and name by thename of the Governor & Company of the Massachusetts Bay in New England & did Grant unto them and their successors divers powers Liberties & Priviledges as in & by the said Letters Patents may more fully and at large appear & Whereas the said Governor & Company of the Massachusetts Bay in New England by virtue of the said Letters Patents did settle a Colony of the English in the said parts of New England in America & divers good subjects of this Kingdom encouraged and invited by the said Letters Patents did Transport themselves and their Effects into the same where by the said plantation did become very Populous And Divers Counties Towns and Places, were created, erected, made set forth, and designed within the s^d parts of America by the said Governor and Company for the time being And Whereas in term of the Holy Trinity in the Thirty sixth year of the Reign of our dearest Uncle King Charles the second, a Judgement was given in our Court of Chancery sitting at Westminster upon a Writ of Scire Facias brought and prosecuted in the s.ᵈ Court against the Governor and Company of the Massachusetts Bay in New England, That the s.ᵈ letters Patents of our s.ᵈ Royal Grandfather King Charles the First bearing Date at Westminster the fourth Day of March in the fourth year of His Reign, made and Granted to the s.ᵈ Governor & Company of the Massachusetts Bay in New England and the enrollment of the same should be cancelled, vacated and annihilated, and should be brought into the said Court to be cancelled, as in and by the s.ᵈ Judgement remaining upon record in the s.ᵈ Court doth more at Large appear : And *Whereas several persons employed as agents* in behalf our s.ᵈ Colony of Massachusetts Bay in New Engl.ᵈ have made their humble application unto us that we should be graciously pleased by our Royal Charter to *Incorporate our Subjects in our s.ᵈ Colony,* and to Grant and confirm unto them such powers, Priviledges and Franchises as our Royal Wisdom should be thought most conduceing to our Interest and Service & to the welfare and happy state of our subjects in New England. And we being Graciously Pleased to gratify our s.ᵈ subjects and also to the end that our good subjects within our Colony of New Plymouth in New England aforesaid may be brought under such a form of Government as may put them in a better Condition of Defence, and considering as well the granting unto them as unto our subjects in the said Colony of y.ᵉ Massachusetts our Royal Charter with reasonable Powers and priviledges will much tend not only to the safety, but to the Flourishing estate of our subjects in the said parts of New England, and also to the advancing of the Ends for which the said Plantations were at first encouraged, of our especial Grace certain knowledge, & Meer Motion, have willed and ordained & We do by these presents for us our Heirs and successors, Will & Ordain *That the Territorys and Colonys commonly called or known by the names of the Colony of the*

Massachusetts Bay, & Colony of *New Plimouth*, The *Province of Main* The Territory called *Accada or Nova Scotia* & all *that Tract of Land lying between the said Territorys of Nova Scotia, and the said Province of Main be Erected, United, & Incorporated*, And we do by these Presents Unite, Erect, and Incorporate the same into one real province by the name of our province of the Massachusetts Bay in New England & of our especial Grace certain Knowledge, & Meer Motion, We have *Given and Granted* & by these Presents do Give and Grant for us our Heirs and successors, unto our Good Subjects The Inhabitants of our said province or Territory of y.ᵉ Massachusetts Bay and their Successors all that part of New England in America *lying and extending from the great River commonly Monomack alias Merimack, on the north part, & from three miles northward of the s.ᵈ River to the Atlantic or Western Ocean on the South part all the Lands & Hereditaments whatsoever lying within the Limits Aforesaid, and extending as far as the uttermost points or promontorys of Land called Cape Cod & Cape Mallabar north and south & in Latitude Breadth & in Length and Longitude of & within all the Breadth & Compass d'oresaid, throughout the Main Land* there from the sᵈ Atlantic or Western Sea & Ocean on the East Part *towards the South Sea or* WESTWARD, as far as our Colonys of RHODE ISLAND, CONNECTICUT & NARAGANSETT Country, and also all that part or portion of Main Land, beginning at the Entrance of Piscataqua Harbour & so to pass up the same into the River Newichwannock, and through the same into the farthest head thereof, and from thence northward untill one hundred and twenty miles be finished, and from Piscataqua Harbour's Mouth aforesaid north Eastward along the Sea Coast to Sagadahock and from the Period of one hundred &. twenty miles aforesaid, to cross overland to yᵉ one hundred and twenty miles before reckoned up unto the Land from Piscataqua Harbour through Newichwannock River and also the north half of the Isles

and Shoals together with the Isles of Capawock &
Nantucket near Cape Cod aforesaid, & also. the Lands
and Hereditaments lying and being in *the. Country and
Territory commonly called Accada or Nova Scotia* and
also those Lands and Hereditaments lying and extending betwen the said country and Territory of Nova Scotia
and the said River of Sagadahock or any part thereof,
and all Lands Grounds, Places, Soils Woods & Wood
Grounds, Havens Ports, Rivers Waters and other
Hereditaments & Premises whatsoever lying within the
Said Bounds and Limits aforesaid and every Part and
parcel thereof: And also all Islands and Islets lying
within Ten Leagues directly opposite to the Main
Land within the said Bounds, & All Mines and Minerals as well Royal Mines of Gold and Silver as other
Mines & Minerals whatsoever in the s.^{d} Lands and
Premises or any Part thereof, To Have and To Hold
The said Territorys, Tracts, Countrys, Lands & Hereditaments and all and singular other the Premises with
their and every of their appurtenances to our said Subjects the Inhabitants of our s.^{d} Province of the *Massachusetts Bay in New England* and their successors to
their only proper use and Behoof forevermore. To be
holden of us our Heirs and successors as of our Mannor
of East Greenwich in the county of Kent, by Fealty
only in free and common Sockage, Yielding & Paying
therefore yearly to us our Heirs and Successors the
Fifth Part of All Gold and Silver Ore and Precious
Stones which shall from time To Time and at all Times
hereafter happen to be found gotten had or obtained, in
any of the said Lands and premises, or within any
part thereof, Provided Nevertheless & we do for us our
heirs and successors Grant and Ordain, that all and every such Lands Tenements & Hereditaments and all
other Estates which any person or persons or Bodys
Politick or Corporate, Towns, Villages, Colleges or
Schools do hold and enjoy, or ought to Hold and Enjoy within the Bounds aforesaid by or under any Grants
or Estates duly made or Granted by any General Court

formerly Held, or by Virtue of the Letters Patents herein before recited, or by any other lawfull Right or Title whatsoever shall be by such person or persons Bodies Politick & Corporate, Towns, Villages, Colleges or Schools, their respective Heirs, Successors and Assigns forever, hereafter held and enjoyed according to the purport and Intent of such respective Grant under & Subject nevertheless to the Rents and Services thereby reserved or made payable, Any matter or thing whatsoever to the contrary notwithstanding, And provided also nothing herein contained shall extend or be understood or Taken to Impeach or prejudice any Right Title Interest or Grant or Demand which Samuel Allen of London Merchant claiming under John Mason Esq: deceased or any other person or Persons, hath or have or claimeth to have hold or enjoy of into or out of any parts of the Premises situate within y.ᵉ Limits abovementioned, But that the said Samuel Allen and all & every such person & Persons may and shall have, hold and enjoy the same in such manner (& no other than) as if these presents had not been had or made, it being our further will and Pleasure that no Grants or Conveyances of any Lands, Tenements or Hereditaments to any Towns, Colleges Schools of Learning or to any private Person or Persons shall be Judged or taken to be avoided or prejudiced for or by reason of any want or defect of Form, but that the same stand & remain in Force & be maintained and adjudged,to have effect in the same manner as the same should or ought before the time of the said recited Judgement according to the Laws & Rules then and there usually practised & allowed and we do further for us our Heirs & Successors Will Establish and ordain, That from hence forth for ever There shall be one Governor one Lieuᵗ Governor or Deputy, and one Secretary of our Said province or Territory, to be from Time to Time Appointed & Commissionated by us, our Heirs and successors, & Eight and Twenty Assistants or Councellors, to be advising or Assisting to the Governor of our Said province or Territory for the Time being as by these presents is hereafter directed and Appointed, which s^d Councellors or Assistants are to be constituted Elected and Chosen in such form and manner as hereafter in these Presents is Expressed. And for the better execution of our Royal Pleasure and Grant in this behalf We do by these Presents for us our Heirs and Successors, nominate ordain, Make and constitute Our Trusty and well beloved Simon Bradstreet, John Richards, Nathaniel Saltonstall, Wait Winthrop, John Phillips, James Russell, Samuel Sewall, Sam! Appleton, Bartholomew Gedney, John Hathorn, Elisha Hutchinson, Robert Pike, Jonathan Corwin, John Jolliffe Adam Winthrop, Richard Middlecott, John Foster, Peter Sergeant, Joseph Lind, Samuel Heyman, Stephen Mason, Thomas Hinckly, Willm Bradford, John Walley, Barnabas Lothrop, Job Alcott, Samuel Daniel, & Silvanus Davis Esq^{rs} The first & Present Councellors & Assistants of our said Province to Continue in their respective Offices or Trusts of Councellors or Assistants (shall be chosen or appointed) untill the Last Wednesday in May which shall be in the year of our Lord 1693 and untill other Councellors or Assistants shall be appointed in their stead in such manner as in these Presents is expressed. And we do further by these Presents Constitute and appoint our trusty and well Beloved Isaac Addington Esqr to be our first and present secretary of our said province during our pleasure, And our will and pleasure is That the Governor of our s^d province for the time being shall have Authority from Time to Time at his Discretion to Assemble and call together the Councellors or Assistants of our S^d Province for the Time being & that the S^d Governor with the said assistants or Councellors or seven of them at the least, shall and may from Time to Time hold and keep a Council for the Ordering and Directing the affairs of our said province, And Further we Will & by these Presents for us our Heirs and Successors do ordain and Grant, that there shall and may be convened held & kept, by the Governor for the Time

Being upon every last Wednesday in the Month of May every year forever and at all such other Times as the Governor of our s.^d province shall think fitt & appoint a Great and general Court or Assembly, which s.^d Great and General Court or Assembly shall consist of the Governor & Council or Assistants for the Time being and such Freeholders of our said Province or Territory as shall be from Time to Time elected or deputed by the Major Part of the Freeholders and other Inhabitants of the respective Towns & Places who shall be present at such Elections each of the said Towns and Places being hereby empowered to elect and depute two persons and no more to serve for and represent them respectively in said Gr.^t and General Court or Assembly, To which Great & General Court or Assembly, to be held as aforesaid We do humbly for us our Heirs and Successors Give and Grant full Power and authority from Time to Time to direct appoint and declare what number each town, County and Place shall elect and depute to serve for and represent them respectively in the said General Court or Assembly, Provided Always that no Freeholder or other person shall have a vote at the Election of members to serve in any Great and General Court or Assembly to be held as aforesaid who at the Time of such Election shall not have an Estate or Freehold in Land within our said Province or Territory to the Value of Forty Shillings per Annum at the least or other Estate to the Value of Forty Pounds Sterling: And that every person who shall be so Elected shall before he sit and act in the said Great and General Court or Assembly take the oaths mentioned in an act of Parliament made in the First year of our Reign Entitled an Act for Abrogating of the Oaths of Allegiance & Supremacy & appointing other oaths, and thereby appointed to be taken instead of the oaths of allegiance & supremacy: And shall make repeat and subscribe the declaration mentioned in the s.^d Act, before the Governor or Lieu.^t or Deputy Governor or any two of the Assistants for the time being who shall be thereunto Authorised and Ap-

23

pointed by our said Governor. And that the Governor for the Time being, shall have full power and
Authority from time to time as he shall Judge Necessary to Adjourn Prorogue and Dissolve all great
and General Courts or Assemblies met and convened
as aforesaid. And our will and Pleasure is, And
we do hereby for us our Heirs & Successors, Grant,
Establish and Ordain that yearly once in every year forever after the aforesaid number of Eight and Twenty
Councellors or Assistants shall be by the General
Court or Assembly newly chosen; That is to say
Eighteen at least of the Inhabitants of or Proprietors
of Lands within the Territory formerly called the Colony of the Massachusetts Bay, and four at least of the
Inhabitants of or proprietors of Lands within the said
Territory formerly called New Plimouth and three at
y⁰ least of the Inhabitants of or proprietors of Lands
within the Territory formerly called y⁰ Province of
Maine and one at the least of the Inhabitants of or
Proprietors of Lands within the Territory lying between
the River of Sagadahock and Nova Scotia. And that
the Councellors or Assistants or any of them shall or
may at any Time hereafter be removed or displaced
from their respective Places or Trust of Councellors or
Assistants by any Great and General Court or Assembly and that if any of the s.ᵈ Councellors or Assistants
shall happen to Die or be removed as aforesaid before
the General Day of Election, that then and in every
such Case, the Great and General Court or Assembly at
their first sitting may proceed to a new Election of one
or more Councellors or Assistants in the Room or
place of such Councellors or Assistants so dying or
Removed. And we do further Grant and ordain that it
shall and may be lawfull for the said Governor with the
Advice and Consent of the Council or Assistants from
from time to Time to nominate and appoint Judges,
Commissioners of Oyer and Terminer, Sheriffs, Pro-
vosts and Marshals, Justices of the Peace and other
Officers to our Council and Courts of Justice belonging.

Provided Always that no such nomination or appointment of Officers be made without notice first given or Summons Issued out seven days before such nomination or Appointment. unto such of the said Councellors or Assistants as shall be at that Time resideing within our s.ᵈ Province. And our will and Pleasure is That the Governor and Lieuᵗ or Deputy Governor and Councellors or Assistants for the Time being & all other officers to be Appointed or Chosen as aforesaid shall before the undertaking the execution of their Offices & Places respectively, take their several and respective Oaths for the due and faithfull Performance of their Duties in their several and respective offices and Places, And also the Oaths appointed by the said act of Parliament made in the first year of our Reign, to be Taken Instead of the Oaths of Allegiance & Supremacy. and shall make repeat and subscribe the Declaration Mentioned in the said Act before such Person or Persons as are by these Presents herein after appointed (that is to say) the Govʳ of our said province of Territory for the Time being shall take the said oaths and make repeat and subscribe the s.ᵈ Declaration before the Lieuᵗ or Deputy Governor, or in his absence before any two or more of s.ᵈ persons hereby nominated and appointed the present Councellors or Assistants of our said Province or Territory, to whom we do by these presents give full power and Authority to give and administer the same unto our s.ᵈ Governor accordingly; and after our said Governor shall be sworn and shall have subscribed to the said Declaration that then our Lieuᵗ or Deputy Governor, for the time being and the Councellors or Assistants before by these Presents nominated and appointed, shall take the said oaths and make repeat and subscribe the said Declaration before our said Governor & that every such Person or Persons as shall (at any time of the Annual Elections or otherwise upon Death or Removal) be appointed to be the New Councellors or Assistants and all other Officers to be hereafter Chosen from Time to Time shall take the oaths to their respective Offices & Places belonging, and also the oaths appointed by the said act of Parliament to be Taken instead of the Oaths of Allegiance & Supremacy and shall make repeat and subscribe the said declaration mentioned in the said Act before the Governor or the Lieutenant or Deputy Governor or any two more Councellors or Assistants or such other person or Persons as shall be appointed thereunto by the Governor for the time being: To whom we do therefore by these Presents give full Power and Authority from Time to Time to give and administer the same respectively according to our True meaning hereunto before declared without any Commission or further warrant to be had and obtained from us our heirs & Successors in that behalf, and our Will and pleasure is & We do hereby require and Command That all and every Person & Persons hereafter by us our Heirs and Successors nominated and appointed to the Respective Offices of Governor or Lieutenant or Deputy Govr. and Secretary of our said Province or Territory (which said Governor or Lieutenant or Deputy Governour and Secretary of our said Province or Territory for the Time being, We do hereby reserve full power and Authority to us our Heirs and Successors to nominate and appoint accordingly) shall before he or they be admitted to the Execution of their respective Offices take as well the Oath prescribed for the due & Faithfull discharge of the s^d. Offices as well as the Oath appointed by Act of Parliament made in the first year of our reign, to be taken instead of the Oaths of Allegiance and supremacy & shall also make repeat & subscribe the declaration appointed by the said act in such manner and before such persons as aforesaid. And Further our will and Pleasure is, and we do hereby for us our Heirs & Successors Grant establish and ordain that all and every of the subjects of us our Heirs and sucessors which shall go to and Inhabit within our said province & Territory and every of their Children which shall happen to be born there or on the Seas in going thither or Returning from thence shall have and enjoy all Libertys and immunities of Free and natural subjects within any of the Dominions of us our Heirs & Successors to all intents constructions and purposes whatsoever as if they and every of them were Born within this our Realm of England. And for the Greater ease and encouragement of our loveing subjects inhabiting our said province or Territory of the Massachusetts Bay and of such as shall come to Inhabit there, We do by these Presents for us our Heirs & Successors Grant Establish and Ordain that forever hereafter there shall be a Liberty of Conscience allowed in the worship of God to all christians (except Papists) inhabiting or which shall inhabit or be resident within our said province or Territory for the time being And we do hereby grant and ordain that the Governor or the Lieu^t or Deputy Governor of our s^d Province or Territory for the time being, or either of them or any two or more of the Council or Assistants for the time being as shall be thereunto appointed by the said Governor, shall and may at all Times & from time to time hereafter have full power and authority to administer and give the oaths appointed by the said Acts of Parliament made in the first year of our Reign to be taken instead of the Oaths of Allegiance and supremacy to all and every person or Persons which are now inhabiting or residing within our said province or Territory or who shall at any time or times hereafter go or pass thither, & We do of our further grace certain knowledge & Meer Motion grant establish and Ordain for us our Heirs & Successors, That the Great and General Court or Assembly of our said province or Territory for the time being convened as aforesaid, shall for ever have full Power and Authority to erect and constitute Judicatories & Courts of Record or other Courts to be held in the name of us our Heirs and successors for the hearing Trying and Determining of all manner of crimes, offences, Pleas Processes Plaints, Actions, Matters, Causes & things whatsoever, arising or happening within our said Province or Territory or Between Persons Inhabiting

or residing there whether the same be criminal or Civil
and whether said crimes be capital or not Capital &
whether said Pleas be real personal or mixt and for
the awarding and making out of Executions thereupon:
To which Courts & Judicatories We do hereby for us
our Heirs and successors give and Grant full Power
& Authority from time to Time to administer oaths for
the better discovery of truth in any matter in controversy or depending before them. And we do for us our
Heirs and Successors Grant establish and Ordain that
the Governor of our said province or Territory for
the Time being with the council or Assistants may
do execute and perform all that is necessary for the
Probate of Wills and Granting of Administrations for
Touching or concerning any Interest or Estate which
any Person or Persons shall have within our said
Province or Territory. And Whereas we Judge it
necessary that all our subjects shall have liberty to
Appeal to us, our Heirs and Successors in cases that
may deserve the same, We do by these Presents
ordain that in case either Party shall *not* rest satisfied
with the Judgement or Sentence of any Judicatories
or Courts within our said Provinces or Territories in
any personal Action wherein the matter in difference
doth exceed the value of three Hundred pounds sterling, That then He or They may appeal to us our
Heirs and Successors in our or their Privy Council,
Provided that such an appeal be made within fourteen
Days after the sentence or Judgement given & that
before such an appeal be allowed security be given
by the Party or Parties appealing, in the Value of the
matter in difference to pay or answer the Debt, or
Damages for the which Judgement or Sentence is given
with such Costs & Damages as shall be awarded by
us, our Heirs and Successors in Case the Judgment
be affirmed, And Provided also that no Execution shall
be stayed or suspended by reason of such appeal unto
us our Heirs & Successors, in our or their Privy
Council so as the Party sueing or taking out execu-.

tion in the like manner give security to the Value of
the matter in difference to make restitution in Case
the said Judgment or Sentence be reversed or an-
nulled upon the said appeal, And we do further for us
our Heirs and Successors Give and Grant to the said
Governor and the Great and General Court or Assembly
of our s⁴ Province or Territory for the Time being full
Power and Authority from time to Time to make Ordain
& Establish all manner of wholesome & reasonable
Orders, Laws, Statutes & Ordinances, Directions and
Instructions, either with penalties or without (so as the
same be not repugnant or contrary to the Laws of this
our Realm of England) as they shall Judge to be for
the Good and Welfare of said Province or Territory and
for the Government and ordering thereof & of the
People Inhabiting or who shall Inhabit the same, and for
the necessary support and defence of the Government
thereof, And we do for us our Heirs and Successors Give
and Grant that the said General Court or Assembly
shall have full power and Authority, to name and settle
annually all Civil officers within the said province such
Officers excepted, the Election and constitution of whom
We have by these Presents reserved to us our Heirs and
successors, or to the Governor of our s⁴ province for the
time being & to set forth the several Duties, Powers &
Limits of every such Officer to be appointed by the said
General Court or Assembly and the forms of such oaths
not repugnant to the Laws and Statutes of this our
Realm of England as shall be respectively administered
unto them for the execution of their respective Offices
and Places, And also to impose fines, Mulcts, Imprison-
ments & other Punishments, & to impose and levy Proportionable & Reasonable rates and Taxes upon the
Estates and Persons of all & every The Proprietors or
Inhabitants of our s⁴ province or Territory to be Issued
and disposed of by Warrant under the Hand of the
Governor of our said Province for the time being with
the advice and consent of the council—for our service
in the necessary defence & support of our Government

of our said province or Territory & the Protection and
preservation of the Inhabitants there, accordingly to
such acts as are or shall be in force, within our said
province, & to dispose of matters and things
whereby our subjects Inhabitants of our s.ᵈ Province may be Religiously peaceably and civily
governed, Protected, and defended, so as their
good life and orderly conversation may win the Indians
natives of the Country to the knowledge and obedience
of the only true God and Saviour of Mankind, and the
Christian Faith which his Royal Majesty our Royal
Grandfather King Charles the first in his s.ᵈ Letters
Patents declared was his Royal Intention, and the
adventurers free profession to be the principal end of
the s.ᵈ plantation. And for the better securing and maintaining liberty of conscience hereby granted to all persons at any time being and residing at any time within
our s.ᵈ Province and Territory as aforesaid, willing commanding and requiring and by these presents for us our
Heirs and Successors ordaining and appointing that all
such Laws, Orders, Statutes and Ordinances, Instructions and Directions as shall be so made and published
under our Seal of our s.ᵈ Province or Territory, shall be
carefully and duly observed, kept, and performed and
put in execution according to the true intent and meaning of these presents, Provided Always and we do by
these Presents for us our Heirs and successors establish
and ordain that in the framing & passing of all such
Orders, Laws, Statutes, and Ordinances, and in all
Elections and Acts of Government whatsoever to be
passed, made, or Done by the s.ᵈ General Court or Assembly or in council the Governor of our s.ᵈ province or
Territory of the Massachusetts Bay in New England for
the Time being shall have the negative voice and that
without his Consent or approbation signified and declared
in writeing no such Laws Statutes or Ordinances Elections or other Acts of Government whatsoever, so to be
made passed or done by the General Assembly or in
Council shall be of any Force Effect, or Validity any-

thing herein contained to the contrary in anywise notwithstanding, And we do for us our Heirs and Successors establish and Ordain that the said Orders Laws Statutes and Ordinances be by the first opportunity after ye making thereof, sent or transmitted unto us our Heirs & Successors under the Public Seal to be Appointed by us for our or their Approbation or disallowance & that in Case all or any of them shall at any Time within the space of three years Next after the Same shall have been presented to us our Heirs and Successors in our or their Privy Council be disallowed & rejected and so signified by us our Heirs and Successors under our or their Sign Manual or Signet in our or their Privy Council unto the Governor for the time being, then such and so many as shall be so disallowed and rejected shall thenceforth cease and determine and become utterly void and of none Effect. Provided Always that in case we our Heirs & Successors, shall not within the Term of three years after the presenting of such Orders, Laws, Statutes, Ordinances, as aforesaid signifying our or their disallowance of the same, then the s^d laws, Statutes, orders, & ordinances, shall and be & continue in force and Effect according to the true intent and meaning of the same, untill the expiration thereof or that the same shall be repealed by the General Assembly of our s^d province for the Time being, Provided also that it shall be Lawfull for the said Governor & General Assembly to make & Pass any Grant of Lands lying within the Bounds of the Colonys formerly called the Colonys of the Massachusetts Bay & New Plimouth & Province of Maine in such manner as heretofore they might have done by Virtue of any former Charter or Letters Patents. Which Grants of Lands within the Bounds aforesaid, We do hereby Will and Ordain to be and Continue forever of full Force and effect, without our further approbation or Consent, And so as nevertheless & it is our Royal Will and Pleasure that no Grant or Grants of Lands lying or extending from the River Sagadahock to the Gulf of St Lawrence &

Canada Rivers & to the Main Sea Northward and Eastward to be made or past by the Governor and General Assembly of our s.ᵈ Province be of any force validity or Effect untill we our Heirs & Successors shall have signified our or their Approbation of the same, And we do by these presents for us our Heirs and Successors Grant establish and Ordain that the Governor of our s.ᵈ Territory or Province for the Time being have full Power by himself or by any Chief Commander or other Officer or Officers to be appointed by him from Time to Time, to Train instruct Exercise and Govern the Militia there, and for the special defence and safety of our s.ᵈ Province or Territory to Assemble in Martial array, & Put in warlike posture yᵉ Inhabitants of our s.ᵈ province and Territory & to lead & conduct them, and with them to Encounter, Expulse, Repel, Resist, and pursue by force of arms as well by sea as by Land, within or without the limits of our said Province or Territory, and also to Kill, Slay, destroy, and Conquer, by all fitting ways, enterprizes & means whatsoever all and every such Person & Persons as shall at any time hereafter attempt or Enterprize the Destruction, Invasion, detriment or annoyance of our said Province or Territory & to use and exercise the Law Martial in time of Actual War, Invasion, or Rebellion, as occasion shall necessarily require, and also from time to time to Erect Forts and to Fortify any Place or Places within our s.ᵈ Province or Territory, and the same to furnish with all necessary Ammunition, Provision and Stores of war, for offence or defence, & to commit from time to Time to the Custody & Govern.ᵐᵗ of the same to such Person or Persons as to him shall seem meet, and the s.ᵈ Forts and Fortifycations to demolish at his pleasure, and. to take and surprize by all ways and means whatsoever all and every such person or Persons, with their Ships arms & Ammunition and other Goods as shall in a hostile manner invade or attempt the invading and conquering of our s.ᵈ province or Territory, Provided Always, And we do by these presents for us our Heirs and successors establish and ordain, That the said Governor shall not at any time hereafter by Virtue of any Power hereby granted or hereafter to be Granted to him—transport any of the Inhabitants of our s^d province or Territory or Oblige them to march out of the Limits of ye same without their free and voluntary consent, or the consent of the Great and General Court or Assembly of the s^d Province or Territory, nor Grant Commissions for exercising the Law Martial, upon any of the Inhabitants of our s^d Province or Territory without the advice and consent of the Council or Assistants of the same. Provided in like manner, & we do by these presents for us our Heirs and Successors, constitute & ordain, That when & as often as the Governor of our s^d Province for the time being shall happen to Die, or Be displaces by us, our Heirs and Successors, or be absent from his Government, that then & in any of the s^d Cases, the Lieu^t Governor of our s^d province for the time being shall have full power and authority to do and execute all and every such acts, matters and things, which our Governor of our s^d Province for the time being might or could, by Virtue of these our Letters Patents lawfully do or execute as if he were personally present, untill the return of the Governor so absent or arrival or Constitution of such other Governor as shall or may be appointed by us our Heirs and Successors in his stead, and that when and as often as the Governor & Lieu^t or Deputy Governor of our said Province or Territory for the Time being shall happen to Die or be displaced by us our Heirs and Successors, or be absent from our said Province and that there shall be no person within the said Province Commissionated by us our Heirs or Successors, to be Governor within the same then and in every of the said Cases, the Council or assistants of our said Province shall have full Power and authority And we do hereby Give and Grant unto the said Council or Assistants of our s^d Province for the time being, or the Major part of them full power and Authority to do and execute all and

every such acts, matters and things which the s.ᵈ
Governor or Lieutenant or Deputy Governor of our
s.ᵈ Province or Territory for the time being might or
could Lawfully do or exercise if they or either of them
were personally present untill the return of the Governor
Lieu.ᵗ or Deputy Governor so absent or Arrival or
Constitution of such other Governor or Lieut or Deputy
Governor as shall or may be appointed by us our
Heirs or Successors from time to time Provided always
and it is hereby declared, that nothing herein shall
extend, or be taken to erect or Grant or allow, the exercise of any Admiral Court, Jurisdiction Power or
Authority, but that the same be and is hereby reserved
to us and our successors and shall from time to time
be Erected Granted and Exercised by Virtue of Commissions to be Issued under the great seal of England, or under the seal of the High Admiral or the
Commissioners for executing the office of High Admiral of England. And further our express will and
pleasure is and We do by these presents for us our
heirs and successors ordain and appoint, that these
our letters Patents shall not in any manner Enure or
be taken to abridge, bar, or hinder, any of our loveing
subjects whatsoever, to use and exercise the Trade of
Fishing upon the Coasts of New England, but that
they and every of them, shall have full Power &
Authority freely to continue the same Trade of Fishing
upon the s.ᵈ Coasts, and in any of the seas thereunto
adjoining or any arms of the s.ᵈ Seas or Salt water
Rivers, where they have been wont to fish & to Build
and Set upon y.ᵉ Lands within our s.ᵈ province, or Colony
lying Waste and not then possessed by particular proprietors such Wharfs Stages & Work Houses, as shall
be necessary for the salting drying, Keeping and Pack-
ing of their fish, to be taken or gotten upon that Coast
and to Cut down and take such Trees and other materials there growing and being upon any Parts or places
lying Waste, and not then in Possession of Particular
proprietors, as shall be needfull for that purpose, and

for all other necessary easements helps, and advantages, concerning the Trade of Fishing there, in such manner and Form as they have been heretofore at any Time accustomed to do, without making any willfull Waste, or Spoil, anything in these presents contained to the contrary notwithstanding. And lastly for the better providing and Furnishing of Masts for our Royal Navy, We do hereby reserve to us our Heirs and Successors all Trees of the Diameter of twenty-four Inches and upwards, of Twelve Inches from the Ground growing upon any soil or Tract of Land within our s^d province or Territory, not heretofore granted to any Private Persons, And we do restrain and forbid all Persons whatsoever upon felling Cutting and destroying, any such Trees, without the Royal Licence of us our Heirs & Successors first had and obtained, upon Penalty of forfeiting one hundred Pounds Sterling, unto us our Heirs and Successors for every such Tree so felled, Cut or destroyed, without such Licence, had and Obtained in that behalf any thing in these Presents contained to the contrary in any Wise notwithstanding. In Witness whereof we have caused these our Letters to be made Patents. Witness ourselves at Westminster the seventh day of October in the third year of our Reign.

By Writ of Privy Seal

PIGOT

The Great Seal of England appending
Pro fine in hanaperio quod
 vagint mareas
  J. TREVOR   l. s.
  S. BARLINO   l. s.
  G. HUTCHINS   l. s.
A true Copy from the Original examined p
  SAM^L TYLEY JUN^R. Clc.
  W^M SAM^L BALLARD Clc.

The Committee for the Province Produced the Original Charter of Plimouth Colony, under a seal. The Committee for the Colony objected that the Livery of

Seizin endorsed upon the back was all one hand writing, and the Agent for the Province allowed it to be so.

The Court ordered that a Copy thereof be taken, examined and attested by two of the Clerks, which was accordingly done and is as Follows:

To all to whom these Presents shall come Greeting: Whereas our Late Sovereign Lord King James for the advancement of a Colony and Plantation in y.ᵉ Country called or known by the name of New England in America By His Highnesses Letters Patents under the Great Seal of England bearing Date at Westminster the third of November in the Eighteenth year of his Highnesses Reign of England &c. Did Give Grant and confirm unto the Right honorable Lodowick late L.ᵈ Duke of Lenox, George late L.ᵈ Marquis of Buckingham, James Marquis Hamilton, Thomas Earl of Arundel, Robert Earl of Warwick, Sir Ferdinando Gorges, Kn.ᵗ and divers others whose names are expressed in the s.ᵈ letters Patents and their Success.ᵒʳˢ That they should be one Body Politique and Corporate Perpetually consisting of Forty Persons, and that they should have perpetual succession and one common Seal to serve for the said Body, And that they and their Successors should be incorporated called and known by the name of the Council established at Plimouth in the County of Devon, for the Planting ruling Ordering and Government of New England in America and further also of his especial grace, Certain Knowledge & Meer Motion, Did give Grant and confirm unto the s.ᵈ President and Council and their successors for ever under the Reservations limitations and Declarations in the s.ᵈ Letters Patents expressed, All that part and Portion of the s.ᵈ Country now called New England in America situate lying and being in breadth from the fortyeth degree of northerly Latitude from the Equinoctial Line to Forty Eight degrees of the s.ᵈ northerly latitude inclusive and in Length of and in all the Breadth aforesaid throughout the Main Land from Sea to Sea, together also with all the firm Lands, Soils Grounds,

Creeks Inlets Havens Ports, Seas, Ports, Rivers, Islands, Waters, Fishings Mines, Minerals, as well royal Mines of Gold and Silver as other Mines and Minerals Precious Stones & Quarries & all & singular the Commodities, Jurisdictions, Royalties, Priviledges, Franchises, & Preheminences both within the Tract of Land and upon the Main and also within the S^d. Islands and Seas adjoining. To Have and to hold possess and enjoy all and singular the afors^d. Continent Lands Territorys, Islands, Hereditaments and Premises Seas, Waters & Fishings, with all and all manner their Commodities, Royalties, Priviledges Preheminences and Profits that shall arise from thence with all and Singular their appurtenances and every part and Parcels thereof, unto the s^d. Council and their Successors and Assigns forever to be holden of his Majesty his Heirs and Successors as of his Mannor of East Greenwich in the County of Kent, in free and Common Sockage and not in Capite nor by Knights service. Yielding and paying therefore to the s^d. late Kings Majesty his Heirs and Successors, the fifth Part of the Oar of Gold and Silver which from Time to Time and at all Times from the Date of the s^d. Letters Patents shall be gotten had & Obtained for and in respect of all & all manner of Duties and Demands Services &c whatsoever to be Done made & Paid unto his s^d. Late Majesty his Heirs & Successors as in and by the s^d. letters Patents amongst sundry other Privileges & Matters therein contained more fully and at Large it doth and may appear. Now Know Ye that the s^d. Council by Virtue and Authority of his s^d. late Majestys letters Patents and for and in consideration That William Bradford and his Associates have for these nine years lived in New England aforesaid and have there Inhabited & Planted a Town called by the name of New Plimouth, at their own Proper cost and charges and now seeing that by the special providence of God, and their extraordinary care and Industry they have Increased their Plantation to near three hundred People, and are upon all occasions

able to relieve any New Planters or other of His Majestys subjects who may fall upon that Coast, Have
given, Granted, Bargained, Sold, Enfeoffed, allotted,
assigned and set over and by these Presents do clearly
and Absolutely Give, Grant, Bargain, Sell, Aliene,
Enfeoff, Allot Assign and confirm unto the s.ᵈ William
Bradford his Heirs and Associates and Assigns, all that
Part of New England in America aforesaid and Tract
and Tracts of Land that lye within or between a certain
Rivulet or Runlet there commonly called Cohasset alias
Conehassett towards the North of the River commonly
called Naragansett towards the South, and the Great
Western Ocean towards the East, and between and
within a straight line and directly extending up into
the Main Land towards the West, from the mouth of the
said River called Naragansett River to the utmost Limits
and Bounds of a Country or Place in New England
commonly called Pokenacutt alias Sowamsett, Westward another like straight Line extending itself directly
from the mouth of the s.ᵈ River called Cohassett alias
Conehassett towards the West so far up unto the Main
Land Westward, as the utmost Limits of the s.ᵈ Place or
Country commonly Pokenacutt alias Sowansett, do
extend, together with one half of the s.ᵈ River of Naragansett, and the s.ᵈ Rivulet or Runlet called Cohasset,
alias Conehassett and all Lands Rivers Waters Havens
Creeks, Ports, Fishings, Fowlings, and all Heredta-
ments, Profits, Commodities and Emoluments, whatsoever situate lying being or arising within the s.ᵈ Limits
and Bounds or any of them, and for as much as they
have no convenient Place either of Tradeing and Fishing within their own Precincts whereby after so long
Travel, and great Pains so hopefull a Plantation may
subsist, and also that they may be encouraged the better to proceed in so pious a work, which may especially tend to the Propagation of Religion and the
great Increase of Trade to His Majestys Realms, and
advancement of the Public Plantation, The said council have further Given Granted Bargained, Enfeoffed

Aliened Sold Allotted Assigned and set over & by
these Presents do clearly and absolutely Give Grant
Bargain Sell Alien Enfeoff allot assign and Confirm unto
the s⁴ William Bradford his Heirs associates and Assigns, all that Tract of Land or Part of New England
in America which lyeth in or Between and extendeth
itself from the utmost limits of Cobicecontee alias
Comusecontee which adjoineth to the River of Kenebunk
alias Kenebeck towards the Western Ocean, and a Place
called the Falls at Nequamkike in America aforesaid
and the space of Fifteen English Miles on each side of
said River commonly called Kennebeck and all the s⁴
River Called Kennebeck that lies within the s⁴ Limits
and Bounds, Eastward, Westward, Northward, Southward, last above mentioned, And all Lands, Grounds,
Soils, Rivers Waters, Fishings, Hereditaments & Profits
whatsoever, situate lying and being, arising, happening,
or accruing, or which shall arise happen or accrue in or
within the s⁴ Limits & Bounds or either of them together with free ingress, egress, regress with ships Boats
shallops and other vessels from the Sea commonly called
the Western Ocean to the s⁴ River called Kennebeck
and from the s⁴ River of Kennebeck to the s⁴ Western
ocean together with all Prerogatives Rights, Royalties
and Jurisdictions, Priviledges Immunities & Priviledges
and also Marine Liberty with the escheats and casualties
thereof the Admiralty Jurisdiction excepted, with all
the Interest Right Title and Demand whatsoever which
the said Council or their Successors have or ought to
have & Claim or may have and acquire hereafter in or
any of the s⁴ Portions or Tracts of Land hereby mentioned to be granted or any of the Premises in as free
ample and Beneficial manner to all intents and purposes
whatsoever, as the s⁴ council by virtue of his Majestys
s⁴ Letters Patents may or can grant to have and to hold
the s⁴ Tract or Tracts of Land of all and singular the
Premises above mentioned to be granted with their and
every of their Appurtenances to the s⁴ William Bradford his Heirs Associates and Assigns forever to the

24

only proper & absolute use and Behoofe of the s⁰.
William Bradford his Heirs Associates and Assigns for
ever yielding and Paying unto our s⁰. Sovereign Lord
the King his Heirs and Successors forever one fifth Part
of the ore of Gold and Silver & one fifth part also to
the President & Council, which shall be had Possessed
and obtained within the Precincts aforesaid, for all services & Demands whatsoever, and the s⁰. Council do further agree & Grant to & with the s⁰. William Bradford
his Heirs Associates and Assigns, and every of them
his and their Factors Agents Tenants and Servants and
all such as he or they shall send and employ about his
Particular Plantation, shall and may from time to time
freely and lawfully go and return Trade and Traffick as
well with the English, as any of the Nations within Precincts aforesaid with liberty of Fishing upon any part of
the sea Coast and Sea shores, of any of the Seas or Islands adjacent and not being Inhabited or otherwise
disposed of by order of the s⁰. President and Council
also to import Export and Transport their Goods and
merchandize at their wills and Pleasures, paying only
such duties to the kings Majesty his Heirs and successors as the s⁰ President & council do or ought to Pay
without any other Taxes, Impositions, Burthens and
Restraints upon them to be impsed, and further the
s⁰ Council do grant and agree to and with the s⁰. William
Bradford, his Heirs Associates and assigns that the persons transported by him or any of them shall not be
taken away imployed or commanded either by the Governor for the time being of New England or by any
other authority there from the business or Employment
of the s⁰. William Bradford and his Associates his Heirs
and assigns (necessary defence of the Country, preservation of the Peace suppressing of Tumults within the
Lands, Tryalls in matter of Justice by appeal upon special occasion only eccepted) also it shall be lawfull and
free for the s⁰ William Bradford his Associates his Heirs
and assigns at all times hereafter to incorporate by some
usual or fit manner to entitle him or themselves or the

People there inhabiting under him or them with liberty
to them and their Successors from time to time to frame
and make orders Ordinances and Constitutions as well
for the better Government of their officers there And
the receiving and admitting any to his or their society
as also for the better Government of his or their People
and Affairs in New England, or of his and their People
at Sea in going thither or returning from thence and
the Same put in Execution by such officers and Ministers as he and they Shall authorise and Depute. Provided that the s^d Laws & Orders be not repugnant to the
Laws of England or the frame of Government by the
s^d. President & Council hereafter to be established
and further it shall be lawful and free for the s^d William Bradford his Heirs Associates and assigns, to Transport Cattle of all kinds, also Powder, shot, ordinance
ammunition from time to time as shall be necessary for
their strength and safety hereafter for their several defence to Encounter, Expulse repel & resist by force of
Arms as well by Sea as by land by all ways and means
whatsoever and by virtue of the authority to us derived
by his s^d late Majesty's Letters patents to take apprehend
Seize and make Prize of all such Persons their Ships
and Goods, as shall attempt to Inhabit or Trade with
the savage People of that Country, within the Several
Precincts and Limits of his and their several Plantations,
or shall enterprize or attempt at any time Destruction,
Invasion, Detriment or annoyance to his and their s^d
Plantation, the one moiety of which Goods, so seized
and taken it shall be lawful for the s^d William Bradford
his Heirs associates and assigns to take to their
own use and behoofe, the other moiety thereof to be delivered by the s^d William Bradford his Heirs associates
and assigns to such officer and officers as shall be appointed to receive the same, for his Majesty's use. And
the s^d Council do hereby covenant and declare that it is
their intent and meaning for the good of this Plantation
that the s^d William Bradford his associates his or their
Heirs and Assigns shall have and enjoy whatsoever

Priviledge or Priviledges of what Kind soever as are expressed or intended to be granted in and by his sᵈ late
Majestys Letters Patents and that in as large and ample manner as the sᵈ Council thereby now may or hereafter can grant, Coining of Monies excepted and the
sᵈ Council for them and their Successors do Covenant
and grant to and with the sᵈ William Bradford his
Heirs and Successors by these presents that the sᵈ Council shall at any time hereafter upon request at the only
proper costs and charges of the sᵈ William Bradford his
Heirs Associates and Assigns do make suffer execute
and willingly consent to any further Act or Acts Conveyance or Conveyances assurance or assurances whatsoever for the good and perfect investing assuring and
conveying and sure making of all the aforesaid Tract and
Tracts of land, Royalties, Mines, Minerals, Woods, Fishings and all and singular their appurtenances unto the
sᵈ William Bradford his Heirs associates and assigns,
as by him or them or his or their Heirs and assigns or
his or their Council learned in the Law, shall be de-
vised and required. And lastly Know Ye that we the
sᵈ Council have made constituted, Deputed Authorized
and appointed Capᵗ Miles Standish or in his Absence
Edward Winslow, John Howland and John Alden our
Attorneys Jointly and Severally in our name and stead,
to enter into the sᵈ Tract and Tracts of Land and other
the Premises with their appurtenances or into some
part thereof in the manner of the whole for us in our
names to take possession and seizin thereof and after
such possession and seizin thereof or of some part thereof in yᵉ name of yᵉ whole had and taken, then for us
and in our names to deliver the full and Peaceable possession and seizin of all and singular the sᵈ mentioned
to be granted Premises unto the sᵈ William Bradford
his Heirs associates and assigns or to his or their certain Attorneys in that behalf ratifying allowing and
confirming all whatsoever our sᵈ attorney shall do in or
about the Premises. In Witness whereof the sᵈ Council
Established at Plymouth, in the County of Devon for

the Planting ruling ordering and Governing of New England in America have hereunto put their Seal, the thirteenth day of January, in the fifth year of the reign of our Sovereign L.ᵈ Charles by the Grace of God King of England, Scotland France and Ireland Defender of the faith &c: Anno Domini 1629.

ROBERT WARWICK (Seal)

The Within named John Alden authorized as Attorney for the within mentioned council, having in their name and stead, entered into some part of the Mentioned Tracts of Land and other the Premises in the name of the whole & for them & in their names, taken Possession and seizin thereof Did in the name of the said Council deliver the Full and Peacable possession & Seizin of all and Singular the within Mentioned to be granted Premises unto William Bradford for him his Heirs Associates and Assigns. Secundum form. Cart.

In Presence of   JAMES CADWARD

        WILLIAM CLARKE

A true Copy compared   NATHᴸ MORTON, Secʸ
with the Original.
p Wˣ SAMᴸ BALLARD Clk.
SAMᴸ TYLEY Junʳ Clk.

Nᵒ 50.   At a Councill Aprill 16ᵗʰ 1675
Present

   The Governor   Mr. Laurence
   The Secretary   Capᵗ Wᵐ Dyer

Resolved that yᵉ Maques Indians be encouraged in their Loyalty and friendship to yᵉ English and yᵉ french to be sent to, not to molest them without Cause and forthwith to release any Hostages they may have of theirs: Engaging to Interpose (or help for due satisfaction to be given from the Maquaes to the French) upon all just Occasions requiring the french Governor promising the like for the Natives in their Limitts.

That Jesuits or other French Residing with the Maques bee sent for to y.ᵉ Governo.ʳ at his Arrivall at Albany, to give an Acco.ᵗ of his being and Acting's in those parts: and if to continue to give such Assurance as is proper for his future Comport.

N.ᵒ 51.   April y.ᵈ 10ᵗʰ 1676.
There was a meeting of th.ᵉ Governo and Councill in th.ᵉ Morning upon occasion of the arrivall of Mr. Samuel Willis and Mr. W.ᵐ Pitkin with a Letter from the Councill of Conecticott; th.ᵉ Letter being read it was not adjudged that the Gent'men mentioned therein were authorized farther than in a Compliment or for advice thereupon they Produced their Instructions, and Read them, butt no further Authority appearing The Governor proposed to them to Deliver their minds in writing to the which hee would Likewise return them Answer in Writing.

Afternoon.   M.ʳ Willis and M.ʳ Pitkin delivered in their Proposalls in Writing to the which after a Consultation of the Governo.ʳ and Councill Together with the Mayor and Aldermen an Answer was made and Publickly read to the Conecticott Gentlemen—the Governo.ʳ and Councill with the Mayor and Aldermen being together and divers Merchants and other strangers admitted to be present.

Ordered that a fair Copy of what was read be given th.ᵉ Gentlemen as an Answer both to th.ᵉ Letter and proposalls.   The tenour as Follows.

The Proposalls.

To the Hon.ˡᵉ Major Edmund Andross Governo.ʳ of his Highness Territories in America.

Sir: Having Presented to your Honor the Letter which we received from y.ᵉ Secretary of the Council of Conecticott Colony According to our Instructions and the import of that Letter as agents sent from the said Councill we do in their behalf desire.

First that yor honor will please to inform us of what Intelligence you have as to ye State &c. place of the Enemys of the Colony of Conecticott and what correspondence th^e Enemy holds with the Maquaes and Sennekes & how ye said Maquaes & Sennekes stand affected towards the said Colony of Conecticott, according as your Honor is advertized or knoweth.

Secondly that your hono.^r will advize us what is best to be done in Exciting the Maques & Sinneks to Prosecute their & our Enemy according as is Propounded in the said Letter and what Present (if any) you will advize us to give them and

Thirdly if your Honor advize us thereunto that you will please to afford your aid and Conduct to us therein an Interpreter with what else may in your Honor.^s prudence best Effectuate ye same.

Fourthly what Liberty your Honor^s. will Graunt us to pass to Albany or any other Convenient place in your Governm^t to Excite y^e. said Indyans According to our Instructions to proceed against our Ennemyes.

Your Hono^{rs} humble Servt

SAM^L WILLIS
WILLIAM PITKIN

New York April 10th 1676.

An Answer to the proposalls of M^r. Samuel Willis and M^r. William Pitkin in th^e name of the Councill of Conecticott from whom they Brought a Letter dated th^e first of Aprill most mistaken and ineffectual.

You are sent agents to salute but not authorized or empowered to treate or conclude by said Councills Letter or otherwise that appears.

I know of no Commerce or Correspondence w^h such Indyans butt upon the Rumor of your Warr (having made fitting Preparations) when s^d. Indyans did approach our Confines were repulsed by our Indyans th^e Maquaes and Sinnekes and (as we are informed) are retreated beyond Conecticott River, but am Ignorant if our Indyans have any particular knowledge of you which should· be Best Known to yourselves.

·2 & 3. Having already taken Fitting orders hope th^e Maquaes &c will do their Duty as they ought to this Goverment on all Occasions and cannot be Subject to two.

4th ·Think it strange that you should ask to treat with any Branch of this Government apart and upon your own Acco^t. And Notwithstanding y^e. Neighbour-hood and all my Endeavours unasked that you have hitherto and Still Keep mee a stranger to all th^e. Concerns of your said Indyans Warr.

New York April 10th 1676.

N°. 52.   At a Councell October y^e. 11th. 1676 Present.

The Governo^r.	Capt. Brockholls
The Secretary	Capt. Dyre
Capt. T. Delavall,	M^r. Philips

Major Treat Deputy Governor of Conecticott being present.

Proposes that one or more of the Maquaes Sachem may come to some of their Towns to renew friendship that they may Acknowledge their Kindness in assisting them against their Enemy y^e. North Indyans and Gratify them and that Prisoners of the North Indyans are in this Governm^t. may be delivered up to him.

It is alledged th^e. Governor received none till themselves made Proclamation to receive all those that would Come in and that he hath Security for them he hath Received.

  And that the Maquaes are our Indyans and are so to be· acknowledged and will be of ill Consequence for the Maquaes to Treat or to make application to another Government th^e. which will breed a distraction amongst them.

N°. 53.   At a Councill April 2d 1677

The Governor proposes a voyage to Albany it being

a Leysure time and a Necessity of going this year.
The which concluded on. That Letters be written to
Boston and Conecticutt about the Governours going up
now to Albany and the Maquaes.

No. 54. From Book of Entries Letter C Nº 18—$\frac{1682}{1683}$.
Entered for Henry Coursey Esqr this following Commission May 31 1677.

THOMAS NOTLEY Esqr. Lieutenant and Chief Governour of the Provinc^e of Maryland under the R^{ht} Hon^{bl}
Charles absolute Lord and Proprietary of th^e Provinces
of Maryland and Avalon, Lord Baron of Baltimore &c.
To all to whome these Presents shall come or any way
appertain^e Greeting in our Lord God everlasting.
Whereas th^e Sasquahannoks Cinnigos and divers others
Nations of Indyans Inhabitting to the Northward of
this Province have Formerly committed divers murders
and other outrages within this Province upon which
there hath ensued a warr between his Ma^{tes} Subjects
residing within this Province under the Governm^t his
said Lordship as well as with those residing under the
Governm^t of his sacred Ma^{tes} Colony of Virginia and
the said Susquahannos and whereas the said Susquahannos have sithence and lately desired to Come to a
treaty of Peace with his said Lordshipp and have (as I
am informed) since ye said overture and submitted themselves to, and put themselves under th^e protection of
the Cinnigos or some other Nation of Indyans residing
to the Northward of this Province and within or near
unto th^e Territoryes of his Royal Highness the Duke of
York Know Yee that I have constituted Ordeyned appointed and authorized, as I do hereby Constitute Ordain
& appoint and Authorize Henry Coursey Esqr one of
his Lordshipps Councell for this Province as Embassa-
dor or Envoy to Treate with and conclude a form^l peace
with the said Susquahannos Cinnigos or any other Indyans now unknown to or Inhabitting or Residing to th^e
Northward of us within or without the Territoryes of
his said Royal Highnesse and from whom wee have already received Injury, or may hereafter reasonably sus-

pect We may receive Injury by the Confederacy between
them and the said Susquahannos upon such reasonable
terms as to them shall seem meet, and convenient according to his Instructions. And forasmuch as the said
Indyans do now Reside for th.^{e} most part wthin the Territory of his said Royal Highness or at least cannott be
treated with but by a Journey to be had through his
said Highness, his Territory and I do hereby constitute
ordain appoint and authorize the said Henry Coursey to
treat with Edmund Andros Esqr seigneur of sausmarez
and Lieut. and Governo.^{r} Gen^{rall} under his Royall Highnesses James Duke of York and Albany &c. of all his
Territory under his Governm.^{t} to the treaty with the Indyans aforesaid and to request his assistance in th.^{e} procuring of a firm and lasting Peace for all his Ma^{tis} subjects in his ma^{tes} colony of Virginia as well as for those
of his Province with the Indyans aforesaid Wherefore I
do request that the aforesaid Henry Coursey (according.
to the Laws of nations) may be Received creditted and
believed Promising to Ratify confirm and approve
whatsoever shall be done by him in the Premises according to this my commission as if it were done by
myself: Given at St Maryes under my hand and th^e
Great Seal of this Province this thirtyeth day of aprill
in the second year of his Lordshipps Dominion Anno
Domini 1677.

THOMAS NOTLEY

N.º 55. At a Council held at Fort James in New York
October the 9th year 1683.
Present.

> The Governor
> Capt. A. Brockholls
> Mr F. fflypson
> Mr Step.^{n} V. Courtland.
> J. Spragge

The Governor acquainted the Sachem of the Ma-
quais, that the reason he sent for them was to tell

them that the King and his Royall Highness had a
great kindness for them, and that he himself would be
gladd to have a good Correspondence and Friendshipp
with them as other Governors before had, and spoke to
them to treat no more with the ffrench, nor goe there if
sent for without leave of his Government and to permit
no ffrenchmen to live amongst then except the Jesuits
and each of them a man and such as shall have a passe
from the Governor of New York and a Seal (of which
they are to have a mark in wax) and that they should
strive to bring as many of their friends as they could
from the ffrench Government and to make peace with
those Indians they now warre against and trade with
them, and if it be thought fitt the Governor will send
one with them, and that they bring the trade to this
Govern! the Governor further required of them to tell
him what the ffrench said to them when they sent for
them to Canada, and they are allso to acquaint the rest
of their neighbours with what hath been now imparted
to them the Governor promissing them that he will
allways look upon them as his children and treat them
with all respect and Kindness accordingly, and by particular order from the King of Great Britain and his
Royall Highness our Master.

The Indians being asked if they were only for the
Maquas, they answered yes; and came from the three
Castles of the Maquas, their names were Odianah, Rodie
Yo non droh Ninok Ogar and Hugar, the names of the
queens were Caunichack Ouyodah harah, they first pro-
duced a Wampum girdle, and presented it to the
Governor to show their sorrow for the Death of Captain
Clark they said he was a Brave man and treated them
as they are now treated in this fort, and was all one as
a Maquas.

The Governor returned them thanks and said the
successor of Clarke should be as kind to them as ever
he was, and they shall receive all the kindness from
this Government, as if they were children of so Great
a King as his ma^{ty} of England, they thanked the

Governor for the title of children and the Governor accepts their tokens.

The Speech of the Sachim Odianah. That as soone as they received the message they came hither, and are very glad to be so well received and that his ma^{ty} hath so great a Kindness for them, as for the Indians that are on to Canada they are very gladd his Hon^r speaks of it and they will endeavour to get them back againe they desire the Governors assistance in it that they may go hand in hand to promote it and they doubt not to get them back again.

That when they were sent for hither they did not know what might be proposed to them &c for Corlear's proposition to make Peace with those Indians they war against they say, that as soone as they come home they will have a general meeting of all the Castles and will tell them what is here proposed, and doubt not but it shall be Effected, for the former Governor said the same, and they obeyed and made peace, and why should it not be also at this time performed for they have been allways obedient to his Govern^t. That his honor hav- ing told them to have an eye to the ffrenchmen, they give his Hono^r their thanks and will allways have an eye to those people, and they desire if any thing happen to be informed for they are and have been allways belong- ing to this Goverm^t and expect no favour from the ffrench, but will put themselves under his Hono^rs protec- tion, that the Governor having wondered why they bring so little Beaver and formerly did bring so much, and that it may be the Governor thinks they carry it to some other Government they answer no, they do not, they never had so firm a Friendship with any, as with this Govrn^t, but the true reason is they having a war with other Indians there Indians would not dare to come on their hunting places, but now they are all in peace, the Indians catch away their Beaver so fast that there be but very few left, His Hono^r having told them they should harbour no ffrench, but the Jesuits and each of them a man, they answer they will never suffer any straggler ffrenchmen amongst them, but those Jesuits who are very good men and very quiet and yet if his honor shall please, they will send them away allso : and that none hath had any land from them and they are resolved never to sell or give them any, or any others except the People of this Goverm^t, that they were sent for by the Governor of Canada, who told them they should make a peace with all the Indians and that the Governor took their axe, and threw it into the water, but did not bury it because if it had been buried it might have been taken up again, and that nothing shall come to their ears but they will acquaint this Government with it, and expect the same from this Government.

They allso say the Governor of Canada promised them to have free passage up all Rivers and Creeks, and said they should suffer all other Indians to have the same, and the Governor took them as his children and told them they should be all of the ffrench Religion.

That all their Land is under the Goverm^t of His Royall High^e that there has been some stranger at Albany to buy the Susquehannah River, but they have considered and will not sell it to them except by the particular leave of His Hono^r

The Governor desired them to make up the Difference amongst themselves about Susquehannah River in a civil and peaceable way that being done to send word to the Governor and that then he will give them further orders about it.

The Sachem spake for himself—

That one Arent Van Corlaer bought all Schannectadi and payed them for it, but now there be some who have bought only the Grasse and pretend to the Land allso, they say allso that they have bought the first flatt, but that is not so, for it belongs to Acques Cornelistin, who is to have it and none else, for he is of their people and it is his Inheritance, that there is writings made of a sale of Land, but it was never sold but only the Grasse, that it may be som Drunken fellows may have made some writings without their knowledge.

That they have only bought the grasse and are now going to live upon it, but they ought to pay for the Land as well as the grasse, and that they had given some to that woman Hillah and another Leach who have the propriety of it, the other have only the grasse.

That now he has declared this matter he desires notice may be taken of it, and says that blame shall never come upon him, as to be found in a lye, that they came down in an open boat, and suffered much cold therefore desires a sloop—upon which it is granted

The Governor desires of them as they are friends, not to trade with the ffrench or any other nation, excepting the Province and the Indians who live afar off as the Octogymists and other remote Indians, as well to the Southward as the Northward, and that they will give them free passage to come through their Countries to Trade hither, and that the Governor would be very gladd for them to bring one or two of the most considerable of them hither, and that they will use all their Endeavors to perswade them to Trade with this Government, and to send an answer as soone as may be what the remote Indians, and particularly the Octogymists say to them.

That no Christians be amongst them or Trade with them but such as have a passe from the Governor under his Seal of which he will give the impression, and that they are to give notice of what is done here to all the other nations who are friends to them, that they when they bring their friends from Canada, the Governor desires it may be in a civil quiet way; and not by force or in a war-like manner.

That all on the side of the lake of Canada, belongs to the Govern.^{mt} of New York, and that the Governor desires that they may be all acquainted with it, and expects their submission.

That if the Governor have any occasion for Land near their Castles, when a Castle may be built or for a greater conveniency of trade with them, that the Governor may have it paying for the-same.

That the Governor as yet knows nothing of any hurt the ffrench intends them, and therefore desires them not to be alarmed, and that if the Governor knows any thing the ffrench design against them he will give them early notice.

That it is the custom of this Government and amongst Christians when they sell the grasse to sell the Land allso, and if they be not payed for the Land they shall be, and that the People of Shannectadi say they sent Acques to purchase the Land in the name of their Town, and that Acques bought it in his own name, and they sent also one Kemel to purchase it for the Towne, the Indians told them that Acques had bought and paid some part of the payment, and they desired them to pay Acques that monie back, and the Towne should have it, which the Towne did, and Acques was satisfied, it is the custom of this place to do justice amongst ourselves if Acques have a better Title than they for it then he shall have it.

N.° 56. At a council at ffort James in New York June [26ᵗʰ 1684.]

Present

The Governor   Mʳ S. V. Cortlandt
Capᵗ A. Brockholls   Collo Lewis Morris
Mʳ F. fflypsen   Mʳ L. Santen

A Letter from the Governor of Canada being read, answered as follows:

Sir:—Yours dated the 15ᵗʰ I received the 23ᵈ of S. V. of this Instant and am very sorry that I did not know sooner of this misunderstanding between you and the Indians that so I might (as really I would) have used all just measures to prevent it. Those Indians are under this Government as doth appear by his Royall Highᵉˢ· his Patent from his majesty the King of England and their submitting themselves to his Governᵐᵗ as is manifest by records, his Rⁿ Highnesses Territories reaching as far as the River of Canada and yet notwithstanding the People of y^r Govern^t come upon the great Lake as allso on this Side of both Lakes, a thing which will scarcely be believed in England.

I desire you to hinder them from so doing and I will strictly forbidde the People of this Province to go on your side of the Lakes this I have hinted that there may be no occasion on your part, as there shall not undoubtedly of mine to break that desireable and fair correspondence between two Kings our masters. I am so heartily bent to promote the Quiet and tranquillity of this Country and yours, that I intend forthwith to go to Albany on purpose, and there send for the Indians and require of them to do what is just in order to a satisfaction to y^r pretences; if they will not I shall not unjustly protect them, but do for your Govern^{mt} all that can reasonably be expected from me, and in the mean time to continue and preserve a good amity between us, I think it convenient and desire that no Acts of Hostility be committed, such differences are of so weighty a concern that they are most proper to be decided at home and not by us.

I do assure you sir that no body living hath a greater desire that there should be a strict friendship betwixt the subjects of this Governm^t and yours than I have and no body more willing upon all occasions justly to approve myself

Sir y^r humble servt.

THOS. DONGAN

[N.° 57.]   At a Council August 30th 1686.
Present

The Governor	Mr N. Bayard
Mr S. V. Courtland	Maj. G. Baxter.
J. Spragge	Arnold, Interpreter.

The Governor gave presents to the Indians, for which they thanked him, after their manner, and he said to them,

Brethren :—I am very glad to see you here, the Business I sent for you is to acquaint you that the great King of England my master hath ordered me to let you know that he looks upon you as he does upon the rest of his Children and subjects in America, and that he will be a loving father to you and with all expects that as you have put yourselves under his protection as Children and Subjects so you are not to make either war or Peace either with Christians or Indians before you shall first acquaint me with it, he being allways ready to protect his subjects provided they begin not the warr without his consent and approbation and therefore I am sorry to hear that some of the Brethren are gone to Cadaracqua for to treat or Trade with the ffrench which is contrary to the promise they made me at Albany contrary to the obedience which children owe to their parents; besides do the Brethren think that it is out of fear to them, that the ffrench do not warr against them? they have thousand men for one of the Brethren, and it is only for fear of disobliging the Great King of England who is your King allso.

I do again renew and confirm wh^t I said to you at Albany towit that you shall not make warr against the ffrench untill they have began a warr against you my meaning is that you shall not meddle with them untill they come with force to disturb the Brethren in their Country, but if the French do them any injury let me know it, and I will take all possible care that the Brethren have due satisfaction.

The great and weighty concern is that the remote Indians called Dionondadies, some of whom you have taken prisoners last year have a mind to bury the Hatchetts with the Brethren and an inclination to enter into ye same friendshipp both in Peace and warr, as the five nations of the Brethren have wth us I know it will be of great advantage to strength to the Brethren and us also and therefore desire that you will send a Sachem of each nation and two from the Sineques and some of Albany whom I will commission for ye purpose

25

to go to the farr and remote Indians and carry them home their Prisoners, and bring two or three of their Sachems to Albany; when I will be present, and we will bury all of Hatchetts and make a firm peace and Alliance that whatsoever shall warre with one shall warre with all of us.

The Governor of Canada hath written a very civil answer to my letter, and says that the reason for putting so much provision in Cadaracqua, is the great length of the winter; which hinders the bringing Provisions to them, that are there, the Brethren need not feare any thing for I have a watchfull eye for their security, and also desire that the Brethren would bring all those of the Brethren that are gone to Canada back again, for I love to have the Brethren strong and united; and what I have promised concerning the Priests and the land shall be performed. I allso desire that neither ffrench nor English go on the Susquehannah River, nor hunt nor trade amongst the Brethren without my passe and seal, the impression of which I will give them, but if they do that the Brethren bring them to Albany and deliver them at the Town house where care shall be taken for Punishing of them (excepting the Priests and one man with each) or either of them although any of them should be married to an Indian Squa, they being only as Spies upon the Brethren.

The Sachems that are with you complain yt you put to death the Poor Prisoners you take and will not suffer them to be Christened. I desire you to do so no more but that you suffer those that commit great crimes may be Christened by the Fathers before they be put to death, and those that are young be kept to strengthen the Brethren or else to bring them to Albany and bestow them on Christians so great as they are and the slighting of them makes the Indians decay, and I should be sorry that the Brethren should do any thing to disoblige the Great God, who hath created the great world sun and moone and gives us all and every thing.

[N̤ 58.]   At a Councill Sepᵣ yᵉ 1ˢᵗ 1686.
Present
> The Governor.   M̤ N. Bayard
> M̤ Stephⁿ V Courtland   J. Spragge.
> Major G. Baxter.

The Indians of the five nations returned the following answer.

The Cayouges and Oneydes answered first and said Brother Corlaer : We are come hither at New York by yᵣ order although the appointed place is at Albany.

We have understood your propositions, that we are no more Brothers, but are looked upon as Children, of which we are glad.

And what concerns the sending the Provisions back again we towit the Cayouges and Oneydes have no hand in taking them, that concerns the Sineques.

What your Honor hath said about the Indians that are at Canada we will do our utmost endeavour to bring them from thence, and do desire that yᵣ Honoᵣ would write a letter to them which would have more influence upon them, than our bare words.

Concerning the Indians going to Cadaracqua that doth not concern us but the Onondagos.

What yᵣ Honoᵣ hath said of the Christian hunters &c &c traders that may come upon the Susquehannah River to hunt or trade without your passe, that we should take their goods from them, and bring their Persons to Albany, we dare not meddle therewith, for a man whose goods are taken from him will defend himself, wʰ made great trouble or warre, and therefore we deliver the Seals to your Honour again.

All that yᵣ Honᵣ hath further proposed, we like very well, and give yᵣ Honoᵣ many thanks for your kindness whereupon they gave a present.

Then a Maquas stood up and said.

All that his Honoᵣ hath proposed we do accept and promise to observe, and concerning the Indian Prisoners it concerns us not, but if it be your Honoᵣ pleasure,

that one of the Sachems shall go along we are willing
to goe.

We desire that your Hono. will order, that Lande
a Priest may be at Saraghtoga, for they will be most
Maquas that return, from Canada and for the reasons
given your Honor by the Cayougas and Oneydas wee
allso deliver your honor the Seals againe—upon that
they gave a present.

The Onondage stood up and said in answer

Brother Corlaer:—We find that you perform what
you told us by Arnout; and give y. Hono. thanks for
it.   We have heard that your Hono. is not well pleased
that some of your People are gone for Cadaracqua.   It
is true our fire burns there allso ; it is not for Politick it
is for Church affairs, for our Priest is gone thither
allso.

The Sinequas have not been guilty of taking Prisoners from the Dionondadies, for we have taken allso some
of them which we redelivered againe, that Dionondadies
are gone for Cadarachqua, where allso our people are gone
to speak with them, they are there by this time, and we
are here, and do speak perhaps of one and the same
Business, that is about the Prisoners, the first time that
our Priest went for Cadarachqua we gave him four
Prisoners, and the second time six more, so that there is
not one of the Prisoners we took with us.   Hearing the
ffrench will make no warre in his majesties Dominions,
hath taken away all fear and care from us and therefore
we will without any fear goe where we have a mind, this
is now for the ffrench, but we are afraid the Seals given
us put us in a new Trouble, therefore we deliver them to
your Honour againe, that we may live whole in peace—
give a present.

The Sineques said

We came the first to Albany, although we live the
furthest of, and do find Corlaer to be a good Brother to
us, therefore did not delay.   I shall speak first of the
Seals—we know the ffrench by their Coats, and other
hristians by their habits, and if we should take their

goods from them, it would create Trouble or warre and therefore deliver the same againe.

The calling of the Indians from Canada back againe is very good we will do our utmost endeavo.ʳ to get them from thence and do desire that your Hono.ʳ will write a letter to them for the same purpose.

We did think allways that the ffrench would not warre against us, for y.ʳ Honour told us years ago, that they should do it because it is upon his majesties Dominions.

The Prisoners that are with us I cannot dispose of being here alone, but I will acquaint the rest of the Nations with it, and do not Doubt but we shall doe what your Honour desires, we have already sent Ayendos one of the Prisoners a great man with two other Prisoners to Dionondadies to fetch off their Indians and to come into our Land to speak of Peace and what shall be done and concluded upon shall forthwith be sent and made known to y.ʳ Hono.ʳ..

So as I have said I say still when Arendos comes back what we then conclude shall be forthwith made known to y.ʳ Honour—give a present.

Then the five nations consulted together, and came to his Hono.ʳ to know when they should return home and that they might have Provisions for their Voyage, and gave his honor many thanks for his gifts and good propositions.

[N.º 59.] Council held at Fort James. Wednesday y.ᵉ Seaventh day of September 1687.
Present
        His Excellency the Governor
        Major Anthony Brockholls
        Major Stephen V. Courtland
        Major ffredrick fflypsen
        Judge John Palmer
        Coll Nicholas Bayard

'Mons.ʳ De Non Ville Governor of Canada his letter in ffrench to His Excell.ʸ read.

Letter from Robert Livingston dated at Albany to his Excell^y read.

Letter from Peiter Schuyler Mayor of Albany to his Excell.

Ordered that Judge Nicholls translate ye Govr of Cannaday letter.

Heads of enquiries taken at Albany by Robert Livingston ffrom John Rosse Inhabitant of Albany who was in Canada with Anthony Lispinar, read

That ye Mayor of Albany send ord^n to ye nute Indians to keep thirty or forty Indyans allways towards Corlaers lake, that ye said mayor if he be in Albany send a belt of wampum to each of the five nations with ord^r that ye Christians Indyans who come from Cannada to them be sent Hith^r to his Excell^y ye Governor and to encourage ye Indians to look out carefully letting them know the Gove^r will be up early there ye next spring. Ordered that Proclamation be drawn up Prohibiting ye bringing any Indyans Corne or Pease out of ye Countys of Albany or Ulster until further ord^{rs}.

[N° 60.] Council held at ffort James ffryday ye Ninth of September 1687.
Present

His Excell^y the Governor
Major Anthony Brockholls
Major ffredrick fflypsen
Major Stephanus Van Courtland
Coll Nicholas Bayard
Judge John Palmer

Information being given to his Excell^y and some of the members of this Board that ye ffrench of Cannada are providing ffifteen hundred pair of snow *shoes.*

Ordered that ye mayor and magistrates of Albany send ord^{rs} to the five Nations to bring down their Wives Children and old men least ye ffrench come upon them in the Winter and none to stay in the Castles but ye young men that they who come be settled some at Cats-

Kill Levingston Land and along y° River wher they can find conveyance to be near us to assist them if they should want and that they send down with them all y° Indyan Corne that can be spared by y° young men who are to stay in y° Castles.

[N° 61.] Council held at ffort James Sonday the 11ᵗʰ of September 1687

Present

> His Excellᵞ the Governor
> Major Anthony Brockholls
> Major Stephanus Van Courtland
> Major ffredrick fflypsen
> Judge John Palmer
> Coll Nicholas Bayard

Letters from Albany giving account that the People there are in great consternation thro apprehension that y° ffrench will come down upon them this Winter. Resolved that every tenth man of all y° Militia Troups and Companys within the Province except who were out y° last year a whaling be drawn out to go up thither.

[N° 62.] Council held at ffort James Monday the thir-tyeth day of Aprill 1688

Present

> His Excellᵞ the Governor
> Major Anthony Brockholls
> Major Jarvis Baxter
> Major ffredrick fflypsen
> Major Stephanus Van Cortland
> Coll Nicholas Bayard
> Mr. James Graham.

Letter ffrom Monˢ De Non Ville Governor of Canada dated at Mont Regall y° 4ᵗʰ of Aprill 1688, to his Excellᵞ read.

Letters ffrom Dirick Wessells (who was sent express to Mons. De Non Ville Govᵗ of Canada) to his

Excell.ʸ dated y.ᵉ 17.ᵗʰ & 27.ᵗʰ of Aprill at Mont Regall read.

Propositions to y.ᵉ Six nations of Indyans by his Excell.ʸ dated y.ᵉ 29.ᵗʰ of Aprill 1688, read and approved.

Major Matts Gregorys account of fifteen pound expended in his journey to and coming from Cannada read and allowed.

Account of Disbourcements made by Robert Livingston at Albany by his Excell.ʸ ord.ˢ maintainance of his Maj.ˢᵗˢ fforces there and for Sundry Gifts and presents made to y.ᵉ Indyans and relief of y.ᵉ ffrench Prisoners from the 11.ᵗʰ of August 1687 to y.ᵉ first day of June 1688, amounting to two thousand sixty seaven pound six shillings and four pence, read.

[N.ᵒ 63.] Council held at ffort James. Sunday y.ᵉ 6.ᵗʰ of May 1688.

Present

    His Excell.ʸ the Governor
    Major Anthony Brockholls
    Major Jarvis Baxter
    Major ffredrick fflypsen
    Major Stephanus Van Cortland
    Coll Nicholas Bayard
    M.ʳ James Graham

Resolved that his Excell.ʸ with all convenient speed go up for Albany that two or three men be sent to lye in each Castle of y.ᵉ Indyans to observe the motions of the ffrench and Indyans and that his Excell.ʸ according to the Exigence of Affairs take such resolutions about sending for y.ᵉ Boston forces as he shall Judg fitt and make such presents to y.ᵉ Indyans as y.ᵉ occasion shall require.

[N.ᵒ 64.] Council held at ffort James Monday y.ᵉ 7.ᵗʰ day of May 1688

Present

    His Excell: y.ᵉ Governor

Major Anthony Brockholls
Major Stephanus Van Cortland
Major ffredrick fflypsen
Coll Nicholas Bayard.

Ordered that a messenger be sent to Minissinks to
order them to send their young men to Albany in ord.ᵣ
to·jòyn with the Six Nations against the ffrench and
likewise that an order be sent with all expedition to
the Sheriffs of this Province to ord.ᵣ the young Indyans
to go with all speed to Albany to assist in y.ᵉ warre
against y.ᵉ Indyans.

[N.º 65.] At a Council held at ffort William Henry
            August the 20ᵗʰ. 1691.
Present
        The Commander in Chiefe,
    Jos. Dudley   ⎫   Steph Van Cortland ⎫
    ffred Phillips   ⎬ Esq.ʳˢ Chidley Brooke   ⎬ Esq.ʳˢ
    Nich Bayard   ⎭   William Nicolls   ⎭

The Council having taken into their consideration
the good services of Derick Wessells at Albany in
maintaining a fair correspondence with the five nations
of Indians for their Maj.ᵉˢᵗˢ service,
    Ordered to be allowed fifty pounds for one year to
commence from the arrival of the Governour at Albany
May last past.

[N.º 66.]   At a Council held at ffort William Henry
            the 3ᵈ of September 1691.
Present
        The Commander in Chiefe
    Jos. Dudley   ⎫   Steph Van Cortland ⎫
    ffred Phillips   ⎬ Esq.ʳˢ William Nicolls   ⎬ Esq.ʳˢ
    Nich. Bayard   ⎭   Gab. Monviell   ⎭

The Governor produced several letters from Governor Nicholson of Virginia also Bills of Exchange for

the sum of one hundred and two pounds fiffteen shillings and nine pence sterling sent by their Governor
and Council for a present to the five nations of Indians
to ty the knott of friendship with them on their behalf.

Ordered that the sums be sett apart for that use
and that it be disposed of into suitable merchandize to
the best advantage that they may be delivered to the
five nations in the name and behalfe of the Governor
and Council of Virginia.

[N.º 67.]   At a Council held at ffort William Henry
the 5th of October 1691.

Present

⸗ The Commander in Chiefe

ffred Phillips ⎫
Steph Van Cortland ⎬ Esq^{rs} Chidley Brooke ⎫ Esq^{rs}
Nich.ᵃ Bayard ⎭   Gab Monvill ⎬

Ordered that the Major and Aldermen of the City
of Albany are provide Indiane Corne for the Schack-
kook Indians and that they keep an account thereof
which they are to transmitt unto the Board for satis-
faccon.

[N.º 68.]   At a Council held at ffort William Henry
the 11th of January 1691.

Present

The Commander in Chiefe

ffred Phillips ⎫   Chidley Brooke ⎫
Steph V. Cortland ⎬ Esq^{rs} Gab. Monville ⎬ Esq^{rs}
Nich.ᵉ Bayard ⎭   William Nicolls ⎭

Upon reading a Lre from the Officers of Albany by
the land post giving an Acc.ᵗ of the Dangers and condition of that Garrison having lately lost a considerable
number of our best Mohaquas by the ffrench at Corlaers Lake amongst whome some considerable Captains
which hath caused great consternation amongst *our*
Indians also many necessary charges arising in the said

Garrison this winter for which they have noe order nor fund to defray the same.

Ordered a warrant issue forth for the payment ot one hundred and fifty two pounds unto the said officers to be disposed as followeth viz. one hundred and thirty pounds into presents for the five nations to be given them with recommendation to confirme the Peace and friendship between them and the Government of Virginia and to encourage them to fight against the ffrench and praying Indians of Canada and the sum of twenty five pounds to be disposed into white string Wampum to be given to the friends and relations of those Indians lately killed neer Corlaers lake to wipe off their tears.

And that the Collec.! doe order his D. receiver at Albany to lett them have the money raised by the 2000£ Act in the City and County of Albany, as they shall have occasion towards the incidentall charges untill the spring of the year that the River be open and that they be wrote unto to be good Husbands thereof watchfull and diligent.

[N.º 69.]   At a Council held at ffort William Henry the 19.ᵗʰ of March 1691
Present
            The Commander in Chiefe
ffred Phillips   ⎫   Chid Brooke   ⎫
Steph V Cortland ⎬ Esq.ʳˢ   Gab Monviell ⎬ Esq.ʳˢ
Nich.ˢ Bayard   ⎭   Willi. Nicolls   ⎭

Upon reading Lre's from Albany of the 16.ᵗʰ of this instant giving account of a great consternation upon the Inhabitants of that Garrison occassioned by the news of the losse of several of our Onondagoes by the ffrench and the great danger which threatens them the company of 100 fusileers being to be discharged the 28.ᵗʰ of this instant and the other 2 Companies on the first of May next following and the principal Inhabitants threatening to desert the place.

Ordered that a lre be sent up to Albany to Capt.

Bradshaw with two hundred and twenty five pounds to pay off the Private Soldiers of his Company and if enough remains to pay the Drummers, Corporalls, & Sergeants and to acquaint the officers that their pay shall quickly follow the s^d sum being what money can be p^{r}sently advanced and that the Soldiers after payment that are willing to continue be listed in the two other Companys who shall in like manner be payed off and discharged the first of May next.

[N° 70.] At a Council held at ffort William Henry the 12th of August 1692

Present

..The Commander in Chiefe

ffred Phillips
Nich^s Bayard
Steph V. Cortland } Esq^{rs}
Gab. Monviell

Chid. Brooke
Willi. Nicolls } Esq^{rs}
John Laurence

Lieutenant Gover^n Nicholson having signified that sundry outrages are committed by Indians passing the Heads of their rivers and desired that our Indians may have passes granted them under some Publick Seal when they goe a hunting or travail to the Southward of Virginia whereby they may be known to be friends.

Ordered that the Mayor of Albany be directed in letter to give the Indians that do travail thither passes on parchment or vellum sealed with the Seal of the City of Albany and that he send down eight or tenne Impressions thereof to be sent to Virginia for comparison.

The Commander in Chiefe being advised that the Gattoras Indians late in war with our five nations of Indians have to the numbers of 100 traveling so far as Delaware River coming hither to negociate a Peace with our Indians which is agreed to contribute to their mut^l Interest in the Province our Sinnequas being much diverted and hindered in their efforts against Canada by reason of the warr.

Ordered that Capt Aront Schuyler be forthwith dispatched to the said Indians with two Belts of Wampum in order to conduct them safe hither and that he have Lett.ᵉ of Credence to Mᵣ Thomas Lloyd of Pennsilvania for his assistance.

Ordered a warrant issue to the Coll. for the Payment of tenne Pounds four shillings currᵗ money of New York to David Jamison for soe much by him advanced and payed to Capt. Aront Schuyler to defray the charges of his journey.

[Nᵒ 71.] At a Council held at ffort William Henry the 17ᵗʰ of September 1692

Present

His Excelly. the Governour

ffred. Phillips			Chid. Brooke	
Steph V Cortland			Caleb. Heathcote	
Will. Smith	Esqʳˢ		Thoˢ Johnson	Esqʳˢ
Nichˢ Bayard			John Young	
Gab Monviell			John Laurence	

The River Indians that had been long absent from their native country with the Shawannoes this morning had the audience of the Governᵣ and Council in the Court of the ffort.

They in yᵉ first place did set forth that they had been long absent from their own Country and did desire to be kindly received as they in former days had received Christians when they first came to America they pray the same likewise in behalf of the strange Indians they have brought along with them. They Publish their intention of settling at the Minissinck Country upon Hudsons River where the fire of their relations now burns and of opening a path to come hither, which they confirm with some Beavers.

They add moreover that they are now come to their own River and those farr Indians have accompanyed them by the Great Gods protection they are poor but come to renew the Covenant Chain with Corlaer the

Mahaggs and five nations and confirm it with the fourth
of their farr Country whither they intend to depart in
20 days.

A Minnissinck Indian rose and spake

Corlaer! These Indians are designed to settle among
us I do acquaint you that we have accepted them as our
friends and relations.

We are very poor and design to goe along with the
Shawannoes Indians to hunt in their Country and ask
some creditt upon the reputation of our journey. Doe
give some Beaver.

His Excellency made answer—

To the Strangers

That they first make peace with the five nations,
and the five nations doe signifie Peace to be concluded
and confirmed unto him then he will extend the same
protection to them as to the rest of the Indians that
live in this Governm!. Therefore he advises them
to goe up and make peace with them in the first place
and gives them some white string Zee-Wamp.

To the Minnissinck Indians

That he would take care to maintaine the Chain of
friendship with them gives them some white string Zee
Wamp.

On consideration of soe considerable a number of
farr Indians coming to settle amongst us will add much
to our strength and the advantage of Trade,

Ordered Coll Cortland do expend the value of twenty
or thirty pounds in suitable presents for them and bring
an account thereof at next meeting to this Board.

[N.º 72.] At a Council held at ffort William Henry
the 10ᵗʰ of October 1692

Present

His Excell.ʸ the Governour

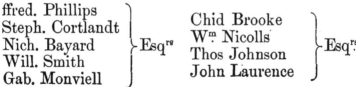

ffred. Phillips
Steph. Cortlandt
Nich. Bayard   } Esqʳˢ
Will. Smith
Gab. Monviell

Chid Brooke
Wᵐ Nicolls
Thos Johnson   } Esqʳˢ
John Laurence

His Excelly. was pleased to acquaint the Council with the reasons of his Private withdrawing to Albany viz: to avoid great charges in consideration of the circumstances of the Revenue and that by his surprize all the ffrontiers be not left be better informed of their condition coming unexpected, that he had strengthened the ffrontiers at Albany with tenne p^s of ordinance and Ammunition conformable, that he had viewed them and was thereby the better enabled to provide what will be necessary to be done next summer. That he had confirmed a friendship between the five nations and farr Indians which he believed was much for the benefit of their majes^y Interest in this Province and caused to be read the minitts of their conference that he saw them confirme the peace by the burying of two Hatchetts in the Ground and that he had viewed Schennectady and the out parts giving what directions & orders he judged most for the benefit and security of the ffrontiers which was well approved by the Council and accepted as an Extraordinary Service for which they did severally return their humble expressions of thankfulness.

[N° 73.] At a Council held at New York the 15th day of ffebruary 1692
His Excellency Ben Fletcher absent gone to Albany against the ffrench.
Present

ffred Phillips		Chid. Brooke	
Steph Courtlandt	Esq^{rs}	Wm Nicolls	Esq^{rs}
Gab. Monviele		John Laurence	

Ordered Lre^s be wrote forthwith to Virginia, Maryland, New Castle, Pennsilvania, Connecticut & Boston giving information of the ffrench and Indians being in 2 of our Indian Castles, of his Excell^y Expedition having embarqu'd yesterday with 200 men for Albany and other detachments of 150 men to follow to day, that they may doe what they conceive to be their duty on such occasion and to let them know that sence we cannot at present expect supplyes of men from them at their distance, we do expect they will at least con-tribute to the charge of this Expedition soe much for their Maj^{ies} service and the common safety.

[N? 73 *a*.] Her Maties Letter to the Governour of Pennsilvania to be assistant to New York.*

To our Trusty and well beloved Benjamin Fletcher Esqr our Captaine Generall and Governor in Chief in and over our Province of Pennsilvania & New Castle County and all the Tracts of land depending thereon in America and to our Chief Governor. *Governor* thereof the time being.

MARIE R. Trusty and well beloved we greet you well. Whereas it has been represented unto us in Council in behalf of our Province of New York in America that the same having been at great expense for the preservation and defence of Albany its fronteers against the ffrench by the losse of which Province the Inhabitants of Maryland and Virginia would not be able to live but in Garrison and having hitherto preser-ved that part the burthen thereby is now intolerable to the Inhabitants there we think it reasonable and necessary that our several Colonyes and Provinces of New England, Virginia, Maryland, and Pennsilvania should be aiding and assisting from time to time to the Governours or Commander in Chiefe of our said Province of New York in the maintainance and defence of it during the present warr and accordingly our will and pleasure is that upon the application of the said Gover nor or Commander in Chiefe you do immediately send him such aid or assistance in men or otherwise for the security of our said Province from the attempts of the ffrench or Indians as the condition of the Plantations under y^r Government shall permitt and our further pleasure is that as soon as conveniently may be you agree with the Governours of New England Virginia

* Book of General Entries 1686-1702.

and Maryland unto whome we have sent the like directions upon a quota of men or other assistance to be given by each Colony or Province for the defence of New York as occasion may require the same. And that you returne a speedy account of y^r proceedings herein to the end such further directions may be given as shall be necessary for securing the ffort of Albany and the Province of New Yorke from the attempts of our enemys in those parts. And so we bid you farewell. Given at our Court at Whitehall the 11th day of October 1692 in the fourth year of our Reigne

By her Ma^{ty} command

NOTTINGHAM

[N<u>o</u> 74.]   At a Council held at ffort William Henry the 28th of July 1693

Present

His Excellency Benjamin Fletcher

ffred Phillips ⎫ Esq^{rs}   Nichol. Bayard ⎫ Esq^{rs}
Steph Cortlandt ⎭   Gab. Monviel ⎭

His Excelly. did acquaint the Council the occasion of his calling them together so late is an express from Albany giving intelligence of the return of the messenger sent to Canada by the Jesuit Milett and that he hath brought a belt of Wampum called a belt of peace, and that the five Nations have agreed to a meeting of their Sachims at Onondago to consider of an answer of the Governor of Canada without his Excelly. our Governors knowledge that Jurian the Indian has brought from Oneydo two letters Dom. Dellius the teacher of our Christian Indians one from the Jesuit Milett who is a prisoner at Oneydo the other from the Superior at Canada.

Ordered the reading of the letter from Coll. Ingoldesby and Major Schuyler and the Examination of Jurian who brought the intelligence from Oneydo. Ordered the letters from the Superior of Canada and Jesuit Milett be interpreted into English.

26

His Excellency did declare that it is a strange surprizall upon him to think that the Indians of the five nations have so little regard to their late Vows as to receive a belt of Peace from the Governor of Canada consent to a meeting at Onondago in orde. to give an answer thereunto and not to have sent him the Packett and deliver up the Jesuit Milett according to agreement and promise so lately made—how little confidence there is to rely upon such a perfidious People who were little better than brutes.

His Excell. did propose to send forthwith Dirck Wessells Esq. with a letter to remind the Sachims of the five Nations of their Vows to disswade their intended meeting at Onondago and to exhort them to cause the Oneydes deliver up the Jesuit Milett in Exchange for the Indian boy according to their promise and agreement with his Excell. at Albany which was approved of and ordered accordingly.

[N. 75.]   At a Council held at ffort William Henry
the 31st of July 1693
Present
          His Excell. Benjamin Fletcher
          ffred Phillips   ⎫   Wm. Pinhorne ⎫ Esq.^{rs}
          Gab. Monvielle ⎬ Esq.^{rs}   John Laurence ⎭
          Wm. Nicolls   ⎭

His Excelly caused the reading of his letter to the Sachims of the five nations which was approved and allowed off.

[N. 76.]   At a Council held at ffort William Henry
the 3d day of August 1693.
Present
          His Benj.ⁿ Fletcher &c
          Steph Cortlandt ⎫   Wm. Pinhorne ⎫
          Nich.^s Bayard   ⎬ Esq.^{rs}   John Laurence ⎬ Esq.^{rs}
          Wm Nicolls   ⎭   Caleb Heathcott ⎭

Ordered a warrant issue for the payment of

pounds sixteen shillings Cour! money of New York to Daniel Honan accoumptant for soe much p? by him to the expresse that brought the intelligence from Albany of the meeting intended by the Sachims of the five nations to confer of Peace with the Governor of Cannada at Onondago.

Coll Stephen Cortlandt and Coll Nich Bayard having returned the account of his Excell? Expedition to Albany and the Presents to the Indians amounting in all to the sum of £99. 10s. 8d. whereof is already payed the sume of £45. 8s. 10d. and list of creditors of the sumes unpaid amounting to £346. 1s. 10d. under their hands. Ordered that Warrants issue for the payment of the severall creditts contained in the said lists amounting in all to three hundred and forty-six pounds one shilling and tenne pence to the respective Creditors pursuant to the said lists under the hands and seals of Coll Stephen Cortlandt and Coll Nich. Bayard.

Ordered a warrant issue for the payment of seventeen pounds eight shillings and six pence to Mr. Rob! Livingston for the charge of rebuilding the Mohags ffort.

[N°. 77.] At a Council held at fforte William Henry
the 17ᵗʰ of August 1693

Present

His Excell? Benj. Fletcher

ffred Phillips ⎫
Gab. Monviell ⎬ Wᵐ Pinhorne ⎫
Wᵐ Nicolls ⎭ John Laurence ⎬

Ordered a warrant issue for the payment of twenty seven pounds to Joseph Penno Merchant for three Barrells powder delivered to Mayor Schuyler for the Indians of Albany.

Ordered a warrant issue for the payment of Eighteen to Mʳ Godfrey Dellius Minister of Albany for the maintainance of 3 Indian boys from October 1692 to April 1693.

Ordered a warrant issue for the payment of thirty pounds to Mrs Margaret Macgregore—widow & relict of Major Hugh Macgregore Dec^d in full for his journey to Canada for their mat^ies service 1688.

[N° 78.]   At a Council held at ffort William Henry
the 4th of September 1693
Present
His Excell^y. Ben. Fletcher

ffred Phillips			Gab. Monviell	
Step^h Cortlandt	} Esq^rs		Wm Pinhorn	} Esq^rs
Nich Bayard			John Laurence	

Major Derick Wessells having arrived yesterday from Albany after his journey to the five nations to prevent their mutiny at Onondago, and to urge the Indians to perform their promise in delivering up the Jesuite Milett.

His Excell^y ordered his journal to be read wherein it is observed that the Indians are wavering and much inclined to a peace with the ffrench.

Major Wessells being sent for was asked the result of his journey who made answer that after much debate they at last declared they would not make peace with the Governor of Canada but they would send him word if he was minded for peace he must apply himself to their elder Brother Cayenguirago whom they own to be their master as well as his mat^r of the ffrench Indians.

[N° 79.]   At a council held at ffort William Henry
the 19th of September 1693.
Present
His Excell^y Benj. ffletcher

Stephen Cortlandt			Wm Pinhorne	
Nich^s Bayard	} Esq^rs		John Young	} Esq^rs
Chidley Brooke			Caleb Heathcote	

Chidley Brooke Esqr presented to this board two

Bonds given to sundry merchants by the members of Council to secure the payment of 300£ with interest at tenne per cent being advanced and payed to M^r. Robt. Livingston to defray the charge of Major Richard Ingoldesbys expedition to Albany May the 4th 1692 which are cancelled the money being repayed out of the Revenue and desired an order for the payment of the Interest thereof amounting to thirty seven pounds three shillings and three pence which is ordered accordingly payable to Coll Ab D Peyster and Robert Darkins Esq^{rs}.

His Excellency caused a letter from M^r. Godfrey Dellius to be read amongst other things giving intelligence that the ffrench of Canada have built above one hundred Battoes for Transportation.

His Excel^y offered his opinion that by all that he could understand their designs are upon our frontier and if the ffrench of Canada should come this winter His Excell^y did express how uneasy he should be to be at such a distance upon such an occasion and therefore bid them to consider of this matter that at lengthe he may have their opinion if it be needfull for their Matie. service and the safety of the Province that his Excell^y goe and remain at Albany this Winter.

[N°. 80.] At a council held at ffort William Henry the 20th of September 1693

Present

His Excell^y Benj. Fletcher

ffred Phillips ⎫
Steph Cortland ⎬ Esq^{rs}
Nich. Bayard ⎭

Chidley Brooke ⎫
John Laurence ⎬ Esq^{rs}.
John Young ⎭

M^r. Adolph Phillips being returned from Connecticut His Excell^y caused a letter which he brought from them signed John Allyn Sec'ry to be read wherein they promised to send a Commissioner but deny the other demands of supplys for Albany.

[N? 81.]   At a council held at ffort William Henry
25ᵗʰ of September 1693
Present
His Excellʸ Benjⁿ Fletcher &c

ffred Phillips ⎫
Gab. Monville ⎬ Esqʳˢ   William Pinhorne ⎫ Esqʳˢ
Chid Brooke   ⎭   John Laurence   ⎬

His Excellʸ did acquaint the Council that he had
appointed the first Wednesday in October for a meeting
of Commissioners one from each of the neighbouring
Colonys and Provinces at New York pursuant to their
matⁱᵉˢ Letters Patents to concerte and agree upon a certain quota of men and other assistance from each for the
ffrontiers during the present Warr and in Answer to
his demand caused Sir William Phips letter of the 18ᵗʰ
instant to be read wherein he denys to give any assistance, to the ffrontiers of this Province or to send any
Commissioner notwithstanᵍ their maᵗᵉˢ command.

Resolved it is requisite His Excellʸ doe send home a
copy of his demand and Sʳ William Phips answer by the
first opportunity to the Lords of the Committee or the
Secretʸ of State.

His Excellʸ did againe reminde the Council to take it
into their consideration his being in Albany this winter
signifying his great apprehensions of the coming of the
ffrench when the river may be shutt up between us and
them.

[N? 82.]   At a council held at ffort William Henry
6 of October 1693
Present
His Excellʸ Benjⁿ Fletcher

Steph Cortland ⎫
Nich Bayard   ⎬ Esqʳˢ   Gab. Monviel ⎫
Wᵐ Smith   ⎭   Chid Brooke ⎬ Esqʳˢ
                       Wᵐ Nicoll   ⎭

Ordered a Warrant issue for the payment of one
hundred and fifty pounds to Daniel Honan towards the

charge of his Excell^{ys} Journey to Connecticut and Albany.

[N.° 83.] At a council held at ffort William Henry 11th of December 1693

Present

His Excelly Benj. Fletcher

Steph Cortlandt			Gab. Monviel	
Nich Bayard	} Esq^{rs}		John Laurence	} Esq^{rs}
Chid Brooke			Ca^b Heathcote	

His Excelly did acquaint the Council that he did call them together to communicate to them intelligence from Albany yesterday arrived that another Belt of Wampum is come from Count ffrontenac Governor of Canada to the five nations of Indians—desire a peace as formerly and ordered the records of the severall papers thereoff.

The Council desire that Major Peter Schuyler be sent up to Onondage to promote the meeting of the five nations to consult of an answer to his belt to be held at Albany—if not to be effected to preserve their making any final agreement with the ffrench.

[N.° 84.] At a Council held at ffort William Henry the 5th of ffebruary 1693–4

Present

His Excelly. Benj Fletcher

ffred Phillips			Thos Willett	
Steph Cortlandt	} Esq^{rs}		Will. Pinhorne	} Esq^{rs}
Nich Bayard			John Laurence	
Gab. Monvielle				

His Excelly. did acquaint the Council that he had received letters from Lt Coll Beekman with new reports of the coming of the ffrench and Indians giving acc^t how the people of Ulster County fly into Kingston from all Parts.

Some of the council signifyed their opinion of the falsehood of those reports.

His Excelly. did offer that there is an use to be made of them—it is high time to consider to have a body of 500 men in readynesse with all things necessary for their march as there may be occasion, there is no time for Sloath and ease. His Excelly. did likewise express his sense of the great hardship upon the People to be harrassed and drawn from their famileys, to march upon every uncertain report, himselfe being always ready to minutes warning, therefore desires the advise of this board.

His Excelly. did signify his inclination to issue forth orders for the next troops of Horse to be in readyness to attend him to the ffrontiers if occasion—which the Council approved of.

[N°. 85.]   At a Council held at Albany the 13ᵗʰ of August 1694.

Present

His Excelly. Benj. Fletcher
Steph Cortlandt   Chidly Brooke
Nich Bayard   Peter Schuyler
Wᵐ. Smith   Esquires

His Excelly. did acquaint this Council that he had received a letter from Sʳ William Phips by the Commissioners which mentions a present to be made in behalf of the Province of Massachusetts Bay to the Indians of the five nations, but the manner is submitted to his Excelly.—which letter was read.

His Excelly. offered his opinion that since he had always given the presents to the Indians in the name of his Master and Mistresse the King and Queen and included all the neighboring Provinces and Colonies in the covenant chain it may now be inconvenient to alter the method and suffer distinct presents to be made by the Commissioners of a particular province and may incense the Indians against the other Colonies and Provinces which have not come to the Treaty to do the like.

Which the Council do unanimously approve.

[N? 86.]   At a Council held at Albany the same
evening 7 o clock.

Present

His Excelly Benj. Fletcher
Coll Andrew Hamilton Governor of the Jerseys
Steph Cortlandt   Chidley Brooke
Nich Bayard   Peter Schuyler
W™ Smith   Esquires

Major Pincheon ⎫
Major Sewall   ⎬ from Boston.
Capt. Townsend ⎭

Coll Allyn   ⎫ from Connecticut.
Capt Stanley ⎭

His Excelly sett forthe the case or circumstances of
this Province with relation to the neighbouring Provinces and Colonies and the present condition of the
ffrontiers and desired the commissioners would not only
assist his Excelly. with their council and advice but contribute to the support of the ffrontiers.

The Commissioners giving no answer His Excelly.
did acquaint them that S⁬ William Phips in his letter
did make mention of some presents to be made to the
Indians in behalf of the Province of Massachusetts
Bay and desired to know their whether they design to
give their presents in the name of that particular Province to which they answer in the affirmative—then his
Excell? gave reasons to the contrary. Coll Allyn
moved that his Excelly. haveing signifyed to them his
reasons, they may have time better to consider of any
answer—which was granted.

[N? 87.]   At a Council held at Albany the 14ᵗʰ of
August 1694.

Present

His Excelly. Benj. Fletcher
Steph Cortlandt,   W™ Smith,   ⎫ Esqᵣˢ.
Nich Bayard,   Chidly Brooke ⎭

Resolved it is needfull to urge to the Commissioners

from New England and Connecticut and the other
neighbouring Provinces to give an annual supply during
the warr for the defence of the ffrontiers of the Province.

The Commissioners from New England and Connecticut came in.

His Excelly desired their answer to what was proposed last night—

The Commissioners do consent that what presents
they have to offer be added to the presents made by
his Excelly and that they be delivered without any
particular marke of distinction in their ma[ties] name on
behalf of all their Plantations.

Present,
       His Excellency [Benj. Fletcher]
       Coll Andrew Hamilton Gov[r] of y[e] Jersey[s]
       Coll Steph Van Cortlandt ⎫
       Coll Nich Bayard | of their Maj[ties] Council
       Coll Will Smith   ⎬ for the Province of
       Chidley Brooke | New Yorke
       Major Peter Schuyler   ⎭
       Coll John Pynchon ⎫ Commissioners from their
       Samuel Sewall, Esq ⎬ Maj[ties] Collony of Massachu-
       Maj. Penn Townsend ⎭   setts Bay
       Coll John Allyn ⎫ Commissioners from their Maj[ties]
       Capt. Stanley ⎭   Collony of Connecticut
Sachims
       Rhode   ⎫
       Sinnenquiwse |
       Onnuchwaranow   ⎬ y[e] Maquas Sachims
       Tosoquatho |
       Tassorandoe   ⎭
       Adogounwa   ⎫
       Caniquane   ⎬ y[e] Oneydos Sachims
       Tokorochjondee   ⎭

Sadakanahtie ⎫
Dekanisore ⎪
Canadgegai ⎪
Carackkendie ⎬ yᵉ Onnondage Sachims
Sagorasintho ⎪
Odaniende ⎪
Orondisacht ⎭

Sorichnowanne ⎫
Debaoyjow ⎪
Tandisso ⎬ Cayouge Sachims
Cadgisso ⎭

Rasadxx ⎫
Radondawvax ⎪
Ottawatta ⎪
Twàdego ⎬ Sennekis Sachims
Tohendaisson ⎪
Carachquino a Squae ⎭

Propositions made by the Sachims of the five nations of Indians viz yᵉ Maquas, Oneydes Onnondages Cayueges and Sinnekas to his Excelly Benj Fletcher Capᵗ Genˡˡ and Governor in Cheiffe of yᵉ Province of New Yorke Province of Pensilvania County of New Castle and yᵉ Territories and Tracts of land depending there on in America and Vice admirall of yᵉ same. Their Maᵗⁱᵉˢ Lieft and commander in chieffe of yᵉ militia and all yᵉ forces by sea and Land within their Majᵗⁱᵉˢ Collony of Connecticutt and off all the Forts and places of strength within yᵉ same. At Albany beginning yᵉ 15ᵗʰ day of August 1694.

His Excelly having ordered yᵉˢ gards of foot to be drawn up before yᵉ place of Treaty and a Troop of Dragoons on yᵉ Right. The Sachims sent to his Excellency to signify their reddinesse to waite upon his Excellency and give in their answer to his Excelly questions put to them in May last. His Excelly sent word he was ready.

The Sachims attends with the other Indians came in order two and two; Rhode yᵉ Sachim of yᵉ Maquase being their leader singing all yᵉ way songs of joy and peace to yᵉ place of Treaty.

Dekanisore one of yᵉ Sachims of Onondage moved to his Excelly for liberty to sing a song or two of peace before they proceed to give *their* answer which his Excelly granted.

Rhode yᵉ Maquase Sachim rose up and addressed his discourse to yᵉ Sachims of yᵉ 5 Nations and said they had reason to rejoice to see their Brother Cayenguirago with so many of them that belong to yᵉ Covenant chain convened together to consult about matters relating to yᵉ Publick good after which they sang two or three songs of Joy and Peace successively.

Sadekanahtie a Sachim of Onnondage rose up and addressing his discourse to the 5 Nations told them how long they had been in Union with yᵉ Christians, and which of yᵉ 5 nations was the first that made the covenant chain and repeated all the acts of ffriendship which happened from time, afterwards proceeded thus.

Brother Cayenguirago

You expected to see us here and we yᵉ Sachims of the 5 Nations are come accordingly to speak to you.

Brother Cayenguirago

You appointed us to meet you here in one hundred days time to give our answer who would be for you and who against you, this is just yᵉ hundredth day, and we are come with the representatives of the five Nations to give you our unanimous answer.   This spring we gave you an account that we had sent messengers to Canada to Treat with yᵉ ffrench for which ill management you did check and rebuke us, butt withall you did receive us into your favour againe and embraced us, Promiseing not to break yᵉ covenant chain, so long as you had blood in your veins and gave us a Belt off Wampum in confirmation of itt.

Brother Cayenguirago

You see that the number of our people is much diminished some of them have been out a hunting lately and have caught a small matter we doe present your

Excelly. with some part of what they have gott. They give some Beavers and Otters.

Brother Cayenguirago.

I shall be *brieff* in what I have to say.

In the days of old when yᵉ christians came first into this river we made a Covenant with them, first with yᵉ Barke of a Tree and afterwards it was renewed by a Twisted with or yᵉ barke of a Tree Twisted, but in process of time fearing that would decay and rott yᵉ covenant was fastened with a chain of *Yron* which ever sence has been called yᵉ Covenant chain—and yᵉ of it was made faste to Onnondage yᵉ center of yᵉ 5 Nations and therefore it was concluded that whoever should violate or molest yᵉ chain or any part of it yᵉ partyes linked in yᵉ chain would unanimously fall upon such and destroy them, they should certainly dye the Death.

Since the time that yᵉ Governours have been here from yᵉ great King of England we made a Generall and more firm covenant which has grown stronger and stronger from time to time and our neighbours seing yᵉ advantages thereof came and putt in their hands into our Covenant Chain. We have had great troubles and struggling with yᵉ common enemy yᵉ ffrench—but Brother Cayenguiragoes hand & ours are tyred and stiff with holding fast yᵉ chain alone, while yᵉ rest of our neighbors, sitt still and smoake it, the greese is melted from our fflesh and drops upon our neighbours who are grown ffatt and live at ease while we become lean, they flourish and we decrease.

Addressing his discourse to all yᵉ English Plantations sᵈ

Brethren: We are envyed by our Enemyes round about, and particularly yᵉ french who are very inconstant and if yᵉ french or any oyʳ enemy fall upon us lett us all joyne together and take up yᵉ Hatchett in our hands, and then we shall be strong enough to destroy our Enemyes and live in Peace afterwards.

Brother Cayenguirago—and yᵉ rest of yᵉ Brethren that are in Covenant with us.

Itt has been an Antient Custome to renew y° Cov
enant chain, and we that are left of y° 5 nations are
come now to renew the same and to make it clean and
bright that it may shine like silver, and we promise y.
it shall be kept on our parts so strong and Inviolable
that y° thunder itself shall not break itt.

Brother Cayenguirago and y°. rest of our Brethren.

We have in y° time that y° Governours of this Province were called Corlear, Planted here in this place a
Tree of peace and wellfare whose rootts and Branches
extend themselves as farr as N England, Connecticutt,
New Jersey, Pensilvania, Maryland, and Virginy, and
whoever touches that Tree which we now make green
and saped or any y° roots of it, to hurt it we must not
only be sensible to ffeel & resent it, but rise up and
unanimously fall upon them that makes that breach to
destroy them.

Wee must acquaint you that it has been an Antient
custom among the 5 Nations to keep their meetings att
Onnondage which we are resolved to continue there and
if upon occasion any be sent for from hence to be present at our Generall meetings, we desyre that they may
come up.

Brother Cayenguirago: We have been disobedient
to your commands in going to Canada to Treat with y°
French, we thought because our Brethren of N England
had Treated with their Enemyes to the Eastward we
might goe and see whether there was any peace concluded or Treaty made to our Prejudice our Jealousy
arising by reasons of the french telling us that that
Chevalliere Do was sent back to consider by them of
New England whom they see in Canada giving them a
piece of money as a token that he was freed by y° English, and therefore it was in vain for us to warr with
them for y° English would relieve them again as soon as
they were taken.

Brother Cayenguirago: We pray that your Excellency may order that powder Lead and Gunns and other
ammunition may be sold cheaper and since account is

coming with some of y⁰ farr of the five nations Itt will be requisite yᵗ such goods may be sold cheap for their encouragement that they may be thereby y⁰ easier induced to come and live among us.

Brethren of New England, Connecticutt New Jersey Pensilvania Maryland and Virginia.

Hearken to what we now have said, we have renewed the Covenant Chain with you all, we always depended much upon you of New England to be the Chieffe of them yᵗ putt in their hand into y⁰ Covenant chain, we put more than ordinary confidence in your integrity and readiness to assist us in the common defence, and that you may see that we are not forgetfull of your engagements, here is your Token (being a fish painted upon paper) which you sent us of your being in covenant with us look upon it Broyʳ Cayenguirago and we present to you our Brother Cayenguirago a Belt of Wampum as a token whereby we acknowledge to you to be head of y⁰ Covenant Chain, and that we desyre to give notice to all y⁰ Governments that we have renewed the Covenant with them and desyre their assistance against y⁰ common Enemy which we pray you to putt them in mind of.

Brother Cayenguirago : We have said what we design to say to night and shall speak to morrow concerning what has been Transacted in Canada by our people, and what tokens we have from y⁰ farr nations called y⁰ Twichtwichs and Dionondadies to whom the Belt of Wampum was sent, and we follow your custom in giving our Present altogether—and so gave a parcel of Beaver and Peltry.

A true Copy Examined by
ROBT. LIVINGSTON.

[N°. 88.] At a Council held at Albany the 6ᵗʰ day of
August 1694.

Present

His Excellʸ Benj. Fletcher
Coll Andrew Hamilton, Governor of the Jerseys

Steph Cortlandt ⎫
Nich Bayard   ⎬ Esq.ʳˢ & the Commissioners
Peter Schuyler ⎭

His Excell.ʸ desired the opinion of the Gent.ˡ present concerning the Belt of Wampum sent to his Excell.ʸ by the Governor of Canada it being his opinion That this is a snare laid by Count·ffrontenac to delude and deceive the Indians to make them believe that a Peace was agreed upon between the English and him & broake on his Excellencys part.

It is the opinion of the Council & Commissioners His Excell.ʸ cannot receive the Belt.

[N.º 89.]   At a Council held at Albany 20ᵗʰ August 1694

Present

His Excell.ʸ Benjamin Fletcher &c
Coll Andrew Hamilton Gov.ʳ of the Jerseys.
Coll Stephen Courtlandt   Coll William Smith
Coll Nicholas Bayard   Maj.ʳ Peter Schuyler
The Commissioners from New England & Connecticut.

His Excellency did signify that he had called them together to advise of some things the Commissioners would have offered in behalf of the Province of the Massachusetts Bay to the Indians and caused it to be read.

Upon the Reading of that article whereby the commissioners desire that the Indians be checked for not condoleing the Blood shed lately in New England.

His Excell.ʸ offered his opinion that it cannot be safe to make any particular Treaty in Behalfe of New England lest it expose and put a mark upon other Provinces for whom his Excell.ʸ is equally concerned and are all to be included in the Treaty telling withall that his Excell.ʸ has resolved to acquaint the Indians that the Eastern Indians of New England have broake the peace and cutt off many people and that his Excell⁷ intends to offer a Belt of Wampum to cause them to joyne with his Excell⁷ in sending others to those Indians to make them bury their Hatchetts.

His Excell⁷ did approve of what the Commissioners would have offered concerning Chevalaer Deaux who made his escape into Canada and was not discharged by the Gov⁴ of New England.

His Excell⁷ did offer that five hundred men is the least number of forces requisite for the preservation and defence of the ffrontiers and to secure the Colonies and Provinces of New England Connecticutt and the Jerseys by reinforcing the Halfemoon Connessagirwena, Schenectady and the fflatts and to prevent any incursions of the ffrench and desired their opinion therein and what number of men may be reasonably expected from each Collony and Province. Coll Andrew Hamilton, the Council of New York and Maj Pincheon give their opinion that five hundred men is the least number requisite for that service.

[N⁰ 90.] At a Council at ffort Wᵐ Henry the 9ᵗʰ of Sepᵗ 1694.

Present

His Excell⁷ Benj. Fletcher
Steph Cortlandt   William Nicoll
Nich Bayard   Caleb Heathcote
Chid Brooke   Esquires

His Excell⁷ did acquaint the Council that this morning he received intelligence from Albany of Count ffrontenac being at Mount Regall with a great number of ffrench and Indians with many Cannoes and Battooes and was to sett out on Monday last (as was intended) against Albany and ordered the letter to be read. His Excell⁷ did offer his opinion that the designe was more probable for rebuilding of Cadaracqui and desired the advice of the board what is proper to be done and par-.

27

ticularly from some of the Council who are best acquainted with the affairs of the Country.

The Council are of opinion that there is no marching of forces to prevent the settling of Cadaracqui being fourteen days Journey to the waterside and neither waggon nor Carrages can passe, that at the water side men must encamp until they can make Cannoes for themselves which will spend a considerable time which will give the Enemy intelligence and they will put themselves in readynesse with all the force they can gather.

His Excell⁷ proposed to send copys of the intelligence to New England, Connecticutt, Virginia Maryland and Pensilvania and to desire their assistance in men or money.

[N⁰. 91.] At a Council held at ffort William Henry the 13ᵗʰ of March 1694-5.

Present

His Excell⁷ Benj Fletcher

ffred Phillips		Wm Nicoll	
Steph Cortlandt	Esq^rs	Peter Schuyler	Esq^rs
Nich Bayard		John Laurence	
Chid Brooke		Caleb Heathcote	

His Excell⁷ did acquaint the Council that the occasion of his calling them before the usual day is intelligence from the ffrontiers that the ffrench are on their march towards Cadaracqui to settle it that his Excell⁷ conceives by all the particular accounts given by Major Schuyler as well as other intelligence it must appear reasonable that they designe to repossesse that ffort that they cannot but conceive the consequences of their neighbourhood to our Indians who must be compelled to make peace with them and if they be able to send numbers enough thither will give law to the five nations and so the five nations must become our Enemyes to the utter ruin of the Indian trade—Albany will be nothing more than a Garrison Town and the Province ruined.

His Excelly did likewise offer that seeing the Indians

have made their application to this Province for Assistance and challenge his Excell[y] upon his promise it may be of ill consequence to turn our back upon them and desired the opinion of the Board.

The Board nemine contradicente, are of opinion assistance must be given to the Indians of the five nations according to his Excell[y] promise.

His Excell[y] did propose to send three hundred fusileers into the Country of Onondage for assistance to the Indians and appointed Coll Steph Cortlandt Coll Nich Bayard, William Nicoll Esqr Major Peter Schuyler and Coll Caleb Heathcote a committe to compute the cost of that expedition and that they make report thereof to his Excell in Council within one hour

The same Committee shortly after made report to his Excellency that to defray the extraordinary charge of the expedition for thirty days (besides pay) there will be wanting seven hundred sixty nine pounds five shillings.

There being sundry goods wanting for the use of the fusileers and Indians shoes &c His Excell did desire the severall members of Council to consider what Goods they can furnish upon the creditt of the Government and appointed William Nicoll Esq[r] and Coll Heathcote to find out two hundred pounds in money (if not otherwise) at the interest of tenn p[r] cent to answer the present exigencyes of the s[d] march.

[N[o]. 92.]   At a Council held at ffort William Henry the 14th of March 1694/5

Present

        His Excell Benj Fletcher

Steph Cortlandt ⎫   William Nicoll ⎫
Nich Bayard   ⎬ Esq[rs]   Peter Schuyler ⎬ Esq[rs]
Chid. Brooke   ⎭   Caleb Heathcote ⎭

William Nicoll Esqr and Coll Heathcote did report that in obedience to his Excell command yesterday in Council they have the promise of one hundred pounds at eight per cent interest upon the personal security of the members of Council from Peter Jacobs Marius and that Lieut Coll Gabriel Monviell will advance the sume of one hundred and eighteen pounds five shillings for six months without interest upon the creditt of the Government towards the expedition to Onondage to assist the Indians against the French of Canada which was approved and the members of Council are resolved to give their personall security to Peter Jacobs Marius for the sum of £100.

Ordered Major Peter Schuyler do receive the said sums and carry the same with him to Albany and that he take the advice of Coll Richard Ingoldesby in the disposition thereof towards the said expedition. But in case the Alarm prove false & Coll Richard Ingoldesby do not proceed to March then it is ordered Major Peter Schuyler to retaine the money by him untill he receive directions for the disposition thereof.

[N⁰ 93.] At a Council held at Fort William Henry the 8ᵗʰ of April 1695

Present

His Excell^y Benj Fletcher

Stephen Cortlandt ⎫
Nich Bayard ⎪
William Smith ⎬ Esq^{rs}
William Nicoll ⎭

Wᵐ Pinhorne ⎫
John Laurence ⎬ Esq^{rs}
Caleb Heathcote ⎭

His Excellency did acquaint the Council that some of the principal Sachims of the five nations of Indians are come from Onondage to treate with his Excell^y. The Council are of opinion that they must be clothed and have presents given them at the charge of the revenue.

Sadekanahtie and Dekanisore came into the Council Chamber. And Sadekanahtie spoke. Major Dirck Wessell Interpreted saying

We come now in behalfe of all the five nations to reisste Cayenguirago and to return our hearty thanks.

We were lately alarmed by the ffrench and their

Indians whereupon we sent to Cayenguirago for assistance of men and ammunition the weather was bad and the men could not march but you sent us many kaggs of Powder and barrs of lead, we are now confirmed in your love to us and return you our hearty thanks.

We find out daily more and more falsehood in Onontis (the Governour of Canada) and that he designs nothing but the hurt and ruin of the five nations and of this Province and therefore seeks to divide us but we will allways be steadfast to the Covenant Chain.

His Excell⁷ made answer that he was always ready to assist the five nations against the ffrench and dare meet Count ffrontenac at any time with his sword in hand to vindicate his Great Master and Mistresses quarrell and his Excell took hold of a great Belt of Seawamp and told them that so soon as he heard the ffrench were coming he had ordered men to be in readiness to assist them, and did design that belt for them with a letter as a token of their coming but the Alarm proved false nevertheless bid them take the belt and letter, they will find some body in their Castle at Onondage that can read it, then bid them hang up that belt in their Chiefe Castle for a remembrance that his Excelly will never depart from the Covenant Chain nor deny them assistance while they continue steadfast.

[N.° 94.] At a Council held at ffort William Henry the 13ᵗʰ day of April 1695

Present

His Excellency Benj Fletcher
Stephen Cortlandt   Chid Brooke
Nich. Bayard   Will Pinhorne
Gab Monville   John Laurence

Sadekanahtie and Dekanisore came before his Excell. in Council, Major Dirck Wessells interpreter, another old Captain, Dekanisore's wife and her child.

His Excell⁰ presented them with red Coats laced with Silver and laced hats wastcoats stockings shoes

shirts Blankets Gunns Powder lead &c then told them
they must remember to be true to the Covenant Chain
and never depart from it nor hearken to the Governour
of Canada and they may be assured never to want the
assistance and Countenance of this Province.

Sadekanahtie promised they would always be steadfast to the Covenant Chain and returned thanks for the
large presents they did receive, then told his Excelly
that their young men were lying in readyness with their
Hatchetts in their hands to wait their orders and desired the advice of Cayenguirago if they shall send
them against Canada. The ffrench have now of late
since the talked of Peace made inroads upon our fronteers, and not tenn days ago have taken away a man
neer Albany let your young men bring a Prisoner from
Canada in his room.

[N.° 95.] At a Council held at ffort William Henry
            the 16.ᵗʰ Day of April 1695
Present
            His Excell.ʸ Benj.ⁿ Fletcher &c
Stephen Courtlandt }   Chid Brooke   }
Nicholas Bayard   } Esq.ʳˢ   Will.ᵐ Pinhorne } Esq.ʳˢ

His Excell.ʸ having proposed the necessity lying
upon him to secure the ffronteers the Assembly having
denyed a supply and professing great unwillingness to
oppresse the Country with detachments—The Council
are unanimous in their opinion, that all means must be
used to lighten the burden of Detachments from Inhabitants of the Province which hath been so great a
grievance to them some years past and advise his Ex-
cell.ʸ that money be taken up at Interest to answer the
present necessity upon the Credit of the Goverment for
the levying of one hundred volunteers to be employed
on the ffronteers for one year allowing forty shillings
to each, levy money and twelve pence p day.

Ordered the sum of two hundred and eighteen pounds
five shillings taken up part upon interest and the per

sonal security of the Council towards an expedition to
Onondage be applyed by Major Peter Schuyler to the
levying of one hundred men for one year to have forty
shillings levy money each and 10^d p day

The accounts of the four Companys are referred to
Coll Cortlandt, Coll Bayard and Chidley Brooke Esqr
for examination.

[N? 96.] At a Council held at ffort William Henry
    in the Evening of the 18th of June 1695
Present
        His Excell^y Benj Fletcher
  Steph Cortlandt   Chid Brooke
  Nich. Bayard   Caleb Heathcote
  Gab Monville   Esquires

His Excelly did acquaint the Council the reason of
his calling them together at this time is intelligence
from Albany by expresse just now arrived from Coll
Ingoldesby that the enemy are upon their march towards
that Garrison and at the same time comes advice from
Maryland that there a fleet of ffrench Shipps with great
force designed to attack this Port being the Key of the
Province.

[N? 97.] At a Council held at ffort William Henry
    the 11th day of July 1695
Present
        His Excellency Benj. Fletcher
  Stephen Cortlandt,   Willi Nicolls and
  Nich Bayard,   Caleb Heathcote
  Chid Brooke,   Esquires

His Excellency did acquaint the Council that having
made application to the neighbouring Colonies and
Provinces for their Quotas he hath received two more
answers from Boston and Pensilvania the other from
Connecticutt they have seene before, so ordered them
to be read.

It appears that no assistance will be had the Lieut Gove.ᶜ of New England says that by their Charter he cannot oblige any of the Inhabitants to march out of the Province without the consent of the Assembly that he hath recommended his Excell.ʸˢ letter to the Assembly who refuse and say they have enough to do to maintain their own ffrontiers.

Governor Markham called his Council and declared he had no directions from the Proprietor to comply with Governour ffletchers demands he asked their consent to have the Assembly called to consider thereof but the Council would not consent the Assembly should meet sooner than their former appointment which is the 9ᵗʰ of September next.

His Excell. taking taking into consideration some part of Lieut. Governor Stoughtons letter desiring our River Indians may be prohibited from coming upon their ffronteer Towns in their return from hunting alledging that under colour of them their ffronteer are viewed by Spyes—asked advice what is to be done.

The Council are of opinion that having formerly prohibited the River Indians from going that way his Excelly may renew his orders.

His Excelly asked the opinion of the Council if they think it needfull for his Ma.ᵗⁱˢ service that his Excelly. go to Albany this season and what presents will be required for the Indians.

[N.º 98.]   At a Council held at ffortt William Henry
the 15th of July 1695
Present
His Excellency Benj. Fletcher,
Steph Cortlandt, } Esqʳˢ William Nicolls, } Esqʳˢ
Chid Brooke; Caleb Heathcote

The proposition of the Sachims of the five Nations and River Indians at Albany the 6th of July instant were read.

His Excellency taking into consideration that Proposition of the Schackhook Indians whereby they desire assistance to the Building a ffort wherein they may live with more safety did desire the opinion of the Council therein and to know what may be the charge.

[N° 99.]   At a Council at ffort William Henry the 15th day of August 1695.

Present

His Excelly Benj. Fletcher,

Steph Cortlandt,   ⎫   Willi Pinhorne,   ⎫
Nich Bayard,   ⎬ Esqrs Peter Schuyler,   ⎬ Esqrs
Willi Nicolls   ⎭   Caleb Heathcote,   ⎭

Resolved it is needfull for the encouragement of the Indians of the five Nations that have lately appeared more brisk in their pursuit of the warre against Canida that his Excelle. make his personal appearance to them at Albany and present them with arms and ammunition and other necessarys also that some of the Council do accompany his Excelly. in this expedition.

Ordered that Major Peter Schuyler do forthwith give notice to the Sachims of the five nations that his Excelly will meet them at Albany on the tenth of September next.

[N° 100.]   At a Council held at ffort William Henry the 18th of August 1695

Present

His Excellency Benjamin Fletcher,
Steph Cortlandt,   Peter Schuyler,
Nich Bayard,   Caleb Heathcote,
Willi Nicoll,   Esquires.

His Excellency did acquaint the Council he had an account from Albany last night that the ffrench were endeavouring with all the force they can spare to resettle Cadaracqui and the Indians call for our assistance which is the reason of his Excelly. calling the Council together this day to have their opinion.

It is the opinion of the Council that as many forces as can be spared from the Companies upon the ffronteers be ordered to march towards the assistance of the Indians so that the Garrison be not exposed to apparent danger and that they must be supplyed with things necessary for such a march.

Resolved it is for his Ma^{tis} service that Major Peter Schuyler forthwith go to Albany and lead those men that are to be detached from his own and the other Companyes with such of the People of the Country as are willing to march unto the Castles of the Mohaques to show the readynesse of this Government to their assistance and acquaint the Indians the reason of their not coming sooner is want of earlier intelligence.

His Excelly did likewise acquaint the Council he hath received a letter from Connecticutt whereby they seem to deny the giving of any assistance to this Province notwithstanding the Royall Commands they acknowledge to have received and his Excelly application to them and expect that if they send any men this Government shall defray their charge.

It is the opinion of the Council that his Excelly do write to them once more and give them account that there is intelligence the ffrench are endeavouring to resettle Cadaracqui.

[N° 101.]   At a Council held at ffort William Henry the 29th day of August 1695.

Present

His Excellency Benjamin Fletcher,

Steph Cortlandt,			William Pinhorne,		
Nich Bayard,	} Esq^rs		William Nicoll,	} Esq^rs
Chid Brooke,			Caleb Heathcote,	

Coll Cortlandt and Coll Bayard do report that in obedience to his Excelly. order in Council they compute the Charge of his Excelly present Journey and presents for the Indians will amount to £600 and upwards.

[N.º 101 a.] At a Council held at ffort William Henry
the 6th of September 1695 Sunday.
Present
His Excelly Benjamin Fletcher,
Steph Cortlandt, ⎫   Willi Nicoll,   ⎫
Nich Bayard,   ⎬ Esqrs Willi Pinhorne,   ⎬ Esqrs
Chid. Brooke,   ⎭   Caleb Heathcote,   ⎭

His Excelly did acquaint the reason of calling them
together is he hath received intelligence from Albany
the ffrench have repossessed themselves of Cadaracqui
for which reason the Sachims have sent to beg leave of
his Excellency for not coming to Albany at the appointed time, whereupon his Excelly desired the opinion
of the Council if they think it for his Maties service
that he be at Albany at the time appointed to wit the
tenth instant or that he remain here.

It is the opinion of the Council that his Excelly remain here—His Excelly did further communicate some
letters and propositions of the Indians at Albany
wherein they desire assistance of 500 hundred men and
claim a Promise of assistance to expell the ffrench from
Cadaracqui.

It is resolved that all the care and endeavours
possible be used to encourage the Indians so far as
this province can that his Excelly appear personally at
Albany and that it is needfull his Excelly do renew his
application to the neighbouring Provinces for assistance.

His Excelly was pleased to communicate a letter
from New England by which it is manifest there is no
assistance to be expected from thence.

[N.º 102.] At a Council held at ffort William Henry
the 24th day of September 1695.
Present
His Excelly Benjamin Fletcher,
Steph Cortlandt,   Chid Brooke,
Nich Bayard,   John Laurence,
Gabr Monviell,   Caleb Heathcote.

His Excelly did give the reasons of his calling of the Council this time that being returned yesterday from Albany and the ffronteers he finds the ffrench have resetled Cadaracqui that notwithstanding his Maties repeated orders to the neighbouring Governments for their giving assistance and his Excellency's frequent application's he hath not been able to procure so much as one man of 1198 appointed by his Majesty that there is a ship now ready to saile for England and that it may be requisite our present circumstances be represented to his Majtys by agents appointed from this Province which his Excellency did offer to the consideration of this Board and desired their opinion. His Excelly. ordered to be read his conference with the Indians and others passages happening during his Excelly being at Albany.

[N.º 103.] At a Council held at ffort William Henry the first of November 1695.

Present

His Excellency Benjamin Fletcher,

Nich Bayard,		Thomas Willett,	
Gab. Monviele,	Esqrs	Wm Pinhorne	Esqrs
Wm Nicoll,		Caleb Heathcote,	

His Excelly did acquaint the Council that he has rec'd some propositions made by some of the Indian Sachims at Albany the 19th of October past by which they appear more insolent than formerly in asserting many things which the members of the board know to be falsehoods and peremptorily demanding assistance. His Excelly therefore desires the opinion of the Council what is to be done.

The Council are of opinion that since his Excelly. has taken all the pains and care imaginable to gett assistance from the neighbouring Provinces which has proved ineffectually notwithstanding his Maties commands his Excelly. do transmitt a copy of the Propositions to the Lds of the Committee for his Maties information.

It is the opinion of the Council that if there be necessity of sending up Christian Forces to the Indian Country it is most proper that Maj.ʳ Schuylers Company of ffusileers who are best acquainted and have more encouragement in pay than the Granadeers be ordered to undertake that march but declare that they knowe no promise nor doe believe his Excelly. obliged to march up forces to their Country being always ready to give assistance upon any occasion of the ffrench ag.ˢᵗ the Castles or Country of the Lower Nations and having recommended to the upper Nations to look out that way and be upon their own defence and having supplyed them with arms, ammunition and clothing for that purpose.

[N.ᵒ 104.] At a Council held at his Maties ffort in New York the 9th of July 1696

Present

His Excelly. Benjamin Fletcher.

ffred Phillips ⎫
Steph Cortlandt ⎬ Esqʳˢ
Nich Bayard ⎭

Gab Monville ⎫
Peter Schuyler ⎬ Esqʳˢ
John Laurence ⎭

His Excellency did communicate intelligence from Albany with the examination of a ffrench Prisoner wherein appears there is great preparation in Canada and a resolution of the Gover.ⁿ.ʳ of Canada to reduce the five Nations this Summer that all the men between fifteen and fifty in Canada are ordered to be in readynesse and that all the ffrench Indians and Ottowawaes are together and that they are to joyne the Dawaganhaes. His Excelly offered his opinion to march up 400 men to the Castle of Onondage to encourage and confirme the Indians.

[N.ᵒ 105.] At a Council held at his Maties ffort in New York the 26th of July 1696.

Present

His Excelly Benjamin Fletcher &c

Steph Cortlandt ⎫
Nich Bayard ⎬ Esqʳˢ
Gab. Monviell ⎭

John Laurence ⎫
Caleb Heathcote ⎬ Esqʳˢ

His Excelly did acquaint the Council from the Governor of Maryland and from the Council and Assembly of that Province alledging they have never paid their Quota of £200 which his Maties is pleased to accept from them in lieu of the former Quota and desired they may be no more applied unto for assistance.

[Nº 106.] At a Council at his Maties ffort in New York the 31ˢᵗ day of July 1696.
Present
        His Excelly. Benjamin Fletcher
        ffred Phillips   Gab Monviele
        Steph Cortlandt   Caleb Heathcote
        Nich Bayard   Esquires

His Excellency did communicate to the Council intelligence from the ffrontiers that the Enemy are upon their March that the Indians of the five Nations have sent to call for assistance of Christian force, and did express his readynesse to go to Albany.

His Excelly did desire their opinion what is to be done being there is no Money in the Coffers.

It is the opinion of the Council that there may be men found upon the ffrontiers that upon encouragement will march to the Indian Country if there were a friend to answer the Charge thereof. His Excellency did declare his readyness to go provided they will find money to answer the necessary charge. Coll Cortlandt profferred his personal credit for £200 towards the expedition. Coll Bayard offered the same. ffred Phillips offers the same Lᵗ Coll Monville the same, Coll Heathcote the same.

His Excellʸ did recommend to them to procure the credit each for £200 forthwith.

[Nº 107.] At a Council held at his Maties ffort in New York the 18ᵗʰ of August 1696.
Present
        His Excellʸ Benj Fletcher

Steph Cortlandt   John Laurence
Nich Bayard   Caleb Heathcote
Gab. Monviele   Esquires.

' His Excellency did communicate papers of his proceedings at Albany which were approved and ordered to be entered in haec Verba.

[N.º 108.] At a Council called by his Excellᵧ at Albany the 7ᵗʰ day of August 1696 the day of his Excellency's arrival there.
Present
His Excellᵧ Benjamin Fletcher.
Coll Nicholas Bayard   Coll Richᵈ Ingoldesby
Major Peter Schuyler   Capᵗ James Weems
Evert Bancker Esq.   Capᵗ Willi Hyde
Lᵗ Coll Lodwick   Capᵗ Peter Mathews
Dirick Wessells Esq.   Mathew Clarkson, Esq.
Doctor Dellius

The Governor said Gentlemen so soon as I had certain notice from you that the Enemy were marched into the Country of our Indian friends and by the number of their forces did seeme to threaten this place and Schenectady I made all the haste I could to your assistance loosing no time but while I wrote to Connecticutt and the Jerseys for such supplys of men as I conceived necessary upon this Occasion by this letter which I rec'd at the same time (with those from Albany) from the Lords of his Maties Council in England you will see that I could not reasonably draw forces from New York nor be well spared from that place myselfe yet by advice of his Maties Council there I am come up with a part of my own Company and desired yʳ advice what is most proper to be done for the King's service and yʳ own safetys and for securing the Indians in their fidelity and renewing the Covenant Chain—this we are to consider that time may not be lost and the Country not burthened by any unnecessary charge. His Excellᵧ further proposed sending thirty men of his own Company nowe brought up with him with a detachment of twenty out of each of the three Company's here into the Indian Country to cover the retreat of our Indians and secure them from their fears.

The Council are of opinion the ffrench being retreated it would be an unnecessary charge. And offer their advice that the Sachims of the Oneydes should be sent for (who are here) and condoled as to their losse which was accordingly done. And they were further of opinion that the Members of the Council present with the officers of the Companyes and the principal Inhabitants of this place should meet and consult with the Chief Indians now in Town about the properest methods for bringing back those Indians that are fled and setting them firm again in the Covenant Chain and make report what they have done therein to his Excell.[y]

In obedience to y.[r] Excellency order of the 7 Instant we under written having mett and considered about the properest methods for bringing both those Indian Nations Viz the Onnondages and Oneydes that are fled and renewing with them and the rest of the five Nations the Covenant Chain and having thereupon sounded the opinions of the Sachims of the Maques and Oneydes Nations and several of their Chiefe men now here at Albany do humbly offer as our Opinion that since we are informed that it is now twelve days ago the ffrench army left the Indian Country and that the Sennekes and Cayouges are still undisturbed in their own country that the Onnondage Nation upon the approach of the Enemy have sett their own Castles on fire and are fled to be out of the Enemies reach that the Oneyde Nation have in like manner left their Castles and great part of them are already come in here to Albany for reliefe of their wants of Provision and Ammunition.

And that the Maquas Nation or great part of them are in like manner come in hither we cannot perceive that it can be any service to send out any great body of

men now to the upper Nations who are seated at that
distance from hence neither can any men be well spared
from Albany here being only three established Companyes in Garrison with a detachment of yor Excell
own Company now broug^t with you besides a few Inhabitants which we judge to be little enough for the
defence of the place. But we humbly suppose that its
of absolute necessity that small partyes be frequently
sent out to clear the coast from such small troops that
may come to annoy the adjacent farms getting in their
harvest and lastly with submission we are of opinion
that the best. method to reduce the Indians that are fled
and to unite them with the rest of this Government as
formerly in renewing the Covenant Chain—[is]

Imprimis that trusty and faithfull Indians be procured and sent to the Sennekes and Cayouges in their
Castles and to the Onondages that are fled, with instructions to acquaint them that his Excellency the
Governor upon the first news of the ffrench invading
their Country came up to Albany from New York in
order for their assistance and reliefe.

2dly. That upon his Excellency's coming hither he
had intelligence the Enemy was already departed out of
the Indian country.

3^{aly}. That is hardly possible to have a Meeting with
all the brethren of the five Nations now to consult with
them what may be proper for their common Good and
to present them with those things which are sent to them
from his Excellency's great master the King of Great
Brittaine.

4^{thly} That therefore your Excellency do appoint the
brethren to meet you in order thereunto at Albany this
day two months but if it should so happen that by reason of the Onondages being fled the brethren could not
then meet in a body at that time that the Onondages
Sennekes and Cayouges will consult and pitch upon the
time and to give your Excellency timely notice thereof
to the end the brethren of the Maquas and Oneydas
may be acquainted therewith accordingly. Dated the

8th of August, 1696. G Dellius, Evert Banker, N. Bayard, Dirick Wessells, Pr Schuyler.

Resolved the Indians of the two Nations of Onondage and Oneyde whose corn is destroyed by the enemy be supplyed the ensuing Winter at the charge of this Government. Ordered no Indian corne be brought down the river from Albany Ulster and Dutchess Countys untill the Indians be supplyed the ensuing Winter and that the Commissioners appointed to treate with the Indians in his Excellency's absence do purchase so much corne as is necessary for them.

[N.º 109.] At a Council held at his Maties ffort in New York the 5th of November 1696.
Present
      His Excellency Benjamin Fletcher
      Steph Cortlandt   Peter Schuyler
      Gab. Monville   John Lawrence
      Willi Pinhorne.   Esquires

His Excellency did communicate to the Council news from Albany come this morning of the good successe of that party that pursued the ffrench having killed seven of them neare the Lake one of which is the Indian guide offering the necessity of rewarding the party according to the former proclamation. Whereupon it is ordered Major Schuyler Major Wessells and Captain Ranslaer do take up two hundred pounds upon interest pursuant to the Act of Assembly to answer that charge.

[N.º 110.] At a Council at his Maties ffort in New Yorke the 20th of December 1697
Present
      His Excellency Benjamin Fletcher
    ffred Phillips   Nich Bayard
                  Esq.^{rs}   Esq.^{rs}
    Steph Cortlandt   Gab Monville

His Excellency did communicate intelligence from

the Lt Governor of Boston of the Peace and the printed Articles and desired their advice.

It is ordered that the Clk of the Council draw up a letter to the Commissioners at Albany desiring them to send the Articles to Mount Reall to prevent further Mischiefe and the Charge of Winter Scouts and to perswade the Indians of this Province to bury the Hatchett.

[N.º 111.] At a Council held at his Maties ffort in New York the 15th of August 1698.

Present

His Excellency Richard Earl of Bellomont

ffred Phillips ⎫
Stephen Cortlandt ⎬ Esq^{rs}.
Nich Bayard ⎭

Willi Smith ⎫
Gab Monville ⎬ Esq^{rs}.
John Lawrence ⎭

His Excellency did order the propositions and answers of the five Nations of Indians in his late Expedicōn to Albany to be read and did acquaint the Council with the address that was presented to him by Principal Inhabitants of Albany and Schenectady wherein amongst other things they have represented the weaknesse of their fforts and prayed that new ones might be built for their future security.

His Excellency also produced several petitions delivered to him at Albany and Schenectady by persons who had given credit to the Government & being most of them necessitous could not afford to be longer out of their money therefore desired payment might be ordered them out of hand which was consented to by the Council after reading petitions.

His Excellency also acquainting the Council that upon Count ffrontenacs haughty answer to His Excell^{ys} letter to him notifying the Peace and proposing an exchange of Prisoners and also upon the grievous complaint of the five nations of Indians to his Excellency at Albany of the Hostilitys committed on them by the ffrench since the peace was proclaimed : And his Excelly.

stepping to his closet to fetch another letter which he had newly writt to the Governor of Canada the Gentlemen of the Council took the opportunity of his Excellency's short absence to agree among themselves that Coll Will: Smith Chief Justice should in the name of the rest of the Council compliment his Excellency upon the successfull pains he had taken with the Indians in his expedition to Albany and the good humour he had put them in: His Excellency being returned and seated Coll Smith stood up and expressed himselfe to his Excell^y as followeth. My Lor^d yor Excellency hath been pleased to shew us the Treaty you have lately had with the Indians of the five nations at Albany which having duly considered my brethren of the Council have prayed me to assure your Lordship they are of opinion the same hath been managed by yor Excellency with such conduct temper and prudence as is very extraordinary: And as we have great reason to hope the effect of it will highly conduce to his Maties service and the great good benefit and welfare of the Province so we do all think ourselves obliged to render yor Excell^y. our humble acknowledgement for the studious care great pains and fatigue yor Excell^y has been pleased to take upon you therein and do pray that it may be entered in the Council book.

His Excellency thanked the Council for the compliment they had paid him by Coll Smith which he said was unexpected to him as was kinde for that he thought the pains he has taken in managing the Indians at Albany, was but a bare performance of his duty to the King and the publick—after which his Excellency did communicate to the Council his letter to Count ffrontenac which being written in ffrench he expounded into English and his Excellency's expostulations therein were thought very reasonable and were approved off.

His Excellency did communicate his instructions left at Albany to Coll Schuyler the Mayor Mr Livingston and other Magistrates relative to the Government of that place in his absence chiefly with relation to the Indians and the charges accruing by them.

[N.º 112.] At a Council held at his Maties ffort in New York the 17ᵗʰ of August 1698.

Present

His Excelly. Richard Earl of Bellomont
Capt John Nanfan Lieut Governour
ffred Phillips   Gab Monviell
Steph Cortlandt   John Laurence
Wᵐ Smith   Esquires

His Excellency told the Council that the occasion of his meeting is an express from Albany and the Onondage County with intelligence that four of the five nations have had a message from Canada that Count ffrontenac refused to deliver up some prisoners of Onondage to their messengers because there came no Delegates from each of the four nations requesting their Belt and threatening to prosecute the warr if they did not speedily submitt and make a separate peace with them whereupon there being a generall Meeting appointed at Onondage of the five nations they desire assistance and that some Christians from this Government may be at their meeting.

His Excellency ordered Dekanisore and the other Indians to be called in with the interpreter and told them that he had taken the advice of the Council upon this message they have brought and that he was fully resolved to succour & protect them that to that purpose he had ordered his Lieut Governour and his Company forthwith to repair to Albany where he is to remain to succour them upon occasions with all the forces upon the ffrontiers and desired them to send out scouts towards Cadaracqui for intelligence.

Dekanisore said it was hard there should be a peace and they have no benefit of it. His Excellency answered that he sent not the Lieut Governour to begin a new warr but to succour them in case the ffrench should break the peace and deny them the benefit of it he will take care they have an equal benefit of the peace with the rest of his Majesties Xtian subjects. His Excellency told them he would send the Mayor of Albany along with them to the meeting at Onondage which Dekanisore said he liked very well. His Excellency told them he had wrote to the Governour of Canada that he will have them comprehended in the generall peace and do his utmost to endeavour to force them to it. Dekanisore said the same rivers that lead to Onondage have branches that lead to Cayouge and Oneyde so that they cannot come to help one another and if they cannot be protected from the ffrench they must make peace with them for the way is farr off for assistance to come up to them. His Excellency told them they should not be losers that if the ffrench came with force sufficient to overcome them then they should send their women and children to Albany where they should be protected & maintained and then he would go with a sufficient force against Canada to revenge the injurys done them and make good to them all their losses. His Excellency told them likewise they must not be discouraged the Great King of England has forced the ffrench King to make a peace and begin the warr upon their own account and will allways support them. His Excellency told them that the ffrench Governour intended only to cozen them and although he does propose peace yet will always endeavour by this stratagem to entice or frighten them to break the Covenant Chain and make them own him as their father but if he do begin the warr upon the account of the Brethren will justify and defend them still.

Ordered Coll Cortlandt do provide suitable clothing for the two Indians.

Ordered by his Excellency and Council that Major Wessells Mayor of Albany as also John Baptista the interpreter do go forthwith to the meeting that's to be of the five Nations of Indians at Onondage and there give them all the encouragement he possibly can and do all other things pursuant to the instructions to be given him by his Excellency and that care should be taken to reward the pains and defray the Journey of the said Mayor Wessels and John Baptista.

Ordered by his Excellency and Council that a Messenger be immediately sent to Canada with a letter from his Excellency to the Governour of Canada upon the subject matter of the Message and alarm brought by the said Dekanisore and another Indian.

[N.º 113.] At a Council held at ffort William Henry the sixth day of October 1698.

Present

His Excellency Richard Earl of Bellomont
Stephen Cortlandt   Samuel Staatts
William Smith   Robt Livingston
Abraham Depeyster   Robert Walters Esquires.

The accounts of the charge of his Excellency's expedition to Albany presents to the Indians &c in July and August last were returned auditted by Coll Nich Bayard Coll Steph Cortlandt and Coll Gab Minville.

Ordered a Warrant issue for payment of the sume of two hundred and ninety pounds one shilling current money of this Province out of the revenue to Coll Abraham Depeyster for strouds, Duffills and linnen for the Indians.

Ordered a Warrant issue for payment of twenty seaven pounds fifteen shillings to Ouzell Van Sweeten for stockings linen lace &c for the Indians.

Ordered a Warrant issue for payment of forty pounds one shilling to Samuel Bayard for Guns for the Indians and Pewter for a Travelling Chest.

Ordered a warrant issue for payment of one hundred and two pounds two shillings and six pence to Johannes Van Cortlandt for sundries for presents for the Indians

Ordered a Warrant issue for the payment of twelve pounds twelve shillings to Rip Van Dam for Table linen for the travelling chest.

Ordered a Warrant issue of thirty pounds fourteen shillings and nine pence to Gab Minville for presents to the Indians.

Ordered a Warrant issue for the payment of thirty two pounds three shillings and six pence to Peter Moria Brazier for thirty five Kittles for presents to the Indians.

Ordered a Warrant issue for the payment of twenty eight pounds four shillings and ten pence half penny. to Stephen De Lancey for plaine Blankets &c for presents to the Indians.

Ordered a Warrant issue for the payment of twelve pounds seaven shillings and six pence to Moses Levi for Tobacco for the Indinas.

Ordered a Warrant issue for the payment of five pounds ten shillings to Arent the Turner for Carriages for the four small Guns.

Ordered a Warrant issue for the payment of one hundred and forty four pounds one shilling five pence half penny to Robert Livingston for presents to the Indians.

Ordered a Warrant issue for the payment of twenty nine pounds nineteen shillings and eight pence to Robert Livingston for charges on his Excellency's Expedition to Albany.

Ordered a Warrant issue for the payment of thirty pounds to Harput Jacobse for the freight of his sloop with his Excellency to Albany and back to New York.

Ordered a Warrant issue for the payment of six pounds to Abraham Provost for the freight of his sloop from Albany.

Ordered a Warrant issue for the payment of ninety five pounds ten pence half penny to Robt Livingston for provisions to the Indians and ffrench prisoners

Ordered a Warrant issue for the payment of Ten pounds Ten Shillings to Doctor James Bradie for his Journey with his Excellency the Earl of Bellomont as Chyrurgion.

Ordered that a Warrant issue for the payment of forty five pounds one shilling and ten pence half penny Current money of this Province out of the Revenue to Robert Livingston for Sundrys paid and delivered by him towards his Excellency's expedition to Albany, amounting to two hundred forty five pounds one shilling ten pence half penny he having already received two hundred pounds by virtue of an order of Council dated the Ninth day of June last.

Severall miscellaneous Accounts being returned to this Board auditted by Coll Stephen Cortlandt . Coll Nicholas Bayard and Coll Gabriel Minville

Ordered a Warrant issue for the payment of twenty seven pounds five shillings current money of New York out of the Revenue to Robert Livingston Esq.r for contingent charges at Albany for sick souldiers and repairing Blockhouses.

Ordered a Warrant issue for the payment of eighty three pounds eight shillings three pence half penny to Robert Livingston for sundrys for the use of the ffort at Albany.

Ordered a Warrant issue for the payment of nineteen pounds two shillings one penny to Robert Livingston for Incidentall charges for the Indians at Albany.

[N.o 114.] At a Council held at ffort William Henry the seaventh day of October 1698.

Present

His Excellency Richard Earl of Bellomont

Stephen Cortlandt ⎱ Robert Livingston ⎱
William Smith ⎰ Esq.rs Samuel Staates ⎰ Esq.rs
Abraham Depeyster   Robert Walters

The Accounts of the Charge of the Expedition of Capt John Schuyler who went expresse with his Excellencies letter and instructions to Canada were returned auditted by Coll Abraham Depeyster and Robert Walters Esq.rs

Ordered a Warrant issue for the payment of thirty pounds nine shillings and nine pence to the said Capt. John Schuyler for sundrys in fitting himselfe for the said expedition.

Ordered a Warrant issue for the payment of thirty

pounds to the said Captaine John Schuyler for his and his negroes Journey to Canada.

Ordered a Warrant issue for the payment of Eighty pounds to Jean Rossie for his Journey to Canada as interpreter of Captain John Schuyler.

Ordered a Warrant issue for the payment of two pounds seaventeen shillings and six pence to Dyrick Vanderheyden for sundry necessaries received of him by Capt John Schuyler on his journey.

Ordered a Warrant issue for the payment of four pounds eighteen shillings to Robert Livingston for money expended in bringing back Hellebrand Lootman who was going to Canada without a passe.

His Excellency and Council taking into their consideration's the extraordinary diligence and nice observations made by Capt John Schuyler at Canada doe order that a Warrant issue for payment of twenty pounds out of the revenue of this province to the said Captain John Schuyler for his said services. It being moved to this board by Capt John Schuyler for an allowance to John Livingston David Schuyler and Dyrick Vanderheyden for their attendance on him the said Capt John Schuyler in his expedition to Canada the said Schuyler being obliged to take the said persons with him in order to perform the Instructions given him by his Excellency— The Instructions given the said Capt John Schuyler being read and it appearing thereby that the said Captain Schuyler was obliged to send an immediate account to his Excellency from Canada by some diligent Messenger in case the ffrench were p'pairing to invade our five nations of Indians or were in motion towards them: And it being considered by the Council that such diligent Messengers could not be procured at Canada—It is ordered that Warrant issue for the payment of the sume of thirty pounds out of the Revenue to the said John Livingston David Schuyler and Dyrick Vanderheyden to each tenne pounds for their Journey to Canada on the said Expeditions.

[N.º 115.]   At a Council held at ffort William Henry
the fourteenth day of October 1698.

Present

His Excellency Richard Earl of Bellomont.

Steph Cortlandt   Robert Livingston ⎫
William Smith   Samuel Staates   ⎬ Esq^{rs}
Abraham Depeyster   Robert Walters   ⎭

Ordered a Warrant issue for the payment of thirteen pounds thirteen shillings and nine pence to. Robert
Livingston Esqr. out of the Revenue for Sundryes delivered to Capt John Schuyler on his Expedition to
Canada.

[No. 116.]   At a Council at ffort William Henry the
seaventh day of November 1698.

Present

His Excellency Richard Earl of Bellomont

Steph Cortlandt   Sam! Staats
Abra^h Depeyster   Ro^t Walters
Ro^t Livingston   Esquires

Ordered a Warrant issue for payment of thirty five
pounds four shillings and three pence to Robert Livingston Esqr out of the Revenue of this Province for Sundryes delivered to the Indians at Albany.

Ordered a Warrant issue for payment of forty four
pounds sixteen shillings to Robert Livingston Esqr for
sundreys delivered to the Indians and ffrench prisoners.

[N.º 117.]   At a Council held at ffort William Henry
31st May 1699.

Present

The Honble John Nanfan Esqr
Stephen Cortlandt   Robert Livingston
Samuel Staats   Robert Walters.
The rest out of Town.

Ordered a Warrant issue for payment of thirty five

pounds Eight shillings and four pence half penny to Robert Livingston Esqr out of the revenue of divers incidentall charges for the Indians at Albany advanced by him from the nineteenth of Oct.ʳ 1698 to the ninth day of March 1698.

[N.º 118.]   At a Council held at ffort William Henry the 31.ˢᵗ of July 1700.

Present.

His Excellency Richard Earl of Bellomont.

Steph. Cortlandt   Sam.ˡ Staats
W.ᵐ Smith   Rob Livingston
Abra Depeyster   Rob Walters   Esqʳˢ

His Excellency acquainted the Council that he just now received an expresse from Coll Schuyler giving an account that Monsieur Mairbour and ffather Bruyas the Jesuit with others to the number of ten were come from Canada to Onnondage, and were tampering with the five nations of Indians and endeavouring to seduce them over to the ffrench, That the Gentlemen appointed for the management of the Indians affairs at Albany upon notice thereof had sent Jan. Baptist Van Eps with an instruction to Onnondage to hinder the Sachims from harbouring or making any treaty with the ffrench, or to allow of any meeting with them and that if the ffrench would propose anything to the Sachims to order them to answer that they expected his Excellency, which was approved of.

Ordered a Warrant issue for payment of six pounds to Johannes De Wandell and the other two men that brought the Expresse from Albany for their said service.

[N.º 119.]   At a Council held at ffort William Henry the seaventh August 1700.

Present

His Excellency Richard Earl of Bellomont
Stephen Cortlandt   Abra Depeyster

William Smith   Rob. Livingston
Samuel Staats   Robert Walters Esqr.ˢ

Ordered a Warrant issue for payment of one hundred and seaventy pounds twelve shillings and one half penny to the following persons Viz. twelve pounds part thereof to Garret Luykasse twelve pounds part thereof to Hendrick Rooseboom, Twelve pounds part thereof to Nicholas Bleeker, and fifteen pounds part thereof to Jan Baptist Van Eps Interpreter, for their Journeys to the Indians at Onnondage. Coll Peter Schuyler, Robert Livingston, Hendrick Hansen Esqʳ and others on account of the Government, and to Robert Livingston the sume of ninety three pounds fifteen shillings and eight pence to Hendrick Hansen the sume of twenty five pounds sixteen shillings and four pence half penny for charges expended &c. things provided by them for the said expedition.

[Nº 120.] At a Council held at ffort William Henry the 13ᵗʰ September 1700.
Present
    His Excellʸ. Richard Earl of Bellomont
    Stephen Cortlandt   Robert Livingston
    Abra. Depeyster   Robert Walters
    Samuel Staats   Esquires

The propositions made by his Excellency at Albany to the five nations of Indians, the Schackhook or river Indians together with the answer of the said Indians to his Lordship were read, and Coll Stephen Cortlandt in the name of the rest of the members of the Board, did thank his Lordship for the great care and diligence his Lordship had used in the said expedition.
Robert Livingston Esqʳ produced at the Board a Comission from his most sacred Majesty dated the seaven and twentieth day of January 1695|6, appointing him Secretary or Agent to the Indians with one

hundred pounds sterling p annum, which he prayed might be entered into the Council Book and was ordered to be entered accordingly and as follows in haec Verba.

[Locus Sigilli.] William the third by the Grace of God King of England Scotland ffrance and Ireland Defender of the Faith &c.° To our Trusty and well beloved Robert Levingston Gentleman Greeting.

Whereas by your Petition to us you have humbly prayed to be confirmed in your severall imployments of Collector of the Excise, Receiver of our Quit Rents in our County and City of Albany and Town Clerk, Clerk of the Peace, and Clerk of the Common Pleas there, with the usuall sallary and ffees to be executed by yourself or your sufficient Deputy, and in the execution of your office of Secretary or Agent for the Government of New York to the Indian nations, and that the ffee or sallary of one hundred pounds a year may be allowed to you for your future encouragement in the said services : And Whereas upon the reports of the Lords of the Committee of Trade and Plantations, and of the Commissions of our Treasury, wee have taken the same into our Royal consideration and reposing especiall Trust and confidence in your Loyalty and fidelity, are graciously pleased for your future encouragement to confirm you and wee do accordingly hereby confirm Constitute and appoint you the said Robert Livingston to be Collector of the Excise and receiver of our Quit rents in our County and City of Albany and Towne Clerk, Clerk of the Peace, and Clerk of the Comon Pleas there, with all the usual ffees, sallarys, perquisites and advantages to the same belonging, to be executed by yourself or your sufficient Deputy or Deputies for and during our pleasure, and we do further in consideration of the long and faithfull services to the Crown for many years past performed by you in all Treaties and negotiations with the Indians our subjects in those parts Confirme Constitute and appoint you the the said Robert Livingston to be our Secretary or Agent of our Government of New York to the Indians To hold exercise and enjoy the said office during our Royal pleasure. And as a recompense of your past services and for your future encouragement in the Diligent performance of the said imployment We do hereby grant unto you an Annuall sallary or ffee of one hundred pounds sterling to be paid Quarterly at the four usual ffeasts or days of Payment out of our Revenew of New York the said sallary to commence from the five and twentieth day of March last past. And we do hereby Comand our Governour or Commander in Chiefe of our Province of New York for the time being to give effectual orders that the said sallary of one hundred pounds sterling p^r annum and the other sallaries ffees and perquisits to the afore mentioned offices belonging be duly payed and satisfied to you according to our will and pleasure herein declared. Given at our Court at Kensington the seaven and twentieth day of January 169$\frac{5}{6}$. in the seaventh year of our reigne.

By his Majesties Comand

Endorsed thus   SHREWSBURY

Entered in the Plantation Office
Lib. New York Vol 3 page 141

[N° 121.]   At a Council held at ffort William Henry
            the Sixth November 1700

Present as yesterday

Ordered a Warrant issue for payment of thirty pounds eight shillings and two pence to Peter Van Brugh Esqr. out of the five hundred pounds raised by Virtue of an Act of Assembly for better securing the ffive nations of Indians in their ffidelity to his Majesty for several necessaries found and provided by him for his journey with Coll William Romer his Majties Ingineer Generall and Hendrick Hansen Esqr to Onnondage.

Ordered a Warrant issue for payment of twenty pounds ten pence half penny to Hendrick Hansen Esqr out of the ffive hundred pounds raised by Virtue of an

Act of Assembly for better securing the ffive nations of Indians in their ffidelity to his Majties for several necessaries found and provided by him for his journey with Coll Willi Romer his Majesties Ingineer·Generall and Peter Van Burgh Esqr to Onnondage.

Ordered a Warrant issue for payment of nine pounds nineteen shillings and three pence to Major Dirick Wessells out of the revenue for the value thereof delivered by him to the five nations of Indians in the years 1697 and 1698.

Ordered a Warrant issue for the payment of two pounds to Garrit Ziell for casting two thousand pounds of lead into small barrs for the Indians.

Ordered a Warrant Issue for payment of Eighteen pounds to Major Dirick Wessells out of the revenue for one journey to Onondage and two to New York on his Majesties service.

Ordered a Warrant issue for payment of twenty four pounds ten shillings and six pence to Capt John Schuyler out of the revenue for goods delivered by him by order of Capt. James Weemes to four Indians who were sent on the publick account with some Christians to Ottowawa.

[N° 122.] At a council held at ffort William Henry this seaven and twentieth day of June 1701
Present as yesterday

Severall accounts were produced to the board of persons of whom rum and other things for presents to Indians had been bought, and for the Governour's expedition to Albany which were ordered to be putt into list and delivered to the Collector, and ordered that the Collector do pay the same which he is to be allowed in his account.

[N° 123.] At a Council held at ffort William Henry this two and twentieth day of August 1701
Present as on the nineteenth instant

The Governor produced at the board a letter sent

expresse to him from the Gentlemen at Albany appointed for managing the Indian affairs dated the nineteenth day of August instant, with a message from the Sachims of Onnondage, informing that the Governor of Canada hath sent to Onnondage seaven persons who are now on the way, and desiring that two wise understanding men who write well may be sent thither, that the managers of the Indians affairs have sent back the said Indians who brought the message, with answer that they would send an expresse to the Governor with their message, and that in the mean time if the ffrench should arrive at Onnondage that the Sachims should not call any meeting or hearken to any proposalls of the ffrench untill they should receive an answer from the Governor. This Board are of opinion that Cap John Bleeker and David Schuyler do immediately repair to Onnondage in order to hinder the ffrench from deluding our five nations of Indians and that they keep a journall of their proceedings there.

The Governor produced at the board the journall kept by Captain Bleeker and David Schuyler during their last journey to and residence at Onnondage, which was read as also the propositions made by his honor the Governor at Albany in July last to the five nations of Indians and the river Indians together with the answers of the said Indians thereto which were read.

[N.º 124.] At a Council held at ffort William Henry
     this sixteenth day of September 1701
Present
    The Honorable John Nanfan Esq.
      Abraham Depeyster   Rob Walters
      Samuel Staats   Thos. Weaver
      Rob.ᵗ Livingston   Willi Atwood Esquires

To the Hono.ᵇˡ John Nanfan Esq.ʳ· Lieut Governor and Commander in Chiefe of the Province of New York
    The humble addresse of the House of Representatives of the said Province in Generall Assembly convened—
29

May it please y.º Honor.

Wee the Representatives of this his Majesties Province out of a deep sense we have of the great services your honor did to this Province in your last negotiations with the five nations of Indians at Albany in your last conference with them. Do in behalf of ourselves and all the Inhabitants of this Province congratulate your honors successe of the same and do render you our most hearty and unfeigned thanks for your care prudence and wise management therin, and humbly pray that for the future no person may be imployed to interpret the conference of the said five nations but the sworn Interpreter Laurence Claesson when he is to be had; so wishing your honor all imaginable prosperity in this his Majesties Government, Wee are Your friends the Representatives in General Assembly convened

By order of the House of Representatives,

ABRAH: GOUVERNEUR, Speaker.

Die Saturn 13ᵗʰ September 1701.

[Nº 125.] At a Council held at Fort William Henry, &c.

Present   The Honᵇˡᵉ John Nanfan Esq.

Abraham Depeyster   Thomˢ Weaver
Samuel Staats   Willi Atwood
Robert Walters   Esquires.

A message sent from the Sachims of Onnondage read —wherein they acquaint that the Waganhaes or farr nations of Indians with whom the ffive nations of Indians have had warr these several years have appointed the ffive nations to meet them in order to conclude a peace Whereof it is ordered that the Clerk of the Council do draw up Instructions for Captain Bleeker in relation to that matter.

[Nº 126.] At a Council held at ffort William Henry this seaven and twentieth day of October 1701.

Present   The Hono'ble John Nanfan Esq.

Abrah Depeyster   Robt Walters,
Saml Staats,   Thomas Weaver Esquires

Ordered a warrant issue for payment of ninety nine pounds Eighteen shillings and ten pence half penny out of the Revenue. To Captain John Bleeker the sume of ffifty pounds sixteen shillings and · six pence for his journey to the five nations of Indians at Onnondage in June last by order of the Government and for necessaries provided by him in fitting himself and others for said journey. To David Schuyler twenty two pounds two shillings and four pence half penny for his journey with Captain Bleeker and for providing himself for said journey. To Laurence Claeson nine pounds for his journey with them as Interpreter, To Jacobus Luykesse six pounds. To Albert Vanderzee six pounds, and to Matys Mack six pounds for their journey with said Captain Bleeker and David Schuyler as aforesaid.

Ordered warrants issue for payments of sixty two pounds thirteen shillings and nine pence out of the revenue viz—To Captain John Bleeker twenty nine pounds ten pence half penny for his journey to the five nations of Indians at Onnondage in August last p^r order of Government and for necessaries provided by him for the said journey. To David Schuyler twenty six pounds two shillings and ten pence half penny for his journey with the said Capt Bleeker, and for necessaries provided by him for the said journey and to Laurence Claeson the Interpreter seaven pounds ten shillings for his journey with the said Captain Bleeker and David Schuyler as aforesaid.

Ordered a Warrant issue for payment of forty four pounds sixteen shillings to Hendrick Hansen and Peter Van Brugh Esqr for goods furnished by them by order of his late Excellency the Earl of Bellomont for fitting severall persons sent by his Lordship to the Ottawawas or farr nations and whereas severall of the goods furnished by the said Hendrick Hansen and Peter Van Brugh Esqr to the said persons were not made use of but returned to them by reason the said persons did not proceed on the said expedition. It is hereby ordered that the Clerk of the Council do write to the said Hendrick Hansen and Peter Van Brugh Esqr to dispose of the same in the best manner they can for the Kings service.

Ordered a warrant issue for the payment of three pounds twelve shillings to Garrett Luykesse and Johannes Luykesse for their journey with Hendrick Hansen and Ryer Schermerhorn Esq^{rs} to the Mohoggs country on account of the Government.

[N° 127.] At a Council held at ffort William Henry the twentieth day of November 1701.
Present

> The Hono'ble John Nanfan Esqr
> Abraham Depeyster   Thomas Weaver
> Samuel Staats   William Atwood
> Robert Walters   Esquires

Ordered a warrant issue for payment of two hundred fifty eight pounds two shillings and four pence out of the revenue to Barne Cosens for so much payed by the Hon^{l} John Nanfan Esqr his Majties Govr and Commander in Chiefe of this Province to severall persons who advanced goods for presents to the Indians and found and provided necessaries for the said Governor's expedition to Albany and during his residence there in July last.

[N° 128.] At a Council held at ffort William Henry this sixth and twentieth day of January 1701.
Present as yesterday   •

Ordered a warrant issue for payment of forty five pounds to William Teller for the hire of his sloop to carry the hono'ble the Governor to Albany to the five nations of Indians in July last.

Ordered a warrant issue for payment of twenty one pounds and three half pence to Johannes Schuyler for sundry necessaries provided by for the Messenger's sent to the Onondage Indians by order of his late Excellency the Earl of Bellomont.

[N.º 129.] At a Council held att Forte Anne in New Yorke this 6ᵗʰ of July 1708.

Present

His Excellency Edward Visco.ᵗ Cornbury, &c.

Gerardus Beekman   John Barberie
Rip Van Dam   Adolph Phillips
Tho.ˢ Wenham   Esquires

His Excellency communicated to this Board an account he lately received from the Managers of the Indians affairs at Albany giving an account that they have received information from the Onondage Sachims that the ffrench are about to build two ffortes at the passes of the Chiefe Hunting places of our Indians viz at Schovehare and Ohneyagre which our Indians desire may be prevented by having a Garrison erected by us and that the french make daily presents to our Indians with design to debauch alienate them from us, Whereupon his Excell and Council are of opinion that in answer to the Indians the managers of the Indian affairs signifyed to them that his Excell.ʸ designs to be at Albany the latter end of August and that the Indians be appointed to meet him on the first of September against which time his Excellency will take care that every thing shall be concerted and provided in the best manner that may be.

[N.º 130.] At a Council held at Fort Anne in New York this 7ᵗʰ day of September 1708.

Present

His Excelly. Edward Viscount Cornbury &c
Peter Schuyler   Killian Van Renssalaer
Gerardus Beekman   Roger Mompesson
Rip Van Dam   John Barberie
Thomas Wenham   Adolph Phillips Esquires.

Mr Robert Livingston having formerly presented to his Excell^y and Council her Maties Commission dated the 29th day of September 1705 restoring him to and confirming in the imployments of Town Clerk, Clerk of the Peace and Clerk of the Common Pleas in the County and City of Albany and to and in the office of Secretary or Agent of the Government of New York to the Indian Nation's together with the sallary of £100 p^r annum. It was ordered that that the said Commission should lye in the hands of the Secretary and that he should inspect the Commission which his late Matie King William granted to him for the afore-said offices and lay the same or the entry thereof before this Board together with the orders or proceedings thereon in Council. In obedience thereof the Secretary having laid before this Board the entry of the said Commission together with the proceedings of Council and a copy of my Lord Bellomont's report to the R^t Hono^ble the Lords of Trade on the s^d Commission. It is ordered on a due consideration thereof that the said Commission be entered at large in the minutes of this Board—And follows in Haec Verba—

Anne by the Grace of God Queen of England Scotland ffrance and Ireland defender of the faith &c To our Trusty and well beloved Robt Livingston Gent^l Greeting Whereas by your petition you have humbly besought us to restore you to and confirm you in your employment of Town Clerk, Clerk of the Peace and Clerk of the Common Pleas in the County and City of Albany within the Province of New York in America and to and in the office of Secretary or Agent for the Government of New Yorke to the Indian nation's with the ffees Perquisites and sallarys to the said Respective offices belonging or granted to you for the Exercise thereof. And whereas our Commissioners for Trade and Plantations, upon our reference of your Petition to them have by their report certifyed to us that you having been very serviceable in managing the Treaties with the Indians, We have taken the same into our

Royall Consideration and reposing special Trust and
confidence in your Loyalty fidelity & ability are graciously pleased to restore you, to and confirm—And
we do hereby restore confirm constitute and appoint
you the said Robt Livingston to be our Town Clerk,
Clerk of the Peace and Clerk of the Common Pleas in
our said County and City of Albany with all the usual
ffees Perquisites advantages and sallarys thereunto belonging and to be secretary or Agent for the Government of New Yorke to the Indians our Subjects in those
parts with the Annual sallary or fee of one hundred
pounds sterling formerly granted to you by our late
Royall Brother King William the third of Glorious
memory and payable Quarterly at the four usual feasts
or days of payment out of our Revenew of New Yorke,
To hold exercise and enjoy the said respective offices in
our Employment by yourself, or your sufficient Deputy
or Deputies with the said respective ffees, sallarys Perquisites and advantages during our Royall Pleasure
and we do hereby command our Governor or Commander in Chiefe &c. of our said Province of New Yorke
for the time being to give effectuall orders that the said
sallary of one hundred pounds sterling p^r annum and
the other sallarys fees Perquisits to the aforementioned
offices belonging be duly paid and satisfied to you according to our will and Pleasure herein declared. Given
att our Castle att Windsor the twenty ninth day of
September 1705. In the fourth year of our Reigne.

By her Maties Command

C. HEDGES

[N° 131.] Att a Council held at Forte Anne in New
Yorke this fifteenth day of Sepr 1708.

Present

His Ex^{ly} Edward Viscount Cornbury, &c

Peter Schuyler	Killian Van Renssalaer
Rip Van Dam	Roger Mompesson
Thos Wenham	Jno. Barberie
Adolph Phillips	Esquires

Two warrants were signed for payment of £25 a piece to Laurance Claesson being for his sallary as Interpreter to the 5 nations of Indians from the 25th of August 1706 to the 25 of Augt 1708.

[N.º 132.] Att a Councill held at Fort Anne in New
　　　　Yorke this 27th of October 1708
Present

　　　　His Exc.^{ly} Edward Viscount Cornbury &c.
　　　　Coll Schuyler　　　　Mr Barberie
　　　　Mr Wenham　　　　Mr Phillips
　　　　Mr Mompesson

Upon reading the report of the Committee of this Board for Coll Schuyler's service in going to Albany Sep.^{tr} last to meet the five nations of Indians by his Excelly.^s orders and the charges they put them too it is Ordered that warrants be prepared for payment of thirty pounds out of the revenew to the said Coll Schuyler for the same.

The Gent.^l of this Board having considered what his Excell.^y told them yesterday concerning a complaint made against him att home off his converting the revenue to his own use, Do unanimously declare (his Excellency having left them alone) that since they have respectively satt at this Board they do not know that his Excell.^y has received any money out of the public revenue other than by warrants past in Council in the usual manner which warrants have been either for his sallary or towards defraying the expences of his Excellency's expeditions to Albany from time to time.

[N.º 133.] At a Councill held at Fort Anne in New
　　　　York this 1st day of December 1708
Present

　　　　His Excell.^y Edward Viscount Cornbury.
　　　　Coll Schuyler,　　　Coll Wenham, &
　　　　Mr Van Dam,　　　Mr Barbarie

Upon reading the report on severall acc.^{ts} of Coll

Schuyler for money advanced and services done by him for the Government amounting to five hundred and thirty four pounds it is ordered that warrants be prepared for payment thereof out of the revenue viz Two hundred seventy four pounds seventeen shillings and seaven pence half penny for his journey to Onondage in 1703.

Two hundred thirty two pounds two shillings and four pence half penny for the out scouts who were sent to the Lake when there was advice that the ffrench was on their march this way, and twenty seaven pounds for building Stockado Fort in the Mohacks country.

[N.º 134.]   Att a Council held att Fort Anne in New York this 19th of Aprill 1708.

Present
            His Excelly John Lord Lovelace Baron of
Hurly.

Coll Schuyler	M.ʳ Rensalaer
Coll Beekman	M.ʳ Mompesson
Mr. Van Dam	M.ʳ Phillips
Coll Heathcote	

Upon reading a paper sent from Albany by the Commissioners for Managing the Indian Affairs dated the sixth day of April signifying that a message was sent by the five Nations to inform that four Nations of Waganhaes with whom they were in warr desire a place to meet in Onondago, that the Sachims of the five Nations desire his Excelly. to send some person to that Treaty and that if he makes any propositions to the farr Nations he must send them Blanketts, Powder, Kettles, Hatchetts and Shirts.

[N.º 135.]   At a Council held att New Yorke this 6th day of May 1709

Present
            Peter Schuyler Esqr. President
      Mr. Van Dam,   M.ʳ Barberie,

Coll. Heathcote,	M! Phillips,
Coll Wenham,	M! Peartree,
M! Ranslear,	M! Provoost.

ANNE R. INSTRUCTIONS for our Right Trusty and Well-beloved John Lord Lovelace Baron of Hurly our Cap! Gen! and Gov! in Chiefe of our Provinces of New Yorke & the Territories depending thereon in America. Given at our Court att Kensington the 27th day of June 1708, in the seventh year of our Reigne.

[Note. There are one hundred and eleven Instructions—but only these here entered relate to Trade & Indian affairs.]

100. AND WHEREAS wee are informed that some of the Colonies adjoining to our said Province under Colour of Grants or upon some other Groundless Pretences endeavour to obstruct the Trade of New York and Albany you are not to suffer any Invasion within the river of New York nor any goods to passe upon the same But which shall have paid the Duties at New Yorke to the end the Chiefe benefit of that trade may be preserved to the Inhabitants and Traders of New York and Albany the same being agreeable to the laws of the said Province to former practices as well as necessary for the Collecting those Custom's and other duty's which are to be raised for the support of this Government there.

101. You are to encourage the Indians upon all occasions as to induce them to trade with our subjects rather than others of Europe and you are to call before you the five Nations or Cantons of Indians Viz the Maquas, Senecas, Cayouges, Oneydes, and Onondages and upon their renewing their submission to our Government you are to assure them in our name that we will protect them as our subjects against the French Kings and you are to give the like assurance to the Schackhook or River Indians and to such other Indians in that neighbourhood as by their Union and Friendship with

the five Nations aforesaid and in conjunction with them shall submitt themselves in the same manner to our Government and when any opportunity shall offer for purchasing great Tracts of Land for us from the Indians for small sums you are to use your discretion therein as you shall judge for the convenience or advantage which may arise unto us by the same and you are to inform us and our Comissioners for Trade and Plantations as aforesaid what has been the consequences of the Treaty of Neutrality agreed between the s.ᵈ five Nations and the French Indians.

[N.° 136.] At a Council held att Fort Anne in New Yorke this 19th day May 1709

Present

The Honoble Richard Ingoldsby Esqʳ Lieut Gov.

Coll. Schuyler,	Mʳ Barbarie,
Coll. Heathcote,	Mʳ Phillips,
Coll Wenham,	Coll Peartree,
Mʳ Mompesson,	Capt. Provost.

Coll Nichollson and Coll Vetch being seated at the Board Mʳ Schuyler brought from the Assembly the letter framed yesterday for the Managers of the Indians Affairs and yᵉ Instructions to be given to the Prisoners to be sent to the five Nations where to yᵉ Assembly do agree which being read att this Board ordered to be copyed fair and signed.

[N.° 137.] At a Council held at fforte Anne in New Yorke this 5th day of July 1710

Present

His Excellency Robert Hunter Esqr.

Coll Depeyster	Mr. Van Dam,
Doctor Staats	Mr. Barbarie,
Capt Walters,	Major Provoost,

His Excellency communicated to this Board a letter

from the Commissioners of the Indians affairs at Albany
of the 27th of June with their proceedings with a
Sachim of the Senekes concerning the farr Nations who
are come into the Covenant Chain—And desiring
money to defray their publick charge but there being
no publick money to defray that charge his Excelly
will discourse the said Commissioners thereon when hee
goes to Albany.

[N.° 138.] At a Council held at ffort Anne in New
    York this 20th day of July 1710.
Present
        His Excellency Robert Hunter Esq.ᵣ
    Coll. Depeyster,   M.ᵣ Mompesson,
    Doctor Staats   M.ᵣ Barbarie,
    Cap.ᵗ Walters,   Major Provoost.
    M.ᵣ Van Dam,

His Excellency communicated to yᵉ Board a Copy
of y.ᵉ Journall of y.ᵉ Commissioners for the Indians Affairs
wherein they signifye to him that the Mohoques have
consented to let y.ᵉ Surveyor Generall Survey Skohare.

[N.° 139.] At a Council held at ffort Anne in New
    York this 29th day of March 1711.

His Excellency communicated to the Councill the
Journall of the Proceedings of the Commissioners for
Managing the Indian affairs at Albany from the 31.ˢᵗ
of October last to the 5ᵗʰ Instant chiefly concerning
the Indians Making Warr against the Waganhaes.
Where upon his Excelly told the Gent.ˡᵉ of y Councill
he will write to yᵉ Commissioners of the Indian Affairs directing them to inform the Indians that his
Excellency would by noe means have them engage in
that Warr to which they have noe late Call, and that
for their own saefty hee would have them stay at home
where they may be ready to assist each other on any
occasion.

That as to their demand of Ammunition it seems only to be for the Carrying on this Warre against the Wagannes, and that he cannot give them because he does not approve of this their undertaking, but when they have any just want for it for a Warr entered into by his Excellencies consent he will take care to supply them.

[N.º 140.] At a Councill at ffort Anne in New York in this 24.ᵗʰ day of Aprill 1711.
Present
      His Excellency Robert Hunter Esqr.
Coll Depeyster,   M.ʳ Mompesson
Doctor Staats,   M.ʳ Barbarie,
Capt Walters,   M.ʳ Phillips.

His Excellency told the Gentlemen of the Councill that he just now received a letter from the Commissioners of the Indian affairs at Albany by express dated the 21.ˢᵗ instant acquainting him that they just then received a Message from Onondage by express telling them that the ffrench officers one Interpreter and thirty men were arived there from Canada. Whereupon the five nations sent seaven hands of Wampum to desire Coll Peter Schuyler to come there with all speed which hee would not doe unless hee had orders and Instructions from his Excellency.

Whereupon it is y.ᵉ opinion of this Board that a letter be written to Coll Schuyler to goe to Onondage and that he take the Interpreters with him and such others as he thinks convenient—that he be instructed to thank the Indians for this notice they have given the Government of the arrival of the ffrench in their Castles.

That for the future his Excellency expects from their allegiance and their former promises that they will not permitt any armed men, Priests or Emissarys from the ffrench to come among them.

That he acquaint the Indians 'tis expected they should have noe private Consults with any of the ffrench who are now among them, but that he be present att all their meetings and debates.

That soe soon as the ffrench have made their propositions and the Indians have answered it if they think fitt to make any answer thereto they oblige the ffrench to leave their Country assuring them if any attempts be made against them from Canada they shall have all the assistance y.ᵉ Government can give them.

That whilst he is at Onondage he send some trusty Indians to y.ᵉ ffronteers of Canada to discover the motions of y.ᵉ Enemy, and if any propositions are making by them either for their Defence or for an Enterprize against her majesties subjects. That by the first opportunity, hee send to his Excellency any account of his proceedings, and of the proceedings of the french and Indians.

[Nᵒ. 141.] At a Council held at ffort Anne in New York y.ᵉ 22ᵈ day of November 1711.
Present
        His Excellency Robert Hunter, Esqʳ.
Coll Depeyster,   Coll Beekman
Doctor Staats,   Mʳ. Van Dam
Capt. Walters,   Mʳ. Byerley.

His Excellency communicated to this Board a letter from Governor Dudley, Governor Saltonstall and Governor Cranston concerning the engaging the five Nations to an actuall rupture with the ffrench in Canada.

Whereupon it is ordered that the secretary lay the said letter before y.ᵉ Assembly and desire them to take it into their consideration: And in regard that if y.ᵉ five Nations be engaged in any actual Warr with the ffrench it will be absolutely necessary that a greater number of the Country Troops be constantly employed on y.ᵉ ffronteers during y.ᵉ Warr four safety and defence which will require considerable sums of money to defray y.ᵉ expence.

His Excellency desires y.ᵉ Assembly to give him

their opinion what they think proper for him to doe on this occasion.

[N.º 142.] At a Councill held at ffort Anne in New Yorke the 15th day of June 1713.

Present
      His Excellency Robert Hunter Esqr.

Coll Schuyler,	M.º Van Dam,
Coll. Depeyster,	Coll Heathcot,
Doctor Staats,	M.º Phillips
Cap.ᵗ Walters,	M.º Byerly.

His Excellency communicated to this Board a letter from the Commissioners of the Indian Affairs of the 3.ᵈ instant as also the propositions of the Senekes Sachims Dekanisore an Onnondage Sachim whereby it is plain that the Tuscarora Indians who are in Warr with her majestyes subjects in Carolina are coming to settle with the five nations are in actual Warr with the fflattheads who are in alliance with her majestyes subjects of Virginia and Carolina and assisted the people of Carolina in their Warr against the Tuscaroras,

It is the opinion of the Board that a letter be writt to the Commissioners of the Indian affairs at Albany directing them to acquaint the five nations that the Tuscaroras having entred into a Bloody and Barbarous Warr against her Majestyes Subjects in Carolina without any provocation given them that they doe not upon any pretence whatsoever receive any of the Tuscaroras amongst them nor permitt them to settle with them nor to give any countenance or assistance untill such time as they have made a peace with her Majestyes Subjects, and that they do not permitt any of their people to comitt any Hostilityes against the fflatheads who are not only in peace with her majestyes subjects but are likewise actually assisting to them in their warr with the Tuscaroras.

[N.º 143.] At a Councill held at Fort Anne in New Yorke this 19th June 1713.

Present

His Excellency Robert Hunter Esqr.
Coll Schuyler,   Mr Barbarie,
Doctor Staats,   Mr Phillipse,
Capt Walters,   Mr Byerley.
Coll Heathcote,

His Excellency communicated to this Board a letter from Laurence Classe of the 18th Instant to the Commissioners of the Indian affaires a Letter from said Com.^{er} to his Excellency of the 11th importing that the five nations have returned the Belt of Wampum given them not to enter into warr with the fflatheads and desiring some of the principal men of Albany may be sent to Onnondage with presents to hinder their entering into that warr. Ordered that secretary lay the said letter before the Assembly and acquaint them that this Board think it absolutely necessary that some Gentlemen of the best note be sent from Albany to Onnondage to prevent the five nations from joining the Tuscaroras and with them entering into a warr with the flattheads the friends and allies of her majestyes subjects in Carolina and Virginia and that it will be highley necessary that these Gentlemen carry such presents with them as may be effectual to direct their present intentions and that those Gen.^{tl} be likewise paid for their Journey, and that this Board does recommend to the Assembly to pass a resolve for defraying their expences out of the Colony's money in the Treasurer's hands.

[N.º 144.] At a Council held at Fort Anne in New York the 6th day of August 1714.

Present

His Excellency Robert Hunter Esqr.
Coll Depeyster,   Mr Mompesson,
Doctor Staats,   Mr Barbarie,
Capt Walters,   Mr Phillipse,
Mr Van Dam,   Mr Byerly.

The Assembly attending his Excellency pursuant to his message he gave his assent to the following Bill:

An Act for the Treasurer paying to his Excell^y a sum of money for presents to the five nations of Indians and for his expence in going to Albany to treat with them.

It is the Opinion of this Board that a letter be writt forthwith to the Comm^{rs} of the Indian Affairs directing them to send immediately to the five nations to summons them to be at Albany to meet his Excellency the 15th of September next which time he will be there to take the Hatchett out of their hands and renew the Covenant chain.

[N° 145.]   At a Council held at ffort George in New York the 28th day of June 1716.

Present

    His Excellency Robert Hunter Esqr.
    Coll Depeyster,   Mr Van Dam,
    Capt Walters,   Mr Byerley,
    Coll Beekman,   Mr Clarke.

At account was presented to this Board for smiths work for mending the Indians Guns and Kettles at Albany amounting to £21. 4^s. 3^d. pursuant to his Excell^y order to the magistrates at Albany the 31st of August last.

Whereupon it is ordered that ye Commissioners of ye Indian affairs do lay before this Board an account of the 300£ received by them of the Treasurer for the last years expences.

[N° 146.]   At a Council held at Ffort George in New York the 24th day of June 1717.

Present

    His Excellency Robert Hunter Esqr.
    Coll Depeyster,   Mr Van Dam,
    Capt Walters,   Mr Byerly.
    Coll Beekman,
30

His Excellency being returned from Albany communicated to this Board the severall conferences he had there with the five nations of Indians as followeth, viz:

The Ten Sachims of the ffive nations private conference with his Excellency the 13 June 1717.

His Excell^y reply to the ffive nations at a private conference held by two Sachims of each nation in Albany the 13 day of June 1717.

Propositions made by his Excell^y. to the five nations ye 13th of June 1717.

The Answer of the five nations to his Excell^y. the 14 of June 1717.

Propositions made by the Sachims of the five nations to his Excellency the 15th day of June 1717.

His Excell^y propositions to the River Indians in Albany the 15th of June 1717.

The Answer of the River Indians to his Excell^y the 15th 1717.

His Excellency likewise communicated to the Board a letter he received at Albany by a Gent^{ln} arrived there express from Virginia from Coll Spotswood the Governor there complaining of a grievous Insult on some Indians under the protection of his majesty and that Government alledged to be done by some of the five nations which letter his Excell^y had likewise communicated to the five nations.

His Excell^y likewise communicated to the Board the propositions made by his Excell^y on the 16 of June 1717, to the five nations relating to that letter he received from Virginia.

As also the answer of the five nations to his Excell^y to the propositions made to them relating to Virginia in Albany the 17th day of June 1717.

[N°. 147.] At a Council held at ffort George in New York the 16th day of September 1717.

Present

His Excellency Robert Hunter Esqr.

| Coll Depeyster | Coll Beekman | Mr Byerley |
| Capt Walter | Mr Phillipse | Doctor Johnson |

A warr: to his Excellency for a quarters sallary
ending the 13th September Instant   £390. 00. 0
To Laurence Clauson Indian Interpreter
    for the like   7 10 0
To his Excellency to be imployed in pres-
    ents for the five nations   400 00 0
To defray the expense of his Expedition
    to Albany, to meet the said Indians   150 00 0
To the Commissioners of the Indian af-
    fairs at Albany for expresses Spies
    Intelligence and other incidents for
    the present year   300 00 0
To John Cuyler and Hendrick Hansen
    Esqr. for fire wood and candles for
    the Garrison of Albany, Schenectady
    and ffort Hunter for one year ending
    the 13th June next   200 00 0

[N°. 148.] ! At a Council held at ffort George in New
      York the 17th day of June 1718.
Present
      His Excellency Robert Hunter Esqr.
      Capt Walter   M^r. Barbarie
      Coll Beekman   M^r. Phillipse
      M^r. Van Dam   M^r. Byerley '

To His Excellency for his Q^r sallary   £390 00 0
To the Commissioners of the Indian af-
    fairs at Albany to be by them im-
    ployed for expresses Spies Intelli-
    gence and other incidents for this
    present year   £300. 00. 0
To His Excellency for support of the
    Government   400. 00. 0
    to be employed in presents to the
    five nations of Indians and one hun-
    dred and fifty pounds to defray the
    expence of his Excell^y expedition
    to Albany to meet the said Indians ;   150. 00. 0

[N°. 149]   At a Council held at ffort George in New
York y° 23ᵈ of August 1718.

Present

His Excellency Robert Hunter Esqr.
Coll DePeyster   Mʳ Barbarie
Coll Beekman   Dʳ Johnson

His Excellency communicated to this Board a letter
from the Commissioners of the Indian affairs at Albany
of y° 18ᵗʰ of August instant and enclosed a copy of y°
propositions made by sundry Sachims of the five nations to the Comᵗ of the Indian affairs on the 17ᵗʰ instant
whereby it appears that the five nations are under some
Jealousie that they are to be set upon and cutt off by
the Christians and desiring that his Excellᵉʸ will be
pleased to give them a speedy answer whether there is
any such resolution on ffoot by the Christians and to
begg his Excelly's assistance of arms and necessaries.

Whereupon It is y° opinion of this Board that his
Excellency will be pleased to goe forthwith to Albany
to Albany to meet the said Sachims and make them
such presents as his Excellency shall think reasonable.

[N°. 150.]   At a Council held at fforte George in New
York the 10ᵗʰ of June 1719.

Present

His Excellency Robert Hunter Esqr
Coll Depeyster   Rip Van Dam   Mʳ Byerley
Coll Beekman   Mʳ Phillipse Coll Johnson

The Memorial of James Logan Secretary of the
Province of Pensilvania by order of the Governor of the
said Province concerning the Indians of the five nations
warring upon the Southern Indians who are in league
with the Southern English Colonies was read.

Ordered that the said memorial be forthwith sent
to Commissioners of Indian affairs and that they do send
Laurence Clase to acquaint them that his Excellency and
Council ot this Province expects that they will not make

away with any of their prisoners lately taken because his Excellency is informed that some of them do belong to Indians who are under the protection of the King of Great Brittain.

[N.º 151.] At a Council held a fort George in New York June 13ᵗʰ 1719.

Present

His Excellency Robᵗ Hunter Esqr

Capt Walter   Mʳ Barbarie   Mʳ Byerley

Coll Beekman   Mʳ Phillipse   Doctor Johnson

To pay unto his Excellency for support of Government four hundred pounds to be imployed in presents for the five nations of Indians and one hundred and fifty pounds to defray the expence of his expedition to Albany to meet the said Indians.

To pay unto the Commissioners of the Indian affairs at Albany for the support of Government three hundred pounds to be by them imployed for expresses Spies Intelligences and other Incidents for the present year.

To pay unto Laurence Clauson Indian Interpreter seven pounds ten shillings for his quarters sallary ending the 13ᵗʰ of June instant

[N.º 152.] Att a Council held at Fort George in New York the 24ᵗʰ of June 1719.

Present

His Excellʸ Robᵗ Hunter Esqr.

Coll Depeyster   Mʳ Barbarie

Coll Beekman   Mʳ Phillipse

Coll Heathcott

The Governor Communicated to the Board a letter from the Commissioners of the Indian affairs at Albany and the propositions from the Oneydas Indians with complaints of wanting ammunition and a great famine among them, and acquainted them that he had sent this morning five hundred weight of powder and one thousand weight of lead according to the request of the said Commissioners.

[N° 153.] Att a Council held at fort George in New York the 9ᵗʰ day of July, 1719.

Present

His Excellʸ Robt Hunter Esqr

Coll Depeyster   Coll Beekman,   Mʳ Phillipse
Coll Schuyler   Mʳ Barberie,   Mʳ Byerley
                Mʳ Clarke.

His Excellency communicated to this Board a letter dated the sixth day of this Instant July from the Commᶦˢˢ of the Indian affairs at Albany inclosing a written relation given to them · by the Canasara one of the Indians of the five nations that the ffrench are building a fort at Yaguah intending to settle a Trade there to intercept our Trade with the farr nations of Indians who come by that passe through yᵉ five nations to Albany with their Peltry and desiring that a present be sent to the five nations to encourage them to hinder that settlement.

It is the opinion of this Board that the Commʳˢ of the Indian affairs do forthwith send one of their own members with the interpreter to the five nations and particularily to the Cinnekes in whose Country Yargreah lies to acquaint them that as this · settlement will prejudice them in their Treaty to Albany and hinder their Correspondence with the farr nations in Amity with them and us, obstruct their own Hunting and be of worse consequence in case of a rupture, that it behoves them to hinder the ffrench from making that or any other settlement in their Country or on the frontiers thereof and to enable them to defray the expense this Board is of opinion that a quantity of strouds and other suitable goods to the value of sixty pounds be sent to the Comʳˢ of the Indian affairs to be by them given out·to such persons in such manner as they shall judge most proper for the Services mentioned.

· But that the Comm^is be directed to acquaint the five nations that the peace now subsisting between the Crown of Great Brittain and France being to be inviolably observed they must take care not to committ any hostilities that may infringe it, and particular caution must be had that no directions be given to the five nations that may countenance any Hostilities to the prejudice or violation of those Treaties.

[N? 154.]   Att a Council held at Fort George in New York the 9th of June 1720

Present

         The Hon^le Peter Schuyler Esqr

         Mr Beekman,   Mr Phillipse
         Mr Van Dam,   Mr Harrison.
         Mr Barbarie,

     His Honor the President communicated to the Gen^tl of the Council a letter from the Comm^iss. of Indian affairs at Albany.

     As likewise a Journal of Myndert Schuyler and Robt. Livingston Junr. concerning their voyage to the Sennekes Castle and their conference with the Sachims then at home which letter and Journall follows.

ALBANY 3^d June 1720.

     SIR:—Inclosed wee send you herewith the Journall of Myndert Schuyler and Robert Livingston Junr Esq^rs who have been at the Sennekiss Castle wee cant all at present being prest by the sloop who stay'd for us a while so remaine with great respect.

           Sir your very humble Ser^t
             JOHN RIGGS
             HENDRICK HANSEN
             JOH^s CUYLER.

Answer made by the Sachims of the Sinnekiss, Cayouges and Oneyde and in behalf of the Mohoggs and Onondage Sachims In Sinnondowdene the 22^d day of May, 1720.

Brother Corlaer & Quider :—You come unexpected though wee are now satisfyed you have taken the usual method by sending seaven hands of wampum from the Mohoggs Castle to acquaint us of our coming there that lodging by the way you are in no neglect you have told us that our brother Corlaer was not yet returned and that you were sent from our Brother Quider and that whilst the Sachims from the other four Castles were then not come to hear your propositions you were in hopes to meet such here as would heartily affect the welfare of the whole house. Wee jointly do assure you that we behold the same affection as our predecessors have had and do promise to shew ourselves heartily inclined for the Interest of the whole house and continue steadfast in the Covenant with our Brother Corlear not doubting but your posterity will follow such an Example. Give a Belt of Wampum.

Brother Corlaer and Quider:—You have told us that you was informed that wee were prepareing to warr against the farr Indians and that severall of them were in alliance with you by which that friendship might breake off, that therefore you desired us to bury the Hatchet not only against those Indians but the other Indians to the southward in alliance with the English Government. Wee own that some of our young men had a designe that way but now wee will hearken to your advice and do assure you that none of our men shall go a-fighting against Indians to the southward in Alliance with the English Governments and they may depend that wee nor none of ours shall no ways molest them 'till they trouble us first neither shall any of our men goe out against any of the farr Indians whilst they remain in Peace with us and wee do further assure you that wee shall use all fair means to keep peace with them and endeavour to encourage them this way towards Albany so that wee may have the benefit of their trade. Give a Belt of Wampum.

Brother Corlaer and Quider:—You have told us that you were informed the ffrench were building a

House at Onjagera which you perceive will prove prejudicial to us and you. It is true they are either yet building or it is finished by this time : Wee do own that some
years agoe the five nations gave Trongsagroende Jeroun-
doquet and Onjagera and all other hunting places westward of ye Crowne to be held for us and our posterity
least other might encroach on us then wee also partition'd the hunting places between us and the ffrench
Indians but sence then they are gone farr within the
limitt and the ffrench got more by settling Trongsagroende and wee must join our opinion with yours that
if wee suffer the french to settle at Onjagera being the
only way toward hunting wee will be alltogether shut
up and debarred of means for our livelyhood then indeed our posterity would have reason to reflect on us
therefore to begin in time wee will appoint some of our
men to go thither to Onjagera and desire you to send
one a long so that in the name of the five nations Jean
Coeur may be acquainted with the resolve of this meeting and for bidden to proceed any further building but
ordered to take downe what erected. Give one Belt of
Wampum.

Brother Corlear and Quider:—You have Desired
that ever any matters offered tending to the prejudice
of us that we ought not to consult the *hater* meaning
the Governour of Canada in such affairs but advise with
you : Wee return you thanks for your advice and promise
that if any matter standing to our prejudice happens
wee will only consult and advise with you therein but
desire you not be slack in your assistance as formerly
when wee required it so much that wee were oblidged to
fly for it for want of help at that time when the ffrench
burned down our Castles and destroyed our Corn therefore let us always lye in your thoughts and act the
Brotherly part in giving assistance when it is needfull
which wee promise shall not be wanted on our side to
you. Give a belt of Wampum.

After they had done wee by a Belt of Wampum desired that Hagnguiractiton alias Blue Beetn ought to

be restored a Sachim again which they accepted and was restored accordingly the 23ᵈ wee left the Sennekies Castles and the Twenty fourth Laurence Claasen Interpreter was to set out with the appointed Indians for Onjagera.

Albany the 3ᵈ June 1720.

MYNDERT SCHUYLER
ROBᵀ LIVINGSTON JUNᴿ

[Nᵒ 155.] Att a Council held at fort George in New York the 28ᵗʰ day of July 1720.

Present

The Honᵇˡᵉ Peter Schuyler Esqʳ President

Coll Depeyster,	Mʳ Barbarie,
Capt Walter,	Mʳ Byerley,
Coll Beekman,	Doct Johnson,
Mʳ Van Dam,	Mʳ Harrison.
Coll Heathcote,	

A Committee of this Board reported to his honour that the following particulars will be sufficient as presents to the Indians of the five nations.

		£		
50	Guns computed at	£65	0	0
5	pieces of strouds	50	0	0
3	packes of Duffels	36	0	0
100	Shirts	27	0	0
27	Kettles	10	0	0
9	Blankets	7	0	0
3	pieces of ½ thicke	15	0	0
12	dozⁿ of stockings	12	0	0
500	Bars of Lead of 1½ lb each	7	10	0
2	Boxes of Bullets	3	0	0
2½	doz of Hatchetts	3	0	0
14	doz of Knives	3	10	0
2500	of Flints	2	10	0
5	Barrells of Pouder	40	0	0
		281	10	0
1	Barrell powder for river Indians	8	0	0

100	Weight of Bulletts	1	10	0
1	piece of strouds	10	0	0
6	Guns	9	0	0

Carried forward	£310	0	0

Out of the Store in Fort George

	Brought forward	£310	0	0
2	pieces of Duffeles	24	0	0
1	Hogshead of Rum	14	0	0
1	Barrell pipes	3	0	0
250	lb. Tobacco	5	0	0
3	Barrels pork	9	0	0
50	Bushells Indian Corne	6	0	0
8	Small looking Glasses	1	0	0
	In Wampum Belts	10	0	0
	Hats	3	0	0
	Bread Pease and Beer	8	0	0
	Oznabriggs for powder baggs	3	0	0
	Caggs for Rum	4	0	0

	£400	0	0

Which report is agreed to by the Majority of this Board. And it is the opinion of this Board that a Warrant be prepared for 150 pounds for the President's expences to meet the five nations of Indians at Albany and for ninety pounds to be imployed in presents for the said five nations.

[N.º 156.] At a Council held at Fort George in New York September 19.ᵗʰ 1721.
His Excellency William Burnet Esqr.
Cap.ᵗ Walter   M.ʳ Van Dam   M.ʳ Colden
Coll Beekman   M.ʳ Harrison   M.ʳ Alexander

His Excellency communicated to this Board a letter from the Governour of Boston of the 7.ᵗʰ of August last complaining of great insults Committed by Indians of the Eastward set on by ffrench Jesuits.

M.ʳ Van Dam Communicated to this Board a letter from Coll.ʳ Fitch of the 14ᵗʰ of this month giving an account of severall Presents transmitted to this place in order to be given to the five nations at Albany to procure their assistance against the Indian and desireing that these presents being for the publick service may be admitted to entry free of duty.

It is the opinion of the Board that these goods ought to admitted to entry free of all dutys.

It is the opinion of this Board that no treaty be made with our Indians without first being communicated to this Government and in such manner and form only as this Government shall approve.

Ordĕred that M.ʳ Van Dam, M.ʳ Barbarie, Mr.ʳ Harrison and Doctor Colden or any other of the Genᵗˡ of the Council be a Committee to inspect the Minutes of Council to see in what manner the neighbouring Governments have been allowed to Treat with our Indians.

[N.ᵒ 157.] At a Council held at Fort George in New York Sep.ʳ 20ᵗʰ 1721.
Present
His Excellency William Burnet, Esq.ʳ
Coll Beekman   M.ʳ Barbarie,   Doctor Colden
M.ʳ Van Dam,   M.ʳ Harrison,   M.ʳ Alexander

M.ʳ Van Dam reported from the Committee appointed to inspect the minutes of Council relating to the matter refered to them and especially the minutes of the following dates the 16ᵗʰ of April 1676, and 2ᵈ of Octo.ʳ following in Governor Androsses time as likewise of the 13ᵗʰ of August 1694 and the 14ᵗʰ and 20ᵗʰ of the same Month in Gov.ʳ Fletchers time and the 18ᵗʰ of October 1711 in Governor Hunters time.

And His Excellency having communicated the following Letter—

Sir:—I am directed by the Governour and Council of this Province to acquaint your Excellency that some principal Gentlemen are appointed to meet the five nations of Maquas with a present from this Government and pray the favour of your Excellency that you will give notice to the Indians that they may be at Albany the sixth day of October next at which time the Gentlemen will be there to meet them.

I am with great Respect Sir Your Excellencys most Obedient Humb. servant,

JOSIAH WILLARD Secr'y

Boston Septem^r 9th 1721.

It is the opinion of this Board that the Secretary do send a copy of the foregoing Minutes to the Governour of Boston and do subjoin to them an Answer to the foregoing letter in the following words (viz)

Sir :—I am directed by the Governour and Council of this Province to acquaint your Excellency that a letter signed Josiah Willard secretary, of the 9th instant, was received by his Excellency our Governour at New York having been forwarded from Albany by an express sent by the Comms^s of Indian affairs for for that purpose and that his Excell^y having communicated that letter to the Gentlemen of the Council—It is the opinion of this Board that this Government cannot consent that commissioners from any neighbouring Colony should meet or treat with the five Indian nations who are a branch of this Province or give presents to them in the name of any particular Government. And that such proposals have been constantly refused as will appear by the Copys of several Minutes of Council sent herewith and therefore that the notice desired to be given to the Indians cannot be complyed with 'till first application is made to the Government in a regular manner concerning what is desired of the Indians in order that the Governour with the advice and consent of the Council may come to a resolution concerning the said proposals how far it may be safe and proper that they may be made to the said Indians and in what manner this Government can consent that the proposals be made and the presents given to the said Indians

I am with great respect Sir Your Excellency's most obed Humb. Serv't.

Is: Bobin D Secry

New York Sep 20th 1721.

N° 158.] At a Council held at Fort George in New York October 9th 1721. Post Meridiem.
Present

        His Excellency William Burnet Esqr
        Capt Walter   Mr Harrison
        Coll Beekman   Mr Alexander
        Mr Van Dam   M^r L Morris Jun

His Exc^y communicated to this Board a letter signed Josiah Willard Secretary by order of the Governor and Council of Massachusets Colony.

After considering considering the contents thereof It is the opinion of this Board that the Deputy Secretary do write a letter to the Commissioners from the said Colony now residing at Albany to the following effect. Viz,

That his Excellency having lately met the Indians and renewed the Covenant Chain with them on the part of all his Majestys subjects on the Continent of America it would alarm them to send for them again so soon for the same purpose which should be avoided unless an absolute necessity required it at this time and the season of the year being intirely improper considering the great distance at which most of the Indians live and their hunting season is now approaching. That this Board does not think fit that the Indians be now sent for—that this Board observes in the Instructions given to Mr Fitch Dudley that in case of his Excelly absence they were to apply themselves to some particular persons only at Albany and not to the Commissioners of Indian affairs as would have been most proper. That notwithstanding in Mr Willards letter of October the 2^d it is sayed that the designs of their Commissioners was only to deliver a present and Brighten the Covenant Chain between them and the five nations—that the Board · observes that there are severall particular matters contained in these said Instructions of no small importance and which may be attended with very material consequences. That the Board does not apprehend that they gave them any reason to believe that they imagined any thing sinister or clandestine to be intended on their part and to assure them whatever the present emergency or any future may be we shall at all times be ready *at all times* to lend them our best assistance but with all that this Board does insist that no treaty be made with or presents given to the five nations but with the previous consent of and in the manner directed by this Government all which may be settled and adjusted when they shall think it necessary to send Commissioners hither to Treat upon that subject.

[N° 159.] At a Council at Fort George in New York the 9th of August 1722.
Present

His Excellency William Burnet Esqr
Capt Walter   Mr Harrison
Coll Beekman   Doctor Colden
Mr Van Dam   Mr Alexander

His Excellency communicated to the Board the two following Letters in haec Verba ::

From on Board his Majesty's Ship the Enterprize at Sandy Hook Augt 9. 1722
I am come hither as Governour of Virginia accompanied by some Gentlemen as members of that Government in order to settle a right understanding and establish a lasting peace between his Majesties subjects of that Dominion and the *five nations of Indians belonging to this province.*

Diverse Embassies Treaties and Negociations have heretofore been set on foot for the same purpose but none I believe has been founded on so many considerations as this present intended Treaty: for first your Indians have insisted on our Brightening the Covenant Chain (as your Interpreter tells us) and seem disposed to continue disturbing our Fronteers until the same be done; in the next place repeated instances have been made on the part of the Government of New York that some Commissioners should be sent to Albany in behalf of Virginia to renewe the Covenant Chain with the said five nations likewise the Lords Commissioners for the plantation affairs at home have urged us to comply with such proposall and also the General Assembly of Virginia have had it for the subject matter of their Deliberations in severall sessions and haveing at length concluded on the expediency of this Treaty both Council and House of Burgesses have with one voice desired me to undertake to manage the same in person. This Sir being the occasion and true grounds of our coming hither at this time, I crave admittance in your Government with the hopes of having the honour to confer with your Excellency and Council in order to take the most advisable measures for rendering your negotiations effectual, and the experience I have already had of your good offices towards bringing *your Indians* to accede to the preliminaries insisted on by Virginia has greatly encouraged me to imbark in the undertaking and engages me to be with great Respect

Sir Your Most Obed
and most Humb Ser^t.
A. SPOTSWOOD.

Sir:—The Province of Pensylvania being happyly situated between his Majesty's Government of Virginia and New York. It has been my greatest care to regulate the Management of the Indian affairs in that Colony so as to render the peaceable disposition of the Inhabitants acceptable to the Indians and consistent with

the concerted measures and wise conduct of the neighbouring Provinces. So soon therefore as I understood
that Coll Spotswood the Governour of Virginia intended
with your approbation and concurrence to hold a Treaty
with your Indians of the five nations at Albany I called
the Assembly of Pennsylvania together and it is by
their advice that I am now come accompanied with
some few members of my Council to intreat that with
your Ex:ellencys permission and in your presence I
may be allowed to renew upon that occasion at Albany
the Leagues of Friendship that have formerly been
made between the Province of Pensylvania and the five
Nations.

The unhappy accident of an Indian being lately
killed in the wood by some of our Traders and renewing our former Instances with this Government to prevent if possible the five nations from going to Warr and
making a path through our settlements upon the river
Susquahanna are the principal points on which I propose at this time to speak to your Indians and as I have
not any thing to offer but what I have reason to believe
will perfectly agree with your Excellencys sentiments
and those of your Council, I am encouraged to hope
you will favourably receive this application.

Sir Your Most Obed Humble Servt

W. KEITH.

New York August 13th 1722.

Upon which the Council advise his Ex. to assure the
Governours of Virginia and Pensylvania that this board
shall think it a great honor and happiness to confer
with them on the best measures to be taken with the
five nations at this time to secure a Generall peace betwen them and the Indians and their neighboring Colonies that they are Rightly satisfied with the just and
honourable intentions expressed in the letters which his
Ex. has communicated to them and shall be very ready
to concur in every thing that shall be for the safety and
prosperity of the common British interest in America.

31

To which his Excellency agreed entirely and promised
to acquaint the Governours of Virginia and Pensylvania
with the unanimous sentiments of this Board.

[N.° 160.]   At a Council held at Albany the 28th day
of August 1722.

Present

His Excelly. Wm Burnet Esqr

Mr Van Dam,   Mr Alexander
Mr Barbarie,   Coll Morris Jun. .
Doct Colden,

His Ex. informed this Board that in order to secure
the five nations to his Majestys interest and to promote
the British trade directly with the Indians he had made
choice of Major Abraham Schuyler as a fit person to be
settled among the Sinneskes with eight men including a
smith for that end, and proposes to the Board that the
sum of One Hundred pounds be allowed to such eight
men as shall go upon that undertaking for one year,
and because a man of distinction will be requisite to induce the Indians to be assisting in that affair and to
have the chief management and directions of the said
company he proposed that one hundred pounds be allowed unto the said Major Schuyler it being necessary
for him at such an expense to make himself respected
by the Indians and that the said sums of one hundred
pounds to Abraham Schuyler and the one hundred
pounds to the eight men be allowed out of the five hundred pounds which the Assembly have resolved to raise
at the next session for the ensuing year for keeping the
five nations of Indians steady to the British interest.

His Ex. also proposed to this Board that the sum
of fifty pounds be allowed unto the said Major Schuyler
and company for presents to the Indians and other incidentall charges in equipping themselves of which a just
account is to be rendered.

It is the opinion of the Board when Major Abraham
Schuyler with not less than eight persons besides him-

self having been for the space of one year upon that
service he shall be paid one hundred pounds and the
men the like sum and also fifty pounds for presents to
the Indians and other Incidentalls to be accounted for as
aforesaid and that the same shall be paid out of the
£500 which the Assembly have resolved to raise at their
sessions for keeping the Indians of the five Nations
steady to the British Interest.

[N.° 161.]   At a Council held at Fort George in New
York June 23ᵈ 1725.
Present
        His Excellency William Burnet Esqʳ
        Capt Walter   Mʳ Abra Van Horne
        Mʳ Van Dam   Wm Provost
        Mʳ Barbarie

The following warrants for Officers Salaries and other
services after being read were signed by His Ex.

N.° 415. To his Excelly for presents to the five
    Nations and his Expedition to Albany   550 0 0
N.° 430. To Laurence Clausen Indian Interp.   15 0 0
    431. To Comʳˢ of Indian affairs at Albany   200 0 0

[N.° 162.]   At a Council held at Fort George in New
York Sept 23ᵈ 1725.
Present
        His Excelly. William Burnet Esqʳ
        Capt Walter,   Mʳ Harrison
        Mʳ Van Dam,   Doct Colden
        Mʳ Barbarie,   Mʳ Alexander.

The following warrants of payment of Officers Salaries and other services after being read were signed by
his Excelly.

N.° 449 To Laurence Clausen Indian Inter-
      preter £15 0 0

451 To Philip Livingston Esq' assignee of
Cap.' Hermanus Vedder for the said
Vedders extraordinary expenses and
management of the said Company
sent with him to the Sennekes Coun-
try for one year 60 0 0
To Philip Livingston Esq' Assignee of
Isaac Staats, Andrus Bradt, Jun.
Hendrich Whemp the Company
sent with Capt Hermanus Vedder to
Sennekes Country for one year . .   55 0 0
To Philip Livingston Esq.' Assig-
nee of Hermanus Vanslyke . .   30 0 0

[N.° 163.] At a Council held at Fort George in New
York, October 27th 1725.
His Excellency William Burnet Esq'.
Cap.' Walter,   M.' Harrison,
M.' Van Dam,   M.' Alexander

A warrant to Laurence Clausen Indian Interpreter
for the sum of twenty one pounds nineteen shillings for
his journey and expences to the Onondage Country,
after being read was signed by his Excellency.

[N.° 164.] At a Council held at Fort George in New
York November the 2d 1725.
His Excellency William Burnet, Esq'
Cap.' Walter   Doctor Colden
M.' Van Dam   M.' Alexander
M.' Barbarie   M.' Morris
M.' Harrison   M.' Livingston

His Ex. proposed to the Board that a smith with an
assistant be sent to the Onondage Country as likewise a
smith and assistant to the Sennekes Country and that
twenty five pounds be allowed to each of the smiths and
ten pounds to each of the assistants besides necessaries
for their journey and tools and that a pair of bellows

be bought for the smith sent to the Onondage country which was agreed to by the Board and that the same be paid out of the first moneys that shall hereafter be leveyed by act of Assembly for securing the Indians to the British Interest.

[N.° 165.] At a Council held at Fort George in New York March 13.ᵗʰ 1725/6.

Cap.ᵗ Walter,   Doc.ᵗ Colden
M.ʳ Van Dam,   M.ʳ Alexander
M.ʳ Barbarie   M.ʳ Abra Vanhorne.

N.° 480. To Laurence Clausen Indian Interpreter £15 0 0

[N.° 166.] At a Council held at Fort George in New York June 14ᵗʰ 1726.

His Excellency W.ᵐ Burnet Esq.ʳ
M.ʳ Van Dam,   M.ʳ Harrison
M.ʳ Barbarie,   M.ʳ William Provost.
M.ʳ Vanhorne,

The following warrants after being read were signed by his Ex.

N.° 485. To D.° for presents to the Indians
& Expedition to Albany . . £550 0 0
N.° 498. To Laurence Clausen Indian Interpreter 15 0 0
" 499. To Com.ʳ Indian Affairs at Albany 200 0 0

[N.° 167.] At a Council held at Fort George in New York October 27ᵗʰ 1726.

His Excellency W.ᵐ Burnet Esqr
Cap.ᵗ Walter,   Doct Colden
M.ʳ Van Dam   M.ʳ Vanhorne
M.ʳ Clarke   M.ʳ P. Livingston
M.ʳ Harrison

The following sums being allowed by the Board for services in the Indian Country warrants were ordered to be prepared accordingly payable out of the monies appropriated by act of Assembly for securing the Indians to the British Interest, viz.—

	£		
To Jacob Brown and Hermanus Vedder Jn.ʳ for their services as smiths at the Onondage Country	25	0	0
And for Tools	5	10	0
To Jurian Hogan and Company for their services as smiths at the Sennekes Country	35	0	0
To presents given to the Indians . .	4	7	0
To carrying the anvil &c	6	19	0
To M.ʳ Philip Livingston for presents given by Mayor Abra Schuyler to the Indians	31	7	6
Smiths bellows at Onondage . . .	5	0	0
To an anvil	7	13	6
To Gretena Schuyler the Widow and Relict of Mayor Schuyler for services in the Indian Country during the space of three months time till his death . .	50	0	0
For Provisions	8	19	1½
To Johannes Muldre and Jacob Moore attendants on Major Schuyler in the Indian Country	22	0	0
To Cornelus Cuyler for a Burch Cannoe .	10	0	0
To Laurence Clausen for his journey to the Sennekes Country in bringing down the Sachims with horse hire and charges of fetching Sachims from hunting . .	32	0	0

£243 16 1½

His Excellency proposed to the Board that there be allowed to Captain Evert Banker for the year he shall remain in the Sennekes Country the sum of £100 on condition that at his return to Albany he declares upon oath that he had not traded directly by himself or indirectly by others during his stay in the Indian Country (excepting for provisions for himself and attendants) and that he be allowed £25 for presents to the Indians provided he declares upon oath the same has been given them according to the best of his judgement for the publick service and then be allowed £30 for the two attendants during the said time and 10 pounds for Interpreter all which was agreed to by the Board.

His Ex. further proposed to the Board that £20 be allowed to Jost Vansysen armourer and Nicholas Whemp smith—together with their services and work in the Sennekes Country till the 1st of May next provided they stay their till that day and £12 be allowed to Evert Bancker in full of all provisions during his stay among the Indians.

Which was likewise agreed to by the Board.

[N.º 168.]　At a Council held at Fort George in New York No.ʳ 3ᵈ 1726.

Present as on the 27º October, except Doctor Colden.

His Excellency laid before the Board a Deed he had obtained in his Majestys name from some of the principal Sachims of the Sennekes Cayouges and Onondages Indians in behalf of themselves and the rest of the Indians for all that Tract of Land which they won with the sword where the Beaver hunting is lying and being sixty miles distant directly from the water into the country beginning from a Creek called Canahoque on the Lake Oswego all along the said lake, and all along the narrow passage from the said lake to the falls of Oniagara called Caraquaragh and all along the river of Oniagara and all a long the Lake Catrackquis to the Creek called Sodoms belonging to the Sennekes and from Sodoms to the hill called Tegorhunkserode belonging to the Coyouges and from Tigerhunkserode to the creek called Cayhenghage belonging to the Onondages all the said lands belong of the Breadth of sixty

English miles—which was read and ordered to be recorded in the Book of the patents in the Secretarys
office notwithstanding it has been proved or acknowledged as the Ordinarie directs and that it be delivered
to Mr Philip Livingston the Secretary of Indians affairs
to be filed in his office.

The Indian deed above mentioned which follows is Re-
    corded in Book of Entries of deeds begun 1723
    ending 1735.
    To all People to whom this present Instrument of
Writing shall come Whereas the Sachims of the five
Nations did on the nineteenth day of July one thousand
seaven hundred and one in a Conferance held at Albany
Between John Nanfan Esqr late Lieutenant Governour
of the Province of New York give and render up all
their Land where their Beaver hunting is which they
won with their swords then Eighty years ago Coorach-
koo our great King praying that he might be their protector and Defender therefore for which they desired
that their secretary might then draw an Instrument for
them to sign and seal that it might be conveyed to the
King as by the minutes thereof now in the Custody
of the Secretary for Indian Affairs at Albany may
more fully and at large appear. We Kanakaugh-
ton, Keayakadoroodon and Sadegeluaghtu, Onnondage
Sachims of our own accord free and Voluntary will do
hereby ratify and confirm Submit and grant and by
these presents do (for ourselves our heirs and success·
ors and in behalf of the whole nations of Sennekes,
Cayouges, and Onnondages) ratifye, confirme submit and
grant unto our most sovereign Lord George by the
Grace of God King of Great Britain, ffrance, and Ireland Defender of the Faith &c. his heirs successors for
ever all the said Land and Beaver hunting to be protected and Defended by his said Majesty his heirs and
successors to and for the use of us our heirs and successors and the said three nations and we do also of our
own accord free and voluntary will give render submit

and grant and by these presents do for ourselves our heirs and successors Lord King George his heirs and successors forever all that Land lying and being sixty miles distant taken directly from the Water into the Country Beginning from a Creek called Canahogue on the Lake Oswego all along the said Lake, and all along the narrow passage from the said Lake to the falls of Oniagora and all along the Lake Catarackquis to the Creek called Sodoms belonging to the Sennekes and from Sodoms to the hill called Tegerhunkserode to the Creek called Cayhunghage belonging to the Onondages all the said Land being of the Breadth of Sixty English miles as aforesaid all the way from the aforesaid Lakes or Rivers directly into the country and thereby including all the Castles of the aforesaid three nations, with all the Rivers Creeks and Lakes within the said Limits to be protected and defended by his said Majesty his heirs and successors and the said three nations In testimony whereof we have hereunto set our marks and affixed our seals in the City of Albany this fourteenth day of September in the thirteenth year of his Majestys Reign Anno Domini 1726.

The Mark of KEAYAKODORODON	A Sachim of the Onnondage.
The Mark of DEKANISOREE	A Sachim of the Cayouges.
The Mark of OTSOGHKOREE	A Sachim of the Cayouges.
The Mark of KANAKAUGHTON	A Sachim of the Sennekes.
The Mark of SADEGUNOOGHTIE	A Sachim of the Onnondage.
The Mark of THAMMTSIONUEE.	A Sachim of the Sennekes.

Signed sealed and delivered in presence of us

PHILIP LIVINGSTON
PETER VAN BRUGH
MYNDERT SCHUYLER
LAURENCE CLAUSEN

[N.º 169.] At a Council held at Fort George in New
York Nov. 11ᵗʰ 1726.

Present

> His Excellency Wᵐ Burnet, Esqʳ
> Capt Walter   Mʳ Clarke
> Mʳ Harrison   Mʳ Abra Vanhorne

Ordered that the Deputy Clerk of the Council do
acquaint the House of Representatives that his Excellency requires their Immediate attendance at the Council Chamber.

The Assembly accordingly attending with their
Speaker his Excellency gave his assent to the following
Bills Enacting the same and ordered them to be en-
rolled—

The Act for regulating and securing the Indian
Trade to the westward of Albany and for defraying the
charge thereof.

[N.º 170.] At a Council held at Fort George in New
York Nov 24ᵗʰ 1726

Present

> His Excellency Wᵐ Burnet Esqʳ
> Capt Walter   Mʳ Harrison
> Mʳ Van Dam   Doct Colden
> Mʳ Barbarie   Mʳ Alexander

The following warrant after being read was signed
by his Ex.

> N.º 517. To Laurence Clausen Indian
>   Interpreter   ·   .   .   £15 0 0

[N.º 171.] At a Council held at Fort George in New
York March 2ᵈ 1726|7.

Present

> As on the 24ᵗʰ of Nov. with Mʳ Vanhorne
> Mʳ Provoost

· It is the opinion of this Board that a Fort be built

at the mouth of the Onondage river and that three hundred pounds given by the late Act of Assembly be employed towards building the said Fort and the buying provisions and necessaries for th[ose] to be posted their.

[N? 172.] At a Council held at Fort George in New York April 13ᵗʰ 1727.

Present

As on the 2ᵈ of March 1726 except Mᵣ Provoost and Doctor Colden.

His Excellency communicated to this Board some letters from the Government of the Massachusetts Bay which were sent to the Comsᵣˢ at Albany to desire their assistance in making a peace with some of the Eastern Indians residing at Canada together with an account of proceedings of the Comsᵣˢ thereon.

This Board approves of the proceedings of the Comsˢ at Albany in this affair and desire that his Ex. will direct them to use the best offices to bring it to a happy issue.

His Excellency communicated to this Board what intelligence and papers he had received from Albany since the last meeting of this Board.

This Board consents to the agreement made by the Comᵣˢ the third instant with the workmen and others towards the building the house at Oswego near the mouth of the Onnondage river.

This Board likewise consents that the defraying the charge of such Battoes and provisions his Ex. shall think necessary for the men to be sent into the Indian Country be defrayed out of the monies appropriated by act of Assembly for that purpose.

[N? 173.] At a Council held at Fort George in New York April the 27 1727.

Present.

His Ex. William Burnet.

M.ʳ Barbarie,   Mʳ Vanhorne and
Mʳ Harrison,   Mʳ Kennedy.
Mʳ Alexander

His Excellency acquainted the Board that he had
privately got eight Battoes made in this place besides
four which were ready at Albany and that he was
thereby enabled to send sixty men with their provisions
to Oswego which would be a number sufficient to finish
the work quickly and defend the work in conjunction
with the trades against any that should offer to disturb
the building and that he had provisions sufficient ready
to send with the detachment for three months, and that
he inclined to send this party up the rather because
he had intelligence that the ffrench had ordered a party
of ninety men from Montreal into the Lake which he
apprehended was designed to hinder the building and
that he had prepared Instructions for the commanding
officer of this party which were read and approved of
by the Board as well as the list of necessaries and provisions, which this Board resolves shall be discharged
out of the three hundred pounds provided for the securing the Trade at the mouth of Onnondages river.

[N.º 174.]   At a Council held at Fort George in New
York May 6ᵗʰ 1727.
Present.   .·
          His Excellency W.ᵐ Burnet Esqr
Mʳ. Van Dam,   Mʳ. Clarke   Mʳ Alexander
Mʳ Barbarie   Mʳ Harrison Mʳ Kennedy.

· His Ex. laid before the Board the last advices that
he received from Albany by which the Indians appear
to have objected strongly against building any stronger
house at Oswego.
Upon which it was the opinion of the Board that
this Government ought to insist upon their rights of
building the said house having had the consent of the
Indians thereto long before and since the French have

built at Niagara without their consent and notwithstanding their positive denial that this Government
has reason to expect the Indians will not any ways
hinder or Interrupt the Building the said house at
Oswego.

[N° 175.] At a Council held at Fort George in New
York June 15ᵗʰ 1727.

Mʳ Van Dam,   Mʳ Provoost
Mʳ Barbarie,   Mʳ Kennedy.
Mʳ Alexander,

The following warrants after being read were signed
by his Excellency.

N° 546. To ditto to be imployed in
presents to the Indians and his ex-
pedition to Albany   .   .   £550   0   0
N° 560. To Laurence Clausen Indian
Interpreter   .   .   .   .   -   15   0   0
N° 561. To Commʳˢ of the Indian Affairs
at Albany, for Spies intelligence and
other services for the ensuing year .   ♦200   0   0

His Excellency acquainted the Board that the Indians had given their consent to the building the house
at Oswego and that the work went on very successfully
and went on without any interruption from the ffrench.

[N° 176.] At a Council held at Fort George in New
York July 31ˢᵗ 1727.

Present

His Excellency Wᵐ Burnet, Esqr
Capt Walter   Mʳ Alexander
Mʳ Van Dam   Mʳ Abr Vanhorne
Mʳ Kennedy.

His Excellency acquainted the board that he had
received an express from Albany with an account that

Governour of Canada had summon'd the Garrison at Oswego to desist from further proceedings on the building there and to leave the same in a fortnight—and threatening other means on failure thereof alledging it to be a Contravention of the Treaty of Utrecht which stipulates that the subjects of the two Crowns shall not incroach upon one another 'till the limits have been regulated by commissaries to be appointed for that purpose.

Thereupon his Ex. observed to this board that the Clause of the 15th Article of the Treaty of Utrecht relates only to those Indians who it is doubtfull whether they are subjects of Britian or France and that it cannot relate to the five nations who in the same article are expressly declared to be subjects to the Dominion of Great Britain.

His Ex. further observed that the five nations have already used and possesed Oswego as they have frequently declared to his Ex. and that they had lately executed an instrument submitting and granting this very Land with all the rest of the Southern Coast of the Lake Cataraqui or Ontario to the Crown of Great Britain in order to be protected in their quiet dwelling therein.

Whereupon it is the opinion of this Board that the ffrench have no just pretence to make such demand and that the works at Oswego ought not to be stayed nor the plan relinquished by this province but our possesions there to be maintained to the utmost of our power especially seeing the ffrench do still persist in an actual infringement of the said Treaty by their lately building and holding the Fort at Niagara not only within the Country of the five nations but also their consent and their representations and this Government to the contrary.

It is the opinion of this Board that officers & soldiers that were sent to Oswego should still remain there and if any of them be come away they should forthwith return back to the same and that sufficient provisions and other necessaries be sent there with all convenient expedition the charge whereof be defrayed out of the first moneys that shall come in on account the like services.

That M.ʳ Banker be directed to send for some of the Chief of the several nations of the five nations to acquaint them that the ffrench and sundry Indians do threaten to disturb the Tradeing house at Oswego, that as to the ffrench we shall think ourselves obliged to defend against them alone but as to any disturbance from any nation of Indians we expect they'll take care to expell all such as come to give them or us any disturbance there.

This Board are of opinion that M.ʳ Banker be sup- plyed with the value of about sixty pounds to make presents with to those Chiefs of the five nations upon this occasion to be defrayed out of the first money pro- vided for such service.

[N.ᵒ 177.]   At a Council held at Fort George in New York Aug.ᵗ 10ᵗʰ 1727.

Present

His Excellency, W.ᵐ Burnet Esqr.

| Capt Walter | M.ʳ Harrison | M.ʳ Morris Jnr. |
| M.ʳ Van Dam | M.ʳ Alexander | M.ʳ Kennedy. |

His Ex. acquainted the Board that some of the Com.ᵉʳˢ of Indian Affairs who were come hither from Albany had proposed to have five or six Indians engaged to stay for a year at Oswego as likewise five or six persons with a smith besides the Garrison in order to make proper improvements for the better maintainance of the men there. This Board is of opinion that such a number of Indians as aforesaid whom the Commiss.ʳ shall think proper be engaged to stay for a year at Oswego upon the best terms they can, and that the like number of christians and a sufficient smith be likewise sent thither for a year in order to make the best improvement they can near the Garrison for the maintainance of the men and that the Commissioners agree with them in the best manner they can and for what necessaries they shall want all which to be defrayed out of the moneys that are or shall be provided for that purpose.

[N.° 178.] At a Council held at Fort George in New York the 6th day of December 1753.
Present.
The Hon^{le} James Delancey Lieut Governor
Mr Alexander   Mr Murray   Mr Chambers
Mr Kennedy   Mr Holland   Mr Smith

A representation to his honor the Governor from the Committee and Commissioners appointed to examine into the Eastern boundaries of this Colony, dated the 14. ultimo containing remarks and observations on the letter from Governor Wentworth of the 23^d of March 1750/1 to the Board of Trade, proposing a division-line between New York and New Hampshire was read & approved of by this Board: And the Council advised his honor to Transmit the same and the papers delivered therewith, To the right Hon^{le} the Lords Commissioners for Trade and Plantations.

To the Honourable James Delancey Esqr. his Majestys Lieutenant Governor and Commander in Chief in and over the Province New York and the Territories depending thereon in America.
The Representation of the Committee of his Majestys Council of the Province of New York and the Commissioners appointed to examine into the Eastern Boundaries of the said Province.
May it please your Honor:
Among the papers laid before us relative to the dispute between this Government and the Province of New Hampshire and Massachusetts Bay touching their extent of boundary we find an extract of a letter from Governor Wentworth to the Board of Trade, dated the 23^d of March, 1750/1 containing a proposal for settling a partition line between New York and New Hamp-

shire which extract together with a letter from the agents for this Colony and the Copy of a letter from the secretary to the Board of Trade, to our agents, were some time since transmitted to M: Clinton late Governor of this Province, that their Lordships might be informed of the sentiments of this Government thereupon on which we humbly beg leave to represent to your honor.

That on the 3ᵈ day of April 1750 Governor Clinton laid before the Council of this province, a letter from Governor Wentworth, desiring information, how far north of Albany this Province extends, and how many miles to the Eastward of Hudsons river, to the Northward of the Massachusetts line, that he might govern himself accordingly in the grants he was to make in New Hampshire and that the Council of this Province then advised Governor Clinton to acquaint Governor Wentworth in answer to his letter that this Province is bounded Eastward by Connecticut river, the letters patent from King Charles the Second to the Duke of York, expressly granting all the Lands from the west side of Connecticut river, to the East side of Delaware Bay.

That on the fifth of June 1750 Governor Clinton laid before the Council of this Province a letter from Governor Wentworth of April 25ᵗʰ owning the receipt of Governor Clinton's letter, with the said opinion of the Council, which he declares would have been satisfactory had not the two Charter Governments of Connecticutt and the Massachusetts Bay extended their bounds many miles to the Westward of the said river, and requesting to be informed by what authority Connecticutt and the Massachusetts Governments claimed so far to the westward. Whereupon the Council advised Governor Clinton to acquaint Governor Wentworth, that the claim of the Government of Connecticutt was founded on an agreement with his Government in or about the year 1684, afterwards confirmed by King William. But that as to the Massachusetts settlements

32

so far to the Westward, It was presumed they were first made by intrusion and since continued thro' the neglect of this Government.

That on the 24th day of July 1750 Governor Clinton laid before the Council of this Province a letter from Governor Wentworth of the 22^{d} of June advising he had communicated Governor Clinton's letter with the said last opinion of the Council of this province, to his Majestys council of the province of New Hampshire who were of Opinion and advised that he should on the part of New Hampshire make a representation of the matter to his Majesty relying that Governor Clinton would do the same on the part of New York, on which the Council of this Province advised Governor Clinton to make representation to his Majesty on the part of this province and to acquaint Governor Wentworth with such his Intentions and that it would be for the mutual advantage of both Governments if they exchanged of Both Governments if they exchanged copies of each others representations to his Majesty on that head and thereupon it was ordered that copies of all letters and papers lately passed between Governor Clinton and Governor Wentworth relating to the boundaries of the two Governments and a copy of that order should be forthwith prepared and delivered to his Majestys then Attorney Generall of this Province to prepare and lay before Governor Clinton a proper state of the case with all convenient speed.

That Governor Wentworth by his letter to Governor Clinton of September 2^{d} 1750, expresses himself in these words—Sir, upon my laying your favour of the 25th of July before his Majestys Council it was advised agreeable to your proposal, that exchanges of the representation made both by your Excellency and myself to his Majesty for determining the boundaries between his two Governments might contribute to the speedy settlement thereof, and without expense on either side. I shall therefore as soon as mine is perfected transmit you an authentick copy thereof, and shall endeavour to make it as short and plain as the nature and circumstances of the matter will admit—upon which letter we beg leave to observe, that we are well assured no copy of any representation by Governor Wentworth on that matter ever came to Governor Clinton's hands until he received the above mentioned extract of a letter from Mr Wentworth to the Board of Trade, the date of which is less than seven months after Governor Wentworths promise in his letter to Governor Clinton last mentioned and we have the more reason to believe that no copy of that representation was sent by Governor Wentworth to Governor Clinton, because no mention is therein made of its being so communicated.

That in pursuance of the order of the 24th of July 1750 the then Attorney General of this province prepared and delivered a representation to Governor Clinton concerning the Eastern boundaries of the Province which was read in Council the 29th day of September 1750, and referred to a Committee of the Council or any three of them to consider, That on the 18th of October 1751 the Committee to whom the said representation was referred, reported to Governor Clinton and Council their approbation thereof, and it was then approved of in Council and ordered to be entered in minutes thereof together with a letter from the Surveyor General of this province on the same subject which were both entered in the minutes of the Council accordingly.

We now beg leave to make a few remarks on Governor Wentworths letter to the Board of Trade, which (had he complyed with his promise made in his letter of Sep^t 2^d 1750) might probably have been rendered needless to have been considered by the Board of Trade for this Government would thereby have had an opportunity of setting him right in sundry matters in which we shall remark he was mistaken by his said representation.

1st Though the Eastern Boundaries of this Province and the Western boundaries of New Hampshire so far as they bound on one another (being both under his Majestys immediate Government) entirely depend on his Majestys pleasure, yet as the Eastern boundary of this Province was by the grant of the King Charles the Second to the Duke of York in 1663-4 fixed at Connecticut river now near ninety years ago where it has ever since remained, so far as concerns New Hampshire, we humbly conceive that his Majesty will make no alteration of the bounds thereof without sufficient reasons and we know not of any nor has Governor Wentworth pointed out any, but sundry persons appear against any alteration which are particularly set forth in the Surveyor Generals letter entered in the minutes of Council of October 18th 1751.

2^{d} Governor Wentworth is pleased to say that the Massachusetts Bay have allowed the Government of New York to extend their claim also twenty miles East of Hudsons river: on which we observe that this is a very new kind of Title, that Governor Wentworth says his Majesty has to a great part of this his province, the allowance of his subjects of the Massachusetts Bay. We apprehend that no good Title can be within his Majesteys Dominions but under valid grants of the board, and know of no valid grant that Massachusetts Bay have to any or Jurisdiction west of Connecticut river, and that they have none appears in a strong light, by a report approved in the Council of this province on the 20th of February last (which contains the substance of and more than the Attorney General's representation before mentioned) which has been communicated to the Government of the Massachusetts Bay and to which no direct answer has as yet been given though again and again requested.

3dly We think that Governor Wentworth has been greatly misinformed as to the Manor of Ranselaerwick suggesting that it is claimed by one person whereas great numbers of persons are owners of Lands within it and the whole City of Albany is situated within the bounds of it: again

We know of no such extent of Land within this Province that has so much bad Land in it as the manor of Renselaerwick.   Also the principal owner of that manor is an Infant and unable to contend with the Massachusetts Bay but his Guardian hath lately petitioned to the Legislature of this Province against the incroachments both of the Massachusetts Bay and New Hampshire on his Pupils estate.

4^{thly} Governor Wentworth is pleased to express himself thus. "Presuming it will be his Majestys pleasure that a North and South line should divide both the Massachusetts and New Hampshire from the Government of New York," on which we observe that had Governor Wentworth been informed, as we believe the truth is, that a North and South line from the Northwest Corner of Connecticutt Colony, would have crossed Hudsons river, some miles Southward or below the City of Albany and would leave that City and a great part Hudsons river, to the Eastward of that line, he would have no reason for advancing that presumption and the rather had he been informed, as the fact is, that the Dutch settled Albany by the name of Fort Orange, and had a Fort and Garrison their about 140 years agoe, many years before the grant to the Council of Plymouth, under which the Massachusetts Bay had their first claim.

5^{thly} Governor Wentworth is pleased to say "I have extended the Western boundary of New Hampshire as far West as the Massachusetts Bay have done theirs, that is within twenty miles of Hudsons River" on which we beg leave to observe that his having done so, after being informed of the boundaries of this province by the minutes of Council of the 3^d of April 1750 before mentioned and by the minutes of June 5th 1750 that the Massachusetts settlements Westward of those boundaries were made by intrusion is very extraordinary, and we are further of opinion, that the intrusions of the Massachusetts Bay within this province could be no good reason for Governor Wentworth to commit the like.

6^{thly} We apprehend that New Hampshire has no concern with the Northern Boundaryes of New York because we conceive that the North two degrees west line the Eastern boundary of New Hampshire, will (if M^r. Popples large map be right) intersect Connecticutt river, the Eastern boundary of this province and if so then New Hampshire is bounded to the West and North by Connecticutt river.

7^{thly} Governor Wentworth has been greatly misinformed the patents made by the Crown to the Duke of York, Viz: of March the 12th 1663–4 and June 29th 1674, both which do grant him in ffee all that Island or Islands commonly called by the severall name or names of Matawacks or Long Island situate and being towards the west end of Cape Codd and the Narrow Higgansetts abutting upon the main Land between the two rivers, then called or known by the severall names of Connecticutt and Hudsons river Together also with the river called Hudsons river and all the the land from the west side of Connecticutt river to the East side of Delaware Bay" and there is nothing in either of those patents (which are all we ever heard of) that would give the least colour or ground for Governor Wentworth's suggestion, that the Dukes grant commences at the Sea, and runs only sixty miles north into the Country; and was that grant such as M^r. Wentworth imagines it to be, the North bounds of it would cross Hudsons river above 100 miles South or below Albany instead of twenty as he supposes, for Albany is 150 miles distant from the City of New York and New York about twenty miles from the Sea.

Upon the whole Sir, we humbly conceive it is highly necessary that the representation, and copys of the necessary papers referred to therein, should be laid before the Lords Commissioners for Trade and Plantations; that their Lordships may be informed of the objections which we conceive may with good reason be made to the Line Governor Wentworth points out, to be fixed as the division Line, between this and the

province of New Hampshire, which papers together
with this our representation, we present to your honor
and humbly pray you will be pleased to transmit the
same to their Lordships.
              By Order of the Committee
                    JOHN CHAMBERS Chairman
              By Order of the Commissioners,
                    PAUL RICHARD Chairman
City of New York
  14ᵗʰ Nov. 1753

                    White Hall Decemᵇ 22ᵈ 1752.
      SIR :—I am directed by the Lords Commissioners for
Trade and Plantations to send you the inclosed extract
of Mʳ Wentworth's letter to their Lordships containing
his proposals for running a boundary line between the
Provinces of New York and New Hampshire and to
desire that you would transmit the same to your con·
stituents by the first opportunity, that their Lordships
may be informed of their sentiments upon it as soon as
possible. I am
              Sir Your most humble servant,
                          THOˢ HILL
ROBERT CHARLES Esqʳ Agent
  for the Province of New York

[Nᵒ 179.] At a Council held at Fort George in the
    City of New York on Friday the 21ˢᵗ of October
    1768
              His Excellency Sir Henry Moore Bart Capt
              Genˡ.
              Mʳ Watts   Mʳ Morris
              Mʳ Reade   Mʳ Cruger

      His Excellency communicated to the Board a letter
to him of the 13ᵗʰ of August last from the Earl of Hillsborough his Majestys principal Secretary of State from
the Colonies with sundry papers inclosed and referred to

therein all which being read, were ordered to be entered on the Minutes and are as follows:

Whitehall 13th of Augt 1768.

Sɪʀ:—On the 18th July I received your letter to me N° 11 acquainting me with your intention of setting out the next day after after the date of it for the Mohawk Country: and I shall be happy to hear that your journey has proved as agreeable to yourself as I dare say it will have been beneficial to the public.

I have only in command from his Majesty to send you the inclosed order of his Majesty in council confirming the boundary Line between New York and Quebec, as agreed upon and fixed by yourself and Governor Carlton for the due execution of which order under the general limitations and restrictions contained in it his Majesty has the fullest reliance on you for, and attention to his service.

Some doubts having occured to the Lords of Trade whether the two last acts passed in New York for making provision for quartering his Majestys Troops: were such a compliance with the British Act of Parliament as to give validity to the subsequent acts and proceedings of the Legislature there, under the restrictions of the act of Parliament of the 7th of the King their Lordships thought fit to make a report to his Majesty thereupon.

This Report has since been referred to his Majesty's Attorney and Solicitor General for their opinions upon the question agitated by the Board of Trade, and they having reported that they are of opinion the Act of Assembly passed in New York in June 1767 is such a compliance with the act of Parliament of the seventh year of his Majestys reign as leaves the validity of the acts and proceedings of the Legislature of the Colony subsequent to the 1st of Oct. 1767. subject to no objection on that account, I herewith inclose to you a copy of his Matyse order in Council thereupon directing the Lords Commissioners for Trade and Plantations to proceed in the consideration of the other laws passed in that province and make their representation thereupon to his Majesty in Council in the usual and accustomed manner. I am your most Obt, humble Serv't

HILLSBOROUGH

At a Court at St James's the 12th day of Augt 1768.

Duke of Grafton	Viscount Falmouth
Duke of Rutland	Viscount Barrington
Duke of Queensberry	Viscount Villiers
Marq^{es} of Granby	Lord North
Earl of Litchfield	Jam^s Stuart Mackenzie Esqr
Earl of Hillsborough	Thos Harley Esqr
Earl of Shelburne	Sir Edwd Hawke.
Viscount Weymouth	

Whereas there was this day read at the Board a report from the right Honorable the Lords of the Committee of Council for Plantation affairs dated the 9th of this instant upon considering a report made by the Lords Commissioners for Trade and Plantations upon an Extract of a letter from Sir Henry Moore Governor of New York to the Earl of Shelburne dated the 16th of January last, relative to the Settling the Boundary line between that province and Quebec. By which report it appears, that it having been mutually agreed upon between Sir Henry Moore and the Commander in Chief of the province of Quebec at a meeting for that purpose appointed that the Line of Division between these provinces should be fixed at the forty fifth Degree of North Latitude, conformable to the limits laid down in his Majestys Proclamation of October 1763, and it having been ascertained and determined by proper observations where the said line would pass; it is therefore proposed that those proceedings above stated should be confirmed by his Majesty. His Majesty taking the said report into consideration was pleased with the advice of his privy council to approve thereof and doth hereby confirm the said proceedings above stated and order that the said line of division be run out and continued as far as each province respectively extends. Provided that nothing herein contained shall extend to affect the properties of His Majesty's new subjects having possession under proper Titles on those parts of the lands on the South side of this line, the Dominion of which was not disputed on the part of the Crown of Great Britain and provided also that this determination shall not operate wholly to deprive His Majestys new subjects of such concessions on the south side of the said line, on which they may have made actual settlements and improvements although the lands may have been disputed by the Crown of Great Britain, but that such possessors shall be entitled to so much of the said concessions as shall be proportioned to their improvement, at the rate of fifty acres for every three of improvement provided they take out Grants for the same under the Seal of the province of New York subject to the usual Quit rents and provided also that the Grant to no one person shall exceed twenty thousand acres, and the Governor or Commander in Chief of his Majestys said provinces of New York and Quebec for the time being and all other whom it may concern are to take notice of his Majestys pleasure hereby signifyed and govern themselves accordingly.

STEPH. COTTRELL.

[N⁰ 180.]　At a Council held at Fort George in New York September the 14ᵗʰ 1727.
Present
His Excellency William Burnet, Esqʳ

| Captain Walter | Mʳ Harrison | Mʳ Alexander |
| Mʳ Van Dam | Mʳ Barbarie | Mʳ Kennedy |

His Excellency communicated to this Board his last advices from Albany that the six nations of Indians have agreed to defend the house at Oswego and to warn all the Indians in Canada and other farr Indians not to attempt any thing against the said house.

[N° 181.] At a Council held at Fort George in New York November 1ˢᵗ 1727.
Present
His Excellency Wᵐ Burnet Esqr.

| Mʳ Van Dam | Doctor Colden | Mʳ P. Livingston |
| Mʳ Harrison | Mʳ Alexander | Mʳ Kennedy. |

His Excellency laid before the Board the following accounts.

Mʳ P. Livingston account for Sundrys delivered Capt Philip Schuyler for presents to the Indians at Onnondage amounting to	£42	0 0
Mʳ Stephen Groesbecks to ditto for like service	30	0 0
Laurence Clausen's account for services in the Indian Country	31	19 0
To ditto for his services with Messʳˢ Philip & Peter Schuyler	15	0 0

Ordered that warrants be prepared for paying the said accounts out of the dutys arising on Indian goods by virtue of an act passed June 1726.

Ordered that warrants be prepared for paying Joseph Vansice the sum of £20 for his services as smith in the Sinnekes Country pursuant to the minute; of the Board of the 27ᵗʰ of October 1726, out of the moneys appropriated for Indian Services. It is likewise Ordered that a warrant be prepared for paying Joseph Clement £22. 2. 6 for repairing the Fort at Fort Hunter out of the moneys appropriated by fines and forfeitures.

[N° 182.] At a Council held at Fort George in New York November 11ᵗʰ 1727.
Present
His Excellency William Burnet Esqr.

| Mʳ Barbarie, | Doctor Colden | Mʳ Alexander, |
| Mʳ Philip Livingston, | | Mʳ Kennedy |

The following warrants for Indian Services after
being read were signed by his Excellency.

To Philip Livingston . . .	£42	0	0
To Stephanus Groesbeck . . .	30	0	0
To Laurence Clausen . . .	46	19	0
To Joseph Vansice	20	0	0
To Joseph Clement	22	2	6
	£161	1	6

Post Meridiem, Present as before.

Ordered that warrants be prepared for paying the
following sums out of the dutys arising on Indian goods
by virtue of an act passed June 1726.

To Philip Schuyler in full of his account of thirty six pounds six shillings for his journey and services in trading with the Indians at Onnondage.	£31	6	0
To Peter Schuyler in full of his account for the like Service	30	0	0
To Guysbert Van Cickel and William Reader for their journey to Onnondage	7	4	0
To Myndert Schuyler for goods sent to Captain Bancker at Oswego by order of the Commissioners of Indian affairs	10	4	6
To Stephen Groesbeck for goods sent to ditto	19	15	0
To Hermanus Wendell for goods sent to ditto	9	7	6

[N⁰ 183.]   At a Council held at Fort George in New
            York June the 25ᵗʰ 1728.
Present.
      His Excellency John Montgomerie Esqr
Capt Walter   Mʳ Clarke   Mʳ Kennedy.
Mʳ Van Dam   Mʳ Alexander,

The following warrants after being read were signed by his Ex. viz.,

617. To his Excell[y] for presents to the
     Indians and to defray the charges of
     his Expedition to Albany.   £400   0   0
631. To Laurence Clausen, Indian Inter-
   ' preter   15   0   0
632. To the Com[rs] of Indian affairs at
     Albany.   200   0   0

In Book A of Warrants of Survey Indian purchases and other entries began March 1st 1721 ending—is contained as follows:
Signed GEORGE R.

George the Second by the Grace of God King of Great Brittain France and Ireland defender of the faith &c. To our Trusty and well beloved Philip Livingston Gen[t] Greeting we reposing especial trust and confidence in your Loyalty ffidelity and ability do by these presents constitute and appoint you to be our Town Clerk. Clerk of the Peace, and Clerk of the Common Pleas in our County and City of Albany within our Province of New York in America with all the usual fees perquisites advantages and salarys thereunto belonging, and to be Secretary or Agent for the Government of New York to the Indians, our subjects in those parts, with the annual sallary or Fee of one hundred pounds sterling payable Quarterly at the four most usual Feasts or days of payment in the year, out of our revenue of New York. To Hold, Exercise and Enjoy the said respective office or employments by yourself or your sufficient deputy or Deputies with the usual respective Fees sallarys, perquisites and advantages during our pleasure and we do command our Governor or Commander in Chief and Council of our said Province of New York for the time being to give Effectual orders that the said salary of one hundred pounds sterling per annum and the other salarys, fees and perquisites to the aforementioned offices belonging be duly payed and satisfyed to you according to our will and pleasure herein declared. Given at our Court of St James's the twenty ninth day of Febuary 1727/8, in the first year of our reign.

By his Majestys Command.

HOLLES, NEWCASTLE.

PHILIP LIVINGSTON Town Clerk &c at New York.

[N°. 184.] At a Council held at Fort George in New York June the 27ᵗʰ 1729:

Present

His Excellency John Montgomerie Esqr

Mʳ Van Dam   Mʳ Harrison   Mʳ Morris
Mʳ Clarke   Mʳ Alexander   Mʳ Wᵐ Provoost.

The following warrants after being read were signed by his Excellency.

N°. 21. for presents to the Indians and
  his expedition to Albany to meet the
  sᵈ Indians   £550   1   1
31. To the Indian Interpreter   17   11   1
32. To the Comrs of Indian affairs for
  this year   211   11   1

[N°. 185.] At a Council held at the Council chamber in the City of New York the 27 March 1744.

Present

His Excellency the Governor

Mʳ Kennedy   Mʳ Cortlandt
Mʳ Chief Justice Mʳ Lane   Mʳ Horsmanden

The following quarterly warrants having been read as usual were signed by his Excellency.

N° 520. To the Indian Interpreter   £22 10 0

[N°. 186.] At a Council held at the Council Chamber in the City of New York 11 May 1744

Present

His Excellency the Honᵗ George Clinton Esqʳ
The same Genᵗ as before.

The following Warrants having been read as usual were signed by his Excell.ʸ

N.ᵒ 537. To his Excellency for presents to be made to the Indians for two years from the 13ᵗʰ June next 1742 to the 13th of June next. £800 0 0

N.ᵒ 528. To ditto for his voyage and expences in going to Albany 150 0 0

[N.ᵒ 187.] At a Council held at his Excellencys House in Albany the 14ᵗʰ June 1744.

Present

His Excellency the Hon.ˡᵉ George Clinton
Philip Livingston   Daniel Horsmanden⁴
James De Lancey   Joseph Murray

Answer made by the Sachims of the Six Nations Viz. the Mohawks, Oneydes, Onondages, Tuskarores, Cayouges and Sennekes To his Excellency George Clinton Esqʳ Governor and Commander in Chief of the Province of New York &c at the City of Albany the 20ᵗʰ June 1744.

Brother Corlaer and Quider:—You spake to us lately & we promised to give you an answer which we now come to do, we have well understood what you have said but cannot repeat it all as you spoke it to us, but we will however answer every article. You told us that you was very glad to see us here to renew and strengthen the ancient Covenant Chain made between our Forefathers and that you had express orders from our Father your Master the Great King to renew and strengthen the same which you have accordingly done on your part, we the six Nations do now also on our part, renew, strengthen and brighten the same Covenant Chain which we will keep so as long as the Sun endures we will preserve it so strong and bright that it shall not be in the power of the Devil himself with any of his wiles and arts to break or dirty the same. Gave a belt of Wampum.

Brother:—You told us that the Great King our Father had sent an Army into Germany which was treacherously attacked by the French, but that our Great King defeated the ffrench army killed some, some were drowned in a river and the remainder fled and that afterwards the ffrench joyned their ships with those of the Spaniards to attack the ships of the Great King our father but were again defeated and that the French were then not yet contented but proclaimed warr against our Father the Great King which our King did also against them and that it has also been declared in this place a few days ago.

We the Six Nations have well understood what you have said concerning the warr, we cannot answer to every particular but do promise that we will keep all our people at home and then expect orders from our Brother and we will be upon our Guard to watch against the Enemy and we answer our Brother in General that we will do all things relating to this warr as you have desired as whereupon we give this Belt.

Brother:—We just now told you that we would do as you desired us. We do yet well remember that we went with you to assist you against the French in the Expedition against Canada—

We look upon ourselves to be a warr like people and never entered into a Warr with any Nation but in the end we have got the better of them but yet we are inclined to peace till the Enemy attack some of his Majestys Subjects and then we will joyn together to defend ourselves against them. Gave a Belt.

Brother:—Concerning the house at Oswego you told us that you expected we would assist in defending it against the Enemy. You also told us that you thought that house very beneficial to us as it supplys us with goods we have thought proper at this time to say some thing concerning the Trade the first year or two after that house was Built goods were Cheap and it was a pleasure to Trade there, but now Goods are sold so dear at that place that we cannot say we think it advantageous to us upon the account of Trade. We would now desire of our Brother that Goods may again be at the same rate as the first two years.

The Commanding officer who is now at Oswego we desire of our Brother that he may stay there we like him better than any other.

We are thankfull that you have sent Cannon to Oswego to defend that place against the enemy.

Brother:—It has always been customary to recommend to us to keep up a correspondence with the farr Nations which has at this time not been done. However we will do all we can to keep friendship with those Nations who are united with us and then we can overcome any Enemy whatsoever. Gave a Belt.

Brother:—You remind us of the promise that Cayouges and the Sennekes made two years ago to remove their Castles and to settle in a Body and you told us how necessary this is Especially at this time of warr of which we are convinced we do now acquaint you that we are busy to do as was promised and the Oneydas also promise to gather together their people and to settle in a Body. Gave a Belt.

Brother:—You also desired that we should not suffer any ffrench to reside amongst us and that if any came into our Country we should either banish them or deliver them to the officer at Oswego we have just now told you that we are inclined to peace and will expect the attacks of the enemy and should we now take hold of any French that come among, we should be the aggressors wherefore we leave it to you to do with the French that may come unto our Country as you shall think proper. Gave half a Belt.

[N.º 187.] At a Council held at Greenwich the 13th day of September 1744.

Present

His Excellency the Governor.

Doctor Colden	M.ʳ Kennedy	M.ʳ Horsmanden
M.ʳ Livingston	M.ʳ Cortlandt	M.ʳ Murray.
	M.ʳ Chief Justice	

33

The following Quarterly and other warrants having been read as usual were signed by his Excellency

N° 549. To the Comm^rs for Indian affairs
for one year ending y° first instant
170£ for extraordinary Incidents y°
further sum of 30£   £200   0   0
551 To the Indian Interpreter for his Q^rs
sallary ending the first instant   22   10   0

[N° 188.] At a Council held in the Council Chamber in the City of New York the fifth day of March 1744.
Present
       His Excellency the Hon! George Clinton Esqr.
   M^r. Kennedy   M^r. Cortlandt   M^r. Moore
   M^r. Chief Justice   M^r. Horsmanden

The following Warrants having been read as usual were signed by his Excellency, Viz.

N° 588. To the Indian Interpreter.   £22   10   0

[N° 189.] At a Council held at the Council Chamber in the City of New York the 6th day June, 1745.
Present as before.
The following Quarterly warrants having been read as usual were signed by his Excellency.

N° 599. To the Indian Interpreter.   £22   10   0

[N° 190.] At a Council held at the Council Chamber in the City of New York the 14th day of June 1745.
Present as before except M^r. Horsmanden.
The following war^ts having been read were signed by his Excellency.

N° 605. To his Excell^y for his Voyage to
      Albany   £150   0   0

[N° 191] At a Council held at the Council Chamber in the City of New York the 6th day of July 1745.

Present

His Excellency the Honble George Clinton
Mr Colden   Mr Chief Justice   Mr Horsmanden
Mr Kennedy . Mr Cortlandt   Mr Murray
Mr Moore

The following warrants having been read as usual were signed by his Excellency Viz.

N° 607. To Messrs Johan Joost Herkinan
and Garrit A Lansingh for the second
half year of the first years contract
for victualling the Oswego Troops
ending the first day of March last   £228 0 0
608. To do for the first half year of the
second years contract   228 0 0
609. To the persons who have resided in
the Sennekes Country for their services from the first of September 1743
to the time of their leaving the said
place   40 0 0

[N° 192.] At a Council held at the City of New
York the third day of September 1745
Present as before except Mr Colden and Mr Chief Justice

The following warrant having been read was signed by his Excellency.
610. To his Ex. the Gov^or for presents to
the Indians for one year from the 13th
June 1744 to the 13th June last.   £400 0 0

[N° 193.] At a Council held at his Excellencys residence in the City of Albany October the 6th 1745
Present

His Excellency the Honble George Clinton
Mr Livingston   Mr Murray
Mr Horsmanden   Capt Rutherford

The Commissioners from the respective Governments of the Massachusetts Bay, Connecticutt and Pen-

silvania having attended his Excellency and produced
to him their credentials from their respective Governm^{ts}
viz. John Stoddard, Jacob Wendell, Samuel Welles
Thomas Hutchinson Esq^{rs} for the Province of Massachusetts Bay, Roger Wolcott Esqr Deputy Governour of the
Colony of Connecticutt, & Coll Stanley Comm^{rs} for the
said Colony; and Thomas Laurence, John Kinsey and
Isaac Norris Esq^{rs} for the Province of Pensylvania, which
credentials were severally laid before the Council.

His Excellency thought proper to appoint two Gentlemen of the Council to confer with the s^d Commissioners touching such matters as should be thought proper
for his Excell^y to offer in his speech to the six nations
of Indians at the publick Interview, and the manner in
which the same should be conducted and was pleased to
nominate Mr Horsmanden & Mr Murray a committee
for that purpose.

Ordered that it be an instruction to the said committee to enquire privately into the causes of the uneasiness amongst the Maquas the last Winter and touching all complaints they may have to make to his Excellency and to report the same.

Read some heads drawn up by the Commissioners
of Indian affairs pursuant to his Excellency's directions
touching what to be proposed to the Indians at the conference.

[N° 194.] At a Conference between the Committee of
the Council and the Commis^{rs} from the neighbouring Governm^{ts} had at Albany the 7th day of October 1745.

Present

Daniel Horsmanden } Esq^s Members of the
Joseph Murray   }   Council of New York.

John Stoddard   }
Jacob Wendell   } Esq^{rs} Comm^{rs} from the Province
Samuel Wells   }   of the Massachusetts Bay
Thomas Hutchinson }

Roger Woolcot   } Esq^{rs} Comm^{rs} from the
Nathaniel Stanley }   Colony of Connecticut

Thomas Laurence } Esq^{rs} Comm^{rs} from
John Kinsey } Pensylvania
Isaac Morris }

The Heads of matter proposed to be offered in his Excelly^s Speech to the six nations at the publick conference prepared by the Comm^{rs} of Indians affairs at Albany : read.

It was moved by the Council of New York whether it was not most adviseable for his Excell^y to speak to the Indians in General, on behalf of the several Comm^{rs} for the other Governm^{ts} now convened here, as well as for this province, For that this method would tend to shew the Indians the happy agreement and union of the several Governments, and their resolution for carrying on the warr in conjunction, and unitedly to support and prosecute the Interest and common cause of all, which might have a very good effect with them, they well knowing the strength and abilitys of these several Colonys whose united force they must esteem sufficient to strike a terror into the enemy ; and if the Indians should be wavering in their Intentions with regard to what part they shall take in the warr at this time between the English and French, they may, from the apprehension of such an union be determined to join with us as the strongest side.

With their sentiments the Comm^{rs} of the Massachusetts & Connecticut entirely concurred, and in general, the Comm^{rs} for Pensylvania, but a majority of the latter intimated that as they were aware that considering the present circumstances of affairs with respect to the warr, something would probably be said by his Excell^y to the Indians upon that occasion, which would not alltogether be agreeable to their religious sentiments: They therefore should choose to speak separately, and though they do so they would be carefull to pursue the main intention of this interview, by avoiding to say any thing which may clash or interfere with what his Excellency should say to them, but the rather to inforce and give aid to it, by observing to them the union of

these several Colonys, and their strength as subjects of
the same prince, who would resent any Injury done to
any one of them as done to the whole. Moreover, That
what they should say, concerning the General Interest,
they would previously, lay before his Excell'. And
further that they had at this time some matters of private concern, relative only to the Province of Pensylvania, which they had to discourse with the six nations,
which made it necessary for those comm^rs to speak with
them separately. As that part of the Heads of His
Excelly's speech prepared by the Comm^rs of Indian affairs, which proposed, (after informing the six nations
of the Infraction of the Treaty of neutrality concluded
between them and the ffrench Indians, with regard to
the present warr, by Hostilitys lately committed by the
last mentioned Indians, by murdering several of his
Majestys subjects on the borders of New England) that
the Hatchet should be offered to the six nations to
strike ag^st the French and their Indians upon his
Excelly's commands signified to them for that purpose,
in case that the six nations could not obtain satisfaction
from those French Indians concerned in the said Hostilitys, and reasonable assurances of their observing in-
voiliable the neutrality for the future, it was thereupon
observed by the Massachusetts Comm^rs that the six nations had in effect accepted of the Hatchet by the last
treaty, upon condition to strike with it against the
French and their Indians in case of any infraction made
by them of the neutrality. And since Hostility's had
been committed by them, the six nations were bound
by that treaty to join immediately in the war with us
against the French and their Indians; and therefore if
the six nations were inclined rather in the first place to
interpose their endeavours to obtain satisfaction for their
Breach, and assurances from the Indians offending in
this Instance of their preserving inviolably a strict neutrality for the future—this was matter which (as the
case stood) would come more properly from the six
nations themselves; which reasoning being allowed to
be just, It was agreed t'wou'd be more proper that his

Excellency should propose to the six nations to take up the Hatchet absolutely and to let the condition be offered by the Indians in their answer.

And agreeable thereto his Excellency's speech was framed.

Answer of the six nations (except the Sinnekes who are absent) To his Excellency George Clinton Esq' Governor in Chief of the Province of New York &c and the Commissioners of the Colonys of the Massachusetts Bay, Pennsylvania & Connecticut at Albany the 12 day of October 1745.

Brother Corlear and Brethren of the Massachusetts Bay, Pensylvania & Connecticut.

1) Two days ago our Brother Corlear and our Brethren of the Massachusets Bay and Connecticut spoke to us & now we are come to give our answer. You must not expect that we can answer exactly to the several Heads you mentioned to us but only to the principal Articles, You have renewed the old Covenant Chain, and we do now renew the same on our parts, It is impossible it can ever rust for we daily wipe off the Dirt and keep it clean, which we will ever continue to do. A belt of Wampum.

2) You thought fit to mention to us that there had been an uproar among us last winter, and told us that we ought not to entertain any such notions of you our Brethren, especially as we had no grounds for any such belief. It is true Brethren such a rumour was among us, but it was immediately buried and forgot. And we did not expect that our Brethren would have mentioned any thing concerning that affair to us at this Interview. And we desire you to think no more of it: We are always mindful of the Covenant between us and our Brethren and here is a certificate * to prove that we are

* A certificate dated 1st of August 1744 delivered by Hendrick with the string of Wampum upon this Article under the hand of Governor Shirley, and the Seal of the Province of the Massachusts Bay, signifying, That Hendrick Sachim of the Maquas and, Kajenwarygoa Sachim of the Onondages Delegates from the eight nations arrived at Boston 22 June 1744, had at several conferences with Governor Council and Assembly confirmed the Treatys made with that Government and particularly the last summer at Albany, and have proceeded on a Voyage and had

in Covenant with our Brethren of Boston. A string of Wampum.

Brother Corlear and Brethren of the Massachusets Bay, and Connecticut.

3) You spoke to us concerning our going to Canada this summer and told us that the Commissioners of Indian Affairs had last winter enjoyned us not to go there. But some of us went. As to what you tell us that we had taken a belt from the Governor of Canada whereby he desires us to take up the Hatchet agains you our Brethren, and that we promised him to consider of it at home:—It is not so, all that passed there the Mohawks and Tuskaroras have given the Com^{rs} of Indian Affairs an account of at their return and we are convinced that that acco^t is true, Brethren. A Belt of Wampum.

4) You have thought fit to relate to us several particulars concerning the war between you and the French, and what reason you had for taking up that Hatchet against the French and their Indians. We thank you for giving us a particular account of the provocations and Inducements you had for declaring war against them. You also mentioned to us that we are one body and one Flesh and that if one of us is touched or Hurt then the other is so likewise. And you informed us that you are molested and attacked by the enemy, and had therefore taken up the Hatchet agst them and desired, as we are one Flesh with you, that we would also take up the Hatchet agst the French and those Indian under their influence, in conjunction with you, we the six nations accept of the Hatchet, and will keep it in our Bosom. We are in alliance with a great number of far Indians, and if we should so suddenly lift up the Hatchet without acquainting our allies with it they would perhaps take offence at it. We will therefore before we make use of the Hatchet agst the French or their Indians send four of our people (who are now

an interview with the Eastern Indians, and faithfully acquitted themselves in enjoyning them to maintain peace with the English and warning them of the consequences of their violating the same.

ready to go) to Canada to demand satisfaction for the
wrongs they have done our Brethren and if they refuse
to make satisfaction then we shall be ready to use the
Hatchet against them *whenever our Brother the Governor of New York orders us to do it.* A Belt of Wampum.

[His Excellency asked them, what time they thought
necessary to try whether the French Indians would make
satisfaction. The Indians answered, two months. His
Excellency asked them that if in case the enemy should
commit any further Hostilitys in the mean time—
Whether they would then *upon his Excellencys commands immediately make use of the Hatchet?* *they
answered yes.* Here the Indians requested his Excellency that as they had given the war shout upon delivering the Hatchet to them, that their Brethren would
now signify their approbation of this Article in their usual
method. Whereupon his Excelly. and most of the
Company joined in shouts with three Huzzas, excepting
the Massachusets Commissioners.]

Brethren

5) You desired us that we should gather togth our
people who are scattered, and settle in a body especially
as it is very uncertain how soon we may have occasion
for them. Your request is very reasonable and we will
use our endeavours for that end. A Belt of Wampum.

Brethren

6) We have now finished our answer and have
nothing further to say, but only one request to make to
you all, which is, that you our Brethren should be all
united in your Councils and let this Belt of Wampum
serve to bring you together. And if any of you have
any thing of Importance to communicate to us, this is
the place where it should be done. A Belt of Wampum.

[Here a note of approbation was given by the Interpreter by his Excelly^s directions for New York Connecticut and Pensylvania.]

Brethren,

7) Trade was the first occasion of our entering into
alliance together, and from time to time goods have
been sold dearer to us, and we have several times ad-

viscd that the price of goods should be lower and more
moderate, but could never get a satisfactory answer.
And now we take this oppertunity to desire our Brother
Corlaer himself and the Comm^rs of the several Provinces
to take it into their consideration that Goods may be
sold cheaper to us.   For how shall we doe now we
have taken up the Hatchet?   We have no powder Ball
nor clothes.   People that go to war ought to be well
provided with ammunition, this is the last time that we
shall speak upon this Head, if we do not succeed now.
A Belt.

His Excellency answered them, that he would do
his utmost that Goods should be sold them as cheap as
they could be afforded.   But that the price of Goods
depended upon the scarcity or Plenty of them and as it
is now war Goods are scarce and consequently dear and
that they shall be furnished with Powder & ammunition upon occasion

[N? 195.] At a Council held at Fort George in the City
      of New York the 24th day of March 1751.
Present
            His Excellency the Hon^le George Clinton &c
            Mr Kennedy   Mr Rutherford
            Mr Chief Justice   Mr Holland

A letter of the 15th Instant from Governor Hamilton (of Pensylvania) advising that the Assembly of that
Government have altogether declined having any thing
to do in the Treaty at Albany as appeared by their
Message in closed which with the letter was read.   And
Mr Hamilton having desired permission of Mr Weiser
to deliver to the six nations at Albany a Message of
Condolence accompanied with a small present of £100
value on the death of Canasatego and some other of their
principle Sachims.   The Council advised his Excellency to signify to Mr Hamilton his approbation of the
said Message and presents being delivered by Mr Weiser
provided nothing be said to the Indians but what shall
be previously communicated and agreed to by his Excelly.

[N°. 196.] The Confirmation of Mr Jeremias Renzlaers Authority and Priviledges in Renzlaerswick.*

By Virtue of my Commission from his Royall Highnesse James Duke of Yorke and Albany, I doe by thes presents Order and appoint, That Mr Jeremias Renzluer shall and may Lawfully Enjoy and Execute all such priviledges and Authority within the Limits of Renslures-wicke, as hee did enjoy and Execute before the Surrender of New Yorke into his Maj^{ties} Obedience; And I do further declare, That all persons in the said Colony of Renslures-wicke shall have and enjoy the benefitt of the Articles made and Agreed upon at the Surrender of New Yorke as fully and effectually as if the said Colony had beene expressly mentioned therein, Provided alwayes, that within the space of one Yeare after the date hereof, the said Jeremias Renzluer doe procure a distict Pattent for the Colony from his Royall Highnesse, and in the meane time, that all the Inhabitants shall take the Oath to his Matie and the present Governm^t; Given under my hand and Seale at ffort James in New Yorke on the Island of Manhatans this 18th day of October 1664.

RICHARD NICOLLS.

[N°. 197.] James Duke of Yorke &c Albany Earle of Ulster &c

Whereas it hath pleased the King^s most excellent Ma^{ty} my Sovereigne Lord and Brother, by his letters Patents to give and Grant unto me and to my heirs and assignes all that part of the main Land of New England beginning at a certain place called or known by the name of St Croix next adjoining New Scotland in America and from thence extending along the Sea Coast unto a certain place called Petuaquin or Pemaquid and so up the river thereof to the furthest head of the same as it Tendeth Northwards, and extending from thence to the river of Kinebequi and so upwards by the shortest course of ye river Canada Northwards

[* These priviledges and authority were renewed and confirmed " till further order " by Governor Nicolls, on the 12th October, 1665.]

and also all that Island or Islands commonly called by the severall name or names of Matowacks or Long Island situate lying and being towards the West of Cape Cod, and the Narrow Higansetts abutting upon the main Land, between the two rivers there, called or known by y.ᵉ several names of Connecticut and Hudsons rivers. Together also with the said river called Hudsons river and all the Land from the West side of Connecticut river, to the East side of Delaware Bay : and also all those severall Islands called or known by the name of Martins Vinyard and Nantukes otherwise Nantukett, together with all the Lands, Islands, Soils, rivers, Harbours, Mines, Minerals, Quarrys, woods, Marshes, Waters, Lakes, Fishings, Hawkings, Hunting, and fowling and all other Royaltys and Proffits, Comoditys and Hereditamˢ, to the said severall Islands Lands and Premisses belonging and Appertaining their and every of their Appurtenances. To Hold the same to my own proper use and behoofe, with power to correct, punish, pardon, governe, and rule the Inhabitants thereof by myself, or such Deputyes, Commissioners or Officers as I shall think fitt to appoint, as by his Majᵗˢ said Letters Patents may more fully appear ; And Whereas I have conceived a Good opinion of the Integrity prudence, Ability and fitness of Major Edmund Andros, to be imployed as my Lieutenant there, I have therefore thought fitt to constitute and appoint him the said Major Edmund Andros, to be my Lieutenant and Governour, within the Lands, Islands and places aforesaid to performe and execute all and every the powers which are by the said letters patent Graunted unto mee, to be executed by me, my Deputy, Agents or assignes. To have and to hold the said place of Lieutenant and Governᵣ unto him the said Edmund Andros Esqᵣ but during my will & pleasure Only hereby willing and requiring all, and every the Inhabitants of the said Lands, Islands, and places, to give Obedience unto him the said Edmund Andros Esqᵣ in all things according to his Maᵗⁱᵉˢ letters patent &c. the said E. Andros Esqᵣ to observe, follow and execute such orders and Directions as he shall from time to time receive from myself. Given under my hand, and Seal at Windsor this first day of July, 1674.

JAMES.

By Command of his Royal Highnesse GEO. WERDEN.

[N? 198.] At a Council at Fort George in New York March the 2ᵈ 1726|7.

Present

His Excellency William Burnet Esqrs.
Capt Walter   Mʳ Barbarie
Mʳ Van Dam   Mʳ Harrison
Mʳ Abrah Vanhorne,   Mʳ William Provoost
Doct Colden   Mʳ Alexander

His Excellency communicated to the Board the Paragraph of a letter from the Lieutenant Governour of Boston to his Excellency dated 9ᵗʰ of January last in answer to his Exˢ letter to the said Governor and the Petition of some of the Inhabitants of New York to his Ex. respecting the lands at Westenhook.

His Excellency likewise communicated to the Board the Resolutions of the Assembly of the Massachusets Bay thereupon in order to have the lines run between this Province and the Colony.

Whereupon it is the opinion of this Board that a copy of the said resolutions be sent to some of the Patentees of Westenhook residing at Albany in order for their observation thereupon.

[N? 199.] At a Council held at Fort George in New York April 13ᵗʰ 1727.

Present

His Excellency William Burnet Esqʳ
Capᵗ Walter,   Mʳ Barbarie   Mʳ Alexander
Mʳ Van Dam   Mʳ Harrison   Mʳ Vanhorne,

Upon his Excellency laying before the Board the answer of the Pattentees of Westenhook to the resolutions of the Assembly of the Massachusetts Bay of the 23ᵈ of November last. transmitted to them the 2ᵈ of March with the minutes of this Board thereupon and the sᵈ Pattentees having not made any objections against the said Resolutions.

It is ordered by this Board that all persons concerned belonging to this Government be prohibited from making any further settlements near the dividing lines between the two Provinces, and that all actions already commenced against any of the people residing at Westenhook cease and that they be put to no further trouble in the law untill the further orders of this Government.

Ordered that the Patentees of Westenhook be served with a copy of this order.

It is the opinion of this Board that the settling the boundaries between the two provinces and naming Commissioners be deferred till the sitting of the Assembly of this Province that provision may be made for that service.

It is the desire of this Board that his Excellency, acquaint his honour the Lieutenant Governor of Boston that this Government has made the aforesaid order.

[N.º 200.] At a Council held at Fort George in New York September 30ᵗʰ 1727.

Mʳ Walter   Mʳ Harrison   Mʳ Vanhorne
Mʳ Van Dam   Mʳ Alexander   Mʳ Kennedy.

His Excellency sent the Deputy Secretary to the Assembly to acquaint that he was ready in the Council Chamber to Qualify them and that he desired their attendance Whereupon those that were in town came and took the Oaths appointed to be taken instead the Oaths of allegiance and supremacy and took and subscribed the Test and abjuration Oath and then His Excellency Recommended to them to return and choose a Speaker to be presented to him.

Then they returned and presented Adolph Philips Esqʳ their Speaker whom his Ex. was pleased to approve of.

Then his Excelly. made the following Speech.

Gentlemen :—The death of our late Sovereign of

ever glorious memory and the happy accession of his most Excellent Ma^{ty} have already, filled our hearts with all that dutifull subjects must feel upon so great an occasion and the choice which the People have at this time made of you to represent them, gives you an early opportunity of expressing their Loyal sentiments upon it.

You find that I have lost no time nor spared no expense in order to secure the five nations to the British Interest by making a settlement of some strength among them convenient for Trade with the far Indians as well as themselves and by supporting it in such a manner as I hope with your assistance will prevent any attempts against it. The Consequence of this undertaking cannot appear better than by the great uneasiness it has given to the French who seem apprehensive that their unjustifiable pretensions & Encroachments upon our Indians and their endeavours to engross the trade with all the far nations will be defeated by it. That they are under so much concern you will plainly see by the Governors of Canada summons to my Officer at Oswego to abandon it and by his Letter to me by the Governour of Trois Rivieres wherein he complains of the enterprise in the strongest terms which papers together with my answer I shall lay before you.

I cannot avoid observing to you that the fund provided by the last assembly for this service has not in any ways answered the greatness of the charge no even any part worth mentioning of what it was intended to produce so that the whole has been performed at my own expense or upon my private credit, and this burden I choose to take entirely upon myself rather than suffer the design to run the risque of being lost as it probably would do by the least delay, I have thus engaged myself upon a full Confidence that you would not fail to provide for the immediate discharge of a debt contracted for the Province when its safety required it in the most pressing manner. The particulars shall be laid before you as far as the accounts are completed—And I hope you will make a large allowance for what is not yet brought to account and make full provision of what shall be requisite for the next year to support and maintain this important Post.

I must remind you of the inconveniences which arise from the limits of the province being undetermined. This is not only a great discouragement to its being all peopled and improved but likewise a constant occasion of quarrels with our neighbours, our late agreement with the Government of Connecticut has indeed put a stop to them for the present on that side but unless you make Provision for compleating the lines to be run in consequence of it, which that Province has made repeated application to have done the mischiefs intended to be prevented by that agreement may possibly happen. You are no strangers to the difference which have subsisted for some years between the patentees of Westenhook and the Inhabitants of the Province of the Massachusetts Bay upon the application of those patentees. I have made an agreement with that Government to abstain on both sides from any new attempts till the line between that province & this shall be run and their Assembly has made a proposal to treat with the Government about those limits and have named Commissioners for that purpose.

I shall lay their resolves before you that you may take such measures on that head as you shall think expedient.

I, JOHN MORIN SCOTT, Secretary of the State of New York, do hereby certify that the aforegoing copies, from the first to the three hundred and sixty third page inclusive; have been by me carefully compared with their respective originals lodged in the Secretary's office of the State of New York and found compleatly to agree with the same. As Witness my hand and seal, at Philadelphia this 13th day of November in the year of our Lord one thousand seven hundred and eighty.

JNO. MORIN SCOTT.

INDEX.

INDEX.

Coursey, Henry, appointed Commissioner by Maryland authorities to treat with Northern Indians, 377 ; his mission noticed, 381.

Court of assizes, first session of, noticed, 76.

Court of Commissioners to settle boundaries of Massachusetts and Rhode Island. Extracts from their proceedings, 338, 365.

Cousseau, James, noticed, 333-336.

Cowdray, M. de, noticed, 50.

Cromwell Oliver, favored in Massachusetts, 86.

Culloden, seventy-four gun ship lost on Montauk Point, 227.

Cumberland County, noticed, 293, courts of Common Pleas and General Sessions of the Peace established in, 295.

Danby, Mr., goes to New Albion, 222.

Dawaganhaes, mentioned, 429. See Waganhaes.

Dayton, Ralph, messenger from East Hampton to Connecticut, 230 ; constable, 235.

Deane, Thomas, letter to the Earl of Clarendon, 68 ; his case noticed, 61, 68, 99, 113.

D'eaux, Chevalier, noticed, 414 ; his escape into Canada, 477.

De Decker, John, noticed, 336.

Dekanisore, noticed, 420, 421, 437.

Delancey, James, noticed, 338.

Delavall, Mr., noticed, 80.

Delaware settled by families from New England, 4 ; settlements broken up by Dutch and Swedes, 4 ; English of New Haven prove their claim to lands there, 6 ; their trade thither interrupted by Stuyvesant, 7 ; discovered and possessed by the English, 9 ; Dutch become masters of the whole river, 9 ; plunder taken at, 78 ; taken from the Swedes and annexed to New Netherland, 115 ; sold to the Burgomasters of Amsterdam, *ib.;* its exchange proposed for the patent of Berkeley and Carteret, 126.

Dellius, Rev. Godfrey, accused by resolution of the New York Assembly, and suspended from the ministry in Albany, 183 ; his case considered, 184 ; his services among the Indians, *ib.* ; noticed, 401 ; paid for maintenance of three Indian boys, 403 ; letter from, read in Council, 405.

Denonville, M., noticed, 174 ; letter to Governor Dongan read in Council, 389 ; translated by Judge Nicolls, 390 ; letter, mentioned, 391.

De Ruyter, rumor of his invasion, 74.

Dionondadies, remote Indians, noticed, 385 ; Dongan proposes treaty with, to the five nations, 386 ; noticed, 415.

Dongan, Thomas, Governor, noticed, 233, 241; his conference with the Maquas, 378 ; letter to the Governor of Canada respecting French encroachments, 383 ; addresses the Indians, 384 ; their

unless confirmed within a year by the Duke, 119.

Lawyer, an able, wanting in New England, 36.

Leete, Governor, noticed, 46.

Leisler, Jacob, his execution referred to, 204 ; difficulties arising from his proceedings, 246, 248.

Leverett, Captain, hinders the reduction of the Dutch, 11 ; agent in England, 24, 39 ; threatens to deliver New England to Spain, 24, 30 ; notice of his return to Massachusetts, 24, 30 ; noticed, 79.

Liberty of Conscience, not allowed in Massachusetts, 27, 30 ; in New York and Massachusetts, 208.

Light-house on Montauk Point, built by John McComb, 226.

Ligonia, the province of, noticed, 21.

Livingston, Robert, certifies the documents relating to the destruction of Schenectady, 172, 176 ; noticed, 390, 392 ; paid for rebuilding the Mohags fort, 403 ; his commission as Secretary or Agent to the Indians, 446 ; commission for his re-appointment, 453.

Livingston, Robert, Jr., journal and conference with the Indians at the Senecas' castle, 471.

Livingston, Philip, Secretary of Indian Affairs, 488 ; commission as Town Clerk, etc. of Albany, and Secretary of Indian Affairs in N. Y., 509.

Livingston, Robert, R., commissioner on part of N. Y. to settle boundary with Massachusetts, 319.

Lloyd, Thomas, Governor of Pennsylvania, noticed, 397.

Locke, John, his Two Treatises of Government quoted, 195.

Logan, James, Secretary of Pennsylvania, noticed, 468.

London, great fire in, noticed, 159.

Long Island, see Manati ; settlers alarmed by hostility of the Indians and Dutch, 11 ; Nicolls's account of, 75 ; production of tobacco in, 117 ; description of, 225 ; representation to Connecticut at the time of the revolution of 1688, 241.

Lovelace, Francis, Colonel, recommended by Samuel Maverick for employment in America, 32.

Lovelace, John, Lord, extract from his instructions, 458.

Ludwell, Thomas, his letters to the Earl of Clarendon, 120, 159.

Lusher, Major, noticed, 79.

Macgregore, Mrs. Margaret, widow of Major Hugh, noticed, 404.

Madagascar, New York trade with, 206.

Maid-stone, original name of East Hampton, 229.

Maine, inhabitants unwilling to remain under either Massachusetts or Gorges, 71, 73 ; Royal Commissioners appoint justices there, 71 ; various patents for the Territory, 72.

Mallebar, Cape, Dutch name of Cape Cod, 3.

Mairbour, M., and other French emissaries, noticed, 444.

Manati, Manitie, Long Isle, petition for grant of, 213 ; the commodities of, 214.

Manatos Island, reduction of the town upon, 58.

Manhattan, memoir concerning New Netherland or, 1.

Manhattans, its settlement noticed, 329.

Manitie, see Manati.

Manchannock, Indian name of Gardiner's Island, 261.

Mann, John, Surveyor-General of Jamaica, noticed, 43.

Map, of the Territory of Massachusetts, 84.

Manning, Captain John, recommended for employment in New England by Samuel Maverick, 57 ; noticed, 337.

Maquas Sachems, propositions of the, to the authorities at Albany, 165 ; answer upon their propositions by the authorities at Albany, 169.

Maquas Indians to be encouraged in their loyalty, 373 ; are N. Y. Indians and so to be acknowledged, 376 ; conference with Governor Dongan, 378 ; acknowledge the Duke's government, 381.

Marlborough, Earl of, noticed, 33, 34.

Mary, Queen, letter to the Governor of Pennsylvania to assist New York against the French, 400.

Maryland, dissent from Virginia in respect to planting, 108 ; sectaries and quakers there, 111 ; Indian hostilities in that province, 377 ; directed to aid New York against the French, 400.

Massachusetts, Book of Laws, 16 ; look on themselves as a free state, 17 ; the key of the Indies, 18 ; swallows up other patents, 21, 41 ; loyalty of the people in, 23 ; oath of allegiance not used in, 23 ; severity of the government there, 23 ; petition and address to the King, 25 ; violation of their Charter, 26 ; stubbornness of the, 73 ; Cartwright's account of, 82 ; just lim-

35

PUBLICATION FUND.

NEW-YORK HISTORICAL SOCIETY.

FOUNDED 1804.

THE PUBLICATION FUND.

THE NEW-YORK HISTORICAL SOCIETY has established a fund for the regular publication of its transactions and Collections in American History. Publication is very justly regarded as one of the main instruments of usefulness in such institutions, and the amount and value of what they contribute to the general sum of human knowledge through this agency, as a just criterion of their success.

To effect its object, the Society proposed to issue One Thousand Scrip shares of TWENTY-FIVE DOLLARS each. Each share is transferable on the books of the Fund, in the hands of the Treasurer, and entitles the holder, his heirs, administrators or assigns, to receive:

I. INTEREST—Until the Fund was complete, or sufficient, in the opinion of the Trustees, to enable the publications to commence without impairing the principal thereof, interest on the par value of his share or shares at the rate of five per cent. per annum.

II. PUBLICATIONS—One copy of each and every publication made at the expense of the Fund, amounting to not less that one Octavo Volume of five hundred pages per annum.

The number of copies of these publications is strictly limited to TWELVE HUNDRED and FIFTY—of which the Society receives for corresponding Societies and exchanges for the increase of the Library, TWO HUNDRED and FIFTY copies—but no copies are offered for sale or disposition in any other manner by the Society.

The conditions of subscription included a pledge on the part of the Society that the moneys received should be applied for these purposes, and no other, and be invested solely in stocks of the United States, the City and State of New York, or on bond and mortgage, and be held forever by the President, Recording Secretary, and Treasurer of the Society, as Trustees (ex officio) of the Publication Fund.

The first proposals for the establishment of this Fund were issued in 1858. Received with much less interest on the part of the members than was expected, its total amount up to 1865 was so small as to suggest the necessity of abandoning the scheme and returning the amount of subscriptions and interest to the subscribers. An earnest effort however in that year brought up the amount to a point which gave the assurance of ultimate and not distant success.

Admonished by the universal change of values, which has taken place within the past few years, and the necessity of increasing the amount of the Fund, the Society determined to terminate the issue of shares at the original price, and to double the price of the remaining shares. Other measures are in view which promise to enhance the value of the shares without failure in the full discharge of every obligation to the shareholders, who will receive all its benefits without any additional contribution to the increased Fund.

Under the authority and direction of the Executive Committee, the series of publications began with the volume for the last year, 1868.

Interest still due upon any shares to January 1, 1868, will be paid to shareholders on application to the Secretary to the Trustees at the Library of the Society, Second Avenue, corner of Eleventh Street, where the volume for the current year is also ready for distribution.

THOMAS DE WITT,
ANDREW WARNER,
BENJAMIN H. FIELD,
Trustees.

GEORGE H. MOORE,
Secretary to the Trustees.

** Any person desiring to procure these publications, may purchase a share in the Publication Fund, by enclosing a check or draft for FIFTY DOLLARS, payable to the order of BENJAMIN H. FIELD, Treasurer of the New-York Historical Society, for which the certificate will be immediately transmitted, *with the volume already published,* as the purchaser may direct.

☞ Address GEORGE H. MOORE, Librarian of the Historical Society, Second Avenue, corner of Eleventh St., New York City.

NEW YORK, *December,* 1869.

ORIGINAL SUBSCRIBERS TO THE FUND.

SHARE			SHARE		
1.	JAMES LENOX,	*N. Y. City.*	35.	WILLIAM B. CROSBY,	*N. Y. City.*
2.	SAME,	"	36.	HORATIO S. BROWN,	"
3.	SAME,	"	37.	JOHN A. HARDENBERGH,	"
4.	SAME,	"	38.	WILLIAM P. POWERS,	"
5.	SAME,	"	39.	SAMUEL MARSH,	"
6.	SAME,	"	40.	WILLIAM H. H. MOORE,	"
7.	SAME,	"	41.	C. V. S. ROOSEVELT,	"
8.	SAME,	"	42.	ROBERT TOWNSEND,	*Albany.*
9.	SAME,	"	43.	DAVID THOMPSON,	*N. Y. City.*
10.	SAME,	"	44.	JAMES STOKES,	"
11.	JOHN B. MOREAU,	"	45.	GEORGE C PETERS,	"
12.	HENRY T. DROWNE,	"	46.	GEORGE T. TRIMBLE,	"
13.	BENJAMIN H. FIELD,	"	47.	WILLIAM CURTIS NOYES,	"
14.	THOMAS W. C. MOORE,	"	48.	THOMAS SUFFERN,	"
15.	GEORGE BANCROFT,	"	49.	RICHARD H. BOWNE,	"
16.	WILLIAM CHAUNCEY,	"	50.	GEORGE H. PURSER,	"
17.	CHARLES H. WARD,	"	51.	JOHN H. CHAMBERS,	"
18.	WILLIAM MENZIES,	"	52.	GEORGE W. PRATT,	"
19.	J. WATTS DE PEYSTER,	"	53.	HENRY A. HURLBUT,	"
20.	EDWIN CROSWELL,	"	54.	AUGUST BELMONT,	
21.	EDWARD EVERETT,	*Boston, Mass.*	55.	GEORGE R. JACKSON,	"
22.	HORACE BINNEY,	*Phila., Pa.*	56.	CLEAYTON NEWBOLD,	"
23.	FREDERIC DE PEYSTER,	*N.Y. City.*	57.	GEORGE BRUCE,	
24.	AUGUSTUS SCHELL,	"	58.	F. A. PALMER,	
25.	ANDREW WARNER,	"	59.	JOHN WARD,	
26.	GOUVERNEUR M. WILKINS,	"	60.	SAMUEL JAUDON,	
27.	ERASTUS C. BENEDICT,	"	61.	THOMAS T. STURGES,	"
28.	JAMES SAVAGE,	*Boston, Mass.*	62.	JOHN REID,	
29.	S. ALOFSEN,	*N. Y. City.*	63.	GUSTAVUS SWAN,	"
30.	ALBERT A. MARTIN,	"	64.	MATTHEW CLARKSON,	"
31.	WILLIAM B. CAMPBELL,	"	65.	WILLIAM A. WHITE, Jr.,	"
32.	JOHN ALSTYNE,	"	66.	WM. M. HALSTEAD,	"
33.	JOHN ARMSTRONG,	"	67.	THOMAS DEWITT,	"
34.	WM. L. CHAMBERLAIN,	"	68.	CHARLES P. KIRKLAND,	"

69. H. G. Lawrence, *N. Y. City.*
70. Edward F. De Lancey, "
71. Cyrus Curtiss, "
72. Shepherd Knapp, "
73. Edward DeWitt, "
74. D. B. Fayerweather, "
75. Mark Hoyt, "
76. Charles M. Connolly, "
77. Cornelius DuBois, "
78. L. C. Clark, "
79. Thomas Lawrence, "
80. David T. Valentine, "
81. H'y Russell Drowne, "
82. John Fowler, Jr., "
83. William Bowne, "
84. Henry T. Drowne, "
85. Nehemiah Knight, *Brooklyn.*
86. William S. Thorne, *N. Y. City.*
87. Alex'r McL. Agnew, "
88. Robert C. Goodhue, "
89. George F. Nesbitt, "
90. John E. Wool, *Troy.*
91. John P. Treadwell, *New Milford, Conn.*
92. Isaac Fryer, *N. Y. City.*
93. Charles J. Martin, "
94. Franklin F. Randolph, "
95. Samuel Coulter, "
96. David Van Nostrand, "
97. Addison G. Bickford, "
98. Jonas G. Dudley, "
99. Theodorus B. Taylor, "
100. William Scott, "
101. David Sloane, "
102. Joseph G. Harrison, "
103. Same, "
104. Same, "
105. Same, "
106. Edward Walker, "
107. John C. Hewitt, "
108. Charles I. Bushnell, "
109. Giles F. Bushnell, "
110. John C. Calhoun, "
111. Thomas J. Lee, *Boston, Mass.*

112. S. Whitney Phœnix, *N. Y. City.*
113. Same, "
114. Same, "
115. Same, "
116. Same, "
117. Same,
118. Same,
119. Same,
120. Same,
121. Same,
122. Same,
123. Same, "
124. J. B. Bright, *Waltham, Mass.*
125. Robert L. Stuart, *N. Y. City.*
126. Same, "
127. Alexander Stuart, "
128. Same,
129. George T. Jackson, "
130. John A. Anderson, "
131. Charles P. Daly, "
132. Evert A. Duyckinck, "
133. Henry C. Carter, "
134. Andrew J. Smith, "
135. Mathias Bloodgood, "
136. J. Romeyn Brodhead, "
137. Jno. A. McAllister, *Phila., Pa.*
138. Nath. W. Hunt, *N. Y. City.*
139. Theo. S. Parker, *Hoboken, N. J.*
140. William M. Brown, *N. Y. City.*
141. And. Brown, *Middletown, N. J.*
142. Joseph B. Varnum, *N. Y. City.*
143. Charles B. Cotten, "
144. Alvin A. Alvord, "
145. Wm. Henry Arnoux, "
146. Same,
147. Same,
148. Same, "
149. Albert Smith, *New Rochelle.*
150. M. C. Morgan, *N. Y. City.*
151. S. Howland Robbins, "
152. Francis Bacon, "
153. A. Spiers Brown, "
154. George C. Colburn, "
155. John Calvin Smith, *Manlius.*

SHARE

156. W. B. EAGER, JR., *N. Y. City.*
157. ISAAC J. GREENWOOD, "
158. FREDERIC R. FOWLER, "
159. ANTHONY DEY, JR., "
160. SEYMOUR J. STRONG, "
161. EBENEZER J. HYDE, "
162. WILLIAM B. TAYLOR, "
163. FERD. J. DREER, *Phila., Pa.*
164. AUG. TOETDEBERG, *Brooklyn.*
165. CHARLES C. MOREAU, *N. Y. City.*
166. CHARLES H. HART, *Phila., Pa.*
167. HENRY PHILLIPS, JR., "
168. FRANCIS B. HAYES, *Boston, Mass.*
169. T. STAFFORD DROWNE, *Brooklyn.*
170. CORTLANDT DE PEYSTER FIELD, *N. Y. City.*
171. JOHN S. CRAIG, *N. Y. City.*
172. CHARLES H. ROGERS, "
173. MAURICE HILGER, "
174. E. A. BENEDICT, "
175. WILLIAM EVERDELL, "
176. GEO. R. DROWNE, *Boston, Mass.*
177. J. WATTS DE PEYSTER, *N. Y. City.*
178. JAMES B. ANDREWS, *N. Y. City.*
179. CONSTANT A. ANDREWS, "
180. LORING ANDREWS, JR., "
181. WALTER S. ANDREWS, "
182. CLARENCE ANDREWS, "
183. WILLIAM L. ANDREWS, "
184. SAME, "
185. JOHN ARMSTRONG, "
186. PAUL K. WEIZEL, *B'klyn, N. Y.*
187. JOHN F. MCCOY, *N. Y. City.*
188. JOSEPH B. HOYT, "
189. JAMES BENEDICT, "
190. J. NELSON TAPPAN "
191. FRANCIS WIGAND, "
192. C. H. ISHAM, '
193. D. B. FAYERWEATHER, "
194. JOHN A. HARDENBERGH, "
195. J. W. WEIDMEYER, "
196. EDWIN FAXON, *Boston, Mass.*
197. F. A. GALE, *N. Y. City.*

SHARE

198. JOHN CASWELL, *N. Y. City*
199. WILLIAM C. DORNIN, "
200. WILLIAM P. COOLEDGE, "
201. JOHN R. FORD, "
202. ISRAEL CORSE, "
203. DANIEL MORISON, "
204. JOHN BRIDGE, "
205. WILSON G. HUNT, "
206. CHARLES H. SMITH, "
207. JOHN P. CROSBY, "
208. ERASTUS CORNING, *Albany.*
209. SAME, "
210. JAMES B. COLGATE, *N. Y. City.*
211. SAMUEL MARSH, "
212. EDWIN PARSONS, "
213. ROBERT J. HUBBARD, "
214. J. WATTS DE PEYSTER, "
215. JAMES A. RAYNOR, "
216. ROBERT J. LIVINGSTON, "
217. JOHN C. BARRON, "
218. HENRY K. BREWER, "
219. JOHN A. NEXSEN, "
220. MARSHALL O. ROBERTS, "
221. WILLIAM N. BLAKEMAN, "
222. HERMAN C. ADAMS, "
223. THOMAS B. GUNNING, "
224. ABRAHAM BOGARDUS, "
225. JOHN E. LAUER,
226. E. M. CRAWFORD,
227. JAMES C. HOLDEN, "
228. SAMUEL COLGATE,
229. WILLIAM B. ROSS,
230. WILLIAM K. HINMAN, "
231. JOHN W. QUINCY,
232. JAMES M. BRUCE,
233. MISS ANNIE MOREAU, "
234. LEWIS HALLOCK, "
235. THE LIBRARY OF THE CITY OF AMSTERDAM, *Amsterdam, Netherlands.*
236. MRS. ANNA BOYNTON, *N. Y. City.*
237. RUFUS D. CASE, *N. Y. City.*
238. CYRUS BUTLER, "

SHARE

239. RICHARD S. FIELD, *Princeton, N. J.*

240. A. O. ZABRISKIE, *Jersey City, N. J.*

241. MICHAEL LIENAU, *Jersey City, N. J.*

242. WILLIAM A. WHITEHEAD, *Newark, N. J.*

243. SIMEON DRAPER, *N. Y. City.*

244. FREEMAN M. JOSSELYN, *Boston, Mass.*

245. THEODORE W. RILEY, *N. Y. City.*

246. JOHN BOYD, Jr.,   "

247. GEORGE K. SISTARE,   "

248. J. WARREN S. DEY,   "

249. WILLIAM H. BRIDGMAN,   "

250. ANSON PHELPS STOKES,   "

251. WILLIAM C. MARTIN,   "

252. A. ROBERTSON WALSH,   "

253. JOSEPH A. SPRAGUE,   "

254. CHARLES A. PEABODY,   "

255. WILLIAM H. MORRELL,   "

256. JOHN V. L. PRUYN, *Albany, N. Y.*

257. FREDERICK JAMES DE PEYSTER, *N. Y. City.*

258. WILLIAM H. MACY, *N. Y. City.*

259. THOMAS PATON,   "

260. DAVID STEWART,   "

261. DAVID STEWART, Jr.,   "

262. JOHN E. WILLIAMS,   "

263. JOHN P. TOWNSEND,   "

264. WILLIAM H. MORRELL,   "

265. HOMER MORGAN,   "

266. JOHN ARMSTRONG,   "

267.   SAME,   "

268.   SAME,   "

269.   SAME,   "

270. N. NORRIS HALSTEAD, *Harrison, Hudson Co., N. J.*

271. WM. C. TALLMADGE, *N. Y. City.*

272. HOWARD CROSBY,   "

273. MRS. MARY E. BROOKS,   "

274. EDWARD HODGES,   "

275. ROBERT W. RODMAN,   "

SHARE

276. JOHN L. RIKER,   *N. Y. City.*

277. WALTER R. T. JONES,   "

278. CLAUDIUS L. MONELL,   "

279. BYAM K. STEVENS, JR.,   "

280. FRANCIS MANY,   "

281. HENRY M. TABER,   "

282. T. M. PETERS,

283. JOHN B. CORNELL,   "

284. S. ALOFSEN,

285.   SAME,   "

286. ROBERT B. MINTURN, Jr.,   "

287. GEORGE TUGNOT,   "

288. RUFUS S. BERGEN, *Green Point.*

289. BENJ'N W. BONNEY, *N. Y. City.*

290. BENJ'N W. BONNEY, JR.,   "

291. JOHN S. H. FOGG, *Boston, Mass.*

292. JOHN H. WRIGHT,   "

293. WILLIAM WOOD,   *N. Y. City.*

294. F. G. VAN WOERT,   "

295. ALEX'R T. STEWART,   "

296. JOHN B. CRONIN,

297. GEORGF D. MORGAN,   "

298. HOMER TILTON,

299. SAMUEL FROST,

300.   SAME,

301. JAMES H. PINKNEY,   "

302. WILLIAM T. PINKNEY,   "

303. CHARLES H. PHILLIPS,   "

304. JAMES EAGER,

305. WILLIAM UNDERHILL,   "

306. JOHN D. CLUTE,   '

307. ABRAHAM B. EMBURY,   "

308. CHARLES L. RICHARDS,   "

309. WILLIAM BEARD,   '

310. JAMES H. WELLES,   "

311. JOHN GALLIER,   "

312. CHARLES LE BOUTILLIER,   "

313. THOMAS LE BOUTILLIER,   "

314. JOHN G. LAMBERSON,   "

315. RUSSELL C. ROOT,   "

316. CLARKSON CROLIUS,   "

317. WILLIAM MURPHY, *Chappaqua.*

318. DANIEL T. WILLETS, *N. Y. City.*

319. CHARLES GOULD,   "

SHARE

320. John B. Bartlett, *N. Y. City.*
321. Mathias Clark, "
322. Robert M. Roberts, "
323. Jas. Hasbrouck Sahler, "
324. Frederic de Peyster, "
325. Same, "
326. Same, "
327. John J. Latting, "
328. David Buffum, "
329. F. H. Parker, "
330. George W. Thompson, "
331. Thomas F. Youngs, "
332. Oliver G. Barton, "
333. Abram E. Cutter, *Charlestown, Mass.*
334. William E. Lewis, *N. Y. City.*
335. John H. Johnston "
336. William B. Clerke, "
337. John C. Connor, "
338. Henry T. Morgan, "
339. Abram A. Leggett, "
340. James Davett, "
341. Erastus S. Brown, "
342. Asher Taylor, "
343. Edward Bill, "
344. William H. Tuthill, *Tipton, Cedar Co., Iowa.*
345. Henry S. Terbell, *N. Y. City.*
346. George W. Abbe, "
347. Sidney Mason, "
348. Charles Shields, "
349. George B. Dorr, "
350. Gardiner Pike, "
351. John C. Beatty, "
352. Lora B. Bacon, "
353. Charles H. Ludington, "
354. James Brown, "
355. Charles O'Conor, "
356. Charles B. Collins, "
357. John H. Wright, *Boston, Mass.*
358. Wm. S. Constant, *N. Y. City.*
359. Geo. W. Wales, *Boston, Mass.*
360. John L. Dean, *N. Y. City.*
361. T. Matlack Cheesman, "

SHARE

362. Maximilian Rader, *N. Y. City.*
363. J. Hobart Herrick, "
364. Louis P. Griffith, "
365. Barrow Benrimo, "
366. Edward F. DeLancey, "
367. Samuel L. Breese, "
368. D. Henry Haight, "
369. John Adriance,
370. Same,
371. Joseph W. Alsop, "
372. Henry Chauncey, "
373. Frederick Chauncey, "
374. William Habirshaw, "
375. Henry A. Heiser, "
376. William H. Jackson, "
377. Elijah T. Brown, "
378. Henry K. Bogert, "
379. Addison Brown,
380. Ernest Fiedler, '
381. J. Watts de Peyster, "
382. William Remsen, "
383. Walter M. Underhill, "
384. Samuel W. Francis, "
385. George Livermore, *Cambridge, Mass.*
386. Same, "
387. Same, "
388. Same, "
389. John F. Gray, *N. Y. City.*
390. Henry G. Griffen, "
391. Thomas S. Berry, "
392. Calvin Durand,
393. Robert B. Minturn, "
394. F. A. P. Barnard, "
395. William Bryce,
396. James Bryce,
397. Augustus Belknap, "
398. Andrew Wilson, "
399. William J. Van Duser, "
400. John C. Havemeyer, "
401. John T. Agnew,
402. Same,
403. Charles E. Beebe, "
404. Nathaniel W. Chater, "

SHARE

405. GEORGE C. COLLINS, *N. Y. City.*
406. WILLIAM H. GOODWIN, "
407. CHARLES G. HARMER, "
408. WILLIAM HEGEMAN, "
409. PETER V. KING, "
410. GEORGE W. LANE, "
411. LOUIS F. THERASSON, "
412. HENRY F. SEWALL, "
413. MISS ELIZABETH CLARKSON JAY, *N. Y. City.*
414. WILLIAM E. DODGE, "
415. WILLIAM E. DODGE, JR., "
416. GEORGE W. ROBINS, "
417. JOHN D. LOCKE, "
418. JOHN MCKESSON, "
419. RICHARD M. HOE, "
420. ROBERT HOE, "
421. PETER S. HOE, "
422. AUGUSTUS W. PAYNE, "
423. WILLIAM OOTHOUT, "
424. EDWARD OOTHOUT, "
425. EDWARD F. HOPKINS, "
426. DAVID E. WHEELER, "
427. JOHN H. SPRAGUE, "
428. THEODORE VAN NORDEN, "
429. GEORGE DE HEART GILLESPIE, *N. Y. City.*
430. BENJAMIN G. ARNOLD, "
431. CORIDON A. ALVORD, "
432. SAME, "
433. SAME,
434. SAME, "
435. J. OTIS WARD,
436. JAMES LENOX, "
437. SAME,
438. JABEZ E. MUNSELL, "
439. ARNOLD C. HAWES, "
440. JACOB W. FEETER, "
441. DANIEL SPRING, "
442. JOHN C. GREEN, "
443. DAVID L. HOLDEN, "
444. JOSEPH W. PATTERSON, "
445. GORDON W. BURNHAM, "
446. SAMUEL WILDE, JR., "

SHARE

447. WILLIAM B. TAYLOR, JR., *N. Y. City.*
448. WILLIAM V. BRADY, "
449. OLIVER HOYT,
450. CHARLES W. LECOUR, "
451. JOHN H. SWIFT,
452. HUGH N. CAMP, '
453. W. WOOLSEY WRIGHT, "
454. JED FRYE, '
455. HENRY OWEN, '
456. WILLIAM A. YOUNG, "
457. JOHN BUCKLEY, JR., "
458. D. RANDOLPH MARTIN, "
459. SAMUEL L. M. BARLOW, "
460. E. W. RYERSON, "
461. SAMUEL SHETHAR, "
462. GEO. BRINLEY, *Hartford, Conn.*
463. AUGUSTUS F. SMITH, *N. Y. City.*
464. WILLIAM H. HURLBUT, "
465. HENRY A. HURLBUT, "
466. MRS. SOPHIE H. SCOTT, "
467. THE N. Y. SOCIETY LIBRARY, *New York City.*
468. THOMAS K. MARCY, *Brooklyn.*
469. JAS. Y. SMITH, *Providence, R. I.*
470. WM. B. BOLLES, *Astoria, N. Y.*
471. GOUV. MORRIS WILKINS, *New York City.*
472. JAMES T. FIELDS, *Boston, Mass.*
473. HORACE P. BIDDLE, *Logansport, Indiana.*
474. A. L. ROACHE, *Indianapolis, Indiana.*
475. MISS ELIZA S. QUINCY, *Quincy, Mass.*
476. ALFRED BROOKES, *N. Y. City.*
477. HENRY YOUNGS, JR., "
478. JEREMIAH LODER, "
479. THOMAS H. ARMSTRONG, "
480. WILLIAM C. BRYANT, "
481. MATTHEW P. READ, "
482. MANNING M. KNAPP, *Hackensack, N. J.*
483. LOCKWOOD L. DOTY, *Albany.*

SHARE

484. WALTER L. NEWBERRY, *Chicago, Illinois.*
485. HAMILTON FISH, *New York City.*
486. WM. B. TOWNE, *Boston, Mass.*
487. SAME, "
488. SAME, "
489. SAME, "
490. SIDNEY W. DIBBLE, *N. Y. City.*
491. CHARLES J. SEYMOUR, *Binghamton, N. Y.*
492. D. A. McKNIGHT, *Pittsburgh, Penn.*
493. CHAS. H. HOUSMAN, *N. Y. City.*
494. JAMES M. CHICHESTER, "
495. WILLIAM W. GREENE, "
496. FRANCIS F. DORR, "
497. CHARLES W. WHITNEY, "
498. ROBERT D. HART, "
499. GEORGE H. MATHEWS, "
500. THOMAS ADDIS EMMET, "
501. ANDREW J. SMITH, "
502. WILLIAM D. MAXWELL, "
503. CHARLES A. MACY, JR., "
504. THOMAS W. FIELD, "
505. CHARLES GORHAM BARNEY, *Richmond, Va.*
506. BENJ. B. ATTERBURY, *N. Y. City.*
507. RICHARD W. ROCHE, "
508. THOMAS H. MORRELL, "
509. SMITH BARKER, "
510. EVERARDUS B. WARNER, "
511. AUGUSTUS T. FRANCIS, "
512. WM. A. SLINGERLAND, "
513. RILEY A. BRICK, "
514. SAME, "
515. WALTER M. SMITH, "
516. HENRY ELSWORTH, "
517. JOHN HECKER, "
518. WARREN WARD, "
519. CHARLES G. JUDSON, "
520. J. MEREDITH READ, JR., *Albany.*
521. JOHN H. VAN ANTWERP, "
522. WM. M. VAN WAGENEN, "
523. WM. T. RYERSON, *N. Y. City.*

SHARE

524. EDWIN HOYT, *N. Y. City.*
525. JOHN VAN NEST, "
526. CLINTON GILBERT, "
527. J. CARSON BREVOORT, *Brooklyn.*
528. SAME, "
529. ISAAC D. RUSSELL, *N. Y. City.*
530. HENRY OOTHOUT, "
531. ALEXANDER P. IRVIN, "
532. BERIAH PALMER, '
533. ROBERT SCHELL, "
534. ALFRED T. ACKERT, *Rhinebeck.*
535. JOHN H. WATSON, *N. Y. City.*
536. ABRAHAM BALDWIN, "
537. EZRA A. HAYT, "
538. WILLIAM L. LAMBERT, "
539. CHARLES S. SMITH, "
540. CHARLES A. MACY, "
541. SAMUEL RAYNOR,
542. LUCIUS TUCKERMAN, "
543. WILLIAM BETTS,
544. WILLIAM K. STRONG, "
545. JOHN D. JONES,
546. SAME,
547. THOMAS C. DOREMUS, "
548. RUDOLPH A. WITTHAUS, JR., *N. Y. City.*
549. FRED'K W. MACY, *N. Y. City.*
550. JOSEPH N. IRELAND, "
551. WILLIAM MONTROSS, "
552. SAMUEL R. MABBATT, "
553. JACOB S. WETMORE, "
554. MARVELLE W. COOPER, "
555. ABRAHAM M. COZZENS, "
556. JACOB VAN WAGENEN, "
557. JOHN H. RIKER, "
558. WM. ALEXANDER SMITH, "
559. GEORGE DIXON, JR., "
560. HAMILTON ODELL, "
561. CHARLES B. RICHARDSON, "
562. HORATIO NICHOLS, "
563. GEORGE T. HALL, "
564. HENRY A. BURR, "
565. FRANKLIN H. DELANO, "
566. JAMES M. DEUEL, '

SHARE

567. RICHARD IRVIN, Jr., *N. Y. City.*
568. DUDLEY B. FULLER, "
569. HENRY A. SMYTHE, "
570. JOSIAH S. LEVERETT, "
571. JOHN S. DAVENPORT, "
572. BRONSON PECK, "
573. WILLIAM A. ALLEN, "
574. WILLIAM DOWD, "
575. DAVID L. BAKER, "
576. JOHN G. SHEA, "
577. CLARKSON N. POTTER. "
578. DAVID D. FIELD, "
579. WILLIAM H. APPLETON, "
580. SAMUEL J. TILDEN, "
581. JAMES W. GERARD. "
582. TIMOTHY G. CHURCHILL, "
583. PARKER HANDY, "
584. NATHANIEL HAYDEN, "
585. JOHN G. HOLBROOKE, "
586. ROBERT H. McCURDY, "
587. RUSH C. HAWKINS, "
588. L. M. FERRIS, Jr., "
589. THEO. ROOSEVELT, "
590. J. BUTLER WRIGHT, "
591. GEORGE PALEN, "
592. GEORGE GRISWOLD, "
593. O. D. MUNN, "
594. FRANK MOORE, "
595. WILLIAM H. LEE, "
596. H. P. CROZIER. "
597. HENRY E. CLARK, "
598. JACKSON S. SCHULTZ, "
599. JOHN CARTER BROWN, *Providence, R. I.*
600. JOHN CARTER BROWN, 2d, *Providence, R. I.*
601. PELEG HALL, *N. Y. City.*
602. CHARLES L. ANTHONY, "
603. GEORGE W. HALL, "
604. J. T. LEAVITT, "
605. JOSEPH HOWLAND, *Albany.*
606. JOHN W. MUNRO, *N. Y. City.*
607. PARKER HANDY, "
608. SAME, "

SHARE

609. PARKER HANDY, *N. Y. City*
610. GEORGE GRISWOLD, "
611. WILLARD PARKER, "
612. ALEX'R W. BRADFORD, "
613. BENJAMIN L. BENSON, "
614. EDWARD SCHELL, '
615. A. B. KELLOGG, "
616. JOSEPH O. BROWN, "
617. E. B. OAKLEY, "
618. NATHANIEL JARVIS, Jr., "
619. DAVID S. DUNCOMB, "
620. AUGUSTUS K. GARDNER, "
621. L. BAYARD SMITH, "
622. LOUIS DE V. WILDER, "
623. WILLIAM E. BIRD, "
624. FRANKLIN B. HOUGH, *Lowville.*
625. THOMAS P. ROWE, *N. Y. City.*
626. SAMUEL OSGOOD, "
627. CHARLES A. MEIGS, "
628. EDWARD H. PURDY, "
629. JOSEPH F. JOY, "
630. HEZEKIAH KING, "
631. HORACE W. FULLER, "
632. WILLIAM H. POST, "
633. EDWARD D. BUTLER, "
634. HENRY B. DAWSON, *Morrisania.*
635. ALMON W. GRISWOLD, *N. Y. City.*
636. S. TOWNSEND CANNON, "
637. THEODORE M. BARNES, "
638. JOEL MUNSELL, *Albany.*
639. SAME, "
640. THOMAS A. BISHOP, *N. Y. City.*
641. SAME, "
642. NICHOLAS F. PALMER, "
643. J. L. LEONARD, *Lowville.*
644. DAVID C. HALSTEAD, *N. Y. City.*
645. THOMAS MORTON, "
646. J. F. SHEAFE, "
647. HENRY A. BOSTWICK, "
648. HIRAM D. DATER, "
649. GEORGE H. WILLIAMS, "
650. O. W. REYNOLDS, "
651. SILVANUS J. MACY, "
652. HENRY J. SCUDDER, "

SHARE

653. N. W. Stuyvesant Catlin, *N. Y. City.*

654. H. Tracy Arnold, *N. Y. City.*

655. Benjamin R. Winthrop, "

656. Same, "

657. Benj. R. Winthrop, Jr., "

658. Egerton L. Winthrop, *N. Y. City.*

659. Franklin Edson, *Albany.*

660. Robert C. Melvain, *N. Y. City.*

661. Archibald Russell, "

662. William I. Paulding, *Cold Spring.*

663. John Romeyn Brodhead, *N. Y. City.*

664. John L. Kennin, *N. Y. City.*

665. James Stokes, Jr., "

666. John A. Russell, "

667. E. M. Wright, "

668. Everardus Warner, "

669. Everardus B. Warner, "

670. John C. Hewitt, "

671. Peter Stryker, *Phila., Pa.*

672. Wilson M. Powell, *N. Y. City.*

673. Samuel H. Brown, "

674. Ellsworth Eliot. "

675. John T. Klots, "

676. Charles H. Dummer, "

677. Henry D. Bulkley, "

678. J. K. Hamilton Willcox, "

679. Appleton Sturgis, "

680. William T. Salter, "

681. William Rockwell, "

682. E. H. Janes, "

683. Thomas B. Newby, "

684. Louis de V. Wilder, "

685. Same, "

686. Samuel Coulter, "

687. Ralph Clark, "

688. Thomas F. De Voe, "

689. John Groshon, "

690. S. L. Boardman, *Augusta, Me.*

691. Charles J. Folsom, *N. Y. City.*

692. George Folsom, "

SHARE

693. Everardus Warner, *N. Y. City.*

694. George C. Eyland, "

695. C. F. Hardon, "

696. F. Wiley, "

697. Alexander Wiley, "

698. John W. Scott, *Astoria.*

699. Edward Anthony, *N. Y. City.*

700. Chauncey P. Smith, *Wolcott.*

701. H'y Camerden, Jr., *N. Y. City.*

702. George Bancroft, "

703. Abraham R. Warner, "

704. James W. Purdy, "

705. Chas. Congdon, *B'klyn, N. Y.*

706. Long Island Historical Society, *Brooklyn, N. Y.*

707. Brooklyn Mercantile Library Association, *Brooklyn, N. Y.*

708. New Bedford Free Library, *New Bedford, Mass.*

709. John David Wolfe, *N. Y. City.*

710. Miss C. L. Wolfe, "

711. George W. Cook, "

712. James L. Woodward, "

713. William Frederick Poole, *Boston, Mass.*

714. Benjamin H. Field, *N. Y. City.*

715. Cortlandt De Peyster Field, *N. Y. City.*

716. John Fitch, *N. Y. City.*

717. Same, "

718. F. Augustus Wood, "

719. John H. Dillingham, *Haverford College, Pa.*

720. F. Augustus Wood, *N. Y. City.*

721. Charles A. Peabody, "

722. Edwin F. Corey, Jr., "

723. John G. Lamberson, "

724. Same, "

725. John E. Parsons, "

726. Gratz Nathan, "

727. B. F. De Costa, "

728. Henry C. Potter, "

729. Henry Nicoll, "

730. George E. Moore, "

SHARE		SHARE	
731. JOHN F. TROW,	*N. Y. City.*	742. GEORGE H. MOORE, *N. Y. City.*	
732. SAME,	"	743. SAME,	"
733. SAME,	"	744. SAME,	"
734. SAME,	"	745. SAME,	
735. SAME,	"	746. SAME,	
736. SAME,	"	747. SAME,	
737. SAME,	"	748. SAME,	
738. SAME,	"	749. SAME,	
739. SAME,	"	750. SAME,	
740. SAME,	"	751. WILLIAM J. HOPPIN,	"
741. GEORGE H. MOORE,	"		

SHAREHOLDERS BY TRANSFERS TO DECEMBER, 1869.

SHARE	SHARE
111. J. K. WIGGIN, *Boston, Mass.*	670. WM. P. PRENTICE, *N. Y. City.*
150. GEORGE H. PEEKE, *Jersey City, N. J.*	714. JOHN EVERITT, "
	716. JAMES M. HUNT, "
167. JOHN H. THOMPSON, *N.Y. City.*	719. HAVERFORD COLLEGE LIBRARY,
187. J. K. WIGGIN, *Boston, Mass.*	*Haverford College, Pa.*
358. ROBERT S. MILLER, *N. Y. City.*	727. DAVID G. FRANCIS, *N. Y. City.*
508. JOSEPH SABIN, "	

Lightning Source UK Ltd.
Milton Keynes UK
UKHW022145130219
337289UK00009B/800/P

9 781333 288600